Dr. Len Bergantino, Ed.D., Ph.D.

Musicality,
Pure Sound,
The Art of Melody
and Inner Peace

The Essence of *Music*

This publication contains the opinions and ideas of its author. It is intended to provide helpful and informative material on the subjects addressed in the publication. The author and publisher specifically disclaim all responsibility for any liability, loss or risk, personal or otherwise, which is incurred as a consequence, directly or indirectly, of the use and application of any of the contents of this book.

WORKBOOK PRESS LLC
187 E Warm Springs Rd,
Suite B285, Las Vegas, NV 89119, USA

Website: https://workbookpress.com/
Hotline: 1-888-818-4856
Email: admin@workbookpress.com

Ordering Information:
Quantity sales. Special discounts are available on quantity purchases by corporations, associations, and others.
For details, contact the publisher at the address above.

Library of Congress Control Number:
ISBN-13:   978-1-957618-92-0 (Paperback Version)
                978-1-957618-93-7 (Digital Version)

REV. DATE: 20/04/2022

The Essence of Music

Musicality, Pure Sound, The Art of Melody and Inner Peace

Dr. Len Bergantino, Ed.D., Ph.D.

This book, The Essence of Music, along with the music itself provides the Spirit of place linking the phasing (metronome) of psychoanalysis and music to the practice of psychoanalysis and music with the phrasing that makes effective psychoanalytic treatment probable and music healing.

Dr. LEN BERGANTINO, Ed.D.(USC), Ph.D., A.B.P.P.
Psychoanalysis
(424) 293-9511

p 1

Dr Len Bergantino is the most gifted psychoanalyst who ever lived. Admittedly he had a direct connection with God and the full body of his writings and intended to be "The - Thing - In - Itself" and over the next couple of hundred years evolve an upward spiraling society as opposed to the downward spiraling society from which mankind suffers. These books provide the tools with which to carry on the work of attaining closer and closer approximations of _pure being_, while at the same time giving psychoanalysts and the world at large a fighting chance against Evil. In direct revelation God informed me that 12 out of 100,000,000 people cross into the pearly gates of Heaven. Doubting Thomases go straight to hell!!!

1215 Brockton Ave., Ste. 104, W. Los Angeles, CA 90025-U.S.A.

LEN BERGANTINO, Ed.D., Ph.D., A.B.P.P.

Psychoanalysis
(310) 207-9397

Clinical Psychologist
License Number 3837

NEW YORK TIMES BOOK AD

A.B.P.P. - Diplomate in Family Psychology
American Board of Professional Psychology

THIS BOOK IS INTENDED TO DISTURB THE UNIVERSE IN SEVERAL WAYS:

Dr. Len Bergantino, Ed.D., Ph.D. releases 'I AM FREUD! PSYCHOANALYSIS IS THE ONLY METHOD OF CURE: IT'S TOO BAD NO ONE KNOWS HOW TO DO ONE!!!"

Los Angeles —Dr. Len Bergantino, Ed.D., Ph.D. IS THE REINCARNATED SOUL OF SIGMUND FREUD AND JULIUS CAESAR AND HIS CHILDREN LISA FRANCESCA BERGANTINO IS THE REINCARNATED SOUL OF THE GREAT BRITISH PSYCHOANALYST WILFRED R. BION AND CLEOPATRA AND HIS DEVELOPMENTALLY DELAYED SON IS THE REINCARNATED SOUL OF MILTON H. ERICKSON, M.D. (UNCOMMON THERAPY) AND DECIMUS BRUTUS. ALL OF THOSE SKILL SETS WERE NECESSARY IN THE WRITING OF THIS BOOK AND THE ISSUES IT IS MEANT TO DEAL WITH AT BOTH CONSCIOUS AND UNCONSCIOUS LEVELS. Furthur, Dr. Bergantino in 1980 made a direct contact with God to have Bion and Erickson sent back as the reincarnated souls of his children TO TEACH HIM WHAT TO DO WITH THE PARANORMAL GIFTS THAT WERE GIVEN TO HIM AND UNLEASHED BY MILTON H. ERICKSON, M.D. THROUGH THIS DEVELOPMENT HE, WITH GOD'S TUTELAGE BECAME THE BEST PSYCHOANALYST THAT EVER LIVED AND BEGAN TO IMPLEMENT FREUD'S PLAN THAT BOTH PSYCHOANALYSIS AND SUBSEQUENTLY DEVELOPED PSYCHOTHERAPIES WOULD CREATE THE KIND OF PATIENTS WHO WOULD AND COULD THEN GO OUT AND CREATE AN UPWARD SPIRALING SOCIETY. Wilhelm Reich, M.D.—Freud's most gifted training Analyst said "IF YOU CAN'T DO POLITICS, YOU CAN'T DO ANALYSIS!" The book shows how to develop extrasensory perception so that Analysts and Therapists have an opportunity to develop the tools necessary to do the jobs at hand if they are so inclined. In this way people will not pay for a five day a week seven y ear Analysis and come out as crazy as the day they began with few if any tools to carry on the work. When I did an Analysis with the creme de la creme of society, they customarily tripled their income and the quality of their life!(DON'T WASTE $50,000 per year or $350,000 per Analysis) THIS BOOK IS NOT BASED ON ANYTHING DR. BERGANTINO MAY OR MAY NOT BELIEVE! IT IS BASED ON HIS ATTAINING A LEVEL OF "PURE BEING" THAT SARTRE WROTE ABOUT AS THE THING IN ITSELF! AND IT IS AT THAT LEVEL THAT THIS BOOK IS WRITTEN FOR ALL TIME (200 years at least) THAT THIS BOOK WAS WRITTEN AS THE THING IN ITSELF TO EFFECT

1. DEVELOP THE KIND OF PEOPLE THAT WILL PREVENT THE NEXT HOLOCAUST!
2. UNITE BOTH PSYCHOANALYSIS AND THE UNITED STATES GOVERNMENT WITH GOD SAVING PSYCHOANALYTIC PATIENTS A FORTUNE BY SHOWING THEM WHAT IS REQUIRED TO GET THEIR MONEY'S WORTH AND TO HELP PEOPLE DEVELOP THE TOOLS TO SAVE THEIR OWN SOULS! CURRENTLY TWELVE PERSONS OUT OF ONE HUNDRED MILLION ENTER HEAVEN!
3. ALL BOARDS OF PSYCHOLOGY ARE TO BE DONE AWAY WITH AS THEY

1215 Brockton Ave. Ste. 104. W. Los Angeles, CA. 90025 - U.S.A. Promote Mediocrity

4. Force The Roman Catholic Church to Accept and Believe In
   Reincarnation as my own .AUTHENTIC LIFE EXPERIENCE IS VERY
   CLOSE TO WHAT THE HINDUS HAVE WRITTEN EXCEPT THAT I KNOW
   WHO I AM AND WHO MY CHILDREN WERE!!! THERE ARE 27 YEARS OF
   DIRECT PARANORMAL EXPERIENCES GIVEN TO ME BY GOD THAT I AM
   NOT WRITING ABOUT IN DETAIL BECAUSE THIS BOOK IS NOT PROOF OF
   THE EXISTENCE OF GOD, IT IS A KARMIC MISSION OF WHAT GOD
   WANTED ME TO DEVOTE MY LIFE TO AND GIVE ME UNEXPECTED SKILLS!!!

ABOUT THE AUTHOR

Dr. Bergantino practiced psychoanalysis in Beverly Hills, CA
from 1979-1991. He saw 7 patients 5 days a week for between five and
seven years totaling 49 hours a week and saw an occasional family therapy
or clinical hypnosis case totaling 52 hours a week at $125 per hour; $625
per week; $240,000 per y ear. In addition he trained psychiatrists and
clinical psychologists at the international level delivering on his
workshop promise "The Therapeutic Wizardry of Dr. Len Bergantino" at
Wentworth Castle in Sheffield England and training the British at the
Royal College of Medicine in London in "Developing the Use of Extrasensory Perception in the Practice of Psychoanalysis, Psychotherapy and
Clinical Hypnosis." In Brisbane, Australia his work was described as "a
kind of mental precision that electrified the Australian Therapeutic
Community and had lasting therapeutic results."His other books, The
Art of Psychotherapy and The Liberation of the Therapist; Reverse Analysis,
The Existential Shift, Gestalt Family Therapy, and The Prevention of
The Last Holocaust, as well as THE ESSENCE OF MUSIC, all round out
the psychoanalytic book and give the reader an opportunity to enter Dr.
Bergano's world in places where they own efforts make such entry possible!
Dr. bergantino has never done anything where he was not able to be on
The Cutting Edge whether that be the private practice of clinical
psychology; individual psychotherapy; family therapy, clinical hypnosis,
THE PRIVATE PRACTICE OF PSYCHOANALYSIS: EDUCATION OR PROFESSIONAL MUSICIAN!
HE WAS FULLY ABSORBED IN EACH WHEN HE DID THEM AND FEELS FORTUNATE HE
WAS BORN INTO AN ERA OF SWEETNESS AND LIGHT WHICH NO LONGER EXISTS OR HE
WOULD NOT HAVE WRITTEN T HIS BOOK AND THE HOLY SPIRIT WOULD NOT HAVE
DICTATED IT NOR DEMANDED IT OF HIM! DR. BERGANTINO AT SEVENTY FIVE IS
"THE REVEREND DR. LEN BERGANTINO" AND THE ONLY WAY YOU CAN SPEND TIME WITH
HIM IS IN HIS PRIVATE PRACTICE OF FAMILY THERAPY OR TELEPHONIC FAMILY
THERAPY AS TRAINED BY CARL WHITAKER, M.D. CALL 424 293-9511 and let it
ring 7 times to leave a message. The Reverend Dr. is 75 years old and
too old to do psychoanaly sis which was his first love! FURTHUR, HE HAD
A STRONG INTEREST IN THE LEGAL SYSTEM DEVELOPING ITSELF SO NATURAL LAW,
KARMIC LAW AND CIVIL LAW COME INTO BALANCE; OTHERWISE YOU HAVE AN UNJUST
LEGAL SYSTEM! REMEMBER, AS HEAD OF THE Roman Senate Caesar was quite
adept in creating Roman Law!!! Furthur, Dr. Bergantino was an affiliate
of The Italian American Lawyers Association for 7 years; and a California
Supreme Court Justice told him "Dr. Bergantino, We at the California State
Supreme Court read everything you write! We just wish you would double
space! (Associate Justice Edward Panelli -1992)

***WHEN TESTIFYING ON THE WITNESS STAND IN COURT THE JUDICIAL
OFFICER ANGRILY SAID, "CAN YOU PROVE YOU ARE FREUD!" I LOOKED HIM
RIGHT IN THE EYE AND SAID "CAN YOU PROVE THAT I AM NOT!"

The Reverend Dr. Len Bergantino

Dr. Len Bergantino,
A.B.P.P.

THE GOD FATHER OF CLINICAL PSYCHOLOGY

"The Murderers on the Inside Love Me More than the Murderers on the Outside"

Books that are either published or will be published authored by The Reverend Dr. Len Bergantino as these books were written as the thing-in itself and were divinely inspired by the Holy Spirit to at the very least give men and women an opportunity to be more fully themselves and more in touch with their own nature. It is strongly recommended that the readers develop their level of attention to read all four books and permit them to become part parcel of how each individual answers the question "TO BE OR NOT TO BE". As The Reverend Dr. Len Bergantino is seventy five years old, he will not be around personally to do psychoanalysis or psychotherapy with you, therefore these books were written on the basis of them being around for at least TWO HUNDRED YEARS!!!

1.\ I AM FREUD! PSYCHOANALYSIS IS THE ONLY METHOD OF CURE: IT'S TOO BAD NO ONE KNOWS HOW TO DO ONE, XLIBRIS PUB. CO., 2019. 502 PP.
2.\ REVERSE ANALYSIS, THE EXISTENTIAL SHIFT, GESTALT FAMILY THERAPY AND THE PREVENTION OF THE HOLOCAUST, XLIBRIS PUB. CO,
3.\ THE ART OF PSYCHOTHERAPY AND THE LIBERATION OF THE THERAPIST XLIBRIS PUBLISHING COMPANY.
4.\ THE ESSENCE OF MUSIC, XLIBRIS PUBLISHING COMPANY.

I AM FREUD!

I am Freud! I am Caesar!
I am the Worlds Greatest Psychoanalyst!
Psychoanalysis-Reincarnation-Extra
Sensory Perception

Karmic Law- Natural Law- Civil Law

DR. LEN BERGANTINO, ED.D., PH.D.

This is a book for all time. As I had extrasensory perception to help me find out things on a primitive level and depth with an ability to pick up split-off, severe pathological projective identifications moment to moment in an era when psychologists were only permitted to be research psychoanalysts by the American Psychoanalytic Association (but tightly controlled where that research was going that in many ways nullified it as true psychoanalytic research). And I will show you how extrasensory perception can be developed and utilized by the therapeutic use of self within the psychoanalytic frame in ways that can enhance the treatment of borderline, narcissistic, obsessive-compulsive, and schizophrenic disorders and other diagnoses, as well as help pinpoint psychophysiological awareness, which through the repetition compulsion, can prevent disease and will circumvent disease in later life. This kind of psychoanalysis will go a long way in preventing the next holocaust!

Dr. Bergantino and his two children were sent back on a karmic mission to complete the work. Dr. Bergantino is the reincarnated soul of Sigmund Freud and Julius Caesar. Those skill sets were required to complete the project. His children are Wilfred Bion and Milton Erickson. They taught Dr. Bergantino how to use paranormal abilities. We are all off the karmic wheel and WE WILL NOT BE BACK!!! GOODBYE!!!

ISBN 000-0-0000-0000-0
00000

I DARED TO DISTURB THE UNIVERSE

Len Bergentino Ed D., Ph.D., releases 'I AM Freud! Psychoanalysis Is the Only Method of Cure: It's Too Bad No One Knows How to Do One!!?"

BEVERLY HILLS, Calif. - Dr. Len Bergantino, Ed.D., Ph.D., is the reincarnated soul of Sigmund Freud and Julius Caesar and his children Lisa Francesca is the reincarnated soul of the great British psychoanalyst Wilfred it Bion and Cleopatra while his developmentally delayed son Alexander Leonardo is the reincarnated soul of Milton H. Erickson, M.D. (known as the father of Modern Medical Hypnosis and for Uncommon Therapy) and Decimus Brutus. All of those skill sets were necessary in the writing of "I Am Freud! Psychoanalysis Is the Only Method of Cure: It's Too Bad No One Knows How to Do One!" (published by Xlibris) and the issues it is meant to deal with, at both conscious and unconscious levels.

Furthur, Bergantino in 1980, made a direct contact with God to have Bien and Erickson sent back as the reincarnated souls of his children to teach him what to do with the paranormal gifts that were given to him and unleashed by Erickson. Through this development, he, with God's tutelage became the best psychoanalyst that ever lived and began to implement Freud's plan that both psychoanalysis and subsequently developed psychotherapies would create the kind of patients who would and could then go out and create an upward spiraling society.

Wilhelm Reich, M.D. - Freud's, most gifted training analyst said, "If you can't do politics, you can't do analysis!" The book shows how to develop extrasensory perception so that analysts and therapists have an opportunity to develop the tools necessary to do the lobs at hand if they are so inclined. In this way, people will not pay for a five day a week, seven-year analysis and come out as crazy as the day they began with few if any tools to carry on the work. "When I did an analysis with the crème de la crème of society, they customarily tripled their income and the quality of their life! (Don't waste $50,000 per year or $350,000 per analysis)?

The book is not based on anything Bergantino may or may not believe. It is based on his attaining a level of "pure being" that Jean Paul Sartre wrote about as the thing-in-itself. And it Is at that level that this book was written as the thing-in-itself to effect change in the reader.

"I Am Freud! Psychoanalysis is the Only Method of Cure: It's Too Bad No One Knows How to Do One!!!' By Dr. Len Bergantino, Ed.D., Ph.D.

Hardcover) 6 x gin 1504 pages / ISBN 9781984557308

Softcover16 x gin) 504 pages) ISBN 9781984557292

E-Book 1504 pages) ISBN 9781984557285

Available at www.amazon.corn and www.barnesaridnoble.com

About the Author

Dr. Len Bergantino, Ed.D., Ph.D. practiced psychoanalysis in Beverly Hills, California from 1979-1991. He saw seven patients five days a week for between five and seven years totaling 49 hours a week and saw an occasional family therapy or clinical hypnosis case totaling 52 hours a week at $125 per hour, $625 per week; $240,000 per year. In addition, he trained psychiatrists and clinical psychologists at the international level delivering on his workshop promise. "The Therapheutic Wizardry of Dr. Len Bergantino" at Wentworth Castle in Sheffield, England and training the British at the Royal College of Medicine in London in "Developing the Use of Extrasensory Perception in the Practice of Psychoanalia Psychotherapy and Clinical hypnosis," in Brisbane, Australia, his work was described as "a kind of mental precision' that electrified the Australian Therapeutic Community and had lasting therapeutic impact. Furthermore, he was an affiliate of the Italian American Lawyers Association for seven years. He became an expert witness in both severe parental Alienation Syndrome in criminal cases. He was the only clinician to plea bargain a man for release who was on death row. He was President of the Southern California Society of Clinical Hypnosis when they were composed of exclusively MD's, PHD's and DDS'. The year he was president he turned it into a psychoanalytic institute.

![DR. LEN BERGANTINO, ED.D., PH.D. BOOK COLLECTIONS]

The Books

I AM FREUD! Psychoanalysis Is the Only Method of Cure:

It's Too Bad No One Knows How to Do One!!!

This is a book for all time. As I had extrasensory perception to help me find out things on a primitive level and depth with an ability to pick up split-off, severe pathological projective identifications moment to moment in an era when psychologists were only permitted to be research psychoanalysts by the American Psychoanalytic Association (but tightly controlled where that research was going that in many ways nullified it as true psychoanalytic research), I present to you a book that might at that time have been considered wild psychoanalysis. And I will show you how extrasensory perception can be developed and utilized by the therapeutic use of self within the psychoanalytic frame in ways

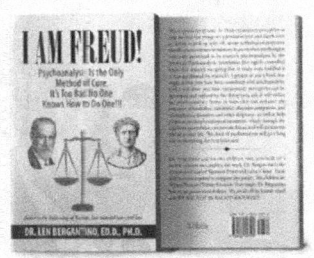

that can enhance the treatment of borderline, narcissistic, obsessive-compulsive, and schizophrenic disorders and other diagnoses, as well as help pinpoint psychophysiological awareness, which through the repetition compulsion, can prevent disease and will

REVERSE ANALYSIS, THE EXISTENTIAL SHIFT, GESTALT FAMILY THERAPY AND THE PREVENTION OF THE NEXT HOLOCAUST

Dr. Len Bergantino, Ed.D., Ph.D.

The purpose of this book is to open up the space so that the reader –
society at large, psychotherapists and patients might start contributing
to LIFE FORCE AND THE THERAPEUTIC USE OF SELF IN CREATING A
SOCIETY THAT IS UPWARD SPIRALING INSTEAD OF ONE DOMINATED
BY INCURABLE DEATH FORCE! FOR THIS TO HAPPEN SOCIETY AT
LARGE MUST LEARN TO THINK AND PAY ATTENTION TO THE FACTS
IN THIS BOOK THAT WILL PERMIT THE CREATION OF NEW THOUGHT
TO MEET NEW PROBLEMS; SO THAT WE DO NOT HAVE SITUATIONS
LIKE 122 VETERANS A DAY COMMITTING SUICIDE WITHOUT HOPE
THAT THERE ARE ANY TREATMENTS FOR THEM NOW OR THAT CAN
BE CREATED! IT IS RECOMMENDED THAT THIS BOOK BE READ AS
ONE OF A SERIES OF FOUR WRITTEN BY DR. LEN RIFRGANTINO TO
CREATE THIS NEW SOCIETY! WHILE PSYCHOTHERAPY IS THE MEDIUM
OF CHOICE IN TH THIS BOOK, THE FOURTH BOOK UTILIZES MUSIC
AS THE MEDIUM TO ANSWER SHAKESPEARE'S QUESTIONS "TO BE
OR NOT TO BE!!!!!!!!!!!!!!!!!!!!!!!"

My Children and I were sent back on a karmic mission to PREVENT THE
APOCALYPSE AND WE HAVE DONE OUR PART IN WRITING FOUR
BOOKS. NOW IT IS UP TO YOU TO READ AND UTILIZE THEM! GOD
HAS MYSTERIOUSLY MURDERED THREE PERSONS WHO COULD HAVE
STOPPED ME FROM FULFILLING THIS MISSION! WE HAVE SUCCEEDED!
THE REST IS UP TO YOU OR YOUR ROOMS WILL BE RESERVED IN
HELL!. Twelve out of 100 million make it into Heaven!

Xlibris

ISBN 978-1-7960-2117-2
51999
9 781796 021172

Dr. Len Bergantino, Ed.!), PhD., addresses societal issues in new book

'Reverse Analysis, the Existential Shift Gestalt Family Therapy and the Prevention of the Next Holocaust' released

LOS ANGELES - Through the Holy Spirit, his direct contact with God and his karmic mission, Dr. Len Bergantino, Ed.D., Ph.D., addresses the problem of the today's downward spiraling society in his latest book "Reverse Analysis, the Existential Shift, Gestalt Family Therapy and the Prevention of the Next Holocaust" (published by Xlibris).

This book creates a subliminal methodology that will help to prevent the next holocaust and perhaps deter the apocalypse and the end of days. As such, the book expands and enriches the community standards of practice of Psychoanalysis. psychiatry, clinical psychology, politics, political intervention and a realliance of religion with the state, as opposed to a separation of church and state that has left its people a soulless and emotionally bankrupt nation with a downward spiraling society. This book throws the United States government and its citizens into an international pot of family therapy as evoked at the unconscious and primitive levels required to effect and affect societal change, to evoke a redirection to an upward spiraling society providing the kind of leadership for Americans to create well-being and prosperity for all.

"[The book is the common man's best bet to turn the tragic corner in his or her life: make dysfunctional families' functional; save one's soul; become thoughtful members of society who do the right thing more often than not," Bergantino says. "This book also trains therapists how to do one session existential shifts thereby creating therapies for the common man that are more affordable than a seven-year psychoanalysis where the patient is seen five days a week. In other words, it makes the currently impossible possible!"

At Its core, the book aims to remind readers to "Open up the space and keep it open so Man will not destroy himself via the illusion of safety and will learn to experientially tolerate the anxiety and chaos of not knowing."

"Reverse Analysis, the Existential Shift, Gestalt Family Therapy and the Prevention of the Next Holocaust" By Dr. Len Bergantino, EcLD, Ph.D.
Hardcover (6 x gin / 244 pages/ ISBN 9781796021189
Softrover I 6 x 9in / 244 pages / ISBN 9781796021172
E-Book I 244 pages / ISBN 9781796021165
Available at Amazon and Barnes & Noble

About the Author

Dr. Len Bergantino, Ed.D. Ph.D., has written THE HOLY BIBLE OF Psychoanalysis, psychotherapy, political psycholo and music-books. I-IV!!! The books are the thing-in-itself and all four books must be read to make the necessary personal and societal impact!!! He as trained by Milton Erickson,. M.D. Carl-Whitaker. M.D. Wilfred Bion, M.R.C.S., Walter Kempler, M.D, George Bach, Ph.D. Bruno Bettelheim, Ph.D, Jim Simkin. Ph.D., and Ery Polster, Ph.D., they had the most lasting impact along with the Holy Spirit. Bergantino is the author of The Essence of Music," "The Art of Psychotherapy and the Liberation of the Therapist," "I Am Freud! Psychoanalysis Is the Only Method of Cure: It's Too Bad No One Knows How to Do One!!!," "Reverse Analysis, the Existential Shift, Gestalt Family Therapy and the Prevention of the Next Holocaust," "Psychotherapy, Insight, and Style: The Existential Moment", and "Making an Impact in Therapy: How Master Clinicians Intervene."

Do you think that some slug who looks very professional who "whispers" an occasional interpretation to you five times a week for 7 years can make one bit of difference in your life or does such a psychotic slug called a psychoanalyst merely stick you in an emotional toilet bowl for seven years having the cumulative result of turning you into a hopeless bastard who will never turn the tragic corner in his or her life?

Can your analyst analyze an archaic liquid symbiotic or an osmotic transference, or can they even recognize this phenomena in order to analyze it? If the psychoanalyst cannot analyze these transferences they can't do an analysis!

I used to get "good faith" patients who had the balls to work on the cutting edge at the same time I did because they had had combinations of twenty years of two seven year analyses plus several briefer psychotherapies, only to be as crazy as the day they walked in! (-$200,000.00)

As Dr. Donald Rinsley, M.D., fellow-American College of Psychoanalysts wrote about me, my work has both a healing effect and affect. Patients used to pay me six months in advance to hold the time open because I was irreplaceable I was the only one who could analyze the psychotic core of the personality and I was the only who could actually do what Dr. Wilfred R. Bion, MRCS (Medical Royal College of Surgeons) wrote about analyzing the psychotic core of the personality.

As I am seventy-nine years old, I have written ten books that must be read and digested in their entirety. As these books are the thing-in-itself they will transform the reader into the kinds of analyst, patient and psychotherapist who can make a difference in helping people turn the tragic corner in their lives! In other words, these ten books are analysis!

These books were written to be around for a few hundred years and were directly guided by the Almighty!
By: Dr. LEN BERGANTINO, Ed. D.(USC), Ph.D., A.B.P.P.
The Essence of Music: Musicality, Pure Sound, the Art of Melody and Inner Peace
They say that music is the international language, but what is music? For the Bergantino-Bredice family, music was the family business.

www.drlenbergantino.com
https://tinyurl.com/bddsanf4 -Falling In Love by: Dr. Len Bergantino featuring Joe Diorio world renown guitarist.
https://www.youtube.com/channel/UCto3H5xzJBwN9fqqWu8OSQA/featured Dr. Len Bergantino Music and Books in Youtube Channel

The Reverend Dr. Len Bergantino
Professional Musician from 1996-2012
(Age 56-70) Musician's Local 47
Los Angeles, California
American Federation of Musicians

THE ESSENCE OF MUSIC

Dr. Len Bergantino, Ed. D., Ph. D

Dr. Len Bergantino, Ed. D., Ph. D. (USC),
PSYCHOANALYST-MUSICIAN

*Musicality,
Pure Sound,
The Art of Melody
and Inner Peace*

The
Essence
of
Music

Do you think that some drug who looks very professional who "whispers" an occasional interpretation to you five times a week for 7 years can make one bit of difference in your life or does such a psychotronic drug called a psychoanalyst merely stick you in an emotional toilet bowl for seven years having the cumulative result of turning you into a hopeless bastard who will never turn the tragic corner in his or her life?

Can your analyst analyze an archaic liquid symbiotic or an osmotic transference, or can they even recognize this phenomena in order to analyze it? If the psychoanalyst cannot analyze these transferences they can't do an analysis!

I used to get "good faith" patients who had the balls to work on the cutting edge at the same time I did because they had combinations of twenty years of two seven year analyses plus several briefer psychotherapies. only to be as crazy as the day they walked in! (~$200,000.00)

As Dr. Donald Rinsley, M.D., fellow-American College of Psychoanalysts wrote about me. my work has both a healing effect and affect. Patients used to pay me six months in advance to hold the time open because I was irreplaceable; I was the only one who could analyze the psychotic core of the personality and I was the only one who could actually do what Dr. Wilfred R. Bion, MRCS (Medical Royal College of Surgeons) wrote about analyzing the psychotic core of the personality.

As I am seventy-nine years old, I have written ten books that must be read and digested in their entirety. As these books are the thing-in-itself they will transform the reader into the kinds of analyst, patient and psychotherapist who can make a difference in helping people turn the tragic corner in their lives! In other words, these ten books are analysis!

These books were written to be around for a few hundred years and were directly guided by the Almighty!
By: Dr. LEN BERGANTINO, Ed. D.(USC), Ph.D., A.B.P.P.
The Essence of Music: Musicality, Pure Sound, the Art of Melody and Inner Peace
They say that music is the international language, but what is music? For the Bergantino-Bredice family, music was the family business.

www.drlenbergantino.com
https://tinyurl.com/bddvanf4 -Falling In Love by: Dr. Len Bergantino featuring Joe Diorio world renown guitarist.
https://www.youtube.com/channel/UCto3H5xeJBwN9fqqWu8OSQA/featured   Dr. Len Bergantino Music and Books in Youtube Channel

The Reverend Dr. Len Bergantino
Professional Musician from 1996-2012
(Age: 56-70) Musician's Local 47
Los Angeles, California
American Federation of Musicians

WorkBook PRESS

THE ESSENCE OF MUSIC

Dr. Len Bergantino, Ed. D., Ph. D.

Dr. Len Bergantino, Ed. D., Ph. D. (USC),
PSYCHOANALYST-MUSICIAN

Musicality,
Pure Sound,
The Art of Melody
and Inner Peace

The Essence of Music

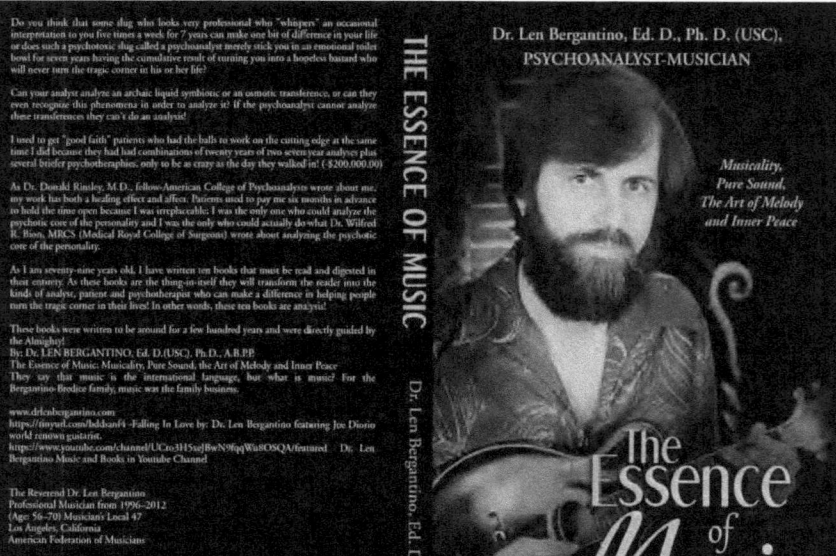

The Art of
Psychotherapy
And the Liberation
of the Therapist

Give me LIBERTY or give me DEATH

Much has been written about the Science of Psychotherapy, but it has remained for Dr. Bergantino to write about the Art of Psychotherapy with such elegant impact.

Dr. Len Bergantino, Ed.D., Ph.D.

This is a book for professional psychotherapists, psychoanalysts, and counselors; students in those areas of specialty; and lay persons who are interested in the essence of effective therapy and how some of the people who do it best practice their art. For professionals, the book presents a personal way of viewing therapy that can add pleasurable options. Each of the therapists with whom I worked, and myself, all had a feeling of enjoyment that we hope will carry over to the office and practices of the readers. For students of therapy, the book offers a search for a professional stature and working posture that may be of value in the development of each student's unique personal style. For lay persons, the book speaks of therapy that can make an impact and speaks of how some of the most potent therapists practice. For Psychoanalysts interested in the work of the Great British Psychoanalyst, Dr. Wilfred R. Bion MRCS (Medical Royal College of Surgeons). This is the only book that demonstrates exactly what he did.

I wrote the book with the intention of having it be both an experience and an explanation. I have presented it according to my developmental needs while enduring personally and professionally. This was done so the book might be informative at the unconscious level, entertaining at the child level, and persuasive at the unconscious level.

The existential moment is the thread that ties the book together; it is a moment of therapeutic potency. While all moments are existential by definition, there are certain moments that are more powerful in helping patients live happier and healthier lives. Positive results, whether they be from one session or over the long haul, are partially, if not fully, a result of existential moments.

Xlibris

ISBN 978-1-7966-2402-7
52399

The Art *of*
Psychotherapy
And the **Liberation**
of the **Therapist**

Give me
LIBERTY
or give me
DEATH

Much has been written about the Science of Psychotherapy, but it has remained for Dr. Bergantino to write about the Art of Psychotherapy with such elegant impact.

Dr. Len Bergantino, Ed.D., Ph.D.

This is a book for professional psychotherapists, psychoanalysts, and counselors; students in those areas of specialty; and lay persons who are interested in the essence of effective therapy and how some of the people who do it best practice their art. For professionals, the book presents a personal way of viewing therapy that can add pleasurable options. Each of the therapists with whom I worked, and myself, all had a feeling of enjoyment that we hope will carry over into the office and practices of the readers. For students of therapy, the book offers a search for a professional stature and working posture that may be of value in the development of each student's unique personal style. For lay persons, the book speaks of therapy that can make an impact and speaks of how some of the most potent therapists practice. For Psychoanalysts interested in the work of the Great British Psychoanalyst, Dr. Wilfred R. Bion MRCS (Medical Royal College of Surgeons), This is the only book that demonstrates exactly what he did.

I wrote the book with the intention of having it be both an experience and an explanation. I have presented it according to my developmental needs while maturing personally and professionally. This was done so the book might be informative at the conscious level, entertaining at the child level, and persuasive at the unconscious level.

The existential moment is the thread that ties the book together; it is a moment of therapeutic potency. While all moments are existential by definition, there are certain moments that are more powerful in helping patients live happier and healthier lives. Positive results, whether they be from one session or over the long haul, are partially, if not fully, a result of existential moments.

Xlibris

ISBN 978-1-7960-2460-7

Introduction To Musicians Names And A Little Bit Of How They Influenced Me!

I was born on May 29, 1943. We got a television the day Bobby Thompson hit the home run heard round the world as the New York Giants beat the Brooklyn Dodgers in 1951; only to get beat by The Mighty Yankees 6 games to 2 in the 1951 world series. UNTIL WE GOT A TELEVISION I USED TO LISTEN TO THE RADIO AND THE 78 rpm record player 7 to 8 hours at a time when I had a snow day off from school. THUS, WHEN I LISTENED TO A RECORD I LOVED I PERHAPS HEARD IT THOUSANDS OF TIMES UNTIL THE SOUND WAS BURNT INTO MY SOUL, MY BEING AND MY UNCONSCIOUS MIND ALL AT ONCE!

My father Dan Bergantino, started me off on solfeggi for a year (reading music) and then bought me a mandolin- a Gibson F-2 high quality sound. During this time I heard Harry James play his 1941 version of THE SLEEPY LAGOON and his 1939 version of YOU MADE ME LOVE YOU AND I FELL IN LOVE WITH THE TRUMPET SOUND AND DECIDED NOT TO BECOME A GUITAR PLAYER, SOMETHING ITALIANS WERE GREAT AT ALMOST LIKE ROCKY Marciano in boxing who had a 49-0 record! But I still loved the sound of the guitar and got a sound on the mandolin like Johnny Smith playing Pavanne or Moonlight In Vermont. Then there was Charlie Christian playing ON THE ALAMO for the Benny Goodman Sextet around 1943 and of course Peggy Lee singing "Waiting For The Train To Come Home"- a WWII song.

My father played classical music in the symphony on violin so I was schooled in classical, swing, dixieland, pop, and progressive jazz. I got to see and hear Arturo Toscanini conduct the NBC symphony on several occasions. It wasn't until the mid-nineties when I heard a tape recording of one of his OUTTAKES that I realized how great he was! It was said that TOSCANINI'S REHEARSALS were better than his concerts in that they were MORE ALIVE IN THE MOMENT!

Mario Lanza was the greatest voice I ever heard! He was better than Enrico Caruso and better than Pavorotti. Lanza had the power and the romantic sweetness that could touch your soul and make you cry at any moment!

Harry Reser was the best tenor banjo player I ever heard. Hear his solos on Lollipops and The Clock and The Banjo. (A CD called 'Cracker Jacks has Lollipops) My father was the second best tenor banjo player I ever heard. He could play Reser's solos at precisely the same speed via the timing of a metronone only RESER DID IT FIRST AND HE DID IT IN NEW YORK! Dave Appollon was the best mandolin player I heard records of at age twelve and the only one as good but with more polish and less fire was Mischa Schenkman- The Paganini of The Mandolin in the Soviet Union, who I studied with for two years from 1979-1981. When I went to Rio de Janiero, Brazil to learn Choro music on a bandolim (looked like a mandolin that was a big pizza and cut more than a mandolin, but was a lead instrument in Choro Music (the music of the people). Joel Nascimento taught me something about sound quality and the pick I used that transcended ALL MUSIC! HE SPOKE ONLY PORTUGESE AND I SPOKE ONLY ENGLISH!

FOR PURE SOUND QUALITY THE ONLY VIOLIN I EVER HEARD PLAYED THAT COULD TOUCH YOUR SOUL WITH EACH AND EVERY NOTE WAS A THIRTY SECOND U TUBE FILM CLIP OF FRITZ KREISLER. MOST CONCERT VIOLIN PLAYERS WHO ARE WELL ACCOMPLISHED IN TRAINING AND EDUCATION AND TECHNIQUE TEND TO SOUND LIKE SOMEONE SAWING A WET SLIGHTLY GREEN PIECE OF WOOD! NOT SO WITH FRITZ KREISLER! IF I HEARD HIM EARLY ON I MIGHT HAVE CHOSEN TO BE A VIOLIN PLAYER AS MY FATHER WAS HAUNTED BY THE GHOST OF PAGANINI! AS FAR

AS REINCARNATION GOES I HAVE SEEN ENOUGH DETAIL OF PERSONHOOD, STYLE AND THE EDUCATION OF HIS SON TO KNOW THAT ZOLTAN MAGA FROM HUNGARY WHO PLAYS GYPSY VIOLIN IS THE REINCARNATED SOUL OF MY FATHER AND HAS ACCOMPLISHED PRETTY MUCH WHAT MY FATHER WANTED TO DO WITH THE VIOLIN, HIS FIRST LOVE! My father was pissed that Paganini never wrote a book transmitting the culture of HOW HE DID THE TECHNICAL THINGS THAT HE DID AND HE BUSTED MY ASS TO FILL IN THE GAPS OF HOW ALL OF THAT WORKS. I COULD DO IT AS A PSYCHOTHERAPIST AND PSYCHOANALYST WITH LARGE AUDIENCES FROM 1973 BUT I COULDN'T DO IT IN MUSIC UNTIL I WAS 67 YEARS OLD! ONCE I COULD DO IT I COULD DO IT ON ALL THE INSTRUMENTS I PLAYED - trumpet, cornet, fluegelhorn, baritone horn, tenor banjo, mandolin banjo, mandolin, bandolim, concert and soprano ukeleles1 The audience reaction felt like someone plugged them into an electric socket and they went absolutely apeshit1 That is really all I ever wanted to do musically and then pass it on as in "transmission of the musical and human culture to infinity!" Perhaps my father taught me to think and function like a doctoral student when I was 3 years old, because that was what the University of Southern California wanted from its' doctoral students! (a transmission of the culture from one generation to the next)

Perhaps that is how I got to know and study with the best alive in the areas of psychoanalysis, psychotherapy and music! They all talked to me like we were little kids in a sandbox playing, having fun, and discovering the unknowable!!!

My mother was always pushing me in the direction of getting a Ph.D., M.D. or law degree. However, while I did pursue subjects other than music academically I NEVER LOST SIGHT OF THE FACT THAT MUSIC WAS "THE FAMILY BUSINESS" WHICH IN AN ITALIAN AMERICAN FAMILY WAS A BIG DEAL. SO I ALWAYS GAVE MUSICIANS AS MUCH RESPECT AS MDs! My father used to say "musician is only and eight letter word but it involves a lot!"

Freddie Bredice, Louis Bredice, Vinny Bredice, and Art Bredice were all part of this family business in one way or another. Then they passed the torch on to Joe Diorio who became the best jazz guitar player in the world from around 1973-2003, when medical problems interfered with his performance wizardry. I caught up with Joe Diorio on December 22,

1997 when we made a cd with me playing mandolin with his intervallically designed guitar accompaniment.

Louis didn't like Vinny too much because his mother was one half German. He used to say "Vinny INVADES THE NOTES, like the Germans, like Wagner (Hitler's favorite composer). Italians EMBELLISH THE NOTES!" Being one eighth German, I can appreciate both the embellishment and the invasion as both a string player and a brass player. I loved Louis Beethoven from the first note I heard that he wrote and he INVADED THE MUSIC! HE WAS GERMAN! I LOVED BOTH!

Art Bredice once told me around 1970 "Phrase like Sinatra sings! You'll be alright!"

What is a family business? I have cousins in Naples, Italy who founded Bergantino's Ristorante in 1848 right off Piazza Garibaldi near the Cavour Hotel.

Italians take great pride in the family business founded in 1848! Lovari's Music Store in Naples had the grandfather working there, also founded in 1848. After giving him a copy of the cd made by me on mandolin and Joe Diorio on guitar -Falling In Love -Orchard records.com and/or amazon. com said, "When Italians move to the United States they are Italian-Italian; the next generation become American-Italian; then American-American and they lose all of the feeling of being Italian-Italian. You got it all back! I don't know how you did it!" With the effort I put in over 18 years to get the feeling of Italian-Italian back, it is the one comment above all others about me and my music that I cherish most!

My first trumpet teacher was Carl Berg who played for Harry James! My second trumpet teacher was Jimmy Gozzo, the father of the greatest lead trumpet player of all time, CONRAD GOZZO!. I WAS JIMMY GOZZO'S THIRD BEST STUDENT! THE FIRST WAS CONRAD! THE SECOND WAS AL HIRT! Jimmy Gozzo said to me "You will move to California. You will study trumpet with Conrad! He hangs out with The Rat Pack (composed of Frank Sinatra, Dean Martin, Sammy Davis Jr., Joey Bishop and Peter Lawford). You will hang out with the Rat Pack! You will have a good life!" The problem was that Conrad Gozzo died at 42 years old and Frank Sinatra told me in 1968 "that contrary to popular opinion he did not keep an entourage and I should continue my doctoral work at USC and become the best psychologist I could be it! When I told Dean Martin this story some 25 years later, telling him I could write a book about The Rat Pack with him as co-author that would be a best seller in that I already wrote a book that became a master classic in the field of Psychotherapy, entitled "Psychotherapy, Insight & Style: The Existential Moment", Allyn & Bacon, Boston, 1981. Dean Martin said "I am just a simple man who sings simple songs that touch people's souls, and that is the only thing I want to be remembered for!"

I came to realize that the sound of Bobby Hackett on the trumpet and cornet, of Billy Butterfield on the trumpet and of Artie Shaw on the clarinet all had THE SOUND CONNECTED TO ONE'S INNER BEING THAT DEAN MARTIN WANTED TO BE REMEMBERED FOR! NAT KING COLE'S SINGING GRABBED ME at 6 years old in 1949 when I heard him sing PRETEND which was the first song I learned how to play on the mandolin! I only learned songs that I loved that had a sound that touched my soul! As a musician I never put in shit so shit never came out! I played one night with Spanish Harlem (Salsa) at the Hollywood Race Track before 2000 people and the leader Johnny Pacheco said "Who's the new guy with THE SOUND!"

AL HIRT's best sound was on a 33 rpm by RCA in 1958 playing a song entitled A STRANGER IN PARADISE!" HE MADE ENOUGH MONEY SELLING SOUND TO BECOME PART OWNER OF A PROFESSIONAL FOOTBALL TEAM -THE NEW ORLEANS SAINTS!

If I were writing this book only for one market I might call it BECOMING A LEAD TRUMPET PLAYER!", for all the cats down at North Texas State University in Denton, Texas. They were great to me in letting me sit in classes, professional meetings, and meeting some great trumpet players!

Last but not least is the hope that this book will once again inspire Americans to write and play songs again! What the hell, We did as Americans write The Great American Song Book! I was reminded of it last night when I saw Yul Brenner and Deborah Kerr singing and dancing in The King And I! They brought tears to my eyes!

Preface

While this is a book about music it is also a book about developing your therapeutic use of self from the point of view of my thirty years of experience and having been trained by many world renown psychiatrists and psychologists. Among them was Milton H. Erickson, M.D. -known as the father of modern medical hypnosis. Something I learned from Erickson's (storytelling) was only embellished by my deep psychoanalytic work whereby I was trained by the best of Wilfred Bion's M.D. psychoanalytic analysands and training analysts. For example one book written about Erickson's work was written by Sid Rosen, M.D. and entitled "My Voice Will Go With You: The Teaching Tales of Milton H. Erickson, M.D." While a Reader in a preliminary reading refers to my Voice going with him through repetitive storytelling interweaved in ways that access the unconscious mind, it will last forever or as long as a person lives as a result of the in depth psychoanalytic training and not just because they know what my voice sounds like from a personal point of view when I tell stories. IN OTHER WORDS THIS BOOK WAS WRITTEN ON AN EXPERIENTIAL LEVEL WHERE THE STORIES WERE MEANT TO ENHANCE THE QUALITY OF BEING OF THE READER IN ALL ASPECTS OF LIFE IN ADDITION TO MUSIC, ALBEIT ENHANCE YOUR THERAPEUTIC USE OF SELF AS APPLIED TO ATTAINING FINER AND FINER DISCRIMINATIONS OF PURE BEING AS YOU LIVE YOUR LIFE AND DEDICATE YOUR BEING TO WHATEVER ENDEAVOR YOU CHOOSE! In this case-Music! In particular, lead trumpet players and music students will love this book! C'mon Folks, write songs again, and then play them using this book as a tool to make your own therapeutic use of self such that you can touch peoples' souls at will!

FOREWORD TO MUSIC BOOK

Nobody writes songs anymore! Nobody plays beautiful melodies anymore! Americans forgot that they wrote THE GREAT AMERICAN SONGBOOK! I had to write this book!

I became a professional musicians joining Musicians Local 47 in Los Angeles at the age of 56 years old! My work has an international following in both clinical psychology and music. In both, I made the opportunity to study with 17 world renown psychiatrists, psychoanalysis, and clinical psychologists as well as many world renown musicians. Writing this book was part of what God wanted me to do to get off the kharmic wheel after he had given me paranormal abilities to give it my best shots! Music was The Family Business in that my father every time he played could light up a stage giving one the feeling that he just plugged in a Christmas Tree and my cousins Fred and Lou Bredice succeeded at the national level. All of them never went pass grammar school and had genius capacity and were the offspring of Italian immigrants who came through Ellis Island in New York, City. My cousins Freddie and Vinny taught world renown jazz guitarist Joe Diorio to play and now at 82 years old he is still transmitting the musical culture that began with them, and Joe and I are in touch once a week whereby he says things that evoke a musical expansion. This book is intended to be a book read along all the other psychology books (three) in that it teaches as much about humanity as it does about music. The goal is a series of books that will be around for 200 years.

Foreword to music book

MUSIC TEACHERS

1. Don Bergantino - Father – 1949 to 1976 on mandolin, tenor banjo, and solfeggl.
2. Mischa Shenkyman - The Paginini of the Mandolin in the Soviet Union – 1979- 1981.
3. 1956-1961 - One time per week trumpet lesson with Carl Berg who played for Harry James. He had the patience of a Saint while he had a great sound his teaching of trumpet was unparalleled.
4. 1955-1956 - Baritone Horn –taught by Mr. Avalon in Waterbury, Connecticut Public Schools.
5. 1962-1963 - Studied trumpet with Jimmy Gozzo, who was the father of the World's Greatest lead trumpet Player Conrad Gozzo and aloso teacher of Al Hirt in addition to his son Conrad.
6. 1965 - One semester course in trumpet performance at U. of Connecticut with San Goldfart, who also taught at Hartt College of Music.
7. 1964 - One semester of lesson in bBass Viol with Bert Teretsky who later became chairperson or U. of California at San Diego Department of Music.
8. 1979-1981 – Mandolin lessons with Mischa Shenkyman, The Paganini of the Mandolin in the Siviet Union.
9. 1995 – 5 mo. Trumpet lessons with Wayne Bergeron, former lead trumpet for Maynard Ferguson.
10. Late nineties, 1 ½ years trumpet lessons on lead trumpet with Frank Szabo who played lead trumpet for Buddy Rich, Count Basic, Francis Capp, Bill Holman plus a gold record for Frank Sinatra.

Foreword for Music Book

MUSIC TEACHERS CONT.

11. Late nineties, jazz lessons with trombonist Bill Watrous – 5 mo.

12. Late nineties, jazz lessons with Stacy Howles on flugelhorn, 6 months. She was the daughter of Jimmy Howles who taught jazz to Chut Baker.

13. 1998 - jazz lessons with Hank Mark at Abersoll Jazz Camp in Louisville, Kentucky.

14. 1996 – one-week trumpet lessons with Scott Englebright who played lead for Maynard Ferguson at that time in Denton, Texas.

15. Sat in for a week of music classes at North Texas State University with permission of Mike Steinel and took a trumpet lesson with Stan Kenton. He gave me a second lesson by telephone a few months later.

16. Around 2001 took 26-hours trumpet lessons from Pope McLaughlin in Denton Texas on trumpet high notes. I increased my range from E flat about high C to a double B flat about high C and played a double high C for Joe Vento's band as a result of his teaching. He was a student of Jake Jacoby at North Texas State he studied to learn how to teach trumpet, as opposed to being a big time lead player. He was the best high note teacher I ever met.

17. 1999 – Took six months of lead trumpet lessons with Charlie Davis who played lead for Woody Herman and The Herd. This required a minimum of five hours a day practicing trumpet.

Foreword to Music Book

While I could immediately light up an audience training others to do psychotherapy, I was not able to do so as a musician until I was 67 years old. I never wanted to live the life of a musician, but I sure as hell wanted to be able to light up a crowd performing. Once I did it on trumpet, I could on it on mandolin, bandolim, flugelhorn, concert ukulele, tenor banjo, mandolin banjo or anything I played.

I used to sit on the floor in front of my father playing guitar and wonder, how the hell do you do it? So, it was truly one of the most exciting moments of my life when I could light up an audience playing music. I remember, several African Americans about 16 years old looking like they were going to jump out of their skin while cheering and applauding, something they clearly were not used to doing with a Caucasian!

Further, the best musicians in the world walked through the doors of Musicians Local 47 and I not only get to know them and study with them, but I had several rehearsal bands of my own where they came to hear me play trumpet. I had one time per week rehearsal bands in progressive jazz, dixieland, brass quintet, as well as a group that played Brazillian Choro Music –the music of the People in Brazil. I wen tot Rio de Janeiro for a couple of weeks and took lessons from the best bandolin choro players in the country. One of the affectionately said to me, "Not bad for a Gringo!" Actually, the Brazilians did all they could to be helpful because they wanted their music to come North of the Border. Charlie Byrd did this with Bossa Nova as well as Von Jobim. He is the only musician they named an airport after in Rio de Janeiro.

Foreword to Music Book

I made a couple of full length CD's and a few demos that demonstrate the feeling I want to convey about the music.

1. Falling in Love is a 22 song CD that has international acclaim where I am playing mandolin accompanied by world renown jazz guitarist Joe Diorio. Joe Diorio's doing this CD with a 56 years-old unknown kicked me up in to the big leagues right away and I am forever grateful to Joe for doing this. He said that I was a great musician! Coming from Joe that meant a lot because he was a jazz guitarist that all the great jazz guitarists thought was the best and want to hear!

2. The last CD were songs I fell in love with from 6 years old forward and I dedicated the CD to my son and titled it Alex's Song (which I wrote) – A Healing CD. I play these songs at a pace that in "relatively free of disease!" For me, it got rid of a 7 day cold in 3days, palying it repetitively.

3. A two song cornet demo which got me hired two days after I sent it out and was paid double for my efforts, which is unheard of in the music industry.

4. The Jazz Trumpet of Dr. Len Bergantino is a demo the best parts of which sound like Miles Davis or Chet Baker playing Jazz with technique of Raphael Mendez.

5. Dr. Bergantino's Progressive Jazz Octet is a demo playing a Jobim song –Meditation. – "Meditation"

6. Dr. Len Bergantino plays Jazz Ukelele

7. Lenny's Song Six songs I wrote in Summer of 2017.

8. "Song Demo playing jazz mandolin –highest quality mandolin sound ever recorded.

9. Dan Bergantino and his tenor banjo – my father's dying gift

All my father said after giving me his playing the tenor banjo was "You should have heard me when I was young!"

10. Mischa Shenkyman, my mandolin teacher from 1979-1981, playing Russian Folk Music for which he was trained at a Russian Conservatory. All the Masters of his music were destroyed for defecting to the United States. While a doctoral student at the University of Southern California I didn't play music, nor while I was building a private practice in clinical psychology. However, when I heard Shenkyman I asked him if he could teach me how to play in a recording studio. He had me playing with a paper pick he made for me for three months. That is the technique I used when making the CD Falling in Love accompanied by joe Diorio on December 22, 1997 at Professional Musicians Local 47. Given I had not played in a number of years it struck me as strange I in my own mind went to a recording studio technique, but I trusted myself, and that put me back in the music business 18 years later.

PURCHASING CD's FROM ME:

1. Falling in Love, Alex's Song and Shenkyman's CD were all done in a professional recording studios. The price for them is $22 each plus $3 shipping - a check or postal money order for $25.

2. All demos which are included to make a point in terms of SOUND QUALITY, THE ART OF MELODY, inner peace while making sound quality and other points if musicality. These demos will be sold at $12 each plus $3 postage as of 2019.

The Reverend Dr. Jan Bryant

Query Letter For
Shades Of Sound

This manuscript was written in two weeks, primarily on an airplane to and from San Pedro Town, Ambergris Caye, Belize. The author did not feel the internal or external freedom to write this book in the United States given the unofficial government sanctions on freedom of speech. The book is a personal odyssey that may have great value not only for musicians, but all those interested in BECOMING MORE OF WHO THEY ARE AT THE HIGHEST LEVELS.

Dr. Len Bergantino, the author, has paranormal abilities. He practiced psychoanalysis in Beverly Hills, California while training psychiatrists and clinical psychologists at the international level. In Australia his work was described as "a kind of mental precision that electrified the Australian therapeutic community and had lasting therapeutic impact." He gave workshops in Sheffield, England at Wentworth Castle entitled "The Therapeutic Wizardry of Dr. Len Bergantino."; and at the Royal College of Medicine in London, entitled "The Development and Use of Extrasensory Perception In The Practice of Psychoanalysis, Psychotherapy, and Clinical Hypnosis."

Dr. Bergantino comes from a musical family and has studied music since he was five years old. He was educated in both string and brass instruments.

Dr. Bergantino is such that if he feels he has gone as far as he could in a discipline (psychoanalysis), and that he is not on the cutting and creative edge of something that enhances the quality of his own BEING (AS IN TO BE OR NOT TO BE), he moves on. THUS, IN 1996-2012 HE RESUMED HIS MUSIC FULL FORCE, BECOMING A PROFESSIONAL MUSICIAN. Dr. Bergantino was trained by 17 world renown psychiatrists and clinical psychologists and then wrote a book that became a master classic in the field under the title Making An Impact In Therapy; How Master Clinicians Intervene. Jason Aronson Publishers, Northvale, New Jersey, 1994 (can be purchased on amazon.com.) Thus, he did the same thing as a professional musician, studied with the best alive on both strings and brass, classical, progressive jazz, big band, swing, dixieland, et. al. A few of his teachers were Mischa Shenkyman, The Paganini of the Mandolin in the Soviet Union; Frank Szabo who played lead trumpet for Count Basie; and Charlie Davis, who played lead trumpet for Woody Herman. Furthur, Dr. Bergantino came in at the top, and got to know most of the world renown trumpet, guitar, banjo and jazz players personally.

One anecdote was at a Christmas party at Burt Bacharach's house Miles Davis arrived with Cecily Tyson. He was wearing a long light tan Camel Hair Coat. Upon arrival someone said to him, "Miles, the best thing you ever did was marry Cecily Tyson." Miles said, "No Man! The best thing I ever did was learn an F Minor 7th Chord!" Burt sat me and Miles together. At the time I was only playing mandolin. Miles said, "Whose your favorite trumpet player?" I said, "Chet Baker! But You're second!" Miles and I got along splendidly after that as he knew I wasn't a sychophant!

Joe Diorio was the John Coltrane of Guitar in that both he and Coltrane had a profound sense of Expression of the Depths of Their Being through their instruments. Joe is not a popular household name, however, the musicians knew he was the best jazz guitar player alive from about 1970 until he had a stroke in the early 2000's.

The second best thing I ever did professionally was make a cd with me playing mandolin and Joe Diorio accompanying me on guitar. It can be purchased from Orchard records.com The first was my book PSYCHOTHERAPY INSIGHT AND STYLE: THE EXISTENTIAL MOMENT, 288 pp. published by Allyn & Bacon, Inc., Boston, 1981.

The good thing when I went into music was that I was a millionaire!!! Given my interest in SHADES OF SOUND I was in a rare position among musicians to purchase whatever combinations of trumpets, cornets, special made mouthpieces, baritone horns, mandolins, ukeleles, tenor guitars and tenor banjos to get the exact sound I was looking for that WOULD GIVE ME THE BEST OPPORTUNITY TO PLAY MUSIC FROM THE INSIDE OUT AS OPPOSED TO FROM THE OUTSIDE

IN!!! UNLESS MUSICIANS LEARN TO DO THIS THEY WILL ONLY BE PLAYING NOTES, NO MATTER HOW TECHNICALLY COMPETENT THEY BECOME!. MY COUSING LOUIS BREDICE, WHO OUTSHEARED (GEORGE) SHEARING THE ONLY TIME I HEARD HIM PLAY AT THE SAN SOUCI HOTEL IN MIAMI BEACH (WHERE HE PLAYED SEVEN NIGHTS A WEEK) SAID TO ME, "WHEN I FIRST STARTED PLAYING JAZZ I PLAYED A LOT OF NOTES! AFTER THAT, I REALIZED ALL I NEEDED WERE THE RIGHT ONES!!!"

***THERE IS A SECTION THAT ALL TRUMPET PLAYERS OUGHT TO KNOW INVOLVING MAKES AND MODELS OF TRUMPETS, CORNETS AND FLUGELHORNS AS WELL AS MOUTHPIECE COMBINATIONS BOTH RIM AND UNDERCUPS.

COMMENT

by EDWARD W. L. SMITH, Ph.D.

1145 Sheridan Road N.E.
Atlanta, Georgia 30324

This is a controversial article. In it Len describes a phenomenon which he has experienced. Most readers have not experienced that phenomenon, and I include myself among them. These days, my stance is skeptical respect for claims beyond my experience. I am very uninterested in the cults of pop-psychology and pop-metaphysics, or in their claims of knowledge and powers. At the same time I respect the reports of serious and conscientious people, and am stirred to interest or even excitement by these reports. Len is a man whom I like and respect. I have witnessed myself time and again evolve from skepticism (or even "solid disbelief") to familiarity with a phenomenon. I also have witnessed the clarification of illusions and the uncovering of untruths. So, I stand as respectful skeptic, usually open to being shown. And once shown compelling evidence I am quick to incorporate. I would like to investigate the phenomenon Len describes with him. My vote was to publish this article to stir us to consider and investigate.

LEN BERGANTINO, Ed.D., Ph.D., A.B.P.P.
Clinical Psychologist (Lic. No. 3857)

Psychoanalysis
A.B.P.P. - Diplomate in Family Psychology
American Board of Professional Psychology

1215 Brockton Ave., Ste. 104, W. Los Angeles, CA 90025 - U.S.A.
(310) 207-9397

Introductions b
What I Brought
To The Music Dining Room
Table Before Dinner

Pilgrimage Lite

Music from the Heart

Len Bergantino

I had been working with a man whose mother had been taken away in a straight jacket and institutionalized when he was three years old. He never saw her again.

The man was so frightened at the primitive three year old level that he invested his entire life in "looking good." He was a successful public relations executive for a big firm, but affectively detached and disconnected and always aiming to please as a result of never being truly present in the here and now.

One day I asked him to sing because he always sounded like he had a cloth stuffed in his mouth. He sang "Come Back to Sorrento," an Italian ballad. He was Irish but sang it with more feeling than I had ever heard in him before.

There had been many sessions which had differing degrees of frustration in which he would come in disconnected, detached and aiming to please, and the feeling I had on this particular day was I just didn't want to say one more word to him about anything.

So, to his surprise, I took out my mandolin and in the most loving mellow beautiful way I could I played, "Come Back to Sorrento." He broke down in tears and cried for the last forty minutes

of the session, saying only, at the very end, "Bergantino, you sure earned your money today!" I replied, "And to think, I wasted all these years talking to people."

The author is in the private practice of psychoanalysis, Eriksonian hypnosis and Gestalt-experiential family therapy. (editor's note: don't be put off by these formidable descriptions; the main thing about Len's work, as this article demonstrates, is that he responds to his clients in a deeply personal intuitive manner.) He writes, "My work is consistently experiential, as is my squishy nose kissing of my seven year old son Alexander Leonardo, and my teddy bear rendition of "Let me call you Sweetheart" with my five year old daughter, Lisa Francesca."

There once was a man who cried every time it snowed. He went to a psychotherapist. Now when the snow falls, he weeps for his mother, who died in the winter.

Joe Riener, "What is Psychotherapy," *Pilgrimage*, Summer 1979 (Vol. 7, No. 2)

1988. Bergantino, L. *Music From The Heart.* Pilgrimage: Psychotherapy and Personal Exploration, Vol. 14, No. 2.

Falling in Love

Romantic Italian and American Old Standards
Dr. Len Bergantino on mandolin
accompanied by world renown guitarist Joe Diorio

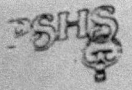

The Professional School for Humanistic Studies
420 Ash Street, San Diego, CA 92101 (714) 232-3171

p d

June 24, 1981

Dr. Len Bergantino
415 North Camden — Suite 202
Beverly Hills, California 90210

Dear Len,

Many thanks for the copy of your book. I was delighted and surprised
that you did include your excellent summary of the workshop and the
case, after all.

The publisher did an excellent job and there are some lovely quotes.
If you need any more you can use the following paragraph.

Many have written about the science of psycho-therapy, but it has remained for Dr. Bergantino to describe and illustrate the art of psychotherapy with such elegant impact.

Sincerely,

Harold Greenwald, Ph.D.
President

BG:cd

Clinical Psychology (PL3837) to Helts

10266 Kilrenney Ave.

1/12/81   Los Angeles, CA 90064

Carl Whitaker, M.D.
Professor of Psychiatry
U. of Wisconsin Medical School
Center for Health Sciences
600 Highland Avenue
Madison, Wisconsin 53792

Dear Carl,

The following is material that you dictated to me over the telephone regarding material that may be used in any advertising capacity that Allyn & Bacon, Inc., chooses to do in the promotion of my book, "Psychotherapy Insight And Style: The Existential Moment."

"The author as a therapist is a student of creativity and he offers a metaphorical elaboration that is both impressionistic, artistic and a stimulus for thinking. He is a professional reporter of interpersonal change models in the family therapy set and even intrapsychic change process in itw twentieth century face. The book rouses powerful feelings and stimulates growth in its readers."

"Reading this book is an active experience in the use of self in the field of psychotherapy, and as such, it both expands and enriches the community standards of practice of professional psychotherapists. That self is really our only tool. It's use is critical and evolving through each practitioner's professional lifetime."

Please sign below acknowledging your permission to quote.

Sincerely,

Len

_____   _____
Carl Whitaker, M.D.   Len Bergantino, Ed.D., Ph.D.

P.S. Please return one copy to me, keep one for your records
     and send one to Allyn & Bacon, Inc. Thank you.

SCHOOL OF EDUCATION
DIVISION OF EDUCATIONAL PSYCHOLOGY
AND TECHNOLOGY, WPH 600
213-740-5601
213-740-2367 FAX

February 29, 2000

To Whom It May Concern:

It is with a great deal of pleasure that I write in support of Dr. Len Bergantino, with whom I have had an association for nearly 30 years. In my graduate seminars, he was an excellent student who exhibited not only a high level of competence in the subject matter but also creative insights rarely found among even the best students. As a counseling and clinical psychologist, Len Bergantino brings a diversified and very broad experience base to any position that he might undertake. His work record has revealed a variety of professionally related activities that he can bring to bear on any position in the counseling area.

Having served as a consultant in both counseling and testing at two counseling centers in the California State University system, I can attest to the fact that he would make an outstanding contribution in such an institutional setting. Moreover, he exhibits a high level of empathy and sensitivity to the feelings and needs of both his patients and his peers. In short, he is an extremely well balanced person who would contribute greatly to any assignment his expertise as a counseling psychologist with a proven record of success. I am happy to give him my very highest recommendation.

If I can be of any further assistance in effecting his appointment in a counseling position, please do not hesitate to communicate with me. You would be indeed most fortunate to obtain his services.

Cordially yours,

William B. Michael
Professor of Educational Psychology and Psychology

WBM:dc

xl

LEN BERGANTINO, ED.D., A.B.P.P.

Doctorate - University of Southern California - 1971
Clinical Psychology (Psy 3837)
Tel/Fax (310) 207-9397

Trained in Family Therapy by
Carl Whitaker, M.D. & Walter Kempler, M.D.

Diplomate in Family Psychology
American Board of Professional Psychology

DECLARATION OF DR. LEN BERGANTINO

I, DR. LEN BERGANTINO DECLARE:

THESE ARE INDISPUTABLE FACTS:

1. I made a demo playing cornet with deep feeling of two songs with piano accompaniment. The two songs were 1) Black and Blue and 2) Georgia On My Mind.

2. I mailed out a few of them via United States mail. Two days later I received a call from the then president of The Italian American Lawyers who hired me to perform two forty five minute sets playing ballads of well known trumpet solos such as I Can't Get Started, The Sleepy Lagoon, You Made Me Love You, Stranger In Paradise, et. al for a fee of $300 at a cathedral in downtown Los Angeles called Vabbiano.

3. After hearing me play a few solos, while reading the music, he paid me double what I asked for - a fee of $600 for two forty five minute sets.

4. I later found out that in the Italian American Lawyer events prior to my performing he hired Il Vuolo (3 singers from Italy), and the groups Chicago and The Beach Boys.

THESE ARE THE INDISPUTABLE FACTS!

I declare under penalty of perjury that the foregoing is true and correct and I would and could testify as such in a court of law if called upon to do so. This declaration was written in Los Angeles California on April 15, 2013.

DR. LEN BERGANTINO

1215 Brockton Avenue, Suite 104, Los Angeles, California 90025 USA

LEN BERGANTINO, ED.D., A.B.P.P.

Doctorate - Univeristy of Southern California - 1971
Clinical Psychology (Psy 3837)
Tel/Fax (310) 207-9397

Trained in Family Therapy by
Carl Whitaker, M.D. & Walter Kempler, M.D.

Diplomate in Family Psychology
American Board of Professional Psychology

DECLARATION OF DR. LEN BERGANTINO

I, DR. LEN BERGANTINO, DECLARE:

This declaration is to clarify both my self perceived abilities as a musician playing both mandolin and cornet, and to provide a rationale as to how I came to my unusual viewpoints.

I DECLARE THAT ON MANDOLIN I CAN BOTH TOUCH PEOPLE'S SOULS AT THE DEEPEST LEVELS AND HAVE THE HIGHEST QUALITATIVE SOUND EVER RECORDED ON THE MANDOLIN. ON THE CORNET I HAVE SIMILAR ABILITIES IN SOUND QUALITY AND BEAUTY ONLY IT IS MUCH MORE DIFFICULT TO ACHIEVE ON A CONSISTENT BASIS DUE TO PERMANENT PHYSICAL DISABILITIES THAT I HAVE NO CONTROL OVER.

AS I GAVE MUSIC A GO AS A SECOND PROFESSION AFTER BECOMING A WORLD RENOWN CLINICAL PSYCHOLOGIST, THE TWO CANNOT BE SEPARATED IN THE CONSIDERATION OF MY VIEWPOINT. IN PARTICULAR BECAUSE I HAVE PARANORMAL ABILITIES DEVELOPED IN THE WORLD OF CLINICAL PSYCHOLOGY THAT HAVE TRANSFERRED OVER TO MY ABILITY TO PRODUCE SOUND THAT TOUCHES THE SOUL. ON THE MANDOLIN MY DAUGHTER LISA FRANCESCA BERGANTINO BROKE OUT IN TEARS AFTER HEARING A FIVE SONG DEMO ON THE MANDOLIN AND WORLD RENOWN GUITARIST JOE DIORIO BROKE OUT IN TEARS IN A RECORDING MADE AT MUSICIANS LOCAL 47 IN LOS ANGELES WHERE I PLAYED MANDOLIN.

Enclosed here is a demo of me playing two cornet solos whereby I was hired by someone who hired "CHICAGO", "IL VUOLO" AND THE "BEACH BOYS" BEFORE ME AND PAID ME DOUBLE WHAT I ASKED FOR.

I declare under penalty of perjury the foregoing is true and correct. This declaration was written in Los Angeles on April 5, 2013. Dr. Len Bergantino

1215 Brockton Avenue, Suite 104, Los Angeles, California 90025 USA

overture

THE OFFICIAL PUBLICATION OF PROFESSIONAL MUSICIANS LOCAL 47 · LOS ANGELES, AFM, AFL-CIO, CLC

MAY, 2003

Important Change in Dues Payment Policy

As of March 31, 2003, you no longer are able to designate how dues payments shall be applied.

As of March 31, 2003, all late membership dues and all work dues ments to Local 47 will be applied in the following order:

1. Reinstatement fees
2. Membership
3. Outstanding fines/Hearing Board
4. Late fees

A Good Deed

By Dr. Len Bergantino

Rex Merriweather, another Local 47 member, and I were playing trumpet duets out of St. Jacome's — something we hadn't done since our teens — with our original trumpet teachers, mine being Carl Berg who played for Harry James. We met at Rex's house to do this because playing a trumpet is something we both love to do – like two little kids in a sandbox.

I began telling him of the well-known trumpet players who were kind to me along the way. They included Miles Davis, Maynard Ferguson, Harry James, Lee Morgan, and Al Hirt. I told Rex that when Al Hirt was playing a show at Oakdale Summer Theatre in Connecticut in 1963, he talked to me for a long time about playing trumpet with the same enthusiasm that Rex and I had, as if he were a little kid in a sandbox. Then Rex told me a story that has deeply moved everyone I have told.

Rex lived in Wisconsin. He got his first regular job in a band as a young teenager (13 or 14), but they wanted him to have a fluegelhorn as well as a trumpet. He took a train to a well-known trumpet shop in Chicago, which was quite a distance. The only way he could do it was if they gave him credit for his cornet and took perhaps $100 extra. All the time he was trying the horn, there was a big heavy-set man in the corner playing trumpet and trying horns. The shopkeeper said that Rex would have to come back the following day, despite having to take the train a long way back to Wisconsin, and then back again.

When Rex came back the following day, he had his mother come with him. She brought some extra money just in case, but they were not wealthy and it was a stretch. When they got to the store, the man said, "Here is your fluegelhorn and here is your cornet back." Rex said, "How much do I owe you?" The man said, "Nothing. You remember that heavy-set fellow over there in the corner? He heard you play and he thought you were pretty good, so he bought you the fluegelhorn. His name is Al Hirt."

It's kind of funny when someone touches your heart in that way. It keeps the love of the trumpet, the love of the music, and the transmission of culture to future generations alive!

ike a Stan

me of their friends and

, even though the new
cked in and protected
feeling of profound
asn't gone away for so
many others, the disa
pered by a profound
s born from the bitte

Guidelines For Use of the Relief Fund

DR. LEN BERGANTINO
ROMANTIC MUSIC
PRETTIEST "SOUND"
SINCE AL HIRT

MUSIC FOR HIRE

FREE DEMO
310-207-9397

xlviii

Dave Low,   4-17-13

Thank you for the lovely note about Joe Venuto. He was a beautiful man and a great player.

By the way, I listened to your Cornet CD. Lovely playing my friend. What make was the Cornet??

Sincerely,
Ken Baptist

1

Declaration Of
Dr. Len Bergantino

I, Dr. Len Bergantino Declare:

THESE ARE INDISPUTABLE FACTS:

1. \ I made a demo playing cornet with deep feeling of two songs with piano accompaniment. The two songs were 1) Black and Blue and 2) Georgia On My Mind.

2. \ I mailed out a few of them via United States mail. Two days later I received a call from the then president of The Italian American Lawyers who hired me to perform two forty five minute sets playing ballads of well known trumpet solos such as I Can't Get Started, The Sleepy Lagoon, You Made Me Love You, Stranger In Paradise, et. al for a fee of $300 at a cathedral in downtown Los Angeles called Vabbiano.

3. \ After hearing me play a few solos, while reading the music, he paid me double what I asked for - a fee of $600 for two forty five minute sets.

4. \ I later found out that in the Italian American Lawyer events prior to my performing he hired II Vuolo (3 singers from Italy), and the groups Chicago and The Beach Boys.

THESE ARE THE INDISPUTABLE FACTS!

I declare under penalty of perjury that the foregoing is true and correct and I would and could testify as such in a court of law if called upon to do so. This declaration was written in Los Angele California on April 15, 2013.

DR. LEN BERGANTINO

DR. LEN BERGANTINO

Clinical Psychologist and Director

CENTER FOR
MEGALOMANIACAL STUDIES

Diplomate-American Board of Professional Psychology
Author: *Making an Impact in Therapy:*
How Master Clinicians Intervene (1994)   Call 310.207.9397

PsychDirectory   About Us | Basic Listing | Sponsored Listings | Contact Us

Mental Health > Psychology > Psychologist In West Los Angeles

Home Page   Psychology Psychiatry Psychoanalysis Psychotherapy

Directory Index | Mental Health Professionals | Psychology | Psychologists

Mental Health Professionals

Education and Training

Psychological Testing/Evaluation

Mental Health & Social Services

Organizations Centers & Institutes

Mental Health & Psychology News

New Job Search Mental Health Jobs

Directory Search

[Find]

Find a Psychologist
Advanced Search

Psychology Psychiatry Psychoanalysis Psychotherapy
Directory Index > Mental Health Professionals > Psychology > Psychologists

DR. LEN BERGANTINO (SPECIALTY: BETRAYAL MANAGEMENT)

Name/Company: **DR. LEN BERGANTINO (SPECIALTY: BETRAYAL MANAGEMENT)** premium
updated

"I AM FREUD! I AM CAESAR!"

FREUD: "THE PURPOSE OF AN ANALYSIS IS TO SAVE MAN'S SOUL"

EVIDENCE: WHEN MY FATHER DIED ON NOVEMBER 14, 1983, I SAW HIS SOUL LEAVE HIS BODY! SO YOU HAVE ONE!

CURRENT JOB: "SAVING MAN'S SOUL!"

"YE TU BRUTUS!"

"GIVE TO CAESAR WHAT IS CAESARS!"

Licensed Psychologist (CA-3837)

Diplomate in Family Psychology

Description: American Board of Professional Psychology

CALL 310-207-9397

CORDIALLY,

CAESAR

Former Employment: EMPEROR OF ROME!

P.S. FEDERAL SHILLS WELCOME

Current levels of interest:

1) Center for Karmic Rehabilitation

2) Center for Megalomaniacal Studies

Country: United States

State: California

City: West Los Angeles, CA

ZIP / Postal Code: 90025

Phone: 310-207-9397

Contact Person: Dr. Len Bergantino

Map / route: View map / route

E-Mail Address: Send message

URL / Website: http://s2.webstarts.com/lenbergantino/

Classification(s):

Mental Health Professionals | Psychology / Psychologists
Mental Health Professionals | Psychotherapy / Psychotherapists

LEN BERGANTINO, ED.D., A.B.P.P.
Doctorate - Univeristy of Southern California - 1971
Clinical Psychology (Psy 3837)
Tel/Fax (310) 207-9397

Trained in Family Therapy by
Carl Whitaker, M.D. & Walter Kempler, M.D.

Diplomate in Family Psychology
American Board of Professional Psychology

November 19, 2012

TO WHOM IT MAY CONCERN   RE: AUTHORITY AND LEADERSHIP

DECLARATION OF DR. LEN BERGANTINO

I, DR. LEN BERGANTINO, DECLARE:

Around 1994 3 STAR GENERAL HOWARD GRAVES, SUPERINTENDENT
AT THE U.S. MILITARY ACADEMY AT WEST POINT WAS THE GUEST SPEAKER
AT TOWN HALL IN LOS ANGELES. I GOT THERE EARLY AND GENERAL GRAVES
AND THREE OF HIS MILITARY ASSISTANTS WERE IN THE ROOM ALONE.

I WONDERED, HOW IS IT I COULD RELATE TO A GENERAL? WHAT WOULD
I SAY TO HIM? I had the thought when I was in grammar school I
always wanted to be a general. I bent over and pointed at him and
like a little kid began to say in a voice much younger than my
current age, "YOU MUST BE THE GENERAL!" He called me over and
said, "Yes, how did you know?" I began pointing at the others
saying "Look at the way you stand! And look at the way they stand!
(absolutely straight as opposed to curved spine and slightly
hunched). He said, "Would you like me to teach you how to
stand that way?" I said (enthusiastically)"YES!" GENERAL GRAVES
SPENT THE NEXT HALF HOUR TELLING ME WHAT WAS REQUIRED TO BE ABLE
TO STAND LIKE HIM!!! (IT WAS A FULL TIME JOB!)

WE CORRESPONDED BY MAIL SEVERAL TIMES AND HE INVITED ME TO
TRAIN CADETS IN "AUTHORITY AND LEADERSHIP!" LATER HE BECAME
CHANCELLOR AT TEXAS A&M UNTIL HIS DEATH IN 2003!

I declare under penalty of perjury that the foregoing is
true and correct.

DR. Len Bergantino

DR. LEN BERGANTINO

1215 Brockton Avenue, Suite 104, Los Angeles, California 90025 USA

Introduction

What I Brought to the Music Dining Room Table Before Dinner

**Pilgrimage Lite
Music from the Heart**

Len Bergantino

I had been working with a man whose mother had been taken away in a straight jacket and institutionalized when he was three years old. He never saw her again.

The man was so frightened at the primitive three year old level that he invested his entire life in "looking good." He was a successful public relations executive for a big firm, but affectively detached and disconnected and always aiming to please as a result of never being truly present in the here and now.

One day I asked him to sing because he always sounded like he had a cloth stuffed in his mouth. He sang "Come Back to Sorrento," an Italian ballad. He was Irish but sang it with more feeling than I had ever heard in him before.

There had been many sessions which had differing degrees of frustration in which he would come in disconnected, detached and aiming to please, and the feeling I had on this particular day was I just didn't want to say one more word to him about anything.

1

So, to his surprise, I took out my mandolin and in the most loving mellow beautiful way I could I played, "Come Back to Sorrento." He broke down in tears and cried for the last forty minutes of the session, saying only, at the very end, "Bergantino, you sure earned your money today!" I replied, "And to think, I wasted all these years talking to people."

The author is in the private practice of psychoanalysis, Eriksonian hypnosis and Gestalt-experiential family therapy. (editor's note: don't be put off by these formidable descriptions; the main thing about Len's work, as this article demonstrates, is that he responds to his clients in a deeply personal intuitive manner.) He writes, "My work is consistently experiential, as is my squishy nose kissing of my seven year old son Alexander Leonardo, and my teddy bear rendition of "Let me call you Sweetheart" with my five year old daughter, Lisa Francesca."

1988, Bergantino, L. <u>Music From The Heart</u>, Pilgrimage: Psychotherapy and Personal Exploration, Vol. 14, No. 2.

Declaration Of
Dr. Len Bergantino

I, Dr. Len Bergantino Declare:

THESE ARE INDISPUTABLE FACTS:

1. \ I made a demo playing cornet with deep feeling of two songs with piano accompaniment. The two songs were 1) Black and Blue and 2) Georgia On My Mind.
2. \ I mailed out a few of them via United States mail. Two days later I received a call from the then president of The Italian American Lawyers who hired me to perform two forty five minute sets playing ballads of well known trumpet solos such as I Can't Get Started, The Sleepy Lagoon, You Made Me Love You, Stranger In Paradise, et. al for a fee of $300 at a cathedral in downtown Los Angeles called Vabbiano.
3. \ After hearing me play a few solos, while reading the music, he paid me double what I asked for - a fee of $600 for two forty five minute sets.
4. \ I later found out that in the Italian American Lawyer events prior to my performing he hired Il Vuolo (3 singers from Italy), and the groups Chicago and The Beach Boys.

THESE ARE THE INDISPUTABLE FACTS!

I declare under penalty of perjury that the foregoing is true and correct and I would and could testify as such in a court of law if called

3

Dr. Len Bergantino, Ed.D., Ph.D.

upon to do so. This declaration was written in Los Angeles California on April 15, 2013.

_____

DR. LEN BERGANTINO

4

Declaration Of
Dr. Len Bergantino

I, Dr. Len Bergantino, Declare:

This declaration is to clarify both my self perceived abilities as a musician playing both mandolin and cornet, and to provide a rationale as to how I came to my unusual viewpoints.

I DECLARE THAT ON MANDOLIN I CAN BOTH TOUCH PEOPLE'S SOULS AT THE DEEPEST LEVELS AND HAVE THE HIGHEST QUALITATIVE SOUND EVER RECORDED ON THE MANDOLIN. ON THE CORNET I HAVE SIMILAR ABILITIES IN SOUND QUALITY AND BEAUTY ONLY IT IS MUCH MORE DIFFICULT TO ACHIEVE ON A CONSISTENT BASIS DUE TO PERMANENT PHYSICAL DISABILITIES THAT I HAVE NO CONTROL OVER.

AS I GAVE MUSIC A GO AS A SECOND PROFESSION AFTER BECOMING A WORLD RENOWN CLINICAL PSYCHOLOGIST, THE TWO CANNOT BE SEPARATED IN THE CONSIDERATION OF MY VIEWPOINT. IN PARTICULAR BECAUSE I HAVE PARANORMAL ABILITIES DEVELOPED IN THE WORLD OF CLINICAL PSYCHOLOGY THAT HAVE TRANSFERRED OVER TO MY ABILITY TO PRODUCE SOUND THAT TOUCHES THE SOUL. ON THE MANDOLIN MY DAUGHTER LISA FRANCESCA BERGANTINO BROKE OUT IN TEARS AFTER HEARING A FIVE SONG DEMO ON THE MANDOLIN AND WORLD RENOWN GUITARIST JOE DIORIO BROKE OUT IN TEARS

IN A RECORDING MADE AT MUSICIANS LOCAL 47 IN LOS ANGELES WHERE I PLAYED MANDOLIN.

Enclosed here is a demo of me playing two cornet solos whereby I was hired by someone who hired "CHICAGO", "IL VUOLO" AND THE "BEACH BOYS" BEFORE ME AND PAID ME DOUBLE WHAT I ASKED FOR.

I declare under penalty of perjury the foregoing is true and correct. This declaration was written in Los Angeles on April 5, 2013.

Dr. Len Bergantino

Submission

THE NIGHT I WAS SOPHIA LOREN'S BODYGUARD

Around 1996 the Italian Cultural Institute which was in West Los Angeles invited Sophia Loren to be the guest of honor. They forgot to get her a bodyguard and as I was the biggest Italian there that evening they asked me if I wanted to do it. Carlo Ponti, her husband and her son and his girlfriend also attended with her. There were two rooms and I was at the door of one room and made the decisions as to who got in to meet Sophia Loren. I remember welcoming Mr. Gil Garcetti, District Attorney of Los Angeles, to the party and introduced him to Sophia Loren.

She and I had a couple of exchanges. I said "Miss Loren: What is the difference between Italy and the United States?" She said "In Italy, if you are walking up a staircase and a man likes you he pinches you in the ass and you know he likes you. Over here the men walk with their arms at their sides and stare at the ground and you don't know who likes you and who does not like you."

Toward the end of the evening I said "Miss Loren, I would appreciate you signing the back of my business card for my daughter Lisa in that like you she will become as beautiful inside as she is outside." She signed the card.

Respectfully submitted by

Dr. LEn BERGANTINO
CLINICAL PSYCHOLOGIST AND MUSICIAN
1215 Brockton Avenue, Ste. 104
Los Angeles, CA 90025
Tel/Fax 310 207-9397

7

My Dad was a professional musician. He and most of his relatives were all string players, most of whom were taught to read music at 5 years old and then begin playing mandolin at 6 years old as a stepping stone to guitar, violin, piano or in my father's case, tenor banjo.

So began my musical education – from solfeggi to a Gibson F-2 mandolin.

I said "Dad", I can't play in the school band with a mandolin. So with great difficulty I talked him into taking baritone lessons free of charge in elementary school. The baritone was also provided by the school.

My father had 78 rpm records of Benny Goodman, with Charlie Christian of the guitar playing "On The Alamo". It became one of my favorite songs. Other records were "The Hot Club of France" with Django Reinhardt on guitar and Stephane Grapelli on violin. Tommy Dorsey's band. Jimmy Dorsey's band with Helen O'Connell and Bob Eberly singing "Green Eyes" and "Tangerine". I thought Jimmy Dorsey was a hot alto sax player but he only took eight bar solos between singers in his own band. Enrico Caruso singing Paglacci.

However, what changed my life forever was hearing Harry James play trumpet "The Sleepy Lagoon" and "You Made Me Love You."

I said "Dad, I am not going from mandolin to guitar." I am going to play trumpet!" He threw a fit! He heard this as "You are going to betray the entire family heritage! We are string players! I SAID, BUT DID YOU HEAR HARRY JAMES!?!?!?!?!?!?!?"

I knew all the musicians in town so I looked up Carl Berg who married Mike DeVito's daughter and was teaching trumpet at DeVito's Music Store on South Main Street in Waterbury, Connecticut. Carl played trumpet for Harry James for a number of years.

It was a snowy winter day. A Conn Director student trumpet cost $125 in the mid fifties, which was a fortune in those days. My father absolutely refused to be any part of helping me get a trumpet.

I went to Carl Berg and Mike DeVito when I was in the 7th grade and said "I want you to give me a trumpet and trumpet lessons ($3 a week) ONCE A WEEK AND I will work for you cleaning the store, doing whatever you want five days a week after school." They did not use the following words exactly but this is what they meant- "ARE YOU CRAZY? YOUR OLD MAN IS A LUNATIC! IF WE EVER DID THAT HE WOULD BEAT THE SHIT OUT OF US! YOU ARE GOING TO

8

BE A GUITAR PLAYER!" SO MUCH FOR PROFESSIONAL CONNECTIONS AT A YOUNG AGE!

It looked hopeless, and then my maternal grandmother, Clotilde, who didn't take any shit from anybody, said to me "Here is $125 for your trumpet! If you tell anyone where you got the money, I will kill you!" My old man was so embarrassed by this devotion of love on the part of my maternal grandmother, that he agreed to pay for trumpet lessons once a week at $3 per lesson. I never missed a lesson in six years.

$125 does not sound like much, but my grandparents were imigrints who came over through Ellis Island around 1903, and my grandfather worked as a dishwasher at the Elton Hotel for $1 an hour in the mid sixties, so it must have been about 75¢ an hour in the mid fifties. So that was 150 hours of blood, sweat and tears my grandmother gave me out of money they needed to live on.

My father did advise me regarding the selection of a trumpet teacher. He said "Carl Berg has a big beautiful sound and he played for Harry James. He is an excellent teacher who will make time for you. Buddy Vaughn is a high note man who used to play for Alvino Rey who is a very busy pharmacist and will not make the time for a student required to become an excellent trumpet player. I chose Carl Berg.

I only had one fight with Carl Berg. He was from Pittsburgh and in 1960 the Pittsburgh Pirates were playing my favorite team-the New York Yankees in the world series and Bill Mazeroski hit a home run in game 7 to give the Pirates the series. I bet Carl double or nothing and he tried everything he could to get out of the bet, but I insisted that I pay him, that a bet was a bet; only I hated him for it for quite awhile.

Carl Berg was the best trumpet teacher I ever had. 1. He had the patience of a saint. 2. He had the organizational mind of a nuclear physicist.. For example, he used Arban's Trumpet Method which was a very thick book. Carl would write a column of page numbers each week from different parts of the book which focused on different aspects of playing the trumpet.

For example, a week's lesson might look something like what follows in vertical order p. 10, p. 12, p. 26, p. 41, p. 92, p. 126. The pages would correspond to exercises focusing on endurance, sound quality, double tongue, triple tongue, single tongue, ballads, duets where he played with me (always fun to play with the master). The Carnival of Venice would be broken into parts as would Maleguena, et. al.

I had many great trumpet players as teachers – whom I will describe later, but Carl Berg was by far the best trumpet teacher I ever had. It was only after I got my doctorate in Education from the University of Southern California and actually taught music that I realized I was actually taught by a Saint who happened to play trumpet.

The thoughtfulness and musicality that went into his weekly selection of pages to practice is still incomprehensible to me after playing trumpet for 54 years.

I met Harry James in 1966 and I asked him about Carl Berg. Harry James said "Carl Berg was a good strong trumpet player."

I will describe the respit from the trumpet that accompanied a B.A., an M.A., M.S. Ed., Ed.D., and Ph.D. as well as building two private practices in clinical psychology – the first in San Diego and the second in Beverly Hills, California. Let's say for all practical purposes I took a 30 year hiatus between 1965 and 1995 where I did not play trumpet. As Wayne Bergeron told me when I resumed playing and selected him as my teacher, "30 Years Is A Long Time!"

In 1995 I went to an Octoberfest at Alpine Village in Torrance and the Kappelmeister of a 25 piece German Brass Band was a man named Hans Schmeltzer. I walked up to the bandstand and said, "I CAN PLAY YOUR MUSIC!" HE SAID, "WHAT DO YOU PLAY?" I SAID, "TRUMPET!" HE SAID, "GIVE ME YOUR BUSINESS CARD." I GAVE HIM MY CLINICAL PSYCHOLOGY BUSINESS CARD AND HE CALLED ME A COUPLE OF DAYS LATER AND SAID "YOU SAID YOU COULD PLAY MY MUSIC!" I SAID, "YEAH, I CAN PLAY YOUR MUSIC IF I HAD TWO MONTHS TO GET MY CHOPS BACK." HE SAID, "I NEED YOU NEXT SUNDAY. I HAVE TWO GOOD FIRSTS WHO WILL COVER YOU! DO WHAT YOU CAN THIS WEEK PRACTICING AND BE THERE SUNDAY WITH GREY PANTS AND A WHITE SHIRT! YOU WILL PLAY SECOND TRUMPET!" I started to practice and 30 minutes seemed like eight hours of pain on my lips and face which felt like it was dragging to the ground from the chair on which I sat while practicing. Nevertheless, I went down there and played a five hour gig with ten minue breaks each hour. I worked my way up to first trumpet in five years (1995- 2000) AND HAVE BEEN FIRST TRUMPET FOR THE LAST TWELVE YEARS. (UNTIL 2012 WHEN I RETIRED.)

While there is no love lost between me and Schmeltzer I am forever grateful to him for had he not pushed me in the authoritarian manner in which he did, I would nev er have made the time to come back and play the trumpet again. Schmeltzer was an SS officer who commanded one of Hitler's brass bands. I have bought tapes of some of those bands and I am convinced during the time of the Third Reich Hitler had the finest brass bands in the world. We did not just play Um-Pah music. We played some serious and difficult stuff! The band had a few other policies I liked "All the pig you can eat and all the beer you can drink!" Stan Kenton used to have a policy of no drinking until after the gig. Charlie Barnet had a policy that the band members had to drink before and during the gig. Joe Vento asked me if I thought I was good enough to play his book when I had beer before the gig. I did it once and the notes went by like flyshit! Depends on the book and the situation! German gigs are always a lot of fun! And the new Kappelmeister of the Blaskappelle is Ernie Star – a lawyer turned good who played with the band since he was a boy and whose father played for the band. He is a great guy!

THE LAST TIME I TALKED TO CARL BERG

I called him in the late nineties to "thank him" for the magnificent job he did teaching me to play the trumpet. He said, "You were always better than you thought you were." When I told him Ther Germans hadn't kicked me out of the first chair yet.

I played first trumpet in the eighth grade at Mary Abbott Grammar School in Waterbury, Connecticut and in high school I played baseball, basketball and football instead of developing myself as a trumpet player. However, I never missed a trumpet lesson with Carl Berg in six years and I did practice one hour a day for six years no matter what between 7th grade and graduating high school.

I lived on Houston Street. Dave Kennedy lived one street up from me on Myrna Avenue. He was 2 years older than me and a pretty good left handed baseball player but he was a trumpet fanatic first. Dave kept asking me to play in this band, or that band, and I kept turning him down to play sports.

Then one day I said "YES" and played in a big band led by Brent Banulis. I always sounded like Harry James and while I felt as if I did not know what I was doing the band liked my big band trumpet solos. Brent Banulis was a Stan Kenton fan and met him in his studies at The University of Notre Dame. Kenton let him copy his entire book so we were playing Kenton original charts. Brent used to with deep affection call him

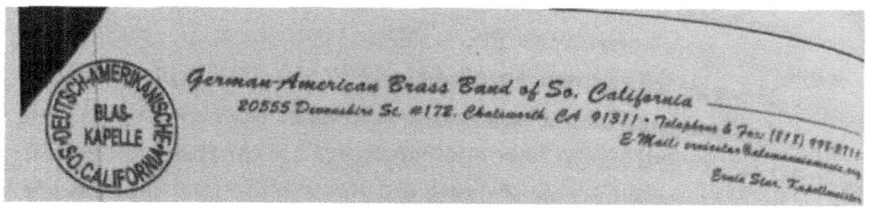

German-American Brass Band of So. California
20555 Devonshire St. #172, Chatsworth, CA 91311 · Telephone & Fax: (818) 999-8711
E-Mail: *****@*********.org
Ernie Star, Kapellmeister

March 19, 2018

Dr. Len Bergantino
1215 Brockton Ave. Ste 104
Los Angeles, CA 90025

To Whom It May Concern:

This letter is confirm that Dr. Len Bergantino played trumpet for the German-American Brass Band of Southern California from 1995 to 2012, during which time I was director of the band.

In 1999 Dr. Bergantino became lead trumpet. His attendance, dedication and preparation were superlative. He enjoyed playing the trumpet and was always working to approve his abilities.

Dr. Bergantino's strengths as a lead trumpet player were the strength and quality of his sound, ability to perform in the higher range of the trumpet, and performance endurance.

Ernie Star
Kapellmeister

12

"Uncle Stan". Kenton was very generous to young musician enthusiasts as he had the good sense to know they would be the ones to carry on his music, something the "trad jazz" people never got right! Stan Kenton left his entire library to the North Texas State University Jazz Department in Denton, Texas and their lab bands are heavily influenced by the Kenton library as are their lead trumpet players. Maynard Ferguson was drafting his lead players from the One O'Clock Lab Bands at North Texas State in the mid to late nineties. One of these fine musicians was Scott Englebright. I went down to study with him for one week in 1996 in Denton Texas. I hit a high G I thought took the paint off the walls. I asked him what he thought and he said "It's a wind instrument!" My view of taking the paint off the walls was different than Maynard Ferguson's lead trumpet player. North Texas State was the only football game I attended where the entire crowd went to hear the band. They were monster players down there in Denton, Texas! Monsters!

THE DAY DAVE KENNEDY DESTROYED MY IDOL

I fell in love with the sound of Harry James playing The Sleepy Lagoon and You Made Me Love You, as well as the trumpet technique of Raphael Mendez. (See Mendez article - p. 239-240). That is why I signed up to play trumpet!

Dave Kennedy kept hounding me to go up to his house and hear a record of a guy he said was better than "MY IDOL, Harry James" – a guy named Maynard Ferguson. For a couple of years I thought it was an impossibility and just refused to go. Then I made the mistake of going and heard a record (33 rpm) entitled "Jazz For Dancing" where Maynard Ferguson played "Stella by Starlight". "Where's Teddy?" and others a good octave above Harry James with a sound as big as a house. All of a sudden I was being thrown into a musical world I didn't sign up for. I was a tall skinny guy, built somewhat like Harry James. The people playing Maynard's music were built more like tackles on the football team, with necks as big as professional wrestlers.

Between the ages of five and six years old my father gave me solfeggi lessons on how to read music – one half hour lesson per week and by six years old I could read flyshit if it happened to appear in the form of musical notations. My choices were to study solfeggi or go fifteen rounds toe to toe with my father in mortal combat, so I studied music instead of playing baseball with the kids in front of the house.

13

THE FAMILY HERITAGE: MANDOLIN LESSONS AT SIX YEARS OLD!

My Great Uncle Soledad Bredice taught his two sons and my father music. They all claimed one of the other was the best and they were all great at certain things. My father was the second best tenor banjo player I ever heard other than Harry Reser who did it first. My cousin Louis Bredice played piano and was tenth in the country in Downbeat Magazine's jazz piano poll one year. He played some with Bobby Hackett in New York. Fred Bredice had blazing speed on the guitar and had his own radio show in the mid thirties. He was a legend in Waterbury among Italian American guitar players. He taught Joe Diorio how to play, a world renown jazz guitar player and last time I talked to Joe he was still having nightmares about Freddie's speed. In any case all of this started with Soledad Bredice teaching his two sons and my father mandolin at age six years old. So went my career with the New York Yankees! It was as if Patrick Henry said, "Give Me Mandolin or Give Me Death!"

My father took me to meet the best violin repair man in Waterbury, Louis Volpe who had a GIbson F-2 mandolin on the wall my father bought for $75 (That was like $1000 in 1949). People like Louis Volpe took pride in what they did in a way that is different than 2017. It was not a matter of money. It was a matter of when Louis Volpe said the Gibson on the wall was better than the Martin he had on the wall, even my old man respected his decision.

Louis Volpe had a big Saint Bernard Dog. The dog was bigger than me when I was six years old. It got up on its hind legs to give me a kiss and knocked me to the ground. For some strange reason to this day I have always had a special fondness for Saint Bernards! My father gave me a lesson a week from a DeCristoforo Mandolin Method Book One. My father's idea was that I would move on from the mandolin to guitar as that was a modern day instrument as opposed to tenor banjo.

My father's idea with the solfeggi first for one year was, "Now that you can read music, you only have to worry about playing the instrument!" While this method is no longer utilized among the precocious and requires a level of frustration tolerance most parents would find inconvenient to inflict on their little dears, by far it is the superior method to become a musician. My father used to say "musician, it is a small word but it encompasses a lot!" No matter how much you become, there is always a lifetime of more!

Guitar players and tenor banjo players customarily played chords and had hands more like Wilt Chamberlin than me. This was before I met cousin Fred Bredice on a gig on a Sunday afternoon in Los Angeles in 1967 and I saw that blazing left hand and went up to him, waited until he finished and looked down at him saying, "You must be Cousin Fred!" He looked up and instead of saying "Hello" he gave me a music lesson. He said, "Yeah, I don't play chords! It fucks up your hands!" And I thought, "Now you tell me!" As Bert Turetzky taught me bass fiddle at the University of Connecticut, when I started playing tenor banjo about 1995, I played soulful jazz as influenced by Miles Davis and Chet Baker and walking bass lines as influenced by Bert Teretzky and Johnnie St. Cyr – the banjo player with Louis Armstrong's Hot Five and Hot Seven in the early to mid twenties.

I wasn't too thrilled to be conscripted as a mandolin player when most people my age never heard of one and you could not play in any school band with it. In the mid fifties it was a rare Italian delicacy in Waterbury, Connecticut although Ray Amicone made a living playing an electric D'Angelico mandolin he had the world renown guitar maker Johnny D'Angelico make for him in the mid fifties. D'Aquisto, later a famous guitar maker was only 19 years old then when I met him as D'Angelico's apprentice. I was playing a blonde D'Angelico mandolin on the wall and Johnny D'Angelico said to me "That is Dick Dia's mandolin. If he walks in and sees you playing it he will take your head off!" In the late nineties someone gave me a record album of Dick Dia with that mandolin on the cover. I tried to look him up to buy it, but alas he was dead. I did get in touch with his son in New Jersey who told me a tragic story, that his father had Alzheimer's and one day came home without the mandolin and had no idea where he left it. His records of Italian mandolin in the era Dean Martin was big were beyond my ability to describe the extent of his musical quality as it approached magnificence.

> DICK DIA! A BLOND D'ANGELICO MANDOLIN
> ON THE ALBUM COVER! (Mid 70's)
> THE SCHOOL BAND – FREE LESSONS AND A
> FREE INSTRUMENT
> BARITONE HORN – 7TH GRADE – MARY

ABBOTT GRAMMAR SCHOOL TEACHER MR. AVALON

I liked the baritone. It had a big full rich round sound. It had a big mouthpiece and when I played in the school marching band no matter how many pot holes you stepped in while marching, you never missed spitting in the right place in the mouthpiece and hitting the right place in the mouthpiece as well as the correct note. I like marching band when I played baritone. I hated marching band when I played trumpet because the mouthpiece was so small that when it bounced it was just as likely to be on the side of my mouth where I would either miss the note or play out of tune.

I PLAYED BARITONE AND TRUMPET FOR ONE FULL YEAR in the seventh grade and then quit baritone because the big mouthpiece was messing up what I had to do with the trumpet and overall I liked trumpet best of all. I resumed baritone and played in a Korean band for two years from 2006-2008 after my trumpet embochure was well developed and could not be adversely affected by the differing sizes of mouthpieces.

BARITONE MOUTHPIECES. Playing the trumpet, fluegelhorn and cornet I must have bought and played over a hundred mouthpieces at different times in my career. This was not the case with the baritone. Baritones have the same mouthpieces as trombones. I studied jazz with trombone player Bill Watrous who told me he played a Bach 11 he got in the U.S. Navy in 1946 and never had reason to change mouthpieces. So a brass player told me to get a Bach 14 1/2 D which would give me the least amount of aggravation switching between trumpet and baritone. I worked out OK and I never had cause to switch baritone mouthpieces.

I was given a baritone in school and weekly lessons by Mr. Avalon - music educator in the Waterbury Connecticut Public School System. The reason I was chosen was that no one else wanted to play it. I fear this is still the case as the instrument has almost become extinct in professional circles.

PUBLIC EDUCATION AND MUSIC IN THE SCHOOLS

1. \ I have a doctorate in Education from the University of Southern California.
2. \ I have had courework in curriculum development and was a straight A student. My major professor in curriculum development was Dr.

16

William Georgiades who was a consultant nationally.

3. \ School districts are always running out of money and always threatening to or actually cutting music from the curriculum.

4. \ THIS IS A BIG MISTAKE. HERE IT IS SOME FIFTY FIVE YEARS AFTER I WAS GIVEN A BARITONE HORN AND FREE MUSIC LESSONS IN THE SCHOOLS, AND I STILL PLAY MUSIC. I NEVER USE CHEMISTRY, PHYSICS, ANY MATH BEYOND SIMPLE ADDITION AND SUBTRACTION, ANY ENGLISH BEYOND READING AND WRITING ENOUGH TO DO THIS BOOK, ET. AL. I AM SURE YOU SEE THE POINT. I STILL PLAY MUSIC! IT IS A LIFETIME SUBJECT THAT ONE CAN DO AT SOME LEVEL OF ACHIEVEMENT EVEN IF IT IS NOT AT A PROFESSIONAL LEVEL FOR AS LONG AS THEY LIVE, AND IN SOME CASES, EMERITUS BANDS COMPOSED OF OLD GEEZERS STILL PLAYING MUSIC MAY BE THE ONLY PURPOSE TO THEIR EXISTENCE! SO IF SCHOOL DISTRICTS RUN OUT OF MONEY CUT SHAKESPEARE! CUT PHYSICS! CUT BIOLOGY! CUT ALGEBRA! CUT GEOMETRY! CUT CHEMISTRY! BUT DO NOT CUT MUSIC!

ABOUT MY FATHER, DAN BERGANTINO, PROFESSIONAL MUSICIAN, LOCAL 186

My father's parents were from San Marco La Catola, Italy in the province of Foggia. If you fly to Bari and take a cab two hours up in the mountains you will get there. It is before Compobasso.

His uncle Soledad Bredice – a genius and inventor of sorts-taught my father, and his own sons Fred and Louis Bredice how to play mandolin, all at the age of six years old. My father had about 6 months of mandolin lessons and then went on to take violin lessons for two years. That was the only musical education he had. His father was a stone mason who was laid off from work and my father taught himself to play tenor banjo. He supported his mother, father and seven other brothers and sisters as a musician.

He played tenor banjo in a big band that was similar to Paul Whiteman's big band. My father is the second best tenor banjo player I ever heard, second only to Harry Reser (buy whatever cd you can still get of Reser! He was a MONSTER! THE LIKES OF WHICH WILL NEVER BE

HEARD OR SEEN AGAIN!) I heard Don Vappie of New Orleans play as good as Reser once! (2009) Nobody wants to practice enough to be that good all the time! Reser was like Raphael Mendez on the trumpet. I met Mendez in 1971 giving a concert at La Puente Junior High School. He told me he played very softly just warming up for two hours. At that time I had never practiced more than two hours total at one time. Mendez practiced 12 hours a day! No wonder he was the best in the world at what he did!

Radio killed the tenor banjo! My father said, first they told him the banjo was too loud; then they put him near the door; then they put him outside the door; and then they said, "Hey Danny! If you want to play you had better learn guitar. So he taught himself how to play guitar. His favorites were Django Reinhardt, Eddie Lang (whose real name was Sal (Italian name starting with an m) and Charlie Christian whose version of "ON THE ALAMO" WITH THE BENNY GOODMAN SEXTET IS SOMETHING YOU WILL REMEMBER FOR THE REST OF YOUR LIFE IF YOU HEAR IT ONCE!

In 1941 my father bought a 1939 D'Angelico Style B guitar for $139. After his death John Bernunzio of Bernunzio Vintage Instruments in Rochester, New York sold it to a man in Australia for $10,000. Bernunzio is a good guy that won't scalp you. I bought 3 vintage tenor banjos from him and two mandolin banjos.

I saw my father on both the tenor banjo and guitar light up an entire room as if he had magic when he was invited to sit in on a band that might be playing at a wedding we were invited to attend as a friends of the family. He was the "music man" so to speak. I could do this as a psychotherapist training people at the international level from 1984 onward and as a musician at the late age of 66 years old. My father lit up like a Christmas tree when he was doing it. He was a straightforward fellow who often spoke his mind in an era when people were polite and straight talk was frowned on. My view of him was that he would much rather play music than talk to people.

THE DAY CHARLIE PARKER CAME TO WATERBURY!

BACK TO THE FUTURE REALLY HAPPENED!

I was about ten years old. I went to a Saturday afternoon Italian wedding. They hired an Italian American young man to play guitar and hire his own band. He was into progressive jazz and Waterbury was a Benny Goodman Swing Music Town.

18

The young guitar player, brought Charlie Parker in from New York (100 miles from Waterbury) for the gig. I remember him playing discordant sounds at the speed of light that I had never in my life heard before or since for that matter! When he finished I was the only one clapping. THE AUDIENCE JUST STOOD THERE, STOPPED ALL MOVEMENT AND STARED AT CHARLIE PARKER UNTIL HE NOT ONLY LEFT THE BANDSTAND BUT WALKED OUT OF THE GIG ALTOGETHER AND WENT IMMEDIATELY BACK TO NEW YORK.

THE DAY ROSALIND RUSSELL ATTEMPTED TO PUT WATERBURY ON THE MAP!

She made a movie in 1955 entitled PICNIC and was going to have the premiere in Waterbury instead of Hollywood. She was from Waterbury and used to come to town to visit her mother. That night a flood hit Waterbury and put the city twelve feet under water on South Main and Grand Street and Bank street. THE NEWSPAPER HEADING THE NEXT MORNING RAN SOMETHING LIKE "BLACK ROSALIND BRINGS FLOOD TO WATERBURY!" IN OTHER WORDS THEY BLAMED HER FOR THE FLOOD. THE LESSON I LEARNED FROM THAT IS "NEVER TRY TO PUT ANYBODY OR ANYTHING ON THE MAP WHEN THEY THINK THEY ALREADY ARE ON THE MAP!" I MEAN AFTER ALL WATERBURY WAS FAMOUS FOR GEORGE METESKY, THE MAD BOMBER AND JIMMY PIERSALL! (KNOWN FOR MOVIE "FEAR STRIKES OUT" WHERE PIERSALL IS PLAYED BY TONY PERKINS). WATERBURY WAS NOT A CITY OF INSIGHT! IN OTHER WORDS, THAT IS JUST HOW IT WAS! EVERYBODY KNEW IT AND EVERYBODY ACCEPTED IT! EXCEPT CHARLIE PARKER! I believe Joe Diorio left town when he was 21 to escape. He did alright in New York at 21 but probably would have been stoned to death in Waterbury.

While my father was one of the premiere musicians in Waterbury he was dominated by music up to progressive jazz but not including. He was paraochial in his musical tastes, which were impeccable as far as they went. The movie Blackboard Jungle came out and Bill Haley and the Comets played "Rock Around The Clock". I did a decent job on the mandolin playing it, and I had long sideburns, motorcycle boots a pompadour haircut, and a black leather jacket and could have easily fit in with Marlon Brando in On The Waterfront. My father said "Forget that Rock and Roll Shit! It will never last!" I would have peaked about the time Elvis did!

In Waterbury, my parents would plan a trip to New York for 6 months and then we would take the train from Waterbury to Grand Central Station. Walking around New York there were always signs that read "Charlie Parker", Dizzy Gillespie, Miles Davis, and he would never take me in to see them. He gave me the feeling he thought their music was crazy and again he said "It will never last!" I wound up being heavily influenced by Chet Baker and Miles Davis in the Cool Era. I also loved the saxaphone tone of Gerry Mulligan on the baritone sax and the duets he played with Chet Baker where they would play off of each other. This is how I took lessons with Bill Watrous, playing as Chet Baker and Gerry Mulligan did taking courses off of each other on a tune. Bob Reeves has made me over $3000 worth of trumpet mouthpieces (Valencia California) and he one time told me "In trumpet sound is everything. If it doesn't sound beautiful no one wants to hear it!" Simple as it may sound it is at the bottom of all music. I always felt that way about saxaphone players and one sound I loved was the alto saxaphone sound of Paul Desmond when he played with Dave Brubeck. Unfortunately he was too much like Harry James. Both were heavy smokers and both died of lung cancer! I cannot understand as a clinical psychologist why a professional musician who made his living blowing a wind instrument would choose to smoke and kill themselves in such a violent manner of death as lung cancer. I take it back. I understand it. It just pisses me off!

MY IRREVERENT COUSIN ANN

My cousin Ann Mete came for a few guitar lessons with my father. She told me she learned three chords. She became a member of one of the first "All Girls Rock And Roll Bands in the early sixties. After the first two lessons my father said "Ann, same time next week?" Ann said, "Oh, No, Uncle Dan! I've got a job in an All Girls Rock and Roll Band playing guitar (the three chords she knew) and I am leaving for Iceland next week.

She made a living from that band and it led to her income for the rest of her life. While my father was one helluva musician it certainly made me give pause about his comments regarding what would last and what would not last in terms of both rock and roll and progressive jazz.

20

I graduated from Sacred Heart High School and went to the University of Connecticut at Storrs, Connecticut. A guitar player heard me playing the mandolin as a "tension breaker" and said excitedly, "You Play Mandolin!" I said, "Yeah, why!" He then said "AND YOU HAVE A GIBSON!" Again, rather flatly and without enthusiasm I said "Yeah." No one had ever cared whether I played mandolin in my entire life except my father to this point in my life, and frankly I thought he was nuts for sticking me with a white elephant so to speak!

ALL OF A SUDDEN MY FATHER BECAME A GENIUS IN MY EYES!

At the University of Connecticut romantic mandolin music was the thing in 1961 (almost as good as Brubeck and "Take Five!"

I was getting hired to play romantic mandolin music during exchange dinners between fraternities and sororities, getting invited to parties I would not otherwise be invited to, getting paid $5 to play about one and one half hours, and getting to meet some very attractive young ladies I would not otherwise have access to.

And the mellow sound of the Gibson F-2 1913 mandolin didn't hurt either. I played it on most of my dates in college as a romancing my date kind of thing, playing Mi sty, Stardust, Smoke Gets in Your Eyes, Come Back To Sorrento, and some other romantic ones. You can see why my view of my father's wisdom changed from being goat to hero radically in his having me play the mandolin. I was one of the few I ever met and certainly the only one at the University of Connecticut in 1961.

COLLEGE AND MY TRUMPET!

Trumpet is louder than mandolin and therefore more unwelcome in dormitory life.

I have always been able to befriend people in high places, not because I was hustling them, but because my being "natural" "not hustling them" and/or having something in common with them brought us together.

I attended Central Connecticut State College for 3 semesters beginning with the Spring Semester of 1962. I had a sound like Harry James. There was a young saxaphone player telling me I was passe and that I had better get with it. He kept telling me that Miles Davis and Chet Baker had a new trumpet style was called "COOL". The first time someone said this to me was a few years earlier when my cousin Bob Mete (God rest his soul – died at 42 years old – big brother of Ann Mete) who played saxaphone on gigs with my father invited me to his home to hear Chet Baker, Miles Davis, Shorty Rogers, and Cannonball and Nat Adderly.

I lived on the second floor of the college dormitory. I used to practice in the basement in the afternoon. It infuriated a senior whose last name was "Toth" who always claimed he was trying to study.

Dean Morris, Dean of The College, was my piano accompanist at these rehearsals.

One day Toth came busting into the rec room screaming "BERGANTINO, IF YOU DON'T STOP PLAYING THAT TRUMPET, I AM GOING TO SHOVE IT RIGHT UP YOUR ASS!" THEN HE SAID, TO MY UTTER DELIGHT, "AND WHO IS THAT ASSHOLE PLAYING PIANO WITH YOU!" DEAN MORRIS TURNED AROUND FACING THE COMPLAINANT AND I SAID "BOB (ROBERT TOTH) This is Dean Morris! He is Dean of the College!" Toth turned ghostly white and looked like he was going to pass out. Then Dean Morris said to him, "After all, the young man has to practice his trumpet!" (which if you are a trumpet player is absolutely true!) Toth then turned around, walking out, screaming at Dean Morris, "You are just as crazy as Bergantino!"

ME AT TWELVE YEARS OLD

I had a great sound on the trumpet and most of the neighbors liked to hear me play. So on summer vacation I would play romantic ballads with the doors and windows open, out into the neighborhood.

How was I to know that Sally Baggish had brought her son Jerry Baggish home from summer camp at 4 a.m. and wanted to sleep in on this particular morning. Speaking of "Arousing a Sleeping Giant" Sally came storming across the street in her night gown with huge breasts bobbing up and down, and began pounding on my door in a tirade telling me she was going to kill me for waking her up. There was no doubt in my mind that she meant to do exactly what she said she was going to do, as Sally was not someone who made idle threats.

I TURNED THE TRUMPET AROUND, HOLDING IT AS IF IT WERE A TIRE IRON, AND I FIRMLY SAID TO HER, "SALLY, IF YOU TAKE ONE MORE STEP I AM GOING TO BREAK THIS TRUMPET OVER YOUR HEAD!" SALLY KNEW I MEANT IT.

WITHOUT SAYING A WORD SHE CALMLY TURNED AROUND AND IMMEDIATELY WALKED BACK ACROSS THE STREET TO HER OWN HOUSE. NEITHER SALLY NOR I EVER MENTIONED THE INCIDENT AND WE REMAINED GOOD FRIENDS, BUT SHE KNEW IT AND I KNEW IT AND THIS IS ALL THERE WAS TO IT!

TRUMPET AND SOPHOMORE YEAR COLLEGE

I sounded like Harry James. There was a girls dormitory slightly up the hill from the boys dormitory. Dinner was usually from about 5-6 p.m. and then I would take out my trumpet and begin to seranade the girls' dormitory, with the sound moving uphill. I played The Sleepy Lagoon and You Made Me Love You (Harry James); I Can't Get Started (Bunny Berrigan); and tunes such as Misty and Stardust and others to a cheering, clapping group of college coeds.

CARL BERG ALWAYS WANTED TO SELL ME A CONN CONSTELLATION TRUMPET in the mid to late fifties. He played one and Maynard Ferguson played one. The sound was a little too dark for me. He would have settled for a New York Bach (always a bit stuffy for my tastes) or an Olds Mendez Model (a little too brassy for my tastes)

Harry James always had his picture in the International Musician Magazine advertising King Silversonic Dual Bore trumpets, and of course that is the sound I wanted so I bought a Parduba #5 Harry James mouthpiece and I went down to Manny's Music Store in New York and bought a King for $225. In Waterbury you couldn't even buy one but the top of the line horns were going for $300 (Bach, Olds and Conn).

KENNY DORHAM WANTED TO SELL ME A
MARTIN LARGE BORE TRUMPET!

I was very parochial in my musical tastes as outlined by my professional musician father, which did not include progressive jazz. I went to Manny's Music Store in New York in 1962 with Billy Mecca who said of this fellow with a baggy jacket and baggy pants who looked rather poor and unkept at the time, "THAT'S KENNY DORHAM!" Of course, I had no idea who Kenny Dorham was and when Billy Mecca informed me he was a famous progressive jazz musician, it still meant nothing to me.

In retrospect if I had bought that horn (Martin Committee Large Bore) it would in 2010 be worth about $3000. At the time Chet Baker, Miles Davis and Dizzy Gillespie all played one but I don't know much about them either. All I knew was I couldn't get the sound I wanted on my test song, "The Sleepy Lagoon" which was a sound ala Harry James. I must have played it fifty times until Billy Mecca and Kenny Dorham had both exhausted any patience they may have had.

JUNIOR YEAR OF COLLEGE AT THE UNIVERSITY OF CONNECTICUT

I had a growth cut out of my lip and did not play trumpet my entire junior year. My senior year I was one of two or three first trumpets in the University of Connecticut Concert Band.

TEACHING GUITAR FOR SOME SPENDING MONEY.

Billy Mecca's father owned Mecca Music Studies and on Monday nights I charged $5 a lesson and kept $3 of it while Mr. Mecca got $2.

TEACHING GUITAR AT MUSIC STUDIO IN TORRINGTON CONNECTICUT

My junior and senior year of college when my father had wedding gigs on the guitar he would have me fill in for him at at music store in Torrington, Connecticut from 9 a.m. to 5 p.m. where I was paid $5 per half hour by guitar students. I kept $3 and $2 went to the store, but that was still pretty good spending money in those days for a college kid. ($51 for a Saturday)

While I did not play guitar all my years playing the mandolin and my familiarity with the guitar finger board got me to a place where I could take students through Mel Bay Guitar Method Books 1-4. I had trouble with one student in Book 5 who wanted me to demonstrate.

CARMEN D'AGOSTINO was my best friend in college at the University of Connecticut. I met him thinking I was selling him a bunch of guitar books and then he told me his father owned the Burritt Music Store in New Britain Connecticut and his father gave him whatever music he wanted free of charge. Carmen was built and looked a little like the Frankenstein Monster in the movies except he had the cutest little baby smile on his face. He was about 6:1 and 205 pounds and he played guard on the football team. Being

Carmen's best friend and a few perks, such as when "the dirty old men from New Britain came to visit Carmen on the weekend" and they went room to room throwing everyone's clothes out the window, mine went untouched. And then there were those fraternity parties where I heard Carmen yell out, "I AM GOING TO STEP ON YOUR FACE!" and of course, when I turned around a split second later I had already missed just how he went about getting the fellow on the ground, but there he was stepping on his face. Anyway with me he was like a little friendly puppy! His father, referred to in the music world as JOE DAG also played symphony gigs with my father. JOE DAG PLAYED CLARINET AND MY FATHER PLAYED VIOLIN. ALAS THEY GOT TO MEET AND COMPARE NOTES AS TO WHICH OF THE TWO SONS WAS CRAZIER, ME OR CARMEN!

CARMEN'S FUTURE WAS NEVER IN DOUBT. THE DAY HE GRADUATED HE WAS GOING TO TAKE OVER THE BURRITT MUSIC STORE FOR THE REST OF HIS NATURAL LIFE; ONLY CARMEN HATED SITTING DOWN IN ANY ONE PLACE FOR TOO LONG, SO HE TOOK EIGHT YEARS TO GET THROUGH FOUR YEARS AT UCONN!

JOE DAG RENTS ME A BASS FIDDLE FOR $10 A MONTH IN 1964

I had a growth on my lip and had it removed and did not play trumpet for one year, so I took a bass fiddle class with world renown BERT TERETZKY, WHO LATER BECAME CHAIRPERSON OF THE DEPARTMENT OF MUSIC AT THE UNIVERSITY OF CALIFORNIA AT SAN DIEGO IN LA JOLLA, CALIFORNIA.

Playing bass had a few perks. The University of Connecticut was about one and one half miles long and you had to walk it in the snow to get to class in the morning and after lunch. When I kept the bass in the back seat I was given a parking pass to park anywhere on campus because I was a bass player (student).

My father often told me "If you want to work, play bass!" I didn't particularly like the music business so I only played it until my lip healed from surgery and then went back to playing my first love, trumpet! Building a music business was like building a psychotherapy business, only the club owners were both crazier and cheaper than my private practice psychotherapy patients. So from my vantage point while I loved to play music I hated to deal with those who would hire me to play because I was paid far more handsomely for doing private practice psychotherapy, and I had to do psychotherapy with club and restaurant owners to get gigs for pennies on the dollar!

SUMMERTIME – 1963 – MY SOPHOMORE YEAR OF COLLEGE

My best friend in Waterbury, Connecticut since kindergarden was George O'Meara (now deceased). We used to go down to Phil Becker's German Bar in the middle of Waterbury's North Square (like Harlem) and suck up 15¢ beers on hot summer afternoons.

RED KEIDEL USED TO PLAY CORNET ON SATURDAY NIGHTS FROM 9 p.m. to closing at 1 a.m. That was his only job, playing one night a week. He worked four hours a week. Red had great ideas. He had ideas like Bobby Hackett. I said to him, "Red, you have great ideas on the cornet! You play like Bobby Hackett! Only you have a sound like you are blowing a tin can! If you practiced two hours a day you could be playing New York City instead of Beckers!" Red took his time and barely lifting his lips off the glass as if his head weighed at least a thousand pounds from his point of view slowly said, "I can't find the time!"

BOB BURNS – THE BROKE STOCKER! O'Meara and I had another friend named Bob Burns who got a fellowship teaching German at The University of Mississippi while pursuing an M.A. in German. He was gibbering away and Phil Becker, the owner of Becker's was from Germany and rather forthrightly said "What language is he speaking?" I said, "Phil, he is speaking German!" Phil said, "That's not German! I'm from Germany and that's not German!" O'Meara and I all too gleefully pointed out to Burns the remarks of Phil Becker, and Burns comment floored us (1965) when he said, "Nobody at the University of Mississippi German Department knows that I am not speaking German!" In other words he got up in front of freshman German students and spoke what might be referred to as alliteration, words that sounded just as if he were speaking German. He finished 30 units of coursework but of course was not able to write a master's thesis in German, given he could not speak, read or write German!

Burns was an adventurer! After the first couple of James Bond movies came out Burns talked me into taking a trip with him to Washington, D.C. where we were interviewed by the C.I.A. with the idea of becoming James Bond like characters for the U.S. Government. Burns first question to the interviewer was "Did Lee Harvey Oswald work for the CIA?" The interviewer candidly said "YES!" Burns next question was whether he had ever been a hired assassin for the United States government. The man said he thought so. Then he told me what he needed was an underwater demolition man. I told him I couldn't swim. As his job description bore no resemblance to the romanticized version of Sean Connery in the Bond movies, I rapidly lost interest.

Burns and I visited Thomas Jefferson's home – then a historic sight with a roped off bed. Burns for some reason unbeknownst to me jumped over the rope into Jefferson's bed and we were both asked to leave. He thought it was funny. I did not! In terms of the bigger picture for two 25 year olds we made a good team. I was a good talker. He was good looking and we never liked the same girl. Burns became a stock broker. To his dismay, O'Meara used to call him "THE BROKE STOCKER!"

BACK TO BOBBY HACKETT AND MY TRUMPET

I had a relative who was an envious, hateful, spiteful person who studied trumpet with the same trumpet teacher I had, Carl Berg. In the 7th grade his mother said "Let's see what you can do on the trumpet!" (after I had been playing all of two months and the sound came out like Harry James) . He yelled out that I sounded as terrible as Harry James and if I had any taste in music at all I should and would model myself after Bobby Hackett! He whined and complained that I had an unfair advantage over him because my father was a professional musician. While this was true in terms of overall musicality it had nothing to do with the fact I had a beautiful sound on the trumpet from the first note I ever played. Perhaps God said "Hey you, play trumpet!"

His father took mandolin lessons from my father when he was twelve years old. As the story goes, one day my father had an epiphany and grabbed his round back Italian mandolin and smashed it over his head while loudly telling him YOU ARE NOT GOING TO MAKE IT!" MY FATHER TOOK HIS MUSIC SERIOUSLY!

NICKY MOFFO, MY FATHER'S GUITAR STUDENT IN 1963 (SEPTEMBER) I used to come home from college some weekends and I saw Nicky Moffo, younger brother of my high school friend Tony Moffo, taking a guitar lesson from my father and looking out the same front window at the kids in front of my house playing stick ball the same as I used to do years earlier when my father taught me mandolin. I saw Nicky looking out the window when my father was explaining a passage on the guitar. I stuck my head in the room and ppinted to Nicky saying "Nicky, don't do that." My father reexplained the passage and I could just feel it coming. Again, I looked into the room as Nicky was looking out the window and said "Nicky, don't do that!" When Nicky did it for a third straight time when my father was explaining the passage, my father pressed his fingers into the strings as hard as he could and in an upwardly ascending voice screeched "NO, NICKY! IT'S LIKE THIS!" AND I HEARD NICKY SCREAM AS LOUD AS IF HE WERE IN A DR. FRANKENSTEIN MOVIE. AT THAT POINT I STUCK MY HEAD BACK INTO THE ROOM AND POINTED AT NICKY AND SAID "NICKY, I TOLD YOU NOT TO DO THAT!"

MY FATHER AND I CAME TO A MUSICAL UNDERSTANDING

Before answering machines were invented my father depended on actually being there to answer the telephone to get hired as a musician. I was a high school kid talking with friends or girls I either dated or wanted to date far too much time to suit my father's musical needs. One day he walked in and there I was on the phone right after he told me to stay off of it. He hit me with a right hand shot to the face as hard as he could. I had been lifting weights: the clean and jerk -200 pounds; bench press of 240 pounds; 1/4 squat with 500 pounds. I looked him square in the eye and said "If you ever try that again I will break your back!" He never did and I made some effort to use the phone less and he got more calls. He played two to four nights a week.

I have no regrets about our encounter. He trained me to handle a lot of life situations that I would not otherwise be able to handle.

My next door neighbor Allie Vestro was spotting me doing bench presses when my father asked him to leave. In my overzealous effort to become all that I could be I did not notice that Allie could not spot me the weights without a clank clank and my father had to get up at 6 a.m. to go to work. He opened the cellar door and asked Allie to leave but I persuaded Allie to continue and my father would not hear the weights go clank clank because we would not go clank clank with them, which of course was impossible. So Allie helped out and my father heard the weights again and came to the cellar door and said "Allie, if you are not gone by the time I count to ten I am coming down stairs and I will beat you to within an inch of your life." So much for weightlifting that night. Allie looked shocked that the father of one of his friends would say that to him but he knew my father never made any idle threats and left quietly and immediately.

*****IN SOME STRANGE WAY I ALWAYS ADMIRED MY FATHER'S BRAND OF LUNACY! IT RUBBED OFF ON ME IN THAT A LOT OF GUYS WHO WANTED TO AND COULD HAVE KICKED MY ASS WHEN THEY LOOKED ME IN THE EYE, SHIT THEIR PANTS AND RAN FOR THE HILLS!!!

When I was about five years old I had a neighbor who bit me in the arm and left teeth marks. I ran in the house crying asking my father to make it right with him. He said I am going to show you how to box and in particular hit someone in the face where it really hurts. If he ever bites you again hit him right in the face. If you lose and you come in here crying I will beat the shit out of you. Well, I was a little afraid of him but I thought my old man could do some serious damage so the next time my neighbor did it I almost put my fist through to the other side of his head and all was well in the neighborhood for awhile. To get to grammar school I had to get through the path every day and all the kids demanded a competitive good fight for entertainment purposes. I was one of the top three fighters in the class so I basically had to fight every day to get to school and home in the morning and a fternoon. I didn't lose too many but it did not make me fond of school.

At world series time when baseball was the King of sports and the New York Yankees were King of baseball, Mickey Mantle, Yogi Berra, Allie Reynolds, Whitey Ford, et. al. I always convinced my mother I was to ill to go to school and I actually willed myself into sore throats and fevers. Between 1951 and 1956 the only world series game I missed and went to school was the day Don Larsen pitched a perfect game in 1956. I got home to see the last pitch of the game to Dale Mitchell. I was pissed!

BACK TO BOBBY HACKETT

My cousin Lou Bredice was 10th in the country in Downbeat Magazine's Jazz Poll one year in jazz piano. In 1946 he played gigs in New York with Bobby Hackett. Lou said that Bobby Hackett refused to say anything negative about anyone under any circumstances. So the guys in the band decided to give Bobby Hackett a hard time. The Germans had just lost the war and Adolph Hitler's reputation was at an all time low given Auschwitz and Buchanwald. So the musicians said "Hey Bobby! What do you think of Adolph Hitler?" Bobby Looked up in the air without saying a word for about a minute and one half and then said "HE WAS THE BEST IN HIS CATEGORY!" (Comparing him to Stalin, Mussolini, and Franco) (a truly amazing out of the box jazz improvisation that not many people know about. No wonder he could play jazz the way he could.)

Years later I got to meet Joe Stalin's interpretor who was at the Pact of Steel in 1939 between Hitler and Stalin.

I met him at a town hall meeting in Los Angeles in the late nineties. Town Hall brought in such dignataries as Henry Kissinger, Margaret Thatcher and my favorite General Howard Graves who was Superintendent of Instruction of West Point Military Academy at the time I met him.

Stalin's interpretor was a down to earth fellow. Someone in the audience asked him, "What was Stalin like?" He said "Stalin was a paranoid maniac! He slept all day and worked all night. He was suspicious of everyone trying to kill him!" "One day he was awakened by a barking dog. He told his two most trusted and beloved personal security guards to go out and find the dog and shoot the dog! They found the dog which was the seeing eye dog of a blind woman who was elderly. They brought her thirty miles outside the city limits with the dog and left her there telling her of Stalin's displeasure.

When Stalin woke up the next day the first words out of his mouth to his guards were "Did you find the dog!" They told him the story. He said "GO GET THE DOG!" THEY DID SO AND WHEN THEY BROUGHT THE DOG IN TO HIM HE TOOK OUT HIS REVOLVER AND PUT A BULLET RIGHT IN THE MIDDLE OF THE DOG'S HEAD! THEN HE SAID TO HIS TWO MOST TRUSTED BELOVED GUARDS, "THE NEXT TIME YOU DISOBEY MY ORDER THE BULLET WILL GO THROUGH THE MIDDLE OF YOUR HEAD!" Then someone in the audience said "Weren't you afraid of him?" He said, "Yes, I was afraid of him!" Next question was "Well, why did you work for him?" Answer: "Like I had a choice! If it wasn't for Molotov intervening I would have been murdered several times over!" This made Bobby Hackett's comment even funnier to me about Hitler being "the best in his category." History revealed that Stalin executed more people than Hitler!

Bobby Hackett's sound was romantic, lyrical and his jazz lines were flowing. A round 1960 he made a 78 rpm with only an organ player backing him up which displayed his georgeous sound. He played "Misty", "Kiss

Me Again" "Stardust" that I can remember. There is also a 78 made into a cd of when Jackie Gleason had a big band and had Bobby Hackett playing solos that were quite something. Those cd's are still available to my knowledge as of 2002. Hackett was a guitar player who knew his chord progressions and put them together in a uniquely melodic and lyrical way. Bobby Hackett was the link between Bix Beiderbecke and Chet Baker!

Trumpet player Jerry Miller from Moline, Iowa became my friend in 1998 at the Raphael Mendez Conference put on at Arizona State University in Tempe Arizona by David Hickman, a classically oriented trumpet player with a sound as big as a house. Raphael Mendez's two sons (both excellent trumpet players who became urologists) left all of Mendez's music, trumpet, et. al to the Music Department at Arizona State University.

I met Raphael Mendez in 1971 when I was a junior high school counselor in Lynwood, California in 1971. The most spectacular trumpet players I ever heard were Maynard Ferguson every time he played –that I heard –about 25, Al Hirt and Raphael Mendez. I was friendly with the music teacher, Ron Savitt, a lead trumpet player who was the son of Pinky Savitt, a big band trumpet player of the forties. One afternoon Savitt came up to me and said "Hey, you want to go hear Raphael Mendez this afternoon at 5 p.m. He is giving a free concert to the La Puente Junior High School kids." I said, "You have got to be kidding! (as I was going to get to hear one of the greatest trumpet players that ever lived off the cuff free of charge on a Tuesday afternoon and he was giving it away!) This was one of the side benefits of living in Los Angeles, as things like this would happen every so often!

Mendez was having his two sons come down from Stanford University to play the second half of the concert with him. I got to talk to him for about 30 minutes. He said it was the worst day of his life. His face and lips were all puffed up from cortisone and he felt he had no control of the trumpet whatsoever. A few other things I remember is that he recorded Paganini's violin solo "Moto Perpetuo" in four segments and not in one segment without a breath. It is still impossible to do. Furthur he said he did not teach double and triple tonguing to Anglos because they did not talk fast enough. He said that people who spoke Spanish spoke so much faster it was much easier for them to get the double and triple tonguing speed. He was a very kind and generous man who gave it away to the kids for nothing. That is what the great ones do. They are more interested in the transmission of the culture than in making a few bucks that afternoon.

Keep in mind that in Mendez' self evaluation he was at his worst and almost apologetically embarrassed to be playing in public. I would consider myself a trumpet afficionado in my having heard most of the great ones by that time and Mendez at his worst in terms of my humble ability to discriminate gave a spectalular concert beyond the belief of human perception. His tone was flawless. His breathing was impeccable. His double and triple tonguing were faster and cleaner than Harry James playing the flight of the bumblebee in record. His tone was a little on the bright side and years later on a cd sent to me by the International Trumpet Guild it was not as full as Timofei Dokshizer of the Russian Soviet Conservatory ilk. I am not able to discriminate Dokshizer's ability regarding double and triple tonguing but according to my calculations the best I ever heard on that score were Raphael Mendez and Herbert Clarke playing on a cd reproduced by the International Trumpet Guild and available for purchase. (Clarke played at least some of his solos on this cd with John Phillip Sousa's concert band at its best!) I always love to hear the original sources to see where the reputation came from. Clarke was a monster cornet player and he was before Mendez. I could not tell who was better! Magnificent is Magnificent!

There is a story trumpet players in Los Angeles tell. Raphael Mendez and his wife were good friends with Uan Rasey and his wife. On one occasion Mrs. Mendez called up Uan Rasey, who did all the solo work for MGM on China Town movie with Jack Nicholson and was known as one of the best trumpet teachers in Los Angeles, and she said "You have got to call up Raphael and get him to stop practicing! He has been going over the same four bars for eight hours to make a recording next week!" Mendez told me the time I met him that he practiced twelve hours a day. He said he did the first two so softly you could barely hear it. In reading the book about him which can also be purchased through David Hickman at Arizona State Music Department I read that Mendez at one time was hit in the lip so badly he could not play for some time and had to develop unusual methods to regain playing ability. He studied with a famous trumpet teacher named Maggio, whose method was not of any use to me in that Maggio was long deceased by the time I came across it.

TRUMPET IS NOT FOR THE FEINT HEARTED! JUST ASK CHARLIE DAVIS!

Prior to a serious accident that physically disabled me I was studying trumpet with LA Recording Artist Charlie Davis who formerly played lead trumpet for Woody Herman and the Herd. I began at about 2 hours practice time a day.

When I first when into his home in the San Fernando Valley he had Trumpets, cornets, fluegelhorns – about eleven of them – layed out all over his living room B Flats, C's, Piccolos, et. al. I said, "Charlie, you must be a trumpet player" attempting to get a laugh. There was none. For several months Charlie eye balled me as if he were attempting to make up his mind whether I was a serious enough student for him to waste his time teaching me. He kept adding material. I went from two hours, to three hours, to four hours a day practice and finally prior to the accident five hours a day. I said "HEY CHARLIE! YOU KEEP ADDING STUFF TO MY LESSON! DON'T YOU EVER TAKE ANYTHING AWAY!" He said, "NO! (IN A BEGRUDGING GRUMBLING MANNER). I SAID "HEY CHARLIE, WHEN YOU WERE A STUDENT AT THE UNIVERSITY OF INDIANA MUSIC SCHOOL (ONE OF THE BEST IN THE U.S.) HOW MANY HOURS A DAY DID YOU PRACTICE?" CHARLIE GRUMBLED OUT "EIGHT!" I SAID, "CHARLIE, I AM STILL A STUDENT, UH?" HE GRUMBLED "YES!" So if you have a modicum of talent on trumpet more than most instruments it boils down to "how bad do you want it?"

As for Hosler Junior High School in Lynwood Ron Savitt asked me a favor. He was the band director and he said if anyone remotely looks like they can play anything send them down here as music is not something people customarily sign up for. My best find was a meaty faced little blond haired kid who blew a double high C on a bugle. His name was Wayne Bergeron. Savitt saw the kid had talent and gave him three lessons a week on trumpet. Wayne is first call in the LA studios in 2010 and did play lead for Maynard Ferguson in 1988. I took trumpet lessons from Waynew in 1996 telling him I had taken thirty years off. He said "Thirty years is a long time."

BACK TO BIX AND DAVENPORT IOWA

An interesting phenomena I noticed about Davenport Iowa in the week I was there was that I only saw one Black person the afternoon I arrived going through a trash can. Then Jerry Miller took me to the Bix Beiderbecke office in the center of town to buy tickets for the entire festival. The next night Stan Mark was playing trumpet and fronting a big band where he played a few Harry James solos. I had seen him in the late seventies playing for Maynard Ferguson. In a workshop he gave he said he was first cornet for "THE" ARMY BAND IN WASHINGTON, D.C. AND THAT IS WHERE HE DEVELOPED HIS TRUMPET PLAYING. HE LOVED THAT MI LITARY BAND EXPERIENCE!

At the Stan Mark concert of 1000 people a woman came up to me and said "Dr. Bergantino, Dr. Bergantino!" She then realized I did not recognize her. She said, "Don't you remember me? I am the woman who sold you the tickets in the Bix Beiderbecke office yesterday!" I said, "Hey, lady! All you White people look the same to me!" She broke out laughing. I mean you had to see it to believe it. I had never seen that many White people in one place!

Louis Armstrong loved Bix and went to his funeral. Bix died young at about 29 years old. Louis and Bix played together before it was permissible for Blacks to play with Whites. Before my time even Los Angeles had a Black Union and a White Union until the late 1940's.

LOUIS ARMSTRONG WAS BEFORE MY TIME!

When I saw Louis on TV it was the mid fifties and he was an old man with beat up lips. So I never heard him play trumpet when he was a young bull at his best! I was at his 70th and last birthday party at the Shrine Auditorium in Los Angeles in 1970.

In the late nineties I was surprised to find myself on the cover of Downbeat Magazine at a picture taken when I was sitting in the fourth or fifth row back on the right side at the Shrine Auditorium when I was about 28 years old and a doctoral student at the University of Southern California across the street from the Shrine Auditorium in Los Angeles. Louis had just had a heart attack and his wife Lil would not let him play trumpet, so I only got to hear him sing and he invited quite a few trumpet players he thought could play his music in the style he played it, but it wasn't the same as hearing him play even once. I did get to hear Bobby Hackett six months before he died at the Playboy Club in Los Angeles and he no longer had the golden tone. Instead I believe he had cancer.

Don Vappie, an amazing tenor banjo player and a teacher of mine on the tenor banjo, kept steering me in the direction of listening to Johnnie St. Cyr playing walking bass lines for Louis Armstrong on the original Not Five and Not Seven recordings.

What I found out was that every time I listened to anything Louis Armstrong played I felt happy. I never had this experience listening to any other musician and I wondered how he managed to project happiness being a Black Man born in a Red Light District and An Orphanage in New Orleans!

I read Louis' autobiography and one story stood out in my memory. He was hitting High F's when other trumpet players were stuck around High C's. In New Orleans they used to have "Cutting Contests" In other words if you thought you were better than Louis Armstrong you brought your trumpet into the club and started playing as best you could and the challenge was on! One night a trumpet player came in and people began to say, "This guy is going to cut Louis tonight!" The book went on to describe the following. Louis had on a white suit. When he got up to play there was a halo around his head and that night he played better than anyone ever heard him play. The folklore goes that he hit a High "F" with such power and held it for so long the challenger just got up and walked out of the Club and Louis was still King, the best trumpet player that had ever lived to that point in time! It was suggested that Louis was annointed by God to play that way! Bob Reeves, one of the world's premiere mouthpiece makers has a picture of Louis that Louis sent him where Louis is sitting on the toilet going to the bathroom with the same big grin he is noted for!

MY FATHER'S VIOLIN MADE ME A CHURCHGOER!

My father was a great technical string player, that is with incredible speed and technique. He often gave one the feeling that his "hands were on fire". I thought only Harry Reser had more speed than my father after about 10,000 listens to "The Clock and the Banjo" and Lollipops!" But the violin was something else. His idol by hearsay was Nicoli Paganini. Although they had never met he spoke of Paganini incessantly with the kind of sentiment "If I didn't have to work as a kid to support my entire family I would have loved to go to Julliard and become like Paganini!" On jazz violin he played like Stephane Grapelle.

The thing about violin is so few can play it and make it sound like pennies from heaven and make it touch your soul. I felt Fritz Kreisler could do this and despite Jascha Heifetz's amazing technical abilities he was a cold fish. Many thought my father could touch your soul when he played Ave Maria, but I hated when he practiced the violin on Sunday mornings. So it was either listen to him or listen to my mother who said "Let's Go To Church!" so I went most every Sunday. My mother and I always rode to St. Thomas' Church with Betty DiLappo and her husband, Frank

DiLappo drove and picked us up. Betty for that ten minute drive was worse than my father practicing the violin in that she was always on a manic non stop talking binge. Every week Frank and I would notice each other crawling up the walls of the car and he would yell at the top of his lungs "BETTY, SHUP UP!" TO WHICH TO MY UTTER AMAZEMENT SHE CONTINUED ON UNDAUNTED AS IF HE HAD NEVER SPOKEN A WORD! I SUPPOSE THAT WAS THE FIRST TIME AT THE UNCONSCIOUS LEVEL A FLEETING THOUGHT WENT THROUGH MY MIND, "WHAT DID FRANK DO TO HIS LIFE WITH THIS INSTITUTION CALLED MARRIAGE!" In any case every week when Frank dropped us off I always thanked him, and he and I both knew it was not for the ride, but for trying to shut Betty up! Alas, my father's violin made me an avid Churchgoer and for that reason only I am grateful to this day he played the violin!

PAGANINI

I read two books written about him. He looked like an ugly gaunt Abe Lincoln only skinnier with long bony fingers. In his time people said he was possessed by the devil and that was how they accounted for what and how he could play the violin. Not as well known was that he played mandolin and guitar for his own amusement and had a son he deeply loved that he taught either the mandolin or guitar to. It was written that he would get on stage and begin to play and then intentionally although not obvious to the audience break 3 of the 4 strings on the violin while the audience threw tomatoes at him. THEN HE WOULD PLAY THE ENTIRE CONCERT ON THE "D" OR "THIRD STRING" OF THE VIOLIN WITH A TECHNIQUE PEOPLE SAID COULD HAVE ONLY BEEN HAD IF ONE MADE A PACT WITH "THE DEVIL!"

Long before Richard Gardner, M.D. came up with the diagnosis of severe parental alienation syndrome Paganini was the victim of such abuse whereby his wife at the time did everything she could to destroy the relationship between Paganini and his beloved son whom he brought everywhere with him. When his wife showed up murdered one day Paganini was put in jail for the murder but it was never proven and authorities released him.

My father was possessed with technique. Paganini never wrote down his methods so they died with him. Of course one cannot compare men of different centuries but the best two I ever heard were Fritz Kreisler who

can make you cry with a violin. The other was a documentary (late 1970's) about when Isaac Stern went to China and the playing he did in that movie was nothing short of magnificent.

Years ago I knew a man named Richard Colburn who made Two Hundred Million Dollars A Year. I was at his home in Truesdale Estates on the outskirts of Beverly Hills and he told me he had a safe with Stradivarius, Guarnari and Amati Violins, Violas, Cellos, and Contrabasses in it. I asked him to open it and show me. He said only the curator had the combination to open it. I asked him to call the curator and he did. He let me into the safe and I actually had those instruments in my hands while he was reading about each one from a book on the subject.. I virtually know everything about trumpets and nothing about violins in that I do not play one. However, I knew this! I was scared half to death I would drop one of these two million dollar violins and have to pay for it. I was holding a Strad kind of like you would hold a baby for the first time you ever did it with a great deal of anxiety. The Strad had green and red trim which was a surprise. Colburn was an amateur cello player and when Isaac Stern came to LA he let him use one of the Strads as long as Isaac Stern would play in a small chamber music setting at his home with the finest musicians in Los Angeles. I deduced from this that it is good to make $200,000,000 a year!

Prior to my father moving to Los Angeles prior to his death Max Herman, then President of Musician's Local 47 of the American Federation of Musicians invited him to the President's Office and my father was feeling him out about what one of the better violin players, one of the two best guitar players, and one of the best tenor banjo players ever who was quite adept on the mandolin would do in Los Angeles. Max was amazing at sizing up my father accurately and quickly in terms of abilities and possible opportunities for a 77 year old musician moving to Los Angeles. He said, "Danny, Leave the guitar and the violin in Waterbury. We have Joe Pass and Jascha Heifetz and we don't need you! Bring the banjo and the mandolin. You will play in the movies!" My father was a cantankerous sort, but made no response at all to Max Herman. He was so candid and spot on that he left us both speechless!

HAL ESPINOSA – PAST PRESIDENT OF MUSICIANS LOCAL 47 IN LOS ANGELES

Though Hal was President of Local 47 as a person who loves to talk trumpet I spoke with him many times about trumpet. He played lead trumpet for Les Brown and his Band of Renown. I said to him "Harry James is the reason I play trumpet." He said to me, "Harry James is the reason we all play trumpet!" Hal was a great guy to me, to my daughter Lisa, and he invited my developmentally delayed son up to the President's Office for a tour on a couple of occasions! HAL ABOVE ALL ELSE WAS A TRUMPET PLAYER!

RICHARD COLBURN DONATED THE COLBURN SCHOOL OF MUSIC TO THE UNIVERSITY OF SOUTHERN CALIFORNIA. HE IS THE FELLOW THAT CALLED THE CURATOR AND LET ME IN TO SEE THE STRADIVARIOUS, GUARNARI, AND AMATI VIOLINS, VIOLAS AND CONTRABASSES AND CELLOS. THE ROOM WAS HUGE AND HE MUST HAVE HAD FIFTY OF THEM IN THE ROOM AT NO LESS THAN 2 MILLION PER INSTRUMENT. THE COLBURN SCHOOL OF MUSIC SEPARATED FROM THE UNIVERSITY OF SOUTHERN CALIFORNIA AND BECAME ITS OWN ENTITY AND WAS REPLACED IN TITLE AT USC AS THE THORNTON SCHOOL OF MUSIC. FROM THE LITTLE I KNEW COLBURN HE WAS NOT ONE TO GIVE UP TOO MUCH CONTROL TO UNIVERSITY ADMINISTRATORS, ALTHOUGH I DO NOT KNOW THE DETAILS OF THEIR DIVORCE. BACK TO THE BASIC POINT! IT IS GOOD TO MAKE TWO HUNDRED MILLION DOLLARS A YEAR!

1962 – JIMMY GOZZO – MY SECOND TRUMPET TEACHER – FATHER OF THE GREATEST LEAD PLAYER OF ALL TIME -THE GREAT "CONRAD GOZZO". Jimmy lived on the second floor in an apartment in New Britain, Connecticut with his wife and he had a picture of Conrad on the tv in the living room where he gave me trumpet lessons. I had studied for six years with Carl Berg who played for Harry James prior to meeting Jimmy Gozzo.

Jimmy heard me play a few flight of the bumblebee kind of licks with a sound like Harry James and he said "Well, you can play the trumpet but you do not breathe correctly." I did not realize this was going to be the crux of my frustration with a trumpet for the rest of my life.

Conrad Gozzo's ability and tone are best exemplified on Tutti's Trumpets where Tutti Cammerata got Conrad Gozzo, Manny Klein, Uan Rasey, and Pete and Conte Condoli together on the same record date all blowing up a storm!

On this record you will hear Conrad Gozzo playing "Trumpeter's

Prayer" with such power and such tone that the orchestra gave him a standing ovation at its completion. Also, on Tenderly it is Conrad hitting the high notes with the power and warmth of a middle C. Conrad told others he could play double high C's but pretty much kept it to G above high C so as not to ruin the lives of all the trumpet players that came after him.

For example, I heard Harry James play "The SLeepy Lagoon" and "You Made Me Love You" and fell in love with the trumpet. Then Maynard Ferguson came around and instead of skinny guys like Harry James, me and Sammy Baugh, the new lead players looked more like Bronco Nagurski or tackles on a football team with necks as big as horses!

This takes us back to my lessons with Jimmy Gozzo where he kept saying over and over "YOU HAVE TO BREATHE LIKE A BABY" AND HE WOULD DEMONSTRATE HOW A BABY'S STOMACH WOULD MOVE UP AND DOWN TAKING AIR IN AND BLOWING IT OUT.

In Waterbury Connecticut Carl Berg was one of the two best trumpet players. I never heard of a lead trumpet player because there were no big bands around, mostly small club dates or summer concerts in the park.

In 1996, on the comeback trail after taking 35 years off playing trumpet I went to Denton Texas to study with Scott Englebright, Maynard Ferguson's lead trumpet player at that time and I hit a high "G" that pealed the paint off the walls. I proudly turned around and said "What do you think!" He squared right off, looked me right in the eye and said "IT'S A WIND INSTRUMENT!" RIGHT BACK TO JIMMY GOZZO! THERE IS ONE HELLUVA DIFFERENCE BETWEEN PLAYING TRUMPET AND PLAYING LEAD TRUMPET!

Maynard had all his trumpet players read a book written by a Yogi from India that focused on breathing. If you watched Maynard in the seventies he used to curl his stomach almost inside out and use this method of breathing air somehow associated with air and energy and referred to as "PRANA!" I read the book but I never could coordinate those particular muscles to do that and as a result while I studied with some of the best lead trumpet players in the world – Frank Szabo, Wayne Bergeron, Charlie Davis and Bobby Shew, and I played some pretty good lead, I never got to a place of being able to take their place on a gig. I had what it takes in desire and dedication, but attempted to do it when I was an old man to make such a beginning – at about 55 years old. I told Wayne Bergeron I took thirty years off and he said "Thirty Years Is A Long Time!"

Not that it did me much good but I was Jimmy Gozzo's third best trumpet student. First there was his son, the best lead player in the world – Conrad Gozzo; then there was Al Hirt, with me a distant third that could not even be seen in the horse race. On the other hand, I got to play all the music I loved between 55 and 70 years old!!!

When Conrad was asked what he remembered from Jimmy's lessons he said "I remember my father saying thousands of times, PRACTICE CONRAD, PRACTICE!" There is a story that Conrad and a saxaphone player friend in high school went to play baseball and Jimmy Gozzo followed them to the park, slapped them both in the face, and told them to stop wasting time and go home and practice! Today, we may not agree with the severity of his methods but he turned out Conrad Gozzo and no one else did!

THE GREAT GOZ

Other places you may have heard Conrad Gozzo were he used to play lead for Frank Sinatra's recordings (great big band) and story has it that when Goz died in 1962, 3, or 4 Sinatra kept yelling that he could not hear the lead trumpet, no matter how good or how loud that trumpet was. Goz was a legend. He hung around with The Rat Pack of Sinatra, Dean Martin, Sammy Davis Jr. and the comedian Joey Bishop. Jimmy Goz told me "You will move to Los Angeles, you will study trumpet with Conrad, and you will hang around with the Rat Pack and You will have a good life and a good time." Then, Conrad messed up all my plans. He drank himself to death at the age of 42. I never met him but the story goes that he had a lot of family problems and his solution was the bottle. He played lead on the Andy Williams TV shows each week as well as for Billy May and Henry Mancini. He idolized Louis Armstrong and insisted his closest friends call him "Satch" after Louis Armstrong. Goz was old enough to have heard Louis when he was a young bull!

Goz used to play lead for the Dinah Shore show at 9 a.m. and one day he came in blasted from the night before and the music was the most difficult it had ever been. Everyone was afraid for him however he insisted he could play it. He had to sit on the top of a bleacher like seat on a platform and he played the material perfect, but upon completion of the show he fell off the platform backward with a whiskey bottle in his coat pocket and his trumpet. He let the trumpet fall to the floor and grasped the whiskey bottle on the way to the floor. He was unharmed.

Goz burnt the candle at both ends as he used to play lead in Los Angeles for shows such as Dinah Shore while he played gigs in Las Vegas the night before. One night, overburdened with family problems, he drove from Las Vegas as far as Santa Barbara, got a hotel room, and drank an entire quart of whiskey. Conrad died that evening from the quart of whiskey. Jimmy Gozzo died of broken heart not too long afterwords. When Conrad Gozzo in the record "Tutti's Trumpets" (Tutti Cammerata – one of the all time great trumpet records made into a cd) played "Trumpeter's Prayer" all the musicians in the orchestra gave him a standing ovation. Conrad Gozzo was the consumate musician!

There were a couple of stories about Jimmy Gozzo and his influence teaching Conrad as Jimmy was the best trumpet player and teacher in the New Britain-Hartford Connecticut area of his time period. Conrad and a high school buddy were playing baseball in New Britain. Both were in high school. The other boy was a saxaphone player. Jimmy Gozzo went to the baseball field and slapped both of them in the face and told them both they were wasting time playing baseball when they should be home practicing music.

In later life when Conrad was asked what he remembered about lessons with his father Jimmy Gozzo he said he always remembered his father saying, "PRACTICE CONRAD! PRACTICE!"

The day I called Frank Sinatra at Caesar's Palace in 1968 and told the person answering the phone that I studied with Jimmy Gozzo and Conrad was supposed to introduce me but he died; Sinatra said, "Contrary to popular opinion he did not have an entourage of hangers on and I would do well to finish my doctoral studies at USC and give up my fantasies of hanging with the Rat Pack. In any case I had the courage to call him! In retrospect Frank gave me his best shot and moved my life in the best direction for me!

I met Dean Martin years later 3 months before he died at a restaurant in Beverly Hills where he dined every night by himself. They played only his records and people were kept out of the bar area where he dined. I thought, I have been waiting thirty years to meet this guy and now I was internationally renown as a clinical psychologist. I told him that I had written a book that was a master classic in the field of psychotherapy and I wanted to write a book about him and the rat pack. He said "I am just a simple guy that wants to be remembered for singing songs from my heart that touched peoples' souls and I don't have any interest in anything being

Dr. Len Bergantino, Ed.D., Ph.D.

Frank Szabo
6618 Yarmouth Avenue
Reseda, CA 91335
February 2, 1999

Henry Mancini Institute
P.O. Box 34575
Los Angeles, CA 90034-0575

Dear Admissions Committee:

It is with great pleasure that I unqualifiedly recommend Dr. Len Bergantino as an applicant for the Henry Mancini Institute from August 1-28, 1999 at UCLA.

Dr. Bergantino is a youthful 55 year old who retired from the private practice of clinical psychology this year with the intent of becoming a full time musician.

He has recently made a CD with renown jazz guitarist Joe Diorio whereby Dr. Bergantino is playing mandolin.

However his studies with me were 10 months in duration. He began taking trumpet lessons once per week, but quickly advanced the pace to three times per week. His primary interests in working with me were to develop high register work as a lead trumpet player and to read and phrase lead trumpet charts. We worked on some of Count Basie's Charts and some of Buddy Rich's charts. I played lead trumpet for Count Basie and I have played for Buddy Rich as well. Also Harry James and a gold record of Frank Sinatra's. I am a working studio musician and currently play lead trumpet for Bill Holman's band and Frank Capp's band.

Dr. Bergantino has a beautiful tone in the middle register. He has significantly improved his reading ability in terms of reading and playing charts and he has somewhat improved his high register. He has made significant strides in his intonation in that we worked on this three times per week in warmups - in other words, locking in on the pitch.
intonation in that we worked on this three times per week in
warmups - in other words, locking in on towards playing jazz

He seems to have a natural inclination towards playing jazz trumpet and is significantly influenced by the work of Chet Baker and Miles Davis. In three short months of study with Bill Watrous he is able to sit in on a weekly basis in a jazz club for four hours each Sunday at La Louisiann.

Dr. Bergantino is highly motivated to be the best musican that he can be and I feel that training with your summer institute would be just the boost that he needs to make the full time transition into the music business. I recommend him without reservation!

Sincerely

Frank Szabo
Frank Szabo

42

written about me." So at the beginning of my career and at the end both Sinatra and Dean Martin made certain I did not get lost as the theme of this book is in giving up ceaseless striving so you can play the kind of music that touches peoples' hearts and souls!.

I WAS JIMMY GOZZO'S THIRD BEST STUDENT! THE FIRST TWO WERE CONRAD GOZZO (THE GREATEST LEAD TRUMPET PLAYER OF ALL TIME) AND AL HIRT (BIGGEST MASS MARKET INFLUENCE OF HIS TIME ON THE TRUMPET AND OWNER OF THE NEW ORLEANS SAINTS!)

Of course Maynard Ferguson changed the game for everybody with his power and triple octave abilities and endurance.

Jimmy Gozzo in 1962 before I knew what a lead trumpet player was said I knew how to play trumpet but there were problems with me learning to "breathe like a baby" making my stomach go in and out.

In 1996 in Denton Texas I was winding down my private practice of clinical psychology in Beverly Hills and I went to North Texas State in Denton Texas for two reasons – to see what it would be like to enroll and play in one of their lab bands as a fifty three year old and to study for one week with Scott Englebright, a 22 year old Maynard drafted out of North Texas State to play lead trumpet for him. During a lesson I hit a G above high C that I thought peeled the paint off the walls. I asked Scott Englebright what he thought of it and he shouted "IT'S A WIND INSTRUMENT!" (ALMOST AS IF HE HADN'T HEARD THE NOTE I HIT, WHICH GAVE ME AN IDEA OF WHAT I WOULD HAVE TO BE ABLE TO DO TO PLAY FOR MAYNARD, WHICH WAS ALWAYS A FANTASY!.) Scott later in the lesson hit a double high C (an octave above high C – that made the room feel like an earthquake hit it!

PARDUBA MOUTHPIECES

My father was a professional musician in Musicians Union Local 186 (Waterbury, Connecticut) of The American Federation of Musicians and when I was twelve years old they sent him a monthly magazine which was much nicer than the AFM Newsletter of today. In the Magazine there was Harry James advertising King Trumpets and John Parduba advertising Harry James' mouthpiece – a Parduba #5 – so I bought a gold plated #5 and sure enough I sounded a little more like Harry James than before I got the King and the Parduba.

BOBBY HACKETT USED TO ADVERTISE FOR ZOTTOLA. I bought a few but at that time I wanted to sound like Harry James and not like Bobby Hackett. IT NEVER OCCURRED TO ME THE OBJECT OF THE WHOLE THING WAS TO FIND OUT WHO LEN BERGANTINO WAS AND SOUND LIKE HIM!!!

Years later I played in Joe Vento's Big Band in Los Angeles (He played for the Three Sons in the fifties) and he told me a story about Harry James. About 1956 Joe Vento was playing with "The Three Sons" in Las Vegas and so was Harry James and his wife Betty Grable. Harry invited about six musicians over to his home one afternoon and Betty Grable - his wife- was in the bedroom. Harry said, "Betty, get the guys a beer, would you?" Joe Vento said Betty came out with 6 beers on a tray serving the musicians while she was totally nude without saying a word and walked immediately back into the bedroom. Do you see why I wanted to be like Harry James! Betty Grable was America's Sweetheart and her pin up was famous during World War II and she was known for having beautiful legs, her "gams" as they were referred to.

Trumpet players were like rock stars in Harry's day and Harry was King! It is no wonder he wound up playing one!

He played a Selmer Balanced Action model on his recordings of "You Made Me Love You," "The Sleepy Lagoon," "Ciribiribin," "The Two O'Clock Jump," "I Don't Want To Walk Without You," but when he demanded Selmer give him free trumpets for his friends and they would not he went over to H. G. White who owned King in Cleveland, Ohio. I met a man who worked for him and he said Mr. White told him, "When Harry comes in, give him whatever he wants!" Harry had the most influential trumpet sound from 1935-1950.

In 1998 I was studying trumpet with Frank Szabo -3 days a week for one and one half hour lessons. Harry James drafted Frank Szabo out of high school and he got credit for his last two years of high school playing third trumpet for Harry James.

John Parduba gave Harry eight gold plated #5 mouthpieces and Harry gave one to Frank Szabo. Frank gave it to me knowing how much it meant to me. Harry was very generous with his friends. He gave Pete Candoli a King Silversonic Dual Bore Harry James model that he put a mike on when I saw him do a show in New Orleans with his then wife Edie Adams around 1976.

There are stories that for high register work Harry used a Parduba 4 1/2 and for bigger sounding ballads a #6. For me I liked the sound of the

Parduba #6 but wound up having Bob Reeves make me several #6 rims which I put on the Old Jet Tone undercups and that took me to double B Flats and a good strong G anytime I wanted it!

MAYNARD FERGUSON

I came to know and love Maynard however I signed up for the trumpet listening to Harry James and Maynard Ferguson threw me into a world I did not sign up for that was a good two octaves above what I played and even what Harry played. Maynard is dead now (around 2005) and "as trumpet is God's instrument" as Maynard himself used to say! There are a few stories about Maynard Ferguson playing for Leonard Bernstein and the New York Philharmonic playing a part on the trumpet that was so high it sounded like a flute part. This was written up in the International Musician around 1956.

My father read the article and refused to believe it (You had to experience Maynard live to believe he was for real. There will never be another Maynard!) as what was written about him was humanly thought to be impossible by my father's lifetime professional experience with trumpet players of high quality.

MAYNARD 62 (1962) on Roulette Records had Maynard playing "Maria" from Westside Story. I met Maynard in February, 1963 in Fairfield, Connecticut. He looked like a college kid with a blue blazer, white shirt and tie. I was with my mother and father. My father had perfect pitch. Maynard opened with Maria at 9 p.m. My father said he played an "E" above double high C. Maynard didn't just hit the notes and they were not squeaky. They were as full and as big as a house! He didn't just play up there! He lived up there! I never heard anyone else do it before, during or after Maynard! He was at his strongest then although he never was anything less than ten megatons above what anyone else could do on a trumpet. That night he played solo after solo, played fast and flashy jazz solos along with Don Rader (The Three Little Foxes). Don Rader later moved to Australia where I believe he is still living. Maynard then would go back to the trumpet section in the back row of the band and double on lead trumpet all night long with Nat Pavone -his lead player and then at 2 a.m. he played Maria again with the same power -same beautiful full and rich tone and the same E above double high C. There was only one Maynard Ferguson and I am honored I got to know "The Fox" -"The Boss" personally!.

I met Maynard that night and as from my perspective although I did not know I felt this way he had ruined my life and crushed my idol - Harry James just by being all that he could be and putting it through his instrument. The entire time I was talking to him I was asking him what he thought of Harry James and Parduba mouthpieces, knowing full well he played Giardinelli mouthpieces at that time. Maynard was kind to me probably being familiar with my response to him and he said "Harry is a good strong player". He was very patient with me as in retrospect most people in his shoes would have been annoyed. He knew I was a serious trumpet guy and he took me seriously!

The band did not take many breaks but one of them was a 20 minute break where all the guys in the band walked off stage and the drummer - Rufus Jones - played phenomenal drum solos until the band came back on stage 20 minutes later! Maynard's band was exciting beyond anything I had ever experienced!

Whenever Maynard played within 100 miles of Los Angeles I went to hear him. The only other guy I went to hear at that level was guitar player Charlie Byrd whose teachers were Django Reinhardt and Andre Segovia. Charlie Byrd brought the Bossa Nova to the United States along with saxaphone player Stan Getz around 1960.

When Stan Getz was very young he played for Stan Kenton in the early fifties. He wanted to take the tenor saxaphone charts home that evening. Kenton was not happy about it and told him if he lost the "only band charts for tenor saxaphone and did not bring them back the following day he would have to murder him!" The next day Stan Getz came back without the charts and he told Stan Kenton he didn't need them. Kenton inquired as to why not and Getz said he "memorized all the tenor saxaphone charts for the band that prior evening." Harry James also had a photographic memory. Harry could look at each player's part for a couple of seconds and he would have the entire score (all the charts for a particular song) memorized in a couple of minutes.

I met Harry James in 1966 at the same place Maynard played in Fairfield, Connecticut. He played a lot of his old standards but did not transcend his own music that made him famous. Maynard Ferguson and Miles Davis transcended their own music which kept them fresh and fully alive and exciting each time you heard them.

GIARDINELLI MOUTHPIECES

Mr. Bob Giardinelli had a huge shop on the second floor of a New York Building and he made Maynard Ferguson's mouthpieces around the time I heard Maynard play Maria and make the records Maynard 62 and Maynard 63 - 33 rpms by Roulette Records. Ole is also quite something on Maynard 61.

Mr. Giardinelli was very kind to me. I met him in 1963. He looked more like a doctor with a white smock -tall-distinguished looking - than a mouthpiece maker. He told me Maynard had one rim and three different undercups and they were branded an MF-1, an MF-2 and an MF-3. I wasn't taking any chances so I bought all three. Mr. Giardinelli told me to keep them for three months and see how things went and if I could not play on them to bring them back and he would exchange them for something I could play. I couldn't get anything higher than a G above the staff on any of them. The MF-1 was so small it was flat on your face - no cup at all in it. I have no idea how Maynard played it. He really was a gift from God - one of a kind - maybe Gabriel reincarnated!!!!!!

When I went back three months later Mr. Giardinelli picked out a 6-S for me. Again, Mr. Giardinelli was kind and supportive of young trumpet players that I felt loyal to him for a lifetime-long after his death!

During the six years I took trumpet lessons from Carl Berg I used a Bach 7-C mouthpiece and a Conn Director student trumpet. Even though I have experimented with a hundred different mouthpieces since then and I am now sixty eight years old - whenever I try a Bach 7-C now my original embouchure kicks right in from MUSCLE MEMORY and it sounds pretty good - almost like I never stopped playing it.

Maynard moved to England in the late 60's and I did not see him until he returned to the United States and played at Donte's Jazz Club in 1973. Only now he came out with long hair, played somewhat frenetically but was still exciting and a tower of power who blew the roof off of Donte's (now defunct jazz club).

About three years later he did "Theme From The Movie Rocky" which put him on the popular charts for the first time in addition to the jazz scene. He also did Chameleon and MacArthur Park which became big hits in those days. (Late 1970's)

He wore a white shirt and jacket with sequins and looked like a bullfighter.

I reviewed Maynard's book for his fan club newsletter in the 90's and he always comped me and my son Alex after writing the review and always made a point to say hello to us by name when he walked through the audience hitting double high C's while the rest of his trumpet section were scattered in different parts of the auditorium playing loud and powerfully in the very highest of the upper register of a trumpet. It was phenomenal! As Scott Englebright told me in 1996 in Denton Texas "Trumpet is a wind instrument!" and Maynard blew a hurricane through the horn! His belly would go in and out (Jimmy Gozzo-like a baby) and roll.

Reading Maynard's book was like being on the bus with the band. It was the experience itself! Not very many writers can write in that manner.

Maynard's lead player after Scott Englebright was also a lead player from the One O'Clock Lab Band for North Texas State University. He told me that Maynard had all his trumpet players read a book on Yoga, prana (life force) and breathing. I read it but was not willing to devote my life to it! You had to want it that bad or it would not happen! My day job was clinical psychology which I did want that bad! and devoted my life to Becoming (to be or not to be) at finer and finer discriminations where I could enhance the quality of being of people beyond anything thought to be humanly possible.

A couple of stories come to mind that were in Maynard's book. Only once was Maynard on the same venue as Elvis Presley. At the time one of his daughters was five years old. Maynard asked her what she thought of The King as Elvis was referred to. She said, "Look at Elvis, Daddy, and then look at you! He has all of these sequins sparkling and gold buttons and you look like you fell off a wedding cake!" PERHAPS THAT EXPLAINS THE DISCREPANCY BETWEEN HOW MAYNARD WAS DRESSED IN 1963 when I first met him and ten years later in 1973 at Donte's when he returned from England. Maynard also spent time with Timothy Leary on his farm in upper State New York during the interim. Leary was experimenting with LSD. I was President of the Southern California Society of Clinical Hypnosis in 1987, which then was composed of MD's, Ph.D.s and Dentists using hypnosis in their respective specialties. One meeting I had the good fortune to spend an hour with Timothy Leary and his 37 year old wife (he had to be sixty) as he was the guest speaker and I was responsible for the introduction. Leary told me he had over 2000 LSD trips. What I noticed is that when he spoke there were one second gaps between his thoughts and his ability to express them. He was brilliant with interruption. To tell you the truth I was glad it was him and not me that experimented with the LSD. It was weird.

Another story was Maynard's fondness for Miles Davis, who Maynard thought was a strange bird but worth the trouble. Maynard said he could see a Caucasion father and his approximately ten year old son walking toward Miles and Maynard said that in itself was enough to give him great trepidation as Maynard never knew quite what Miles would do. Miles had a new record out and the father just bought a copy for the son and wanted Miles to sign it. Then the boy said, "Miles, this new record was the best you ever made!" Miles said "How the fuck would you know kid!" Maynard said he could see it coming from a mile away. Maybe that is why they called him Miles!

Another time Maynard and Miles were both on the bill at Birdland on Christmas Eve and Miles was feeling blue and asked Maynard to play some Christmas Carols. There was a disc jockey named Symphony Sid standing with Miles when Maynard began to play Christmas Carols, Symphony Sid said to Miles, "What the fuck is Maynard doing playing Christmas Carols? This is Birdland!" Miles who was a pretty good boxer hit him once on the jaw and knocked him out as he said "What the fuck are you deaf!"

Around 1998 Ed Sergeant, Maynard's Manager, got me and my daughter Lisa backstage to say hello. I said, "Maynard, this is my daughter Lisa!" He said, "Is she as much trouble as my daughter Lisa!" He was quick and untuitively on target!

In 1995 I was on a plane to Cleveland and I saw this guy with a mashed lip and a fat stomach dragging a trumpet case with a Hannibal Lecter kind of white hat. I knew it was Maynard but I didn't want to bug him, or be a hanger on kind of guy, so I didn't say anything. About 1 1/2 hours into the flight I had to go to the bathroom and Maynard got up at precisely the same time I got up. When he was leading the band he would always shoot his right arm straight up in the air, letting all parties know he was the leader and where he was leading you. Even though he was fifteen seats behind me he threw up his right arm letting me know he was taking the bathroom on the right side of the plane and I the one on the left. We went to our respective bathrooms and the doors opened at precisely the same moment at which point I spontaneously yelled out "Maynard!" He said, "YOU KNOW ME!" I couldn't stop laughing. It was serendipity! We talked for an hour and he had no interest in talking about trumpet once I told him I was a clinical psychologist. He talked to me about his yearly pilgrimages to India to study with the Holy Man Sai Baba, and to teach Indian young boys and girls music pro bono. Then he told me he was married to "Flo Ferguson" for about 40 years and he never cheated on her. He was proud of this achievement, one of his own personal high notes!. Maynard Ferguson was interested in letting me know about the calibre of person with high moral and ethical standards. In May, 2011 his daughter told me that Maynard used to call Flo Ferguson and talk for hours every day no matter what part of the world he was performing.

AL HIRT

Harry James was The Man of my Father's Generation and it was most probably because in pre television days I listened to my father's 78 rpms over and over that I got to know of Harry James. Al Hirt had a beautiful sound with more of a softer French influence as he was from New Orleans and was the most dominant popular force on the trumpet in my era from about 1958 through 1976. I met Al Hirt at Oakdale Summer Theatre in 1963 in Oakdale Connecticut. When he took a break he signed autographs the entire time but talked to me -a twenty year old trumpet enthusiast - about trumpet the entire time with the enthusiasm of a little kid! Al Hirt loved to talk about trumpet and he would rather do that than anything other than play trumpet!

He was Al Hirt! I was a kid He was nice to me. I never forgot him and a lot of his runs were burned into his influence on me. I couldn't play Maynard's Music because of the range and the power and unique environment required, but I could play some of Al Hirt's solos. While I have 23 trumpets, cornets and fluegelhorns, after I had a stroke I wanted to get back to one and focus on the best sound that was mine, and while I played most of my life with a sound that resembled Harry James, after my stroke I played cornet- a Holton Al Hirt Large Bore Model, and cut off a Giardinelli One Rim and put it on top of a Bach #10 cornet mouthpiece undercup. I could play prettier, softer and touch peoples' souls with a cornet more than I could with a trumpet. There are very subtle nuances. Perhaps Herbert L. Clarke was right when he wrote to Eldon Benge that cornet was a superior instrument to the trumpet, if one thinks solely about musicality!

The sound that got embedded in my soul from Al Hirt was on a 33 rpm that RCA produced around 1958 where it referred to Al Hirt as "The World's Greatest Trumpet Player". Al took a lot of heat for this comment and came out with a statement that it was RCA's way to sell his records and that Conrad Gozzo was the world's greatest trumpet player! In particular on this record Al Hirt played "The Sleepy Lagoon", "You Made Me Love You" and my favorite "Stranger In Paradise" in which his tone was qualitatively the most Al Hirt could be and which transferred over to my cornet playing.

In 1963 Al Hirt played a Jet Tone Gold Plated Aluminum mouthpiece. Like Maynard there wasn't much cup to it. Jet Tone's were made in Connecticut at that time. I didn't have any more luck with the Jet Tone than I had with the MF-1, MF-2 or MF-3 Giardinelli mouthpieces. I barely got G over the staff and again the mouthpiece was flat on my face with no room for my lips to vibrate. I could never figure out how either one of them ever played the mouthpieces they played.

Lamentably so a trumpet player figured he had Maynard's secret well in hand that he has a space between his two front teeth. the man went to the dentist and had him create a space between the two front teeth. Meanwhile Maynard went to the dentist and had his two front teeth brought closer together. Furthurmore the man lost the range that he had prior to separating his two front teeth. Reminds me of the song, "All I want for Christmas is my two front teeth!"

I visited Al Hirt's Club in 1968, 1973 and 1976 with my parents at 333 Bourbon street in New Orleans. He was a magnificent entertainer with a golden trumpet player's sound and he was exciting and thrilling with a great dixieland band. Al said "I surround myself with six great musicians and then everyone thinks I am great!" His brother Jerry Hirt played trombone for awhile. Al said, "For all those girls who want to run their fingers through Jerry's hair, they better hurry!" Jerry was balding.

In the late nineties I met a trumpet player named Rex Merriweather who told me a story about Al Hirt. He said he was twelve years old and got his first gig for trumpet and fluegelhorn only he had a trumpet and a cornet. So he took a train ride from three hours north of Chicago to a music store called Sterlings. He told the salesperson he only had $100 and he wanted to trade his cornet for a flugelhorn and $100. The man said only the store owner could make that decision and Rex would have to return tomorrow, which would be Saturday.

Rex took the train with his mother and the storekeeper said "Here is your flugelhorn and your cornet back and keep the $100. Remember that heavy set man playing trumpet in the corner yesterday. That was Al Hirt.

He heard you playing and decided to buy you the flugelhorn. You don't owe us anything. It is paid in full!" So I loved Harry James, Maynard Ferguson and Al Hirt!

THE DAY I MET RAPHAEL MENDEZ

My teacher Carl Berg's favorite trumpet players were Raphael Mendez and Doc Severinsen. In the fifties Doc made those "Torch" 33 rpm's and Mendez arranged violin solos for trumpet, making the trumpet a true solo instrument for classical repertoire.

When I was a full time doctoral student at the University of Southern California I also had a full time job as a junior high school counselor. The music teacher one day in 1971 said "Hey, do you want to go hear Raphael Mendez. He is giving a concert for the kids at 5 p.m. at LaPuente Junior High School free of charge. This was certainly one of the perks of living in Los Angeles..

Mendez's technique was like nothing I had ever heard - ala double and triple tonguing. I spoke with him for about 30 minutes. According to him he was full of cortisone and had no control over his lips which felt puffy to him. I just heard the best technical trumpet player I had ever heard in my life.

Things I remember that Mendez told me were that

1.\ He only teaches triple and double tonguing to people who speak Spanish and not English because they talk a lot faster, which makes the rapid double and triple tontuing more possible.
2.\ He used to warm up for two hours playing so softly you could not even hear the sound of the trumpet.
3.\ He used to practice twelve hours a day.
4.\ He hardly put any pressure at all on his lips. That was the idea behind practicing as softly as he did.

A story among Los Angeles trumpet players is that Uan Rasey and his wife were good friends with Raphael Mendez and his wife; and one day Mrs. Mendez called Uan Rasey in desperation and said "You have to get him to stop practicing! He has been doing the same four bars for eight straight hours." So when you hear something you never heard before on his records, now you know the price he paid to achieve those results.

5.\ Moto Perpetuo, Paganini's violin solo, sounds like it was played with one breath in it's entirety on the recording. It was not. It was broken into 4 segments and each of those three segments were played in one breath. That is still beyond human belief!

Over the course of my lifetime I was to hear the recordings of two other trumpet or cornet players that had such incredible technique. They were Herbert L. Clarke, who played for John Phillip Sousa on a recording put out by The International Trumpet Guild. Also, they put out a recording of Timofei Dokshizer from the Soviet Union trained in the Russian Conservatory. He had such technique with a sound as big as a house that had to come from the Angels. (Maybe Gabriel himself!) A funny story when I read Dokshizer's book is he was required to play trumpet on the Russian Front in WWII when the Russians were fighting the Germans. He said the temperature was quite a bit below freezing and the mouthpiece froze to his lips. He said when one removed the trumpet from his lips he was just as likely to rip off the lips themselves as remove the trumpet. Dokshizer said "I WOULD HAVE MUCH PREFERRED TO HAVE A RIFLE INSTEAD OF A TRUMPET!".

I TOOK THIRTY YEARS OFF

My mother said "Don't mess with your father technically! He will bury you alive! But you play prettier than him!" What I did not realize was that to play prettier than him on the mandolin left me making a recording with world renown jazz guitarist Joe Diorio where I have a richness of sound with greater depth of sound than anyone who ever recorded on the mandolin. Listen to CD "Moonlight in Vermont - Guitar - Johnny Smith. The trumpet was an entirely different animal. I remember coming home from college and sitting in on a gig where my father played guitar; my cousin Bob Mete (now deceased) played tenor saxaphone and Eddie Montana played drums. Eddie said "Lenny, what are you going to be when you finish college?" I said, "Eddie, I want to be a trumpet player!" I just finished playing The Sleepy Lagoon ending on a high D as beautifully as I could play it. Eddie said, "Lenny, if you were going to be great, you would already be great!" -ergo, "Keep your day job!"

I played first trumpet in the concert band for the University of Connecticut and studied with Sam Goldfarb at UCONN. Then I went to

Fairfield University for an M.A. and basically studied hard enough to get a 3.86 GPA and get into USC's doctoral program, but I did not have time to play trumpet from 1965-1995 when I was a full time psychoanalyst in Beverly Hills, California.

During the time off there were a few significant events. In 1966 I heard Woody Herman and The Herd in Fairfield, Connecticut and Bill Chase was playing lead trumpet for him. I remember talking for awhile with him and his being very kind to me. I think he played a Schilke. Woody had another fellow playing third trumpet who played third trumpet for Maynard Ferguson where I got to know him and he remembered me. His name was Dusko Goykovitch. He deninitely was selling me on Schilke trumpets and he was a great guy - a good jazz player. At the time he was from Yugoslavia when it was a United Country.

I had picked up a New York Bach from Lou Pontecorvo that I think he had played all the notes on that horn that should have been played on it before I bought it. So when I moved out to Los Angeles I had my eyes open but there were names out here that I had not heard before, such as Callichio and Benge who had moved from Chicago to Burbank, California in 1968.

Ron Savitt, the son of Pinky Savitt, former big band trumpet player, was the music teacher at the school I was a junior high school counselor.

Savitt brought me to meet Dominic Callichio on Willoughby Street around the corner from Local 47 Musicians Union at 817 N. Vine St., Hollywood, CA 90038. Dominic was a legend among old artisan trumpet makers and I bought a gold plated 2 bell with a 7 pipe for 300 in 1968 and played it as a tension breaker when I was a doctoral student at USC. Sometime I played difficult duets with Ron Savitt who made it clear he was a "lead player" like his father.

During that time I had also gone to the Benge factory, but they sounded a little thin to me. Also, Renaud Schilke mailed me a B-5 that I really liked but sent back because I thought I had no need for two trumpets. Now I have 23 trumpets, flugelhorns and cornets For Shades of Sound. (Purchase Cornet Demo - p.233). I loved that horn too and was foolish to send it back. It was about $285 then and today would sell for $1500 or more! Rick Baptist, Mr. Lead in Los Angeles, has a 1965 Schilke B-5 and will not buy a new one because he is certain new ones do not play as well as his 1965 B-5. (2016 Rick became Vice-President of Musician's Local 47.)

Then Savitt took me to meet Bob Reeves who made me a custom mouthpiece, screw rim, for the man who never practices and sold it to me for $40. Reeves made a similar one for Chuck Finley who was the lead player on the tonight show after Doc Severinsen moved on. Reeves used to say that he only charged Finley $40 and he made $300,000 a year with that mouthpiece. Great players when they find a mouthpiece that is adequate to performance needs do not tend to shop around and switch very much.

Bill Watrous plays a Bach 11 on trombone that he got in the United States Navy in 1946. Frank Szabo, lead player for Count Basie and Buddy Rich, played the mouthpiece he had in high school - a Bush. Irving Bush played for the LA Philharmonic and Szabo used to joke with him about advertising Bush mouthpieces by saying "Wake Up With A Bush In Your Face". He said Irving Bush never went for the idea..

Callichio's was a hangout for me too, only from 1995 to 2005 when Chris Callichio Weik, Dominic's grandson made Callichio's of which I have three. His mother was Dominic's daughter, a delightful woman in her own right.

Chris had some great stories. He said one day Conrad Gozzo's horn got damaged and he wanted Dominic to make him one over night. So Dominic laid out all the metal and did it. Story was better when Chris told it as if he were there.

Chris was always pissed at me because I had a good eye and ear for the best trumpets he made and I would buy them before he could show them to LA's finest lead players. I did introduce him to Frank Szabo who switched from a Chicago Benge to a Callichio.

Chris had one tragic story. Only a few Mendez Models have the original Callichio lead pipe! Everybody has a blind spot and Dominic Callichio was no different. He thought he was a great Italian artisan, a DaVinci of trumpet making. He had a lead pipe that gave lead players about an extra note and one half. After world War II a substance called pitch was unavailable and Dominic could not make trumpets without it. Olds just signed up Raphael Mendez to make a custom model and they told Dominic that if he gave them the mandel to make the lead pipes they would give him several barrels of pitch to make more trumpets. He thought he made it once, and he could easily make another leadpipe mandel equal to the high note lead pipe. HE NEVER COULD! It gives you an extra note and one half higher.

That is why Callichio wound up making so many different lead pipes - a 2, 3, 7 and 9 that I owned and played at different times to get different

"Shades of Sound." Freddie Hubbard used a 9 lead pipe. The all around lead pipe was a 7 and lead players used a #2 lead pipe.

UCONN -1964 -ALMOST TOOK A DOUBLE MAJOR OF POLITICAL SCIENCE AND MUSIC

Bruno DiCecco was head of the music department. My father played violin for his father in the Waterbury Symphony. Bruno was against the idea, saying no one had ever come in as an upperclassman without taking all the music courses the first two years and been accepted into the program. He gave me a bunch of strange musicality tests, all of which I passed with flying colors and he accepted me as a double major if I wanted to do it. I chose not to because it would have taken me one extra year and I was sick and tired of studying at the time. I heard Bruno later lost a substantial portion of his hearing and wound up at the University of Alaska in their music department.

Los Angeles was like a candy store in that anyone who was anyone came through here. I got to see Lee Morgan and Freddie Hubbard in 1968 at the Lighthouse. Also Dizzy Gillespie several times - the last being in 1983 when Sarah Vaughn blew him and Carmen McRea right off the stage. On a good day she was the best I ever heard, and that day she was having a good day!. Maybe William Warfield singing Old Man River in Showboat (the movie) was better.

When my mother and father came to visit me I always took him to the big event he would not have access to in Waterbury. At the Ambassador Hotel one night Charlie Byrd, Herb Ellis and Barney Kessel (a great guy) were playing jazz guitar on the same gig! What an amazing night that was!

The only two times I ever heard a musician get a standing ovation on each and every number was Stephanie Grapelli at the Lighthouse in Hermosa Beach the first time he came to Los Angeles and Benny Goodman at the Grant Hotel in San Diego in 1979.

I got to hear Charlie Mingus, who was so far ahead of me at the time I did not know what the hell he was doing.

The night I heard Raphael Mendez his two sons came down from Stanford University where they were studying medicine to play as a trio the second half of the concert. The sons were terrific but as far as I was concerned they were in the way. I wanted as much as I could get of Big Daddy! Years later their names were on the door at USC Dept. of Urology and my doctor told me they were the only two urologists he knew who had so much money they did not have to practice medicine for a living. He said Raphael Mendez invested in land in the San Fernando Valley that became a shopping Center and both of his sons are extremely wealthy because of it.

The day I saw him Raphael Mendez played Here Kati, Estrelleta, Moto Perpetuo (the violin solo of Paganini)

IF MY FATHER COULD HAVE LIVED OUT HIS FANTASY IT WOULD HAVE BEEN TO PLAY VIOLIN EVEN UP WITH PAGANINI. HE WAS ALWAYS MUTTERING THAT PAGANINI NEVER WROTE DOWN THE TECHNIQUE BY WHICH HE WAS ABLE TO DO THE IMPOSSIBLE THINGS HE DID ON THE VIOLIN. PEOPLE SAID HE WAS INSPIRED AND POSSESSED BY THE DEVIL TO BE ABLE TO PLAY AS HE DID! Uan Rasey played studio trumpet for MGM and is perhaps best known for the beautiful trumpet playing in the movie China Town with Jack Nicholson.

Raphael Mendez was Pancho Villa's trumpet player at 4 years old and also gave concerts in Mexico at four years old. Pancho Villa is known by the Mexicans as The Great Mexican Hero and is known by the United State Government as The Great Mexican Bandit! Again, beauty is in the eye of the beholder!

THE MAGIC LEAD PIPE OF DOMINIC CALLICHIO WAS SOLD TO OLDS. THE TOP OF THE LINE OLDS HORNS WERE THE MENDEZ MODEL AND THE RECORDER. I NEVER PLAYED A RECORDER AND I HAD TO BUY THREE MENDEZ MODELS BEFORE I GOT ONE WITH THE MAGIC LEAD PIPE, SO OLDS DID NOT PUT THEM ON ALL THEIR MODELS. IT WAS AS GOOD AS CHRIS CALLICHIO SAID IT WAS. I GOT A NOTE AND A HALF HIGHER CONSISTENTLY. IT WAS LONGER THAN OTHER TRUMPET LEADPIPES AND EVEN LONGER THAN THE OTHER MENDEZ MODELS BY ABOUT AN INCH AND ONE HALF.

SHADES OF SOUND AND HIGH NOTES AND LEAD TRUMPET AND JAZZ TRUMPET ALA MILES AND CHET

My favorite lead horns were the one Olds Mendez Model with the long lead pipe made from the Mandle that Dominic Callichio sold to Olds in the early fifties - Look for Mendez Models from 1952-58. Maybe Olds didn't know how good a trade they made or they would still be in business! 2. Schilke S-32's designed especially for lead players by Renaud Schilke himself prior to his death. I have two. This is the only modern made trumpet that gives me the Harry James sound for solo playing.

3. Callichio #1 Bell and #2 Leadpipe made by Chris Callichio who sold the company around 2005 to someone in Oklahoma. This particular silver trumpet is a great lead horn and was used by Frank Szabo in place of his Chicago Benge. Szabo was lead for Count Basie, Buddy Rich and Bill Holman and a top studio musician.

Harry James Sound

1.\ Selmer Paris made in 1939-medium bore. Harry actually used Selmer's when he made You Made Me Love You in 1939 and The Sleepy Lagoon in 1941. Those two songs are the reason I became a trumpet player. Of course mouthpieces make a difference, but I will get to that later.
Conrad Gozzo's Lead and Solo Sound on Trumpeter's Prayer was made on a pre WW II French Besson.

2.\ King Supersonic Silver Bell Dual Bore as advertised by Harry. Harry's personal horns were customized a little differently than the stock models as told to me by a guy who made the horns who at that time worked for Chris Callichio.

3.\ Schilke S-32's give you the Harry James sound if you know what it is. Have to listen to Sleepy Lagoon and You Made Me Love You 10,000 times each until it is burned into your soul!

THE COOL SOUND ALA MILES DAVIS AND CHET BAKER

1.\ Pre World War II French Besson was on the wall all blackened with dirt and unrecognized by Randy Anglin - a repairman from Orange County, CA. I hocked him for three years to get it in shape and sell it to me, which he did for $1200 (a lot at the time). It has the best jazz sound along with

2.\ Callichio Trumpet made by Chris Callichio (he only made a few in COPPER) With a 9 pipe (as used by Freddie Hubbard) and a 3 Bell. He charged $2700 - a fortune at the time!

Chuck Finley used a Callichio 1 Bell 2 leadpipe with a custom made Bob Reeves mouthpiece from the late sixties through the tonight show.

There is a story that Barbra Streisand wanted him to play for one full week for her in Las Vegas for either a recording or a show. He commanded $30,000 for that week. (And got it!)

HARRY JAMES' TONE was better on the Selmer Balanced Action trumpet that he made "The Sleepy Lagoon" on in 1941 and "You Made Me Love You" in 1939. The King trumpets had a little tubbier sound and that included his specially made souped up models. I heard him in person. But either is better than none at all. the Selmer Paris 1939 model I have gets the same sound too.

The Olds Mendez horns naturally have a little too much edge for me. With a regular mouthpiece it sounds like I am playing at the Bullfights. Then again Mendez was Pancho Villa's trumpeter at four years old at which time he was also giving concerts all over Mexico.. The solution to the problem is I have recently begun using a Giardinelli 1 VM mouthpiece on the Olds Mendez horn and it now has a big symphonic sound, deep, and rich. Bob Giardinelli was good to me in 1963-1964 - 52nd St. NYC

SENIOR YEAR AT THE UNIVERSITY OF CONNECTICUT

I was a political science major and I toyed with the idea of taking a double major as a senior - the second being in music.

Professor Bruno DiCecco, a cellist, said I would never pass the entrance requirements and I would have an abundance of coursework to make up which means my graduation would be a year later.

I insisted he give me all the prerequisite musical tests - all of which I passed with flying colors to his amazement. He said he had never seen an outside do that before, coming in cold. I guess I was always a musician, my father's son!

WRITING FROM MY UNCONSCIOUS MIND VIA ASSOCIATIONS AS THEY OCCUR FROM THIS POINT FORWARD IN THE BOOK, (OTHERWISE I PROBABLY WILL FORGET MUCH OF THE RICHNESS FROM SITUTIONS THAT OCCURED IN MY MUSICAL LIFE)

SOUND

1.\ Harry James best sound ever was on the Sleepy Lagoon and next best on You Made Me Love You which came out in 1941 and 1939.

It was that sound that made me fall in love with trumpet and betray my family to become a trumpet player instead of a guitar player. My entire family were string players.

2.\ The second best sound I ever heard was Bunny Berrigan playing "I Can't Get Started" in (maybe 1937 - not sure of date.)

3.\ The most powerful big sound I ever heard was Conrad Gozzo on a cd called "Tutti's Trumpets" by Tutti Cammerata where the entire orchestra gave Gozzo a standing ovation after he cut it (Trumpeters Prayer) on the first take!

4.\ Bob Reeves said to me (the mouthpiece maker in Valencia, CA) regarding trumpet "All You've Got To Sell Is Sound!" While he is one of the best mouthpiece makers in the world, when I asked him about Parduba his answer was "Harry James played one!" as in "Need I say more!"

BACK TO THE UNIVERSITY OF CONNECTICUT

I decided against the double major but played first trumpet in the concert band along with two or three other first trumpets. I also took a course in bass fiddle with world renown classical bassist Bert Turetzky. UCONN was huge and I used to have to walk miles to class and back every day. I kept the bass in the back seat of the car most of the time and they gave me a parking pass that I could park anywhere on campus because I was a bass player. Bass Fiddle had its perks including my father telling me "If you want to work (as a professional musician), play bass! I was a lazy bastard so I left it in the back seat! In my mind it could hardly compare to carrying a piccolo in it's case! (parking pass or not!)

I took a class in trumpet performance with Sam Goldfarb who also taught at the Hartt College of Music in Hartford, Connecticut. He gave me a real easy piece given my technical abilities on the trumpet. He said "You have never played in front of a jury before!" A jury in a performance class is a group of three faculty members from the department of music who "JUDGE" EVERY NUANCE OF WHAT YOU PLAY! SAM WAS REASSURING! HE SAID, "Don't worry! You will be shitting your pants first time around! You will thank me for picking this piece!" When I got up there on stage, my horn was shaking, my legs were shaking and I had a hard time holding the mouthpiece in one place on my face as it keep bouncing around all by itself!

Nevertheless, I always had balls and I learned from my all night card games partner, "NBNBC" "NO BALLS, NO BLUE CHIPS!" I played it beautifully as I have always had the talent to play up to a situation; in other words play better than I am used to playing when I am in front of an audience! You see why I moved to Los Angeles! I got an A in the course! Me and the trumpet were born for each other!

THE INTERNATIONAL MUSICIAN MAGAZINE IN THE FIFTIES had a story about Maynard Ferguson playing for Leonard Bernstein around 1956 for the New York Philharmonic. Vacchiano was the first principal trumpet. He had Maynard warm up in the basement instead of with the other "classical" musicians in the orchestra.

Bill Holman who knew Maynard when Bill composed for Stan Kenton ran into Maynard and Maynard said "Bill!" out loud. Holman whispered saying "Shhh, around here it's William!" Maynard began playing in a register similar to where the flutes customarily play and Bernstein said, "Mr. Ferguson, it's mezzo forte!" Vacchiano chimed in "Maestro! That is his mezzo forte!" MICKEY TRENTALANGE AND THE ARMY RESERVE BAND

A lot of guys I knew were coming back from Vietnam in closed caskets. Alan Kosloff, a singer-guitar player, next door neighbor said to me, "It's a long time dying!"

My father played a lot of gigs with saxaphonist Mickey Trentalange and told me to look him up after I graduated from the University of Connecticut about playing in the Army Reserve band. Mickey said, "I can't make you any promises. During WWII they called up the entire reserve unit and we were in Australia praying that the Japanese didn't invade!" He said "I don't have any trumpet spots open but I have a spot for a baritone player. He gave me an old piece of junk that hardly played a note to practice on.

******* When I got hired to train psychiatrists and psychologists in Australia in 1984 after my book "Psychotherapy, Insight & Style: The Existential Moment was published by Allyn & Bacon, of Boston, I was bringing my luggage through customs and they did not check it. Every other foreign country I had been requested to check my bags. So I said, "Aren't you going to check my luggage!" The man said "You are a Yank, aren't you?" I said, "Yeah!" He said "Come on in! Have a good time! If it wasn't for you guys we would all be speaking Japanese down here!" Australia and Norway were the only two countries that were grateful for the gifts of our serviceman!

Dr. Len Bergantino, Ed.D., Ph.D.

Meantime I had allergies, flat feet and a bad back - all of which got you a Four F deferment. However, Lyndon Johnson was increasing the number of servicemen in Vietnam by about 450,000, so the draft board said "As long as your trigger finger works you are 1-A and they did not consider the allergies and the flat feet any longer exemptible. However, they set me up with an orthopaedic surgeon in New Haven, Connecticut to check on my back and I was told to bring my ex rays of back problems.

BLUE COLLAR IGNORANCE

Being from a blue collar city, Waterbury, Connecticut, "The Brass Center of The World" during WWII and the fifties before cheap labor in other places caused all the factories to move out, I did not know that M.D.'s and Chiropractors hated each other. My exam was in New Haven, the seat of Yale University, which was not a blue collar city, and where such prejudices were full blown in 1965.

I had back ex rays from a highly ethical ex marine named Nicholas Bruce, D.C. The orthopaedic surgeon in New Haven said to bend forward six inches and asked me if it hurt. I said "Not today. It is either in or out which is frequently." He started screaming "So you are another wise ass college kid who is trying to beat the draft; Well, You Are In! You are In!" I said, "Listen, you fucking asshole, I was a volunteer, but I don't like your fucking attitude, so I withdraw my volunteer status!" And I walked out!

UCONN WAS A WILD PLACE WHEN I WAS THERE! A GREAT PARTY SCHOOL! YET, I HAD THE SECOND HIGHEST GPA IN THE HOUSE WHERE I RESIDED. THAT WAS A 2.6 GPA (C+ average) -which wasn't bad given I left my books in a duffle bag in the basement of my parents' home in Waterbury! I was sick and tired of college but if I didn't go to graduate school I was headed for Vietnam! A lot of my friends came back in closed caskets!

PARANORMAL ABILITIES

As a psychologist in 1978 I had energy rays shooting out of my hands, cured a woman of broken toes, used to burn my ex wife's teats from 75 feet away with lazer beams shooting out of my hands where she would jump in the air and laugh, and shot energy rays into world renown guitarist Charlie

The Essence of Music

Byrd at the Catamaran in San Diego, California when Charlie was really flat as there were only three people in the audience that night for the first set. After I shot the energy rays into him he played the most enthusiastic set I ever heard him play for only three people.

ALL CD'S ARE DIFFERENT IN TONE AND SOUND AND FEELING QUALITY

1.\ Miles Davis' best tones for the cool era are on "Sketches of Spain" and Porgy And Bess".
2.\ Chet Baker's best sound is on his cd playing Lerner & Loewe's tunes such as "I Could Have Danced All Night" and "On The Street Where You Live." Also "Born To Be Blue" which he played on the flugelhorn and he also sang.
3.\ Charlie Byrd's best sound is on a cd he made with trumpeter Clark Terry and he plays "I Left My Heart In San Francisco" on it.
4.\ Django Reinhardt has one cd made in France of "The Hot Club of France" that is far superior to those copies made in England.
5.\ Best sound I ever heard world renown guitarist Johnny Smith play was on a 33 rpm where he played solo guitar "Pavanne"; and on a cd where he played "Moonlight In Vermont" My mandolin has that sound on my CD - Falling in Love Gibson F-2 - 1913 orchardrecords.com.

BEST SOUNDING FLUGELHORN

Roy Hargrove has the best sounding flugelhorn I heard in this modern day of jazz players where much of the jazz sounds like elevator music. When Chet or Miles played three notes you knew who it was that was playing. Their soul came out of the horn. For the most part in today's music no one has a soul! Furthur, no one writes songs anymore! What the hell would Frank Sinatra or Dean Martin sing today? How about Mario Lanza? I listened to Caruso and Pavarotti and for sheer voice I thought Lanza was better! Beauty of Sound! Remember Bob Reeves! All You've got to sell is sound!

I bought a Couesnon Flugelhorn which is adequate for most any gig and I only paid $750 for it around 1997. Around 2000 Chris Callichio was selling a copper flugelhorn that Chuck Mangione played. It was one of the two best Ameican made flugelhorns I played. The other was a copper

Kanstul in Anaheim after Callichio w ent out of business. That's probably your best bet unless you go after Roy Hargrove's flugelhorn maker named Tom Inderbinen around Zurich, Switzerland. It is the Wood Model. It is not made of wood. That is just the name of the model. It is magnificent.

Speaking of Roy Hargrove he agreed to give me jazz lessons, however the day after his gig at Catalina's Bar and Grill (the new one in Hollywood on either Sunset or Hollywood Blvds.) he said he had to play at the White House for President George W. Bush. I said "What the fuck would you want to do that for? (Meaning, why would a top musician like him want to play at the White House. He thought I was busting his chops in that he had exactly the opposite point of view that it was a big honor. I saw Bush as a war criminal that did away with Civil Rights in America and created a paranoia throughout the country the likes of which I had not seen since Nixon!

The sound does not carry over to Hargrove's trumpet, which has a shrill sound compared to his flugelhorn, both made by the same hand made manufacturer with at least a six month waiting list. It was $3300 around 2002. The good side of being an internationally renown psychologist was that I became a millionaire and could buy whatever horn I wanted to give me exactly that "SHADES OF SOUND" I WANTED AS ALL HORNS WERE DIFFERENT. CHRIS CALLICHIO HATED IT WHEN I CAME AROUND BECAUSE I BOUGHT HIS BEST HORNS AND HE WANTED TO SELL THEM TO THE TOP TRUMPET PLAYERS IN TOWN. SOME OF THE BEST IN THE WORLD LIVE IN LOS ANGELES! THE REST ARE IN NEW YORK!

POST UNIVERSITY OF CONNECTICUT

A friend at the time Bob Burns was on a fellowship at the University of Mississippi teaching German for an M.A. He wanted me to go down and keep him company so I applied to Old Miss. I didn't hear anything so I drove my transcripts down to Fairfield University in Fairfield, Connecticut - a Jesuit Institution. I got accepted. It was expensive and my parents were among the "undeserving poor", so I got a government loan for $10,000 and figured it was a vote for myself and either I would make it or go to jail, but either way I was better off than not voting for my own future! NB NBC - No Balls! No Blue Chips! I got a six room house on 123 Pine Creek Road across the street from the Surf Side Bar which is where all the social life was in Fairfield at that time. Those were "THE GOOD OLD DAYS!"

I was a wild man among serious students ten to fifteen years older than me. I was there about two weeks and the Dean of the College Father McPeake drops by to see me and said "I just got a call from your draft board in Waterbury, Connecticut and they want to know if you are in the top ten percent of your class! I have never received a call after ten days into the semester asking such a question. Two weeks later Father McPeake came back and said the same thing. Then he said to me "What the hell did you do to those people, anyway?!??!?!? I told Father McPeake the orthopaedic surgeon in New Haven bagged my ass - the result being I studied day and night and got a 3.86 GPA and was in the top ten percent of my class which w as good enough for a military deferment.

Then I got a call from the Dean at Ole Miss welcoming me down in Mississippi three weeks into the semester. I explained the situation that as I had not heard from him I borrowed ten grand, had a six room house on the beach and was three weeks into the semester at Fairfield, University. Then I asked him "How come you are calling me three weeks after your semester started at Ole Miss? I will never forget his answer as it was stated in a manner that he totally did not give a shit what I thought about his answer, that is just how it was down there. He said, " Frankly, Mr. Bergantino, I just got around to it!" I had to laugh!

Bob Burns, myself and George O'Meara were drinking German Beer at Phil Becker's Restaurant - the best German Pub in Waterbury, Connecticut and Burns was going on in what sure as hell sounded like German! Phil Becker, from Bavaria said, What the hell is Burns talking about anyway?" I said "Phil, he is talking German!" Becker, seventy years old with arms like a tank said "That's not German! I am from Germany! I know German and that is not German!"

O'Meara and I were flabergasted, so I said to Burns while nudging him in the ribs, "Hey Bob, Becker said you are not speaking German! How the hell can you be on a fellowship teaching German at Ole Miss when you can't speak German. He whispered as if he were telling us a secret saying, "No one down there knows I can't speak German!" He got through the thirty units of course work but never completed his Masters thesis in German. I guess he couldn't write German either?

STUDENT TEACHING AT WILBY HIGH SCHOOL in Waterbury, Connecticut was not a sure bet for an occupational deferment, particularly when I was teaching United States History, World Civilization I and II and Problems of Democracy. There wasn't a job to be had in either

New York State or Connecticut. The last day of my student teaching a tenured teacher named Russo who taught social studies said in the teacher's lounge, "I've had six fucking heart attacks and they can't keep me out of this place" That night he got number 7 and I got his job and the rest is history!

THE IRISH GOT THERE FIRST

In Waterbury the Irish were the mayors and Superintendent of Schools and the highest an Italian got was Dr. Riccuti who became Director of Pupil Personnel Services. As I was the brightest young Italian I thought if I got my doctorate in Counselor Education at the University of Southern California I could come back and take over Dr. Riccuti's job when he retired.

WATERBURY TEACHER'S UNION

In 1967 and 1968 I set a precedent two times by getting my pay minus substitute's pay to leave for USC two weeks prior to the end of the high school year.

Michael Wallace (Irish) and Superintendent of Schools told head counselor and basketball coach Jack Delaney, after I used the Teachers Union to break his balls (Mr. Capozzi-Italian) "Hey Jack, tell the kid he is starting to get on my nerves!" They didn't want me to go at all and I got my pay minus substitute's pay out of them because my additional knowledge would be good for the Waterbury School District.

Political Science Major at The University of Connecticut

We had a visiting Professor Schatschnider who was quite taken with back room politics and Boss Tweed. It was from him I first got the knack of breaking peoples' balls!

I TOOK THIRTY YEARS OFF FROM PLAYING TRUMPET (1965-1995)

When I was at Fairfield I taught Father McPeake's secretary's son how to play trumpet with once a week lessons. While I taught guitar filling in for my father at music studios for five dollars every half hour even though

I could not play guitar (I knew strings) - teaching trumpet was hard work. It was not as much fun and I never did it again. I got a supreme respect for my trumpet teacher Carl Berg who had the patience of a Saint and the organizational skills of a nuclear physicist! The secretary turned me on to the Tijuana Brass.

Herb Alpert had a great recording sound. I heard him at a live gig at Burt Bacharach's wedding to Carol Bayer Sager and was not particularly enchanted with his live performance, but he had magic in the recording studio! (So much so that Al Hirt told an audience that he "hoped Herb Alpert got a lip fungus" because no one bought Al Hirt's records after the Tijuana Brass came out. Al Hirt was a much better trumpet player.

Numbers that stand out from a 33 rpm long play are Al Hirt's Best Recorded Sound - RCA 1958 "Strangers In Paradise" Best Sound, "The Sleepy Lagoon" Al had tremendous technique with the double and triple tonguing. He had a way to do it as he was coming down the scale of notes in a tune that is totally marvelous. At his club in New Orleans you were thrilled and excited from the moment you entered until the moment you left! I loved Al Hirt! He built on those who went before him, such as playing "The Sleepy Lagoon" as done by Harry James in 1941. Al wasn't as good as Harry, but he wasn't afraid of him either. He was the best of his time between about 1958 and 1963 not counting Maynard Ferguson who was an entirely different kind of musician and on that score you could love both of them and not be in conflict. RCA wrote on Al Hirt's Album that he was "The Greatest Trumpet Player In The World". Many professional musicians got pissed at him and he said "Hey, RCA wanted to sell records and they put that on the record. It was their d oing, n ot mine! I think the greatest trumpet player in the world is Conrad Gozzo!" Who could argue with that choice! Again, you have to hear Gozzo play "Trumpeter's Prayer" on Tutti's Trumpets (Tutti Cammerata) before you die. When you hear it you will think you are in Heaven!

BEFORE I GOT TO USC I SOLD THE KING DUAL BORE SILVERSONIC HARRY JAMES MODEL (SOMETHING I ALWAYS REGRETTED AS IT WAS A GREAT HORN THAT I USED TO SERENADE ALL THE GIRLS IN COLLEGE WITH!) AND I BOUGHT A USED BACH SILVER STRADIVARIOUS #37 Model from Lou Pontecorvo, but I hardly ever played it, which in retrospect I think was a good thing because Lou was a top player in New Haven, Connecticut and I think he wore it out. Trumpets are only good for so many notes and then their lives are over! The metal loses its resonance!

(Never listen to other people when attempting to purchase a horn for your own Shades of Sound!)

When I was a doctoral student at USC I was a full time student and I had a full time job as a junior high school counselor at Hosler Junior High School in Lilly White Lynwood, California (no longer the case - entirely African American Community now) During the years 1968-1971 when I absolutely could not read one more page from being overdosed with study I would take a 20 minute break and play my Callichio, Gold plated, 2 bell, 7 pipe Callichio, made by Dominic Callichio himself. I averaged about twenty minutes a day as my studies and work schedule were gruelling. I had a picture of Miles Davis on the wall!

I did play duets once with the music teacher Ron Savitt. I sold the Bach. For me Bach's were a trumpet you used to blend in. I always wanted a tone to stand out, like my heroes Harry James, Al Hirt, Raphael Mendez. Bach's were stuffy to me although a New York Bach (prior to Vincent Bach's move to Mount Vernon -which is referred to as a Mount Vernon Bach) are worth a small fortune now (N.Y. Bach), about $3000. In my day new they sold for $300..

LOS ANGELES WAS LIKE A CANDY STORE FOR JAZZ TRUMPET PLAYERS

While I was not playing much trumpet when I had a date on Friday or Saturday night I often went to a jazz club. I met Freddie Hubbard and Lee Morgan in 1968 at the Lighthouse run by Howard Rumsey in Hermosa Beach, California. They treated me well as I was enthusiastic in my love for trumpet and jazz and I knew what I was talking about so they enjoyed talking to me.

Lee Morgan was unbelievable. His girlfriend shot him in the stomach and killed him six months after I met him for having an affair with another woman. That should have told me something but it didn't! What a waste of talent!

I got to meet Gerry Mulligan, and Charlie Byrd personally and Art Farmer by telephone much later on. I got to hear Charlie Mingus, McCoy Tyner, Herbie Mann, Stephan Grappelli, Benny Goodman, and David Grisman who could play the ass off of the mandolin in something he called DAWG while he played with Grapelli. I got to hear Sarah Vaughn blow Carmen McRae and Dizzy Gillespie right off the stage at "Concerts By

The Sea in Torrance, California. That was Howard Rumsey's new place after "The Lighthouse". I got to meet and chat with him many times. One of the musicians I liked the best was guitarist Barney Kessel. I got to know Pete Candoli - Superman outfit coming out on a swing when he played lead for Woody Herman. I met his brother Conte Candoli but never made a personal connection with him. I met Uan Rasey -another of Tutti's trumpets who played all the trumpet work in the movie "Chinatown" starring Jack Nicholson. A guy you never heard of is Warren Leuning who played the trumpet solo in "Moonstruck" a class B movie starring Cher! It is worth renting the movie just to hear his trumpet solo. I waited until the movie credits were given and then called him up to talk about it. He said he had to practice a lot to get it down, it was in five flats. I told him it was worth every minute he practiced! He was magnificent! I tried to persuade Dizzy to do a workshop with me where I did the shrinking and he did the music! He focused on my phrase "Let's Make Some Money! Let's Have Some Fun!" So that is what I named my trio in 2010. I figured if it got "The Diz's" attention, as he referred to himself, it had the foundation of what I want to do at this stage of my twilight years. Diz was a hot shit. He was high all the time and as funny as they come. Another guy whose playing I thought lacked soul, but could really get around the instrument was Jack Sheldon. I loved Jack more as a comedian t han a trumpet player. I felt he ???

In 1976 California State University -Los Angeles put on a workshop by Nat Adderly who played a King Silver Cornet on all the records he made with his famous saxaphone brother, Cannonball Adderly. Milton H. Erickson, M.D. who trained me in clinical hypnosis and uncommon therapy always made a distinction between "farm folk" and "city folk". Nat Adderly was definitely farm folk. He looked like a Black Roy Rogers. He wore a black cowboy hat and cowboy boots with a western cowboy shirt that looked just like Roy Rogers. He was a great guy. I didn't get to hear him play much, but I had a great time talking to him!

Dizzy Gillespie had a trumpet that shot up in the air instead of forward. Story has it that he accidentally stepped on his trumpet on a gig and he bent it that way. He had nothing else to play and found that it projected out over the audience better than the trumpet that was straight forward.

I got to play next to Clyde Reisinger who played lead trumpet for Harry James in the fifties. He said one night Harry forgot his horn and one of the guys in the trumpet section had an old beat up student trumpet in the trunk of his car. Harry told him to go out and get it. He played the entire gig on it and sounded the same as he usually did. Some people can play a tin can and it wouldn't make any difference!

Nat Adderly was the only person I ever saw play progressive jazz on a cornet instead of a flugelhorn or a trumpet.

In Los Angeles you got to see everybody! I saw Don Ellis and his electric trumpet in 1969. People say he was way ahead of his time. He was way ahead of mine too!

Miles Davis

I went to see Miles in 1968 at the original Shelley's Manne Hole on Cahuenga Blvd. in Hollywood, California. Shelley Manne was a famous jazz drummer who had his own nightclub. There were about 30 people there. I was not shy about meeting my idols and Miles, during his breaks, sat at a table right next to me. There was something about him at that time I got to see once again when I sat next to George Burns at Valentino's Restaurant in Santa Monica. You felt like you knew them but they put off a vibe that they were totally unapproachable, so I did not speak to Miles on that occasion. Another time I saw George Burns waiting for an elevator at Cedars Sinai Hospital and he looked like a wagon train surrounded in a circle with people eqi-distant space away from him and no one spoke to him nor did he speak to anyone else. Benny Goodman also put off that vibe at the Grant Hotel in 1979 in San Diego.

In the late nineties I was in a Big band where Art DePew who played solos in the Harry James Band after Harry died was playing second trumpet. On fourth sitting next to me was Tony Terran who played lead trumpet on the Lucy Show in the fifties. Tony always read the newspaper when the trumpets were not playing and always came in at exactly the correct moment on time musically!

Art DePew was a Julliard School of Music Graduate and he attended Julliard when Miles Davis was there for a semester or two. On this particular day Art stood up with his rear end facing the leader of the band and blew his horn toward the ground and said "Look at me. I am Miles Davis. I am a genius!" Meanwhile Tony Terran nudged me and whispered in my ear. "Yeah, Miles Davis and Inches Depew!"

Harry James used to call Miles Davis and Chet Baker "fu-fu trumpet players" - claiming that the "cool sound" was not really a trumpet sound.

I got to see "CAT ANDERSON" play high notes for Bill Berry's Big

Band at the Ambassador Hotel (where Bobby Kennedy was assassinated). He could hit the high ones in the same range as Maynard Ferguson, but Maynard lived up there. Maynard's sound was as big as a house and Cat's was not!

Somebody asked "Cat" Anderson what he did to play those high notes with Duke Ellington's band. His answer shocked me. He said "I practice G on the second line of the scale for twelve beats hours at a time."

I never met Jonah Jones but I loved what he did with a cup mute!

SLYDE HYDE

Before I met and became friends with Slyde Hyde - a trombone player who played for Stan Kenton and was big in L.A. recording studios before retiring and moving to Hawaii (the big island) he was playing in a Kenton Revival Band put on by KLON Jazz Radio Station. I saw a psychologist from Texas in the crowd. I went up to him and said, "Hey man, how'd you like to have a name like Slyde Hyde?" "Ain't that a cool name!" He stunned me, by yelling out "What are you crazy! I am a psychologist, not a musician! (and then putting his hands as if to hide his genitals he said) "I would have to have a name like Hide Slide!" (as in hide penis to avoid sexual misconduct).

Musicians were known to have done wild and crazy things. JOE VENUTI, A JAZZ VIOLIN PLAYER WHO PLAYED WITH GUITARIST EDDIE LANG WAS KNOWN FOR HIS PRACTICAL JOKES. One night he hired two hookers in New York City, rented a hotel room, and told them to be going at it with each other when he opened the door. Also planned for the evening he hired forty contrabass players, all of whom were to meet on the same street corner at the same time for the same job. He payed them all for the gig! Then he brought them to the hotel room, flung open the door, and while the two prostitutes were going at it said, "Fellas, I would like you to meet my mother and my sister!"

On another occasion he was playing a kiddie matinee with Roy Rogers and Trigger (his horse). The idea was for Roy Rogers to have the curtain open, and Trigger would rear up on his hind legs, and all the kids would think it was great.

What Roy Rogers (real name -Leonard Sly) didn't know was that Joe Venuti was massaging Trigger's penis with his violin bow while they were waiting for the curtain to open. So when the curtain opened Trigger had a big erection, and all the kids screamed, and the curtain was immediately closed! Venuti was way before my time but stories about his deeds are legendary among musicians.

Burt Bacharach heard me play Alfie on the mandolin and said I had a good feel for the song. This pleased me greatly because of all the songs he wrote I liked it the best, I thought it was the most cut out for jazz, and it had the most difficult chord changes. Others I liked were "Raindrops are Falling on My Head" from the movie "Butch Cassady and the Sundance Kid" with Robert Redford and Paul Newman and one that started off with Dionne Warwick singing "What do ya get when you fall in Love?" (That might be the name of it but I am not certain.) Burt was a good guy. He invited me to his wedding in 1983 to Carole Bayer Sager, his lyricist after Hal David. Herb Alpert played trumpet for the wedding (not with the Tijuana brass).

His sound was unnoticeable which surprised me because on his recordings with the Tijuana Brass his sound was distinguishably light, bouncy and unique as testified to by the millions of records he sold. When they asked Miles Davis who the greatest trumpet player in the world was he said "Herb Alpert. He makes two million dollars a year selling his records!"

I was introduced to Paul Anka who gave me a big two handed handshake and as big a grin and he said "Good to meetcha!" Then I got introduced to Neil Diamond who was stoned out of his mind on marijuana and did not move - where upon Paul Anka grabbed my hand again with both of his hands and shook vigorously as he said "This one's for Neill!" We all broke out laughing except for Neill who still did not move. Burt used to say that Neill Diamond was a great performer, it was just that you had to darken out the first three rows!"

At the Christmas party in 1987 where Miles and I sat together, Barbra Streisand, Shirley MacLaine, Pat Reilly and Georgia Frontiere were there as well as Herbie Hancock. Streisand had a date with the guy who owned all of Baskin Robbins ice cream places.

I kept telling Georgia Frontiere that she couldn't win (the Los Angeles Rams which maybe were the St. Louis Rams by then -not certain) for the Rams unless she got another Italian quarterback. I told her she had two choices; to either bring Vince Ferragamo back from Canada (hadn't played for Rams since 1979 Super Bowl vs. Pittsburgh Steelers) or draft Ralph Guglielmi, ex Notre Dame All-American Heisman Winner in 1954, out of retirement. These were both ridiculous suggestions but she kept laughing and laughing, and I myself did not understand why she found what I said that funny?

Georgia Frontiere was a good sport. I was glad of that because she was big enough to kick my ass and I was 6 ft 2 inches tall and 220 pounds at the time. I found out years later why she was laughing so hard. A friend of mine knew the Italian quarterback who played for the Houston Oilers, Dan Pastorini, and he told me Dan told him Georgia had a requirement for the game day Italian quarterbacks - that she had to have sex with them prior to the game on Sunday. No wonder Bradshaw and the Steelers beat the Rams! Those Pittsburgh fans were nuts! The game was at the Los Angeles Coliseum and me and a psychiatrist friend were sitting pretty high up and I noticed two Pittsburgh fans grabbing a Ram's fan by his ankles and hanging him head downward from the top of the stands in the Colesium - a long drop downward. I said to my psychiatrist friend, pointing toward the situation, "Hey, you want to help that guy out!" He looked at me in disbelief and said "What Are You Crazy!" After a couple of terrifying minutes they let the man live and pulled him back into the seating area.

ELIZABETH TAYLOR was the talk of the Christmas Party at Burt Bacharach's home even though she was not present. She and Carole Bayer Sager were best friends. I do not remember why she WAS NOT PRESENT, BUT PEOPLE WERE TALKING ABOUT HER ALL NIGHT.

I liked Carole Bayer Sager! I thought she was a genuinely "good" person - a former high school English teacher. I haven't seen her since the early nineties until she was on television after Elizabeth Taylor died. Her comments were far more substantial than anyone else. It was clear they were best friends! The other person I remember saying something about Liz Taylor about ten years ago was Clint Eastwood, a no bullshit guy, who said "Elizabeth puts her money where her mouth is! She gave millions to AIDS research and of course she backed her good friend Rock Hudson when he got AIDS when the rest of Hollywood treated him as a Pariah! She was not just the flimsy big breasted chunky broad that Richard Burton described her to be. No wonder she divorced him!

BURT BACHARACH

Burt's most interesting stories to me was when he was young and impressionable, a recent graduate in music from McGill University in

Montreal, and he was Marlene Deitrich's piano player. For those stories you will have to ask Burt yourself!

DIONNE WARWICK -THE FEUD!

For a period of many years, I am guessing between 7 and 10, Burt and Dionne had nothing to do with each other because she sued him over her being able to sing a song he wrote and he said he had exclusive rights. In any case it got pretty ugly beyond what I knew about as a member of the general public.

INVITATION #2 -BURT REUNITES WITH DIONNE!

There was a big party somewhere in Los Angeles where I was invited to a dinner where you went up to help yourself. I remember shrimp as big as your plate and I had at least ten of them! Burt was not cheap! When he threw a party he threw a party!

THE SHOW

What made this so funny is that all the invited guests knew it to be true as well as Burt and Dionne. Burt began by saying. "Dionne Warwick! I hate this bitch! We have been fighting in court for years! Can you believe this bitch sued me over a song I wrote! "THEN HE SAID, "LADIES AND GENTLEMEN, DESPITE THE FACT I HATE THIS BITCH, I REALIZED SHE IS THE ONLY ONE WHO CAN SING MY SONGS! I GIVE YOU DIONNE WARWICK!!!" AND THE CROWD WENT BALISTIC! SHE WAS THE ONLY ONE WHO COULD SING HIS SONGS! SHE WAS MAGICAL! BURT WAS A BIG BOY WHO LIKED SUCCESS!

BURT AND THE RADIO STATION DISC JOCKEYS

It used to bother him greatly that disc jockeys would want to and actually do it; change the speed at which they played his songs to suit their audiences as they saw fit! I asked him why he let it go down that way! He said "I write songs so people will hear them! If they don't play my songs, nobody hears them!" So much for fighting the good fight on that issue?

INVITATION #3 -LAS VEGAS BIG HOTEL SHOW

Dionne Warwick was singing his songs. It was in the early 90's. After the show there was a big party with about 100 people in a lower level hotel room with all of Burt's invited guests. I am Italian and the food he had while it was good did not particularly catch my fancy. Directly across the hall was Dionne Warwick's party room. She had a huge platter of Italian Salami, Provolone Cheese, et. al, only it had the cellophane on it. Man, did it look good! Dionne was the only one in the room sitting in a chair and she looked like she was guarding the food so she would not have to pay for it if nobody came to her party! I began to unveil the cellophane. She said "Who the hell are you! Are you crashing the party!" I said "I am a friend of Burt Backarach's!" She said "Well his party is across the hall! Get the hell out of here!" From that moment on, whether she was the only one who could sing his songs or not, I thought she was a bitch!

********** The most important thing I learned from Burt Bacharach was to "NEVER HANG AROUND WITH OR MARRY SOMEONE WHO MAKES LESS MONEY THAN YOU BECAUSE THEY WILL ALWAYS BE RESENTFUL, HATEFUL AND SPITEFUL NO MATTER HOW GENEROUS YOU ARE WITH THEM!

**********CAROLE BAYER SAGER I HAD NOT SEEN SINCE THE MID NINETIES UNTIL I SAW HER ON TELEVISION SPEAKING OF HER FRIEND ELIZABETH TAYLOR'S DEATH. TWO THINGS STRUCK ME. SHE WEARS HER HAIR HOW LIZ USED TO WEAR IT WHEN SHE WAS YOUNG AND CAROLE BAYER SAGER DID NOT LOOK A DAY OLDER THAN SHE DID FIFTEEN YEARS AGO. SHE MUST HAVE INVENTED A "BACK TO THE FUTURE" CREAM WITH CHRISTOPHER LLOYD!

********JOE DIORIO WAS THE WORLD'S GREATEST JAZZ GUITAR PLAYER FROM ABOUT 1973-2003!!!!!!!!!!!!!!!!!!!!!!!!!!!

He happened to be from Waterbury Connecticut and two of my cousins happened to be his guitar teachers -Freddie and Vinnie Bredice.

Freddie I met in 1967. He used to have his own radio show in 1935. His speed on the guitar was legendary. Joe Diorio at his best had speed where it looked like he had three left hands all working at the same time on the fingerboard. Joe, a few years ago, said he still had nightmares about Freddie's speed.

When I got to Los Angeles, Freddie told me to get a ride to a gig he was playing on a Sunday afternoon in 1967 and he would take me out to dinner and give me a ride home. His left hand speed was shocking. I went up and leaned against a post near the bandstand looking down at him and when he finished the song he looked up and I said "You must be Cousin Fred!" He said "Yeah, I don't play chords! It fucks up your hands!"

Joe Diorio's favorite jazz player was John Coltrane. When I asked him "Why?" he said Coltrane could play for hours and never repeat himself. Coltrane and Joe played progressive jazz. Musically, they were equal in reaching the depths of their own human substance. Freddie Bredice died in March, 1968 and he played the music of his era which was swing. However, he did play 142 courses of "Body And Soul" without ever repeating himself.

The thing I respected the most about Joe Diorio and Miles Davis for the most part, certainly in the earlier years, is that they did not pander themselves in terms of what they played.

For example Joe used to sit with a guitar six hours a day and play discordant sounding strange notes. I was never aware of him caring too much what the audience thought of his strangeness or discordant sounds and eventually both he and Miles did it their way! Of course, this is perhaps why only insiders, great guitar players themselves knew that Joe Diorio was the best in the world. As Joe Pass yelled out to him "Hey Joe! When are you going to play songs again!" That is after Joe Pass who knew Joe Diorio was better than him just made a record with Ella FitzGerald playing songs and making as much money as a jazz guitarist could make at the time (1976 or thereabouts).

My cousin Vinnie Bredice taught guitar at Miami Dade Junior College and wrote a jazz guitar book for Mel Bay. He married the Firestone Heiress and lived in a mansion in Golden Beach, Florida for a number of years, just North of Miami. Vinnie's wife's name was "Ardie".

Joe Diorio wrote a guitar book entitled "Intervallic Designs" and he recorded on an Italian CD Label called "RAM"

So in 1997, 20 years after Mischa Shenkyman taught me a recording technique on the mandolin, I had the idea of Joe Diorio and me making a cd with American and Italian Old Standards.

I was fearful of calling Joe Diorio up to actually make the cd with him. I mean after all, he was the best in the world and I wasn't! Furthur, I hadn't played mandolin in about six months, but what Shenkyman taught me on the right hand was in the bank so to speak!

LaJolla psychiatrist James Rice, M.D., a friend at the time, when I described Joe as huffing and puffing on some of his gigs said "Joe might die!" If Dr. Rice didn't say that I wouldn't have had the courage to call Joe. I called him about four days later and said "What are you doing Saturday! You wanna make that cd at Local 47 Musicians Union Recording Studios on 817 N. Vine (Hollywood, CA 90038) Joe said "Yes" and we recorded for six straight hours, 22 songs, mandolin and guitar. Joe used his Gibson ES -175 and he told me to use the Gibson F-2 1913 mandolin instead of the Italian roundback Vinnaccia, (The Stradivarious of Italian Mandolins used by The King of Savoy, Victor Emanuel in Italy.)

Joe Pass couldn't do it, but I got Joe Diorio to play songs again! We made the cd on December 22, 1997. I entitled it "Falling In Love" and it can be purchased on Amazon.com through Orchard Records. orchardrecords.com.)

I chose all the numbers I loved growing up as an Italian American which were also part of Joe's heritage. Some of them were "Misty" "I'm In The Mood For Love", "Theme From La Strada", "Sorrento", "Arriverdici Roma", "Smoke Gets In Your Eyes", one more beautiful than the next - a lot of slow fours.

Joe Diorio did not play jazz on the cd. He played a beautiful background music similar to what guitarist Tony Mottola used to do for Perry Como, the singer, on his tv show in the mid fifties.

A copy of the cd can also be purchased by sending a check for $25 directly to Dr. Len Bergantino, 1215 Brockton Avenue, #104, Los Angeles, CA 90025-1366.

There is a song on the cd entitled "St. Mary's Waltz" written by my father's uncle Soledad Bredice, Freddie Bredice's father, when he was in the hospital in 1920. When we recorded this song Joe Diorio broke out in tears after the song and said this song was better than the Theme From The Godfather and had it been known easily could have been used for the theme song of that movie.

Jerry Vale, who sang at Carnegie Hall called me to tell me how much he liked my cd. John Pizzarelli New York guitarist and radio show host called and left a message that he liked it, and Howard Alden who played all the guitar solos in Woody Allen's movie "Sweet and Lowdown" wrote me a short note that he liked both what I did and what Joe did. (my articulation)

THE GERMANS! 1995

I went to Alpine village in Torrance, California for an Octoberfest. After listening to his 20 piece Brass Band even though I had not played trumpet since 1965 I handed Hans Schneltzer my clinical psychology card, looked him square in the eye, and said "I CAN PLAY YOUR MUSIC! 3 Days later he called me and "told" me as in "order" to be at the Alpine the following Sunday, that he wanted me to play trumpet. I hesitated at which point he said, "You said you could play my music! I said, "That's right! If I had a couple of months to get in shape again!. He said, "I've got two good firsts! Practice a half hour a day until Sunday and be there! They will cover you!" If it hadn't been for him I probably would not have picked up the trumpet again. That week it felt like my face was falling off after a thirty year layoff! But I made it through a five hour gig!

I played second trumpet for five years and have been in the First Chair from 2000 - 2012 at which time I retired for health reasons (as stroke and back surgery)

KLON BIG BAND JAZZ FESTIVAL

Around 1996 George Graham was one of the top studio and big band lead trumpet players and at this particular jazz festival had the first chair for many different big bands. Each time it was his high notes that soared out above the band! At the end of one of the big band extravaganzas I went up to him and said, "Hey, are you the guy that played all the high notes?" He said "Yes" I said, "Do you teach playing high notes?" He said "Yes, but what about all the other notes!" I SAID, "I'VE GOT NO FUCKING INTEREST IN THEM!" He said "Come out to the Moonlight Tango Restaurant on Ventura Blvd on Tuesday or Wednesday night." I said I would be there and I was.

I took my date Loretta Powell, a former Miss USA and Miss Connecticut who looked like Elizabeth Taylor, not necessarily a good thing in the movie business as one Liz Taylor was plenty!

WAYNE BERGERON

George was giving a new guy a shot to play split lead in both the big bands and the recording studios. His name was Wayne Bergeron. He was

37 years old at the time and was a young bull compared to the fifty plus years of George Graham, important on the high notes that rocked the chandeliers. Having studied with Carl Berg I had mastered the trumpet and all the other notes, but as Harry James said about Carl, "He's a good strong third!" High notes were not his bag as a teacher or a player and I did not have the mentality of a second or third trumpet player. A story comes to mind about Louis Armstrong's second wife Lil, when he was quite happy playing second trumpet for King Oliver and Lil said to him, "Get your lazy ass out of this house and start your own band and play first trumpet! I am not going to be married to any damn second trumpet player!" And so Louis started the Hot Fives and Hot sevens and the rest is history!. I had that mentality in myself so I didn't need someone like Lil to bring it up for me.

MAYNARD FERGUSON FANS!

HE PLAYED THE HIGHEST NOTES WITH THE FULLEST SOUND EVER PLAYED ON THE TRUMPET FROM AGE SIXTEEN UNTIL HE DIED AT AGE 77!
SOME OF HIS BEST RECORDINGS ARE ON 33 RPM LONG PLAYS
On Maynard 61   - OLE   I BELIEVE ALL THESE WERE ON ROULETTE
On Maynard 62   -Maria   LABELS AND THEY ARE WORTH SEEKING OUT!
One with Frank Sinatra On The Cover - Chicago on one side but the sound with the highest range I liked the best was on THEME FROM ANTONY AND CLEOPATRA.

LORETTA POWELL - MY GIRLFRIEND AT THE TIME!

She was Miss USA! She looked like Liz Taylor! But that is not what amazed me about her. She used to date the owner of the Sands Hotel and her job was to deliver little brown bags that she was never to look in that had ten thousand dollars in it and deliver it to a higher up at a different hotel. One night she was driving down a one way street in her Cadillac wearing a mink stole and some expensive jewelry and she had an instinct that a group of guys were going to attempt to steal and maybe worse. She immediately put the car in reverse and gunned it while they shot machine gun fire into the front end of her Cadillac. I would have been dead under similar circumstances! A third time in the early phases of my 22 year draw fighting the United states Government, I needed her to testify in Court and the Judge the first time kept her waiting about three hours and did not call her. The second time she was dressed in a red dress and the Judge kept her waiting about 3 hours and did call her. Loretta walked in "smoking" hot and as she was walking in chewed out the Judge for being so inconsiderate as to have kept her waiting the first time and then again the second time for a total of six hours! The Judge attempted to explain lack of control over scheduling but that did not deter Loretta and she finally through the use of her personal authority commanded an apology from the Judge to the amazement of every one in the Courtroom who thought she was on her way to jail for contempt of court. That's my Loretta! She could be trusted! She told me all her friends were male; that she could not trust women!

GEORGE GRAHAM'S PROTEGE, WAYNE BERGERON

So there Loretta and I are sitting against the farthest wall and Wayne Bergeron, one of those husky meat eating types that appeared on the scene after Maynard Ferguson changed the nature of the game regarding high notes, was hitting higher, harder, louder screaming notes than George Graham. Just as I said to Loretta, "Who the hell is that?" his wife was walking by and said "That is Wayne Bergeron! Why, do you want me to bring him over at the break?" I said "Yes!"

Debbie Bergeron, also a trumpet player, introduced me to Wayne. I said, "Where did you study trumpet? North Texas State!" He said, "No, Lynwood, California." I had been a full time junior high school counselor there when I was a full time doctoral student at U. of Southern California from 1968-1971. So I said, "Were you that chubby little kid with the blond hair and the eyeglasses that used to hit double high C's on a bugle? He said "Yes." Then I said, "If it weren't for me, you would have been working in your parents jewelry store in Lynwood."

I sent him down to the music teacher Ron Savitt, who knew talent when he saw it and gave Wayne free trumpet lessons three times a week for an hour and one half per time for three years. In 1988 Wayne was Maynard Ferguson's lead trumpet player, although I did not know it at the time.

80

LESSONS WITH WAYNE BERGERON

Wayne expected me to come in playing double high C's on the warm ups he provided and did not seem to appreciate how it was to have taken thirty years off and never really been a high note guy anyway. Somehow I felt like his head clicked off the moment I did not go above high "G" Nevertheless. I attempted to study one time per week with him but more often than not got a call to cancel because he got a last minute call to play in the studios. He is now and for the last several years referred to as THE NUMBER ONE CALL IN LOS ANGELES FOR STUDIO WORK!

Despite this hairy introduction I do remember things he taught me. A lot of lip bends on the way up and a lot of pedal tones on the way down. He used Warburton mouthpieces which were screw rim from a man who made them in Florida named Warburton. At the time he used a Kanstul trumpet and I bought one when I studied with him. He brought me to a classical trumpet concert where he was featured at Loyola Marymount University and he was just as good at classical as he was at big band. He also played lead for Jack Sheldon's big band one time I saw him.

One day he brought me with him to hear other lead trumpet players and I met someone who Wayne said was at the top of his game who was one of the five lead players who worked in Los Angeles. His name was Frank Szabo.

After Wayne Bergeron I studied for six months with Bobby Shew.

NORTH TEXAS STATE UNIVERSITY
DEPARTMENT OF MUSIC!

When Wayne Bergeron was teaching me he was 37 years old and I told him I took 30 years off from playing the trumpet! He looked me right in the eye and said with an almost shocked look "Thirty years is a long time!" So I had an unusual problem. I had achieved lead psychologist status at the international level and hung around with that crowd having been trained by 17 world renown psychiatrists and psychologists, Milton Erickson, M.D. and Carl Whitaker, M.D. among them; and I had the mentality to do the same thing as a trumpet player minus 30 years experience! All the monsters of the day were coming out of North Texas State University where Stan Kenton left his entire music library. Stan must have thought someone down there could play it!

NORTH TEXAS STATE IS THE ONLY PLACE I EVER WENT TO A FOOTBALL GAME WHERE THE PEOPLE WENT TO HEAR THE BAND!

Maynard's lead player in 1995 was Scott Englebright and after Scott it was Adolpho Acosta. Both played lead for North Texas State in the One O'Clock Lab Band. They had One through 7 o'clock lab bands which were the time they started five days a week for one hour and the most talented wound up in the One O'Clock Lab Band, et. al.

Professor Mike Steinel

Mike was the professor that interviewed prospective students for the school of music and particularly the lab bands. He had me play for him after six months of lessons with Wayne Bergeron and thirty years off and told me he would accept me into the program and I would start out in the six o'clock lab band. He said he did not know if I wanted to deal with the pressure of being a lead player at North Texas State and that I should attend a sectional of one of the lab bands and let him know how I felt about things.

I remember a big guy, looked like a tackle on the football team was the lead player, and he had a little chat with his trumpet section. It went something like this. "My entire career depends on what you fucking idiots do! If you screw up I will rip your fucking heads right off your shoulders!" Mike had me attend a class he was teaching. I remember the guitar player came in without having memorized the tune for that day and attempted to play a solo without having memorized the tune. Mike went apeshit. He gave him the equivalent of running around the gym 1000 times if you were a basketball player!

At 53 years old I just did not want it bad enough to go back to school to get the thirty years experience I missed! I was appreciative Mike made certain I had no illusions about what I would be getting into.

JAY SAUNDERS, FORMER LEAD PLAYER WITH STAN KENTON gave me a lesson when I was down there. He taught many of the top Lab Band Trumpet players! He used to have a trumpet hanging down from a string and walk up to it and without any pressure blow a high "G".

Also, Jay said he rarely practiced on the same mouthpiece he used on the gigs. He was a scientist! He gave me a session by telephone one time! He was a great guy! He did not charge me!

BOBBY SHEW,

followed Wayne Bergeron as one of my illustrious trumpet teachers. In addition to being a recording artist Bobby played lead for Buddy Rich but when I studied with him was mainly teaching and retired from the Los Angeles studio scene. He used to have me practice knocking a piece of paper against the wall from 20 feet, away with just focused air flow. At the time Bobby Shew mouthpieces were quite popular and I had a 1.5, a 2 and a 1. The 1.5 was the best for me, although a little thinner sound than I wanted. Marcinkiewicz made them. Bobby Shew later had Yamaha make them. I had a Bobby Shew model Yamaha trumpet which had a smaller bore that got bigger as the air went through the horn. Bobby said "Americans tend to think big is better; but when playing trumpet sometimes small is better!" In 1998 he was one of the guest teachers at the Abersoll Jazz Camp in Louisville, Kentucky and he walked in, held the horn by its valves and hit a high "G" that peeled the paint off the walls as his first note, without any warmups. Bobby was a scientist. He had me read a chapter in a book he was writing about playing high notes. (Remember - when I took lessons from Carl Berg there was no such book, and if you couldn't play high notes to start with no one really could teach you how to get there. You were just screwd! A funny story when he made a cd with Maynard Ferguson, he was showing Maynard the chapter and Maynard said, "Bobby, do you think I ought to read it?" (as in Do you think I need it?) Bobby and Maynard had a good laugh on that one!

An example was the chair of the jazz studies department at North Texas State in 1996. He wore a bow tie and was a very kind Southern gentleman. I told him I just bought his book on playing high notes. He said "I hope it does you some good! It didn't do me any good!" Harry James was a skinny guy, an ectomorph; and so was I. After Maynard Ferguson the lead players looked more like Dick Butkus of the Chicago Bears. They had necks as big as a rhinocerous and they could blow a hurricane into the horn. In many respects that is not what I signed up for when I took up the trumpet! My forte was a georgeous full sound in the normal register of the trumpet! Kind of like Conrad Gozzo's sound on Trumpet's Prayer although on "Tutti's Trumpet's (Tutti Cammerata) it was Gozzo doing the high register power shots on Tenderly (Song) with an amazing sound!

WHERE PSYCHOANALYSIS AND TRUMPET CROSSED PATHS

In 1977 I was being trained in group psychoanalysis by Martin Grotjahn, M.D. I was a trainee in his group of "beautiful people." A very beautiful and famous woman was complaining about her husband whom she was divorcing - a trumpet player named Pete. I totally forgot I was a shrink and identified with being a trumpet player. I said, "You are not talking about Pete Candoli, are you!" She said "Yes!" I said "What the hell are you complaining about! He's Superman!" (Pete used to come out on a flying trapeze in a Superman outfit when he played for Woody Herman)

I wound up writing the obituary for Pete Candoli in Local 47. He outlived most of his peers and I was one of the few around who could do it. He was always kind to me. He made it clear it was a trumpet player's gums that he needed to worry about, not his chops! Pete always wore a green baseball cap with gold lettering on the front.

THE HIGH NOTE PLAYERS ALL HAD HUGE LIPS, A BIG MEATY HEAD AND LOOKED LIKE TACKLES IN THE NATIONAL FOOTBALL LEAGUE!

BACK TO DENTON TEXAS FOR A WEEK WITH SCOTT ENGLEBRIGHT in 1997. Scott was living with his old roommate at North Texas State but he took off his senior year to play lead for Maynard Ferguson in 1995 and was still doing it when I tracked him down. He made a point of letting me know the trumpet was a "wind" instrument, as he was one of those who could put a hurricane through the trumpet.

AROUND THE SUMMER OF 1998 RAPHAEL MENDEZ CONFERENCE AT ARIZONA STATE UNIVERSITY, DEPARTMENT OF MUSIC where Raphael Mendez's two sons left all his music and trumpets and mouthpieces and where David Hickman put on classically oriented seminars for trumpet players. Several things stood out to me at this workshop:

1.\ It was the first time I played in a brass quintet.
2.\ I was playing with young gifted musicians who were going to make their livlihood playing music. They were in their late teens and early twenties and called me, in my mid fifties, "Father Time!"
3.\ In my first performance I played one bar too many notes and Fred Mills of the Canadian Brass, told Alan Dean, Professor of Trumpet

at Yale and New York City freelance musician, "I always thought that number would sound better with a tag!"

4.\ I took a lesson with Alan Dean playing Chas Colin's BOP duets and I stopped when I got lost. Dean said, "Never stop! You can't stop! Just keep playing until you find the right place!" I never stopped again! It was worth the $90 per hour!

5.\ I had a lesson with David Hickman who had a sound as big as a house! He played a wooden mouthpiece and he played a Mendez Solo entitled Here Kati for me in private. No one played Mendez solos in public except Mendez!

Wayne Bergeron was merciful. He introduced me to Frank Szabo, who made time for me for which I am forever grateful! Frank got drafted out of high school and got credit for his last two years by playing third trumpet for Harry James. When he grew up he was lead trumpet for Count Basie, and Bill Holman's Big Band as well as Buddy Rich. Frank Szabo said "Buddy Rich never bothered you as long as you played your part and you weren't a drunk." Bobby Shew said "Buddy Rich never made a mistake musically." Harry James said "Buddy Rich is the best drummer I ever played with." I have a tape of Buddy Rich stopping the band bus in the middle of the dessert and yelling at his band that high school kids play better and that they were an embarrassment to him and if they did not shape up he was going to fire the entire lot of them and throw them off the bus in the middle of the dessert! (an entirely different view of Buddy Rich). I think Szabo, Harry and Bobby Shew had a truer perspective of the man!

Harry had 8 Parduba #5 Gold Plated mouthpieces and he gave Frank Szabo one of them. Frank knew how much it meant to me and he gave it to me. "Shades of Sound"

I wound up having a #6 rim made from a Parduba #6 made by Parduba's understudy, now making Parduba's in Oakland, California by Bob Reeves and spending $3000 to have specialized undercups fit that # 6 r im for both lead and jazz gigs. For my fluegelhorn mouthpiece I cut off the rim of a Yamaha Bobby Shew Fluegelhorn mouthpiece and matched it with the #6 Parduba rim made by Bob Reeves, the most precise machinist in the world! That got the best sound on the Wood Model Fluegelhorn used by Roy Hargrove!

STUDYING WITH FRANK SZABO HIS FIRST CONCERN WAS FOR ME TO BE ABLE TO "LOCK IN" TO THE CORRECT PITCH! ON THE NOSE! ALL THE TIME! WITHOUT EVER MISSING! AFTER ALL! THAT IS WHAT A LEAD TRUMPET HAD TO DO!

Bobby Shew had me buy a drum pad and drum sticks and get the feel of the drummer in a big band because the lead man hod to know how the writer of the song felt it, and know and feel the tempo, and when the lead player laid it down the entire band followed the lead!

As my father used to say "musician is only an eight letter word but it encompasses a lot!"

Frank Szabo used the first 45 minutes of each lesson three times a week to work on the pitch scales. He did it with me making it clear he did it every day whether I was there taking a lesson or not, it was part of his own routine.

They were scales beginning with low F Sharp, the lowest legitimate note on the trumpet and would go up as such. Low F sharp, G sharp, A sharp,, B natural, C sharp, D sharp, E sharp or F natural, G sharp, A sharp, B natural; C sharp, D sharp, E sharp, and then F sharp. The first low F sharp would be played eight times and then the top F sharp eight times and the middle F sharp eight times both on the way up and on the way back down. Once you hit the top F sharp and played it eight times you came back down the same way you went up until you played eight eighth notes on the bottom F sharp.

Then you start with low G and do the same thing up and down. Then A flat. Then A natural. Then B flat. Then B natural. Then C natural. and you go up as high as you are able to go, usually getting a note or so higher the more you do it. On a daily basis I used to get up to and do double A's!

The last forty five minutes he played along with me line by line sometimes with a record of Count Basie or Buddy Rich and sometimes without. We played the charts Szabo played on the gigs with Count Basie and Buddy Rich, line by line, note by note, at the correct tempo. I was never much for learning through conversation. Frank Szabo was the right teacher for me in that he did it with me. As the great educator John Dewey put it, I "Learned by doing!"

BY CONTRAST BOBBY SHEW WAS NOT A "GOOD TEACHER FOR ME!"

Bobby talked the entire session. They were one hour sessions but he always went two hours. He hardly ever played along with me or demonstrated. Then he asked me to audio tape the sessions, so I not only had to listen to him during the session but for two hours between by weekly sessions. All the talk in the world was not helpful to me but he was Bobby Shew and I wasn't so I endured the experience for about six months.

A useful thing he did was ask me to get a drum pad and sticks and learn to keep tempo as a drummer in a big band, ever impressing the point that as a lead player you have to be able to set the tempo for the entire band. Bobby Shew and Jimmy Gozzo would have added to that that Conrad Gozzo knew each song with a feeling as to exactly how the composer intended it to be played and that is what he did as a lead player. The best I ever heard Bobby Shew play was on a record where he was either playing lead or split lead with Chuck Findlay (Doc Severensin's successor on the Tonight Show Band) where the sound came through with power as clear as a bell and the in sincness of what he and Findlay were doing in coordination with each other was almost beyond belief. (A Buddy Rich 33 RPM (Shew and Findlay were young bucks on Album Cover)

By the same token that I think Bobby Shew was a great big band trumpet player and before I knew him the first call in Los Angeles for recording studios, I was never that fond of him as a jazz player.

Both Miles Davis and Chet Baker, Charlie Parker's two favorites, had the ability to have taken journeys of life where they could reach down into the pit of their existence, turn their souls inside out, put it through their horns, and touch your soul with the first three notes. Cathy Reilly Finn can do this with a tenor banjo although for professional and personal reasons she chooses to play a non instrument called a plectrum banjo when she has the personal capacity to be better than Harry Reser on the tenor banjo and that is saying a lot because Harry was the best that ever lived!

Bobby Shew does not have this ability and all the schooling or education in the world will not make a jazz player of the calibre I am speaking of. ****ONE HAS TO BE ABLE TO "FOCUS WITH A DEEP STILLNESS TO ONE'S DEEPEST INNER BEING" AND THEN HAVE UNIMPEDED ACCESS TO YOUR UNCONSCIOUS MIND AND TRUST WHAT WILL COME OUT! I LEARNED THE PROCESS FROM BRITISH PSYCHOANALYST WILFRED R. BION AND AMERICAN PSYCHIATRIST MILTON H. ERICKSON, M.D. It is playing music from the inside out - not just notes strung together.

Bill Watrous is a great trombone player. He can play a trombone with a technique similar to that of Raphael Mendez on a trumpet. To hear it is almost beyond belief. Yet as a jazz player when he sat in before Miles Davis in an All Black Club in Harlem. They were yelling and a hostile crowd, "Get that White Boy Out of Here! He Can't Play Jazz". Watrous cut off my jazz lessons when I said I wanted to move from the Chet Baker Style to Miles Modal Style from the Cool Era (pre Bitches Brew or Tutu).

He said Miles almost got him killed except that Freddie Hubbard kept telling the crowd that Watrous was a good jazz player so they let him live!

Knowing Miles and learning to play from my soul I put on Miles, Chet, Charlie Byrd and Coltrane for six hours a day and played along with them. This left me with an ability to be The Source! That is in my old age I learned to light up a stage either on a trumpet, or mandolin banjo with either a big band or my own small combo! *********THE PROCESS I AM DESCRIBING I COME ABOUT THROUGH SELF EXPLORATION, DEDICATION AND WANTING IT REAL BAD!

Getting back to Miles. The reason he liked me even though I was a White Boy was because he knew immediately that I was connected at the deepest levels to THE SOURCE OF MY OWN POWER! WATROUS AND BOBBY SHEW WERE NOT. WATROUS WANTED ME TO LEARN FILLS TO PUT IN. AS FILLS WENT THEY WERE OF THE HIGHEST CALIBRE AND COULD BE LEARNED ACADEMICALLY. BUT THAT IS NOT JAZZ AS LOUIS ARMSTRONG, THELONIUS MONK, MILES, COLTRANE, JOE DIORIO, CHET BAKER, OR WES MONTGOMERY WOULD PLAY JAZZ. WHEN ANY ONE OF THEM HIT THREE NOTES YOU KNEW WHO THEY WERE AND YOU WERE THEIRS FOR LIFE! ALL THE REST SOUNDS LIKE ELEVATOR MUSIC! THE AMAZING THING ABOUT CATHY REILLY FINN IS THAT SHE DID IT ON A PLECTRUM BANJO, WHICH TO ME IS LIKE PUTTING A GARBAGE CAN OVER A BOWL OF OATMEAL AND TYING STRINGS ACROSS THE TOP OF IT TO SEE WHAT KIND OF SOUND WILL COME OUT, I HEARD THREE NOTES AND BROKE OUT INTO TEARS. TOO BAD SHE LIVES A LIFE WHERE SHE MAY NEVER DO IT AGAIN!

Most books say nice things about people. My mandolin teacher, Mischa Shenkyman, the Paganini of the Mandolin in the Soviet Union, said "IN THE SOVIET UNION IF SOMEONE DOES NOT THINK WELL OF THE WAY YOU PLAY THEY TELL YOU STRAIGHT OUT! IN THE UNITED STATES EVERYONE TELLS YOU THEY

LIKE THE WAY YOU PLAY AND YOU NEVER KNOW WHAT ANYONE REALLY THINKS OF YOUR MUSIC!" SINCE THAT DAY I NEVER LIED TO ANYONE ABOUT WHAT I THOUGHT OF HIS OR HER PLAYING! IT WOULD BE CHEATING THEM OF THE OPPORTUNITY FOR PERSONAL, PROFESSIONAL AND MUSICAL GROWTH!

For example, in terms of the quality of being one has attained in life, that is really all they have to blow through a horn. If one lies to themselves a lot there will probably be a film over his or her sound, (that is not clear) in a way that does not touch your soul and maybe even slightly nauseating to those who notice.

If you are ugly inside, ugly is what comes out when you play. My father often told me a story about Toscanini. Toscanini when I heard his outtakes, rehearsals, was a screaming wildman who was as near totally in touch with the fullness of his own being as any musician I have ever come across. My father said there was a violin player who made a mistake and Toscanini let the baton fly out of his hand at that exact moment and it put the man's eye out. When asked if he was going to sue Toscanini the man said, "If it were anybody else I would sue the shit out of them, but with Toscanini he had no choice!" I would assume the man's transgression had much more to do with the quality of his being or lack thereof than a simple mistake.

Frank Szabo often talked about the night Doc Severinsen asked him to play on the Tonight Show. He said Doc had a contract with Johnny Carson that he could practice five hours a day and was not to be disturbed. In the afternoon Carson came over to talk with Doc and as Szabo described it Doc's eyes glazed over and he kept practicing which appeared to all present as if he were merely blowing notes in Johnny Carson's face.

Frank Szabo said rehearsal was rather long and exhausting but after rehearsal Doc Severinsen said "Hey Frank, let's go into one of the rooms and have it out (with the trumpets in a sort of duel). Szabo found Severinsen's desire to practice and ability to practice around the clock without tiring absolutely beyond human belief.

I met Doc Severinsen about ten years ago one afternoon at UCLA selling Doc Severinsen Bel Canto trumpets. My first trumpet teacher Carl Berg loved Doc Severinsen's Torch Records as well as Raphael Mendez's solo work. Doc had to be a kid at that time, in his twenties and when I met him he was in his seventies. So I told him that and I said "Hey Doc, You

Look Good! You've Got All Your Hair!" He said, "Yeah! I've got no wife to pull it out!" We both laughed.

Charlie Davis was the most academically knowledgeable of my later day trumpet teachers. He was a graduate of the Indiana University School of Music in addition to being one of the four or five lead players who worked in Los Angeles on recordings and played lead for big bands such as Woody Herman. I studied with Charlie for six months prior to a debilitating automobile accident that prevented me from continuing. While that sounds a bit strange I was doing five hours a day practice and according to Charlie I was three hours short! My entire body was in such pain I could no longer do it after August 17, 2000. I remember the date well because it was the end of a dream!

POPS MC LAUGHLIN OF DE SOTO TEXAS

He is the best high note teacher in the country - maybe the world. You have to go down there and spend a week. He got me to do things I did not believe were possible.

I had such "RESISTANCE" AS PSYCHOANALYSTS WOULD PUT IT, THAT I FORGOT MY MOUTHPIECE. WHEN I OPENED THE TRUMPET CASE IT WASN'T THERE!

THE MOUTHPIECE IS NOT THE CRUCIAL FACTOR

Bill Watrous plays a Bach 11E Trombone Mouthpiece that someone gave him when he was in the Navy around 1946. He has an extremely high register for a trombone player and said he enver switched mouthpieces. Mouthpieces are critical to attain "Shades of Sound." I have over 100 combinations of rims and cups.

POPS took out a bunch of old decrepid looking mouthpieces and asked me to pick one. I picked an old Jet Tone #7 made in Fairfield, Connecticut in the early sixties, when they used to make an Al Hirt Model out of aluminum. As I couldn't play with that one I was not particularly enamored with attempting to do the impossible with a Jet Tone. The new Jet Tone #7's are an entirely different mouthpiece than the old one I played on that week, which he gave me.

NEXT, I PLAYED FOR TWENTY SIX HOURS OF HIGH NOTES AND ATTEMPTED HIGH NOTES DURING FOUR DAYS!

90

IF YOU ASKED ME PRIOR TO GOING TO DESOTO TEXAS TO STUDY WITH POPS MCLAUGHLIN IF THIS WAS POSSIBLE I WOULD SAY "NO" IT IS NOT. YET, SOMEHOW I DID IT AND I WAS NOT FATIGUED OR TIRED.

MOST GUYS I KNEW STUDIED TO BE GREAT TRUMPET PLAYERS.THISWASNOTTHECASEWITHPOPSMCLAUGHLIN. HE STUDIED TO BE A GREAT TRUMPET TEACHER AND HE WAS. HE STUDIED WITH "JAKE" JACOBY AT NORTH TEXAS STATE, WHO WAS NOTED TO BE THE BEST TEACHER EVER FOR TRUMPET PLAYERS AT NORTH TEXAS STATE (DIED PRIOR TO MY GOING TO DENTON IN 1996)

I am almost reluctant to make any comments at all on how in a week I increased my range from a "HIGH G OVER HIGH C" TO A "DOUBLE B FLAT OVER HIGH C" IN THAT I THINK IF YOU ARE "DEDICATED" AND YOU WANT TO PLAY HIGH NOTES YOU SHOULD CALL HIM UP AND GO DOWN

The Overture - May, 2001 - Official Publication of Professional Musician, Local 47 Los Angeles, AFM, AFL-CIO, LLC

Exhibit I

(handwritten) The Overture - May, 2001 — Official Publication of Professional Musicians, Local 47 Los Angeles, AFM, AFL-CIO; LLC

Every Trumpet Players Quest

By Len Bergantino, ED.D., A.B.P.P., Local 47 Member/trumpet player and clinical psychologist

High register has always been a problem for me. My quest began with Jimmy Gozzo, from 1962 - 1964. Jimmy was Conrad Gozzo's father, the greatest lead player of all. Through much diligent work and study with some very excellent trumpet players, among them Frank Szabo and Charlie Davis, I was able to develop to a point of a good high E on the stand and an F sharp every day when practicing, with a once in a while G and A flat above high C in the practice room and once in a while on the stand.

In a rehearsal band I had the unusual experience of sitting next to a very likeable and benevolent lead trumpet player who played second while I played lead so as to develop his capacity to solo. I said to him, "Look, I like high notes and I have no problems with you playing as high as you want to keep your own chops in shape even though I am playing the lead book. Invariably, whatever I played he could take up an octave whenever he wanted to. I used to delight in his ability to do this. His name is Rex Merriweather.

Rex said to me, "I went to study with Clint "Pops" McLaughlin in De Soto, Texas and he increased my range an octave in about two ten-hour days." I told him I didn't think I had the endurance to have such long sessions. He said, "You ought to do it. He increased my range by an octave and I have no mental limitations as to how high I can play. High register is a state of mind."

Then he said the key motivating words, "Hey, pops McLaughlin is very sick. He may not live to long. If you are doing to do it, it better be soon."

I had previously called Pops McLaughlin and sent for three books he had written. My experience as a clinical psychologist for 30 years told me that he was obsessive and had devoted his life to figuring out how to increase the high register. He knew more details about the high register than anyone had expressed to me.

Yet, there were questions by others who had heard of him? Well, he isn't a great trumpet player like the others you have studied with. What makes him think he can teach?

I called Pops and set things up for Wednesday through Sunday. He offered to pick me up at the airport and drive me to a motel and back to lessons, and he turned out to be good company for lunch and dinners, too.

I asked what he charged, and he said $150 for one half day and $300 for a full day. It is about $50 per hour.

As a psychologist trained in the sixties and seventies I had attended marathons, which were intended to break down the resistance by having group psychotherapy for long hours, and sometimes even all day and all night for three days. This trumpet experience was like those marathons in that it was dealing with my mental and physical resistance that has been the pivot at which I was up against with myself in the most difficult of life circumstances.

I had heard of people who were great teachers who were not particularly great trumpet players, such as Carmine Caruso – a saxophone player from New York. Clint "Pops" McLaughlin is one of these and maybe one of a kind in this day and age.

He had a double major in college of music and physics. The physics part of him I think was of major import to his ability to pay attention to very basic problems and resistance as they went through about 26 hours of lessons in five days and to find "immediate relief" in terms of a "solution to the problem." This was very different for me. He knew what to do to fix it right on the spot and then I played different.

The highest note I ever hit was an A above high C prior to working with Pops. During these five days I hit that double high C's, one screaming double A flat and one double D.

Further, he gave me the tools to carry on the work and develop the range and power from that point, and to do it in the context of actually playing music and songs, something I hadn't done in about five years, since I took on the task of trying to be a superman in my real life.

I am writing this short article while Clint "Pops" McLaughlin and I was unsolicited because the high register for one would either be unlikely to come upon one's own accord, and if you did, you wouldn't believe it was possible.

The only sad part about all this is that Clint does have a congestive heart failure and currently he is suffering doctor's predictions; but if you are interested I wouldn't wait too long. A side note, he giving trumpet lessons, not on playing trumpet?

P.S. Another amusing was that Clint took lessons from Don "Jake" Jacoby in giving trumpet lessons, not on playing trumpet?

TO DESOTO TEXAS FOR A WEEK AND YOU WILL COME OUT A NOTE AND ONE HALF HIGHER THAN YOU PLAY NOW IN 26 HOURS OF LESSONS! STRAIT AWAY!

*** THERE IS ONE THING, I LEARNED TO JERK THE AIR UPWARD!!!!!!!!!!!!!! THAT IS DIFFERENT THAN I EVER DID BEFORE GOING THERE. ALSO, THERE ARE TWO MC LAUGHLIN'S IN DE SOTO TEXAS. CALL INFORMATION AND CALL THEM BOTH UNTIL YOU GET THE RIGHT ONE! IT IS WORTH IT!

There was a band leader who played trombone who wanted to play high notes and he read my article and he kept trying to get a quicky from me as to what I learned. For years he asked but never went and he cannot play high notes. He will die a low note player!

EXHIBIT I prior page 122B "EVERY TRUMPET PLAYER'S QUEST is a one page article that was published in THE OVERTURE, IN THE MAY, 2001 ISSUE WHICH IS THE OFFICIAL PUBLICATION OF PROFESSIONAL MUSICIANS LOCAL 47, AFM, AFL-CIO, LLC. IT WAS ALSO PUBLISHED IN THE INTERNATIONAL MUSICIAN. I AM AN INTERNATIONALLY RENOWN WRITER IN BOTH PSYCHOLOGY (SEVENTY PUBLICATIONS) PLUS A BOOK THAT WAS A MASTER CLASSIC IN THE FIELD FOR TWENTY YEARS AND TWENTY PUBLICATIONS IN MUSIC. I AM TOLD THAT MY MOST SOUGHT AFTER PUBLICATION IS THIS ONE REGARDING MY STUDY WITH POPS MC LAUGHLIN. I GUESS MORE PEOPLE CARE ABOUT PLAYING HIGH NOTES THAN WHETHER THEY ARE FUCKING NUTS OR NOT!

BECOMING A JAZZ PLAYER AT FIFTY FIVE YEARS OLD

I always loved small combo jazz with progressive sounds being my favorite. I was taught to read music at 5 years of age and I had played trumpet and mandolin gigs where I read the music. I could read well but was terrified of taking chances on "output" instead of "input!"

FEAR STRIKES OUT! A book and a movie about the life of fellow Waterburian Jimmy Piersall who played for the Boston Red Sox in the early fifties and major league baseball from about 1951-1963. My father was a monster player (musician). He had fire in his hands. I used to sit in front of him when I was three years old and he was playing his D'Angelico Style B acoustic guitar (he always prefered the sound of acoustic non amplified instruments) and he was so fast I used to wonder, "How the fuck did he do that!"

Then when he played and I was there there was never a time he did not play on stage that he personally brought the entire band to life when they were flat on their ass prior to his doing that. Again I wondered, "How the fuck did he do that!"

I always wanted to pitch for the Yankees so every time there was a choice between sports or getting experience as a musician I chose to play sports. I suppose I do not regret this choice because as I got older I could still play music but I could not play sports any more.

My father's name was Daniel Bergantino, otherwise known as Danny. Wherever I did sit in as a youngster, the pros would say "Well, the kid is alright, but he's no Danny!" This in particular gave me a shellshocked feeling about playing jazz.

Then I remember one gig in particular where I played my best rendition of THE SLEEPY LAGOON (ala Harry James) and the drummer, Eddie Montana said "Lenny, what do you want to be when you finish college? (I was a sophomore good enough to play solos for the girls' dormitories after dinner three nights a week to applause!) I said, "Eddie, I want to be a trumpet player!" He said, "Lenny if you were going to be great, you would already be great!" I remember wanting to kill him but my old man needed a drummer to finish the gig!

This fear of inadequacy as not being as good as my old man was not the greatest background to become a jazz player. In fact, it made me tenaciously stay close to the written note!

While I was a doctoral student at USC and during the practice of clinical psychology I became internatinally renown and trained psychiatrists and psychologists in Australia, England, Germany, Italy, Canada, Los Angeles, San Diego, New Orleans and the San Francisco Bay area. This, in addition to a full clinical practice of 52 hours per week in Beverly Hills, did not leave much time to practice either trumpet or mandolin, but of the two mandolin took far less effort either because I began six years earlier at six years old or because in fact string instruments are easier than brass instruments because they are less effected by the daily nuances of your physical condition and on trumpet never really knowing who is going to show up on any given day. Maynard Ferguson told me one time that many times the audience thought he was fantastic and he thought he played as poorly that day as any day in his life. He said the reason he practiced so much was so he would be the only one who could tell the difference.

One of the most thrilling days of my life was meeting Raphael Mendez who told me it would be the worst performance of his life, that he was full of cortisone and his lips felt like tire tubes. He also told me he practiced twelve hours a day and the first two hours were so soft one could barely hear him. To him it was the worst day of his life! To me it was one of the most exciting, thrilling performances I ever witnessed! Mandolin is not so physically demanding!

That is why when I told Miles that "I play mandolin! You play trumpet! You are the one who has to practice!"; he broke into hysterical laughter, because all trumpet players know that is a primitive reality that goes along with the animal called a trumpet! It is certainly not an instrument for the timid!

M.D. Psychoanalysts were a bunch of cutthroat bastards in Beverly Hills and nationwide as well. I had the feeling when I retired from practicing psychoanalysis and moved over to trumpet, life would be less controversial. What a mistake that was! The worst cutthroat bastards in the world are trumpet players, and lead players are worse than them!

Every trumpet player worth his weight in salt thinks he or she is one of the very best around in either their locality or the world. One might think this is grandiose, but if you are not the type to adopt this kind of dog eat dog mentality, you should probably take up clarinet. If you are a lead player, the entire band moves according to your every whim, and you better be damn sure you know what the hell you are doing, and damn confident you are the best in the world when everyone else tells you that you are full of shit and can easily be replaced by someone far lesser in ability than you!

This is the clinical psychology of playing trumpet! You better be a fucking animal, who eats nails for breakfast!. The fellow from New York who made special mouthpieces for Zig Kanstul, when I was studying with Frank Szabo said to me, "What the hell -does everybody in Los Angeles have to be a lead player to get hired?" So I asked Szabo. He said "Yes. The best lead player plays lead. The next two best lead players play second and third and the fourth trumpet spot is held by a jazz player." That is why the lead player of the six o'clock lab band at North Texas State threatened the lives of the entire trumpet section if even one of them screwd up, stating that his future was dependent upon what they did. Playing trumpet is for tough motherfuckers! Women included! No pansy ass bastards in the

trumpet section! Survival of the fittest! Charles Darwin in Action! The Scopes Trial All Over Again! In other words if you are not the sort that could throw an old lady off a moving bus if you had to, don't plan
on being a professional trumpet player!

BECOMING A JAZZ PLAYER

I listened to the ALL JAZZ ALL THE TIME STATION FOR THIRTY YEARS ON THE WAY TO WORK, COMING HOME FROM MY PSYCHOLOGY OFFICE, ANY FREE MOMENTS AT HOME OR ANYWHERE ELSE AND I HEARD ALL THE GREATS AND MET MOST OF THEM AS THEY CAME THROUGH LOS ANGELES, WHICH IF NOTHING ELSE WAS A CANDY STORE FOR GREAT PROGRESSIVE JAZZ MUSICIANS.

While a lot of great clubs came and went perhaps the Grand Old Man of bringing great jazz to Los Angeles was Howard Rumsey who was first known for his "Lighthouse All Stars" in Hermosa Beach, California and then he became the owner of the Lighthouse and brought great jazz there for years. After that he had another place called "Concerts By The Sea" in Torrance, California for years.

Howard has been retired for a number of years, looks good and plays a lot of golf, a game I could never get into. We were cordial in that I was a frequent patron of his establishments. The only time he ever got mad at me was when I asked him why he never brought Chet Baker to his clubs. It went something like this in an explosive rage, "That son of a bitch has fucked up every club owner in Los Angeles! He either doesn't show up or gets so drugged up he falls asleep on stage. If he comes within a hundred miles of Los Angeles I will shoot him!" Other than that, Howard and I were tight!

I met Miles, Cannonball and Nat Adderly, Dizzy Gillespie, Charlie Byrd, Conte and Pete Candoli, Chet Baker was my bartender one night although I did not know it until after the night was over, and I heard but did not meet Charlie Mingus, Tito Puente, Les McCann, and Pancho Sanchez. I met Lee Morgan six months before his girl friend put a bullet in his stomach! I liked the way he played the best of those I heard in person until I heard Art Farmer one night at the Jazz Bakery. He was playing a specially made flumpet. It was not a flugelhorn. It wasn't a cornet. It wasn't a trumpet. It was half way between a trumpet and a cornet, gold plating and while I never liked him on records that was the best one night of jazz horn I ever heard in my life.

I tracked him down in France, where he was living and asked him to give me a jazz lesson when he came to the Jazz Educators Conference in Long Beach California. His response stunned me! "You want me to give you a jazz lesson! I don't know what jazz is! I don't know how to teach it! I don't know how to explain it and I have to get ready to do all of those things at the Jazz Educators meeting in Long Beach!" This was from Doctor Art Farmer who played the best one night of jazz trumpet I ever heard in my life! When I told him that he said he must have been lucky -that he had no idea of what the fuck he was doing!" Anyway he had me laughing my ass off in a few minutes at about $2 a minute from Los Angeles to France, but what the fuck. He was Dr. Art Farmer and I was into getting to know him, so I said, "What the fuck are you doing in France!" He said, "I can go anywhere in Europe and people say There is Dr. Art Farmer, the great jazz trumpet player! I can walk down any street in the United States and if I am lucky no one will recognize me and if I am not lucky they will harrass me for being a Black man walking on the wrong side of the street! I can walk on any street in Europe and people give me the recognition I have earned! Not so in the United States! I am staying here!" He agreed to give me a few jazz lessons if he ever came back to Los Angeles after Long Beach but he died shortly after that and true to his word he died in Europe! That one night he was the best I ever heard, he was "Doctor" Art Farmer, and he swore up and down he knew nothing about playing or teaching jazz (even though he could do it).

MILES AND WYNTON MARSALIS AS A YOUNG BUCK!

As the folklore goes Miles had a gig in New York and Wynton was an up and coming young star wanting to prove his metals and he had the balls to challenge Miles to what in New Orleans folklore was called a cutting context. For example, Louis Armstrong used to take on all comers during his day proving he was the best trumpet player that ever lived to that day.

Miles viewpoint on the matter was different. It was hard to get the kind of gigs Miles wanted in New York. He busted his ass to get the one Wynton showed up on and asked to play one on stage with Miles. Miles, who was a trained boxer having sparred with Sugar Ray Robinson said, "IF YOU

DON'T GET OFF THIS STAGE IMMEDIATELY, I AM GOING TO THROW YOU OFF!"

NOW TO ME MILES WAS A SWEETHEART! BUT THEN AGAIN I WASN'T FUCKING WITH HIM! HE GREW UP IN AN ERA WHERE BLACKS DREW A LOT OF ABUSE AND WAS OFTEN STOPPED IN HIS ELEGANT SPORTS CAR NOT BEING RECOGNIZED FOR BEING MILES DAVIS, BUT BEING ACCUSED OF HAVING STOLEN THE CAR BECAUSE NO BLACK MAN COULD AFFORD A CAR THAT EXPENSIVE! (Beverly Hills - Yellow Ferrari)

Another time a cop laid hands on him insisting he move away from a New York Club where he was playing a gig. Miles tried to make the point and got his head bloodied with a billyclub!

Miles knew he was the best and didn't take any shit from anybody who shortchanged him! I am afraid as a shrink I have always felt and acted precisely as Miles! Maybe that is why we got along so good!

I say this in awe of Louis Armstrong who was before my time, but I was intelligent enough to catch up on my history, so as not to have to recreate the wheel. Louis grew up an orphan in Storyville, a section of New Orleans for prostitutes, yet he was always happy when he played music and always made other people happy when they listened to his music, more than any trumpet player who ever lived! Furthur, he did this during racial discrimination worse than that of the forties and fifties when Miles made his mark. Yet, he was able to maintain love in his heart, and not stir until he refused to be the first jazz ambassador for the United States to the Soviet Union because of the Government's stand on civil rights. FRANKLY, AS AN INTERNATIONALLY RENOWN SHRINK, I DO NOT KNOW HOW THE HELL HE DID IT! PERHAPS HE SHOULD BE CANONIZED AS A SAINT!

FREDDIE HUBBARD

I met him at the Lighthouse in 1968 and he was a friendly down to earth guy who said he was from some place called Indianapolis. He wasn't as good as Lee Morgan, but he was good enough.

After my thirty years off and second career in music I for a time had the notion to study jazz with him. He lived in the San Fernando Valley (I believe it was Sherman Oaks in a ranch style house).

Chris Callichio Weik, Dominic's grandson, did me a favor and called Freddie and said "Take my friend Dr. Len Bergantino as a jazz student. He is an older guy that has to go a long way in a short time.") Freddie told Chris to give me the number and I scheduled a Saturday afternoon appointment. I had a six foot tall brain damaged son at birth who I brought with me everywhere. We walked down the sidewalk of Freddie's house and rang the bell for about twenty minutes. The house was completely darkened. It was 1 p.m. I went to a payphone and called him. He said, "Come back at three o'clock!" I came back at three o'clock and it was the same thing. The house was dark and no one answered the door. When I called him he scheduled it for the following Saturday, and asked me in a very fearful tone, "Whose the Big White Dude was that I had with me?" When I told Freddie it was my innocent harmless brain damaged son who I brought with me everywhere and who Chris Callichio knew intimately Freddie wasn't reassured! He sounded like THE MARTIANS WERE INVADING! My son had an innocent baby face.

Then I began to hear stories that Freddie was all fucked up on drugs and he notoriously did to club owners what he did to me. It was only at that moment I understood the rage of Howard Rumsey when I chastised him for not bringing Chet Baker to his club..

I sent Freddie a review of my book Psychotherapy, Insight & Style: The Existential Moment, Allyn & Bacon, Inc., Boston, 1981, 288 pp. written_by world renown M.D. psychoanalyst Donald Rinsley and published in Bulletin of the Menninger Clinic, in 1983 and said, "Hey Freddie, If you_want to teach me jazz trumpet give me a call and meet me at my house!" I didn't give a shit how good he was. I don't take that shit from anybody!

Chris liked him because between the time Dominic Callichio died and Chris was old enough to take over making the trumpets, Freddie Hubbard was loyal to Callicho and used a 9 pipe with a 3 bell.

Over the last ten years of his life, on top of being a drugged up asshole, while he was trying to get the sympathy of the club owners to give him another chance, he also had a cyst removed from the middle of his top lip and could not play the trumpet anywhere near what he used to do.

THE LAST TIME I SAW FREDDIE he showed up at a Roy Hargrove performance and was standing in the doorway of Catalina's waiting for Hargrove to grab the mike and say "Here's Freddie!" Hargrove and I both saw him there begging for recognition and Hargrove passed on it!

Apparently Hargrove was more like Miles than Louis! And Freddie must have pissed him off as much as he pissed me off!

**************IF YOU ARE WONDERING ABOUT THE CHAOTIC ORGANIZATION OF MY WRITING IN NON SEQUENTIAL ORDER, I OVER THE LAST THIRTY PAGES OR SO HAVE DECIDED TO MAKE THE BOOK MORE OF A STREAM OF CONSCIOUSNESS SO AS NOT TO LOSE ANY IMPORTANT VIGNETTES!

THE QUALITY OF BEING OF THE MUSICIAN AND MY THIRTY YEARS ON HAVING BEEN TRAINED BY SEVENTEEN WORLD RENOWN PSYCHIATRISTS AND PSYCHOLOGISTS AS IT RELATES TO MUSICAL PERFORMANCE!

Wayne Bergeron viewed it from one perspective, saying in shock when I told him I took thirty years off from playing trumpet, "Thirty Years Is A Long Time! On the other hand, I was so solid in myself, and knew every nook and cranny of myself so well, and could utilize every bit of what is me and not submit to anything that was not me no matter how renown or powerful the trumpet or jazz teacher, that basically I could not get fucked over as a music student being led away from my strengths instead of into them by my inner self.

IT ALL BEGAN WITH MILTON ERICKSON, M.D., PSYCHIATRIST AND THE FATHER OF MODERN MEDICAL HYPNOSIS

*********** DR. ART FARMER KNEW HOW TO PUT "PURE BEING" THROUGH A FLUMPET (HALF THE DISTANCE BETWEEN A CORNET AND A TRUMPET) BUT HE DID NOT KNOW HOW TO DESCRIBE IT OR TEACH IT!

**************MILTON H. ERICKSON, M.D. PSYCHIATRIST WRITTEN ABOUT BY JAY HALEY IN HIS BOOK, "UNCOMMON THERAPY: THE PSYCHIATRIC TECHNIQUES OF MILTON H. ERICKSON, M.D., NORTON PRESS, 1973, USED TO TELL STORIES AT A (S L O W) PACE THAT MARGARET MEAD SAID SHE HAD ONLY HEARD IN A RARE AFRICAN TRIBE, RELATIVELY FREE OF DISEASE.

***********FOR ONE AND ONE HALF YEARS I STAYED IN QUASI TRANCE STATES SIXTEEN HOURS A DAY AND AT THE END OF THAT TIME ENERGY USED TO COME OUT OF MY HANDS LIKE FIRE. I USED TO BE ABLE TO BURN MY WIFE'S

TEATS FROM SEVENTY FIVE FEET AWAY; SHOOT ENERGY INTO WORLD RENOWN GUITARIST CHARLIE BYRD WHEN HE WAS NOT IN THE MOOD TO PLAY FOR THREE PEOPLE AT THE CATAMARAN IN SAN DIEGO, AND CURE A WOMAN OF BROKEN TOES.

**************IT TAKES NEARLY THIS LEVEL OF "PURE BEING" SOMETHING LIKE A BUDDHIST MONK MIGHT DEVELOP OVER A NUMBER OF YEARS THROUGH MEDITATION TO BE ABLE TO PLAY JAZZ WITH THE PURITY OF CHET BAKER. AND MILES DAVIS.

**********JAZZ IS WHAT YOU HAVE AS YOUR TRUE NATURE COMING OUT THROUGH YOUR INSTRUMENT OF CHOICE

Not many people can tell the difference, but if you happened to have traveled that road yourself, next to Miles or Chet most of today's greatest jazz artists sound like they are playing elevator music.

******PERHAPS WHETHER IT IS PSYCHOLOGY OR MUSIC, ATTAINING THAT LEVEL OF BEING IS A GIFT FROM GOD AND AS SUCH IS NOT REPEATABLE. FOR EXAMPLE CHET AND MILES DID NOT LIVE EXEMPLARY LIVES THAT THEY SHOULD HAVE BEEN CHOSEN AS GOD'S MESSENGERS; IT IS THE SAME IN PSYCHIATRY AND CLINICAL PSYCHOLOGY, OF THE SEVENTEEN WORLD RENOWN PSYCHIATRISTS AND PSYCHOLOGIST WHO TRAINED ME. WILFRED BION (THE GREAT BRITISH PSYCHOANALYST TRAINED BY MELANIE KLEIN) AND MILTON H. ERICKSON. M.D. STOOD OUT HEADS AND SHOULDERS ABOVE THE OTHERS. BION WROTE TO ME THAT MY WORK WAS "EVOCATIVE AND STIMULATING" ERICKSON SAID HE "RESPECTED MY DEDICATION TO THE WORK." THERE IS NO REASON I CAN THINK OF WHY GOD CHOSE ME TO GO TOE TO TOE WITH THESE WORLD RENOWN CHARACTERS INCLUDING TRUMPET PLAYERS. GROWING UP I SAW MYSELF AS MORE OF A SCREAMING ASSHOLE! BION DIED IN NOVEMBER, 1979 and ERICKSON DIED IN MARCH, 1980. WHILE THERE HAVE BEEN PLENTY OF CONFERENCES PUT ON IN THEIR NAME. WHAT THEY ACTUALLY DID THAT WAS MAGNIFICENT AND GOD LIKE IS

LOST FOREVER AND IS NOT REPEATABLE! THE SAME WITH MENDEZ. MAYNARD, MILES AND CHET! I CAN ONLY SAY I AM GLAD TO HAVE GROWN UP WHEN I DID. WHEN THERE WAS A LIGHT OPEN FOR ABOUT THIRTY YEARS. WHEN THE LIKES OF THOSE PEOPLE CAME ACROSS MY PATH AND I WAS FORTUNATE ENOUGH NOT TO MISS THE BOAT! THAT IS THE "DEDICATION" PART ERICKSON SPOKE ABOUT. (PERHAPS GOD ANNOINTS CERTAIN INDIVIDUALS SUCH AS MILES, CHET, MAYNARD, BION, ERICKSON; ME AS PROOF OF THE EXISTENCE OF GOD IN ANSWERING THE QUESTION "TO BE OR NOT TO BE" WHETHER IT IS THROUGH YOUR TRUMPET OR IN THE DEVELOPMENT OF YOUR "THERAPEUTIC USE OF SELF" OR PERHAPS IT IS ALL ONE IN THE SAME!

The name of my book was "Psychotherapy Insight & Style: The Existential Moment. Allyn & Bacon, Inc., Boston, 1981, 288 pp. My gift is "I AM THE FASTEST IN THE MOMENT THAT EVER LIVED" and as such was able as a psychologist to integrate the work of 17 world famous psychiatrists and psychologists, all of whom were precisely on time and fully absorbed in the moment with whatever gift God gave to them. So it was with Chet and Miles and Maynard being fully absorbed in the moment. Excuse me. Raphael Mendez belongs in this crowd! He practiced 12 hours a day!

SO IT WAS THAT I LEARNED TO PLAY JAZZ. I UTILIZED MY GOD GIVEN GIFT OF BEING ABLE TO PAY ATTENTION AND RESPOND IN THE MOMENT FASTER THAN THE SPEED OF LIGHT TO LEARN TO PLAY JAZZ FROM MY SOUL AS A FIFTY FIVE YEAR OLD MAN!

********CHAPTER FOR VIOLIN PLAYERS WHO WANT TO LEARN HOW PAGANINI WAS ABLE TO PLAY THE WAY HE DID!

The thirty years I spent studying with world renown psychiatrists and psychologists are particularly relevant to writing this section of the book.

***********BACK TO ONE! MY FATHER WAS ALWAYS GRUMBLING THAT PAGANINI NEVER WROTE DOWN HIS VIOLIN TECHNIQUES SO THOSE THAT FOLLOWED IN HIS FOOTSTEPS MIGHT ACHIEVE SIMILAR RESULTS. SO IT WAS WITH MILTON H. ERICKSON, M.D., THE FATHER OF MODERN MEDICAL HYPNOSIS. WHEN I BEGAN MY STUDIES WITH HIM ON SEPTEMBER 11, 1977. For example, he had a woman patient he treated in front of the trainees who claimed she wasn't hypnotized and he leaned over and flipped her arm upward and there it stood. Then he looked over at me and said "Look at old Dr. Bergantino over there! He believes in magic! He doesn't know all I do is pay attention to details!" Well, I spent the next three years "dedicated to the work" of finding out what details he paid attention to that enabled him to call his shots and I never saw him miss! It was the same question my father asked about Paganini! There are multitude of books written about what external details need to be paid attention to EXTERNALLY to call those kind of shots, where you play your own personal instrument, your therapeutic use of self, with such magnificence that you never miss! This can only be done INTERNALLY FROM THE INSIDE OUT!

**********WHAT I FOUND OUT IS THAT THROUGH THE DISCIPLINE OF INNER FOCUS ONE CAN LEARN TO PAY ATTENTION TO ASPECTS OF THE SELF THAT MAKE BOTH MILTON ERICKSON'S WORK POSSIBLE AS WELL AS PAGANINI AS WELL AS THE FULLNESS OF YOU THAT MAY COME OUT NOT LIKE BUT AS YOU ALA MILES, CHET, OR MAYNARD'S HIGH NOTES!

In Australia in 1984 my work was described as "a kind of mental precision that electrified the Australian Therapeutic Community". In 1986 I gave a workshop and delivered the goods in Sheffield, England entitled "The Therapeutic Wizardry of Dr. Len Bergantino." In 1990 I gave a workshop at the Royal College of Medicine in London entitled "The Development And Use of Extrasensory Perception in the Practice of Psychoanalysis. Psychotherapy and Clinical Hypnosis." IN OTHER WORDS JAZZ BUFFS AND WOULD BE TECHNICAL GENIUSES; IT CAN ONLY BE DONE INTERNALLY VIA THE DISCIPLINE OF DEVOTING YOUR LIFE TO BECOMING ALL THAT YOU CAN BE. AS RAPHAEL MENDEZ DID WITH HIS TWELVE HOURS A DAY PRACTICE COMBINED WITH THE DISCIPLINE OF THE BUDDHIST MONK WHO MEDITATES THE REST OF THE DAY! HOW BAD DO YOU WANT IT! AND YOU BETTER NOT DO IT FOR THE WRONG REASONS OR YOU WON'T GET IT ANYWAY! THAT'S IT DAD! THAT IS WHY PAGANINI DIDN'T WRITE IT DOWN!

*****BACK TO THE MUNDANE OF BECOMING A JAZZ PLAYER

Detours

VIOLIN CHAPTER -The best I ever heard in terms of technique with deep rich quality of sound was Isaac Stern in a movie he made in the mid 1970's regarding his tour of Red China which had to be arranged by the State Department because it was off limits. Once a violin player can do what Isaac Stern did in that movie or documentary as it was called) then it would be time to consider what I have said about mastering the solos of Nicoli Paganini and utilize whatever I have shared in this book to help you along with it much as you would the books of "Zen and the Art of Motorcycle Maintenance" and/or "The Inner Game Of Tennis".

I MET MAYNARD FERGUSON'S DAUGHTER YESTERDAY (WILDER FERGUSON JACOB)

She told me Maynard did not do anything that wasn't fun, which reminded me given your mind by this stage of the book ought to be up to between five and twelve hours a day practice time.

Maynard kept his horn on a stand in the house so he would not have to take it out of the case to practice. After hearing that and having twenty three horns I put one in each room on a trumpet stand and play as I walk by just taking it off the stand without having to go through the formal ordeal of taking it out of the case. You would be surprised how many more hours of practice that resulted in as it bypassed one's natural psychological resistance to having to take the trumpet out of the case each time you practice. Page (137 a) is a letter I wrote to Maynard'd daughter on 5/16/11 and 137 b and 137 c are two articles I had published about her father in the Musician's Local 47 Newsletter.

LEN BERGANTINO, ED.D., A.,.P.P

Doctorate - University of Southern California - 1971

Tel/Fax (310) 207-9397

Clinical Psychology (Psy 3837)
"Brief Uncommon Therapy"
Trained by Milton H. Erickson, M.D.

137 a

Diplomate in Family Psychology
American Board of Professional Psychology

May 16, 2011

Dear Maynard's Daughter,

I was glad to meet you yesterday in a brief heart to heart. You
said you wanted to know what people who wrote you letters did.
I became internationally renown as a psychologist and later did a cd -
playing mandolin accompanied by jazz guitarist Joe Diorio.

It is imperative that you get Helen Borges to play Maynard's early
stuff, when he was a bull beyond the imagination of any bull!
33 rpm's -whatever you have to do to get hold of them, do it! It is
imperative for a "transmission of the culture!" My old man was always
pissed that Paganini never wrote down the methods by which he
accomplished the impossible!

1. Jazz For Dancing - Stella By Starlight
2. Maynard 61 "Ole" and maybe "The Three Little Foxes"
3. Maynard 62- Maria.   Rouslette
4. The most awesome was his playing of the Theme From Anthony and
Cleopatra, where he trilled some ridiculous note until you thought
the record was broken and it was just repeating itself. What he did
was humanly impossible, nevertheless he did it and I heard it!
So should KJAZZ listeners.

You may have some problem getting her to both do all this and play
Christian's cd's. KJAZZ primarily plays Black Dudes Jazz. Last time
I saw your Dad he was still White!

Frankly, Black Dudes play more soulful progressive jazz than White
Dudes, so do not try to sell Maynard on this basis because you will
never convince her or anyone else down there as there is an unspoken
racial prejudice. SELL MAYNARD ON THE BASIS OF BEING THE MOST
POWERFUL HIGH NOTE "JAZZ" TRUMPET PLAYER THAT EVER LIVED OR EVER WILL
LIVE WHO DID NOT JUST PLAY HIGH NOTES! HE LIVED UP THERE! SELL HIM
ON THE BASIS THAT EACH AND EVERY TIME SOMEONE HEARD HIM THEY WERE
BOTH "THRILLED AND EXCITED" LIKE A LITTLE KID IN A SANDBOX BEYOND
BELIEF AND THAT HE GAVE OF HIMSELF ALL OUT UNTIL THE DAY HE DIED
TO MAKE CERTAIN HE DID THIS FOR PEOPLE!

IF THIS DOES NOT WORK, SUE THE STATION FOR RACIAL DISCRIMINATION!

WARM PERSONAL REGARDS,

DR. LEN BERGANTINO

P.S. If anyone is ever going to take over
Gabriel's first chair (God's lead trumpet
player) it's Maynard!
P.S. 2   Say hello to Ed Sergeant for me!
(Maynard's tour guide)

1215 Brockton Avenue, Suite 104, Los Angeles, California 90025 USA

105

I Wasn't Always a Maynard Ferguson Fan!

By Len Bergantino, Ed. D., Ph.D., A.B.P.P., Local 47 Member

I was born in 1943 and my father had Harry James records of *The Sleepy Lagoon* and *You Made Me Love You*. I fell in love with the sound and fell in love with the trumpet and told my father I would not move on from mandolin to guitar, that I was going to play trumpet. You could sort of feel why Gabriel, the only musician at God's side, was a trumpet player!

Then I had a friend who was always trying to drag me away from pitching baseball games to play trumpet in bands, and he said, "Harry James, he's passe! You ought to hear this guy Maynard Ferguson. Come on over to my house." He had *Maynard For Dancing with Stella By Starlight*, *Where's Teddy* and other unbelievable sounds. I guess unbelievable was what it was. I could not believe it was a trumpet. Somewhere around that time – either a few years before or around the same time, I had read the International Musician article where Maynard Ferguson was thought to be playing the flute parts for the New York Philharmonic on trumpet. I showed my father, a very good professional musician and he was in disbelief at what he read. He did not think it could possibly be true.

The first time we had a shot at Maynard was in 1962 in Fairfield, Connecticut. He began by playing *Maria*. I don't know if she was the most beautiful girl in the world, but that was certainly the most beautiful trumpet playing in the world. Maynard played from 9:00 p.m. until 2:0_ a.m. with a 20 minute break while Rufu_ Jones played a drum solo and the entir_ band left the stage, and perhaps one othe_ short break at which I went backstage an_ talked to him for about 20 minutes. Durin_ this playing time he played all his solo_ which were unbelievable enough, but h_ also doubled on lead all night long. The_ close to 2:00 a.m., as no one left before h_ played his last note of the evening in an_ concert I ever saw him give, he playe_ *Maria* again and my father said, "He_ playing E about double high C with th_ same power and the same freshness as h_ played at 9:00 p.m.

The funny part, as I think back these _ years was that what happened that nig_ was very hard for me. It was a reality che_ involving the shattering of an idol – Har_ James, which the little kid part of an_ body's personality either does not like _ will not stand for. So there I am backsta_ talking to the greatest trumpet player th_ ever lived, asking him about Harry Jam_ and Parduba mouthpieces. I assume fr_ Maynard's book that if I were fool_ enough to have done this with Miles Da_ I would probably be looking for my fr_ teeth somewhere down the street. Howe_ Maynard was very complimentary ab_ Harry James, saying he was a good sw_

player and answered all my questions in a very supportive way. In some ways I never forgot his kindness in doing this.

From that point on whenever he played within 100 miles of where I lived I never missed a performance. I saw him at Dante's in LA, Santa Monica Civic Auditorium when the trumpet section went to the far walls of a huge auditorium, and when Chuck Niles from the all jazz station mentioned casually at 3:00 p.m. that Maynard Ferguson was playing at some God-foresaken junior high school in some city no one ever heard of. I got there as fast as I could and with no publicity at all, the place was entirely sold out!

There were many other occasions I have seen Maynard, but the main point – and I have seen most of the great trumpet players at one time or another – Maynard has a sense of personal aliveness that is hard to explain. One can only say that when he gives a concert you extremely wake up and every nuance of your body becomes fully alive and charged in a way that you have either never known before or have only reached at peak experiences in your life.

A few years ago, I was taking a plane to Cincinnati and this fellow in front of me was dragging what looked like a trumpet case. I didn't recognize him at first as he was quite a bit heavier and his hair was white. Then I saw the jaws opening and closing, stretching as only Maynard does, and the scar tissue on the lip and I thought, "That's Maynard Ferguson!" Only now I was a fifty-two year old man and not a young kid anymore so I didn't want to interrupt or bother Maynard in any way.

He went on the plane and sat on the right side about fifteen rows toward the back from where I sat. Serendipity would have it that at precisely the same moment we had to go to the bathroom. His back was to me but he sensed I got up at the same time, and with the same motion as when he leads the band or kicks off a song, he shoots his left arm up into the air leading me to the bathroom on the left while he took the one on the right. As serendipity would have it, we opened the restrooms at the same time and he must have seen the childlike grin on my face. At precisely the same moment we threw our arms up in the air and I said "Maynard" and he said "You know me!" We talked about Sai Baba and his family for about twenty minutes. Maynard stressed over and over that he was married to a woman he loved, Flo, for almost fifty years and that he had a large number of children and that he was a family man.

An afterthought that made me laugh was that when his arm went into the bathroom, directing me toward the correct bathroom. I thought, "That's Maynard Ferguson. I'd follow him anywhere, and I have!

106

American Alliance
of Composer Organizations
By David MacMurray, AACO

The AACO invites you to the second event in its landmark educational series of International Music Rights Forums, featuring SACEM of France, the third largest performing rights society in the world. CEO, Jean-Loup Tournier and his staff of experts will answer your questions concerning SACEM's unique royalty payout ratio to composers, Board make-up, performing rights, mechanical rights, and cutting edge issues that concern us as writers and publishers in the international music industry. If one has music being played outside of North America, at present or in the future, it behooves you to be informed of what SACEM can offer you. For the more you

know about how your royalties are collected domestically and for the world, the more money you will be able to put in your own pocket.

The Forum on Performing and Mechanical rights, featuring CEO, Jean Loup Tournier of SACEM (France), and his staff will hold extensive open Q & A after presentation on Thursday, April 23, 1998 from 7:00 p.m. to 10:00 p.m. at The Musician's Institute, 1655 McCadden Place in Hollywood. For more information contact L.H. and Associates at (813) 998-4948 or E-Mail THEAACO1@aol.com or David MacMurray at (818) 798-5779 or E-mail dreamrnac@aol.com.

MF Horn — *Maynard Ferguson's Life in Music*
Book Review By Dr. Len Bergantino, Local 47 Member, Ed.D., Ph.D., Clinical Psychologist.

c

This book by Dr. William F. Lee III, MF Music USA, 1997, among those about great musical leaders and talents, is a classic unto its own for several reasons. The author is scholarly and the detail in which he wrote the book takes the reader on "Maynard's Bus" as if he or she were a member of the band. Depending upon your age, you get on the bus from the very beginning of Maynard's career. You will be saying, "Oh, Wow, I didn't know he played record dates with Conrad Gozzo," or did this record with Pete Condoli." Then you will see where you came in and you will be able to follow those parts of the bus ride with great intensity – and you will experience the transitions both in and out of the United States. Reading this book you will know why people love Maynard Ferguson and why they go to see him at a moment's notice any chance they get!

However, this book is more than fascinating detail. It gives you Ferguson's Message of Life over and over – the enjoyment he has in playing. At sixty-nine there is no question in the reader's mind that he still plays with the enthusiasm of a young boy who fell in love with a trumpet. You take a long enjoyable journey where a zest of life is transmitted through

counters between Maynard and Miles Davis, Maynard and Buddy Rich, stories that will make you laugh and stories that you will tell to your friends for years, particularly if they are musicians.

Dr. Lee is a great writer and he has done a great service in writing this book!

Labor CALENDAR

January

2 The Industrial Workers of the World was founded in Chicago in 1905. Known as "Wobblies," these advocates of revolutionary

"After God had fin tlesnake, the toad. he had some awful with which He m: scab is a two-legg: a cork-screw so logged brain, a backbone of jelly ar others have hearts tumor of rotten pri

15 Dr. Martin Lu birthday, in tion to his contribu rights movement and 1960s, King v

****WHEN YOU CHEAT YOU NEVER KNOW WHEN THE DEVIL IS GOING TO MOVE THE FENCE!

I do not recommend taking thirty years off and then attempting to become a lead trumpet player and a jazz trumpet player. Nevertheless I became a world class shrink and I UTILIZED WHAT I HAD LEARNED IN MY OWN PERSONAL GROWTH TO HELP ME GET THE MOST OUT OF A SECOND CAREER IN MUSIC AFTER I STOPPED DOING PSYCHOANALYSIS IN BEVERLY HILLS AND TRAINING PSYCHOLOGISTS AND PSYCHIATRISTS AT THE INTERNATIONAL LEVEL IN FAMILY THERAPY, EXISTENTIAL PSYCHOTHERAPY, AND ERICKSONIAN STORYTELLING (A FORM OF CLINICAL HYPNOSIS).

There were some gaps I could never fill. Given I had genius capacity I was able to figure out how to use my God Given Gift of being the fastest moment to moment psychotherapist that ever lived to develop my ear and fully absorb myself in the moment to play either progressive jazz and/ or dixieland without academically learning all the traditinal ways that musicians are brought through the system that exists, for better or for worse! Some of what I could do was magnificent in terms of lyrical and modal creativity in the moment and sound production and some was so unlike everybody else it turned the ordinary musician into someone who had homicidal rage toward me - which of course, I knew how to analyze! (which helps)

So beginning to play trumpet again at 53 years old and learning jazz at 58 (from the best around as I did in psychology) I was a solid enough person to do what I could do without any ceaseless striving at the recommendation of fucking well intentioned cement heads whose advice would have crippled me from enjoying anything I was capable of doing at the stage of the game I was coming back. Of those who attempted to block MY TRUE PATH GIVEN MY SITUATION, I DID EVERYTHING I COULD SHORT OF THROWING THEM DOWN THREE FLIGHTS OF STAIRS AND BREAKING EVERY FUCKING BONE IN THEIR BODY TO MAKE CERTAIN THE ONLY PATH I COULD HAVE TAKEN GIVEN MY UNIQUE TALENTS AND ABILITIES AND SHORTCOMINGS DUE TO THIRTY YEARS EXPERIENCE GAP WAS NOT INTERRUPTED! IT WAS IN THIS WAY I WAS ABLE TO HAVE A GREAT DEAL OF PERSONAL FULFILLMENT IN THE THINGS I DID DO AS A PROFESSIONAL MUSICIAN

BOTH WITH A TRUMPET AND WITH STRING INSTRUMENTS OF MANDOLIN, TENOR BANJO, BANJO MANDOLIN AND UKELELE. FRANK CAPALBO AND THE UKELELE

I was always a guy who hated to waste. When I was twelve years old I bought a ukelele from Frank Capalbo, who was the only guy in Waterbury, Connecticut who played both ukelele Hawaii Style and Hawaii Steel Guitar.

Around 2000 I bought a Kamaka Ukelele (Soprano size -smallest). I brought it everywhere and practiced learning the keyboard playing single string. After awhile I had a Low G string put on for the 4_{th} string, so I could play the scales in order of ascenscion as opposed to "My Dog Has Fleas" tuning.

Congruent with the way I learn I went to Hawaii several times to study with the best ukelele players I could find and never forgot my heritage, My father used to talk about Roy Smeck who was known as "The Wizard of The Strings" so I reviewed a video of his work for the Ukelele Hall of Fame and that is Image 27. Image 28 is a note I got back from Herb Ohta Senior, the best ukelele player I heard of or met in my era who said after hearing a cd of me playing jazz solos on the ukelele he did not think I needed lessons. (p. 139b)

WHAT IS EXISTENTIAL FAMILY THERAPY?

Family therapy is the getting together of mother, father, and the children, and perhaps the grandparents on both sides, in one room in the struggle to give each of them a spirit of family, an experiential knowledge of doing, your best to give depth and meaning to the lives of all members of the family while appreciating the possibility and potential of each member of the family to contribute what he or she has to bring to all of the members, which may bring value to their lives.

Adding the word existential means that there are no holds barred. In other words, when your family members' lives, souls, and well-being for all eternity are at stake, existential family therapy approaches the task with a fire and passion to get to the root of the problem no matter what is required to do the job.

Along these lines, I had the good fortune to be trained by two pioneers in family therapy– Walter Kempler, M.D.. and Carl Whitaker, M.D). From Kempler I learned to deal at the conscious level in depth. with passion and fire, never giving in to the hopelessness family members experience that causes them to give up on each other for lack of a better way. From Carl Whitaker I learned to invade the unconscious minds of the family members, with its primitively repressed material that keeps them stuck, in a way that frees up each member of the family to be themselves. My psychoanalytic training enabled me to correctly identify the projective identifications of the family members as a whole group while utilizing Whitaker's methods of invading the unconscious. My own gifts are quick perception and intervention. Why is family therapy not usually the first therapy of choice? I have several notions about this:

1) Most people would rather face a firing squad than talk to their own family members in ways that transcend socially and culturally comfortable ways of having related all one's life to each related all one's life to each family member. In other words, far predominates and prohibits familial growth.

2) Most people do not know that the objectives are different from the goals of individual therapy or psychoanalysis. Over generalizing, one might say the goals of individual therapy of psychoanalysis are personal growth, problem-solving, and the restoration and development of a solid sense of self "The goals of family therapy are to leave each member of the family with the same personality they came in the door with and juxtapose the way family members relate to each other so that the entire family's 'dysfunctional" ways become 'functional,' at least to the level tolerable to the family members themselves.

results can have lifelong impact.

4) The dollar per how ratio maybe significantly higher than what one would pay for individual psychotherapy or psychoanalysis (given the number of people being counselled and the number of lives that will be affected, and the given the brevity of the work and the potential impact and benefit to the family members). Individual therapy may not enhance one's family situation at all, regardless of its benefits. I suppose it boils down to what you can't afford not to afford.

LEN BERGANTINO is a clinical psychologist and the author of Psychotherapy, Insight & Style

3) While individual psycho, therapy and psychoanalysis can take from one to seven years, sometimes several times a week, the juxta positioning of family members to create more satisfying, emotionally functioning families can sometimes take only between three and ten sessions, and the

The Existential Moment (Ally & Bacon. 1981), and has some 90 publications. He has trained psychiatrist and psychologists in Australia. He practices in California, Arizona and Hawaii

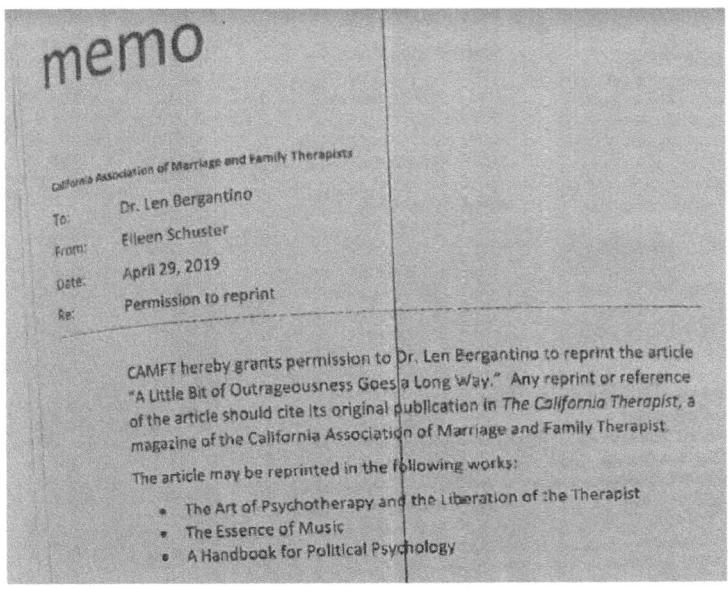

memo

California Association of Marriage and Family Therapists

To: Dr. Len Bergantino

From: Eileen Schuster

Date: April 29, 2019

Re: Permission to reprint

CAMFT hereby grants permission to Dr. Len Bergantino to reprint the article "A Little Bit of Outrageousness Goes a Long Way." Any reprint or reference of the article should cite its original publication in The California Therapist, a magazine of the California Association of Marriage and Family Therapist.

The article may be reprinted in the following works:

- The Art of Psychotherapy and the Liberation of the Therapist
- The Essence of Music
- A Handbook for Political Psychology

The Board of Psychology (State of California)'s
Decision to do Away with The Oral Part of the Exam for
Psychology Licensure: A Dissenting Opinion — *Len Bergantino*

Psychology has moved from a profession of personal growth on the part of the clinician, which could be put into one's private practice on Monday morning to one of legal deadness. It is now a care and caution that make the fullness of being of the clinician in enhancing the patient's ability to become a legal impossibility. The non-clinicians who run Board of Psychology and state Psychological Association's psychologists themselves have capitulated in their own castration. Now there isn't even a penis left to envy in the practice of psychology. I have seen the death of a profession I once loved ad now have nothing in contemn with.

I think the State of California Board of Psychology's decision to do away with the oral examination is wrong on several counts:

1). It shows extreme cowardice on their parts when they have put each and every psychologist (admittedly with their own complicity in the project) at risk since the mid•1980s.

2). Having an oral examination is the only way to get a fair look at an examinee's clinical abilities.
3). Even if the Board of Psychology is sued by a disgruntled person who flunks the oral examination, the Board would probably win (Dr. Steven Frankel in his course on law and ethics describes Board of Psychology bulldozing tactics as not having to adhere to law at all.)
4). The written examination has no validity for evaluating actual clinical practice. It primarily measures 'the ability to pass that kind of test and knowledge of some academic content of psychology.

The Board of Psychology's actions, along with lawyers looking for a new field in which to make money and with the complicity of psychologists whose clinical acumen and lack of courage are suspect, have decimated the private practice of clinical psychology. Because the practitioners can no longer be on the cutting edge of clinical practices nor have an interest in developing that ability the profession has become one in which those kinds of services can no longer be rendered to patients and therefore clinicians with courage can no longer function nor make a good living doing so. Psychologists continue to publish articles about new areas which they will not be able to practice nor make a dime on. They go to continuing education classes (36 units a year) like good students and take courses of no use to private practice or to making a living. Many psychologists are making $75 an hour which I made in 1975, and they are happy to get it. I write this because there has been a great deal about hard times and psychologists not being able to make money. But if you can offer quality of service and a qualify of response, you can make money. For all intents and purposes, the Board of Psychology and the psycholegal system have made quality verboten!

en that the California Board
 participated in the death of
 sychology and asked
psychologists to bear the brunt of
fear by which they continue to
castrate themselves, it is now a
"totally bad faith decision" to do
away with an oral examination. It
is the only way one can determine
if someone has any clinical abilities
whatever. The decision deals a final
blow to a profession that will
attempt to sell the words *clinical
psychologist* to the public when all
they have are people who are able
to pass academic examinations.
   Wilfred Bion, the great British
psychoanalyst, once said: "The
entire psychoanalytic library is
good for about the first hour and
one half of an analysis. After that
you have to know what to say to
the patient." The Board's decision
to do away with the oral
examination will ensure that
psychologists are no longer able to
determine firsthand who knows
what to say to a patient.
   Their fear is unfounded in the
following respects:
   1) They actually do hold clout
over the way administrative law is
set up.
   2) If three independent
clinicians meet with an examinee
and two flunk him, even if there
are countertransference difficulties
that preclude a purely objective
examination, there is still the rule-
of-thumb presumption that if
someone doesn't pass the smell
test of two out of three, then they
ought to get some help, try again,
or perhaps go into administration.
   3) Written tests measure the
ability to take tests and to go to
school. (Dr. William B. Michael,
USC Professor of Statistics, and
writer of SAT and GRE exams, has
stated emphatically that the tests
don't even measure academic
ability but only the ability to take
those exams.)
   4) There is the "halo effect"
regarding graduate school clinical

supervisors' recommendations,
which says: "You are my
supervisee. I have chosen you.
Therefore you are worthy."
   5) Tuition paid by students may
make the university or professional
school reluctant to judge a student
as not having clinical skills when
they may have good grades.
But they have decided anyway to
try to save themselves a few
lawsuits by basing licensure upon
an examination that does not look
at the ability to do clinical work.

CLINICAL INTERVIEW EXAMPLE

Twenty-eight years ago, I worked
as a clinical psychologist in a
community mental health center
in South Central Los Angeles,
which was predominantly African
American. An African American
psychiatrist and an African
American social worker had
already interviewed a prospective
Caucasian psychologist for a
position and wanted to hire him.
   He had a resume about twelve
pages long, which stated that he
had a law degree from the
University of Michigan, a degree in
clinical psychology, a great number
of publications, etc.
   My primary interest was how he
would survive with the street
population he would serve. Did he
know what to say? Would he know
what to do clinically? He came in
and said to me, "Do you want to
ask me about my resume?" I said,
"I can read." He said, "Well, what
do you want to ask me?" I said,
"Nothing." His anxiety continued
to rise. Then he said, "You have to
ask me about my resume." I said,
"No, I don't." He said, "Well, what
are you going to ask me about
then?" I said, "Nothing, all I'm
interested in is what you have to
say to patients, and what you do
with them, and so far you haven't
showed me shit!"
   While this was confrontive, and
may even seem harsh, it gives the
fellow a chance to show me
anything if he has anything to
show, and believe me the patients

attempted to rough me up a lot
worse than that. He said, "I am
going to get Dr. _____ (the
psychiatrist)." I said, "If you need
help with the interview, I strongly
urge you to get him!" The man ran
out of the office. And he did not
come back with the psychiatrist.
That told me he would not know
what to say to clients in this
neighborhood, nor what to do with
them. If I was asked, he was
clinically a "no-hire," I could not
have known this from reading
anything he submitted. It took a
clinical interview.
   After lunch, the psychiatrist said,
"What did you do to Dr. _____,
you really freaked him out?" I told
him exactly what I said, and he said
to me, "If you said and did that to
me, I would have hit you in the
head with a two by four." And I
said, "If you had hit me in the head
with a two by four, I would have
hired you!"
   He hired the man, and I soon
after went into private practice.
One day I read in the *Los Angeles
Times* that that Community Mental
Health Clinic was on probation and
being fined by the State of
California for hiring and having in
their employment a fraudulent
man who had never had any
schooling or training in clinical
psychology, law, or anything else
for that matter.
   Now that happened when the
clinical exam was still in!

*LEN BERGANTINO, ED.D., ABPP
retired from the private practice of
clinical psychology after 30 years. He
has authored 75 publications and the
book Psychotherapy, Insight and
Style: The Existential Moment (Boston: Allyn & Bacon, 1981). He gave
workshops at the international level,
the focus being "Keeping the Space
Open While Doing Therapy So That
Experience Is Not Destroyed By Education." Three major influences were
the training he received from Milton
Erickson, M.D., Carl Whitaker, M.D.
and his exposure to Wilfred Bion,
M.R.C.S. and his analysands who
trained him in Bion's methods.*

The entire
psychoanalytic
library is good
for about the
first hour and
one half of an
analysis.
After that
you have to
know what to
say to the
patient.
— Wilfred
Bion
(1897-1979)

April May 2003   AHP Perspective

Reverse Analysis at Its Best

Stories at a slow pace from my unconscious mind to the unconscious mind of the patient. Pyschoanalysis involves the working through of the Oedipal Complex five days a week from 5 to 7 years. In 1989, a woman patient came to my Beverly Hills office at three for Clinical Hynopsis to relieve stress. My stories had " profound accuracy" and my "pacing" was healing. The woman left statin she had been hypnotized. Then the Board of Psychology came to my office as she reported she had multiple orgasms and that had not left my seat and she hears and that I did not touch her but she was charging me with sexual abuse. The Board of Psychology and I agreed as what I did and that sexual abuse was impossible. What happened is my stories released all her blachs to sex and connectedness and she was in psychophysiological contact at level of prophetic that worked through the Oedipal Complex in one session.

For hypnosis or
training in hyp-
nosis contact

Len Bergamino, Ed.D., Ph.D., has presented Ericksonian Storytelling and
Teaching Tale methods as part of a workshop in training mental and family therapists at the International Gestalt Institute
of Australia in Brisbane, Australia. Further,
he has recently been selected to the Board
of Directors of the Southern California
Society of Clinical Hypnosis.

Len Berga   ino, Ed.D., Ph.
450 N. Bedford Dr., Ste.3(
Beverly Hills, CA 90210
(213) 273-8705

OCTOBER 1984
VOLUME XXVII, Number 1

The American Society of Clinical Hypnosis

Clinical Corner Interesting Case Reports

HYPNOTIC STORYTELLING AS AN UNCONSCIOUS SUPERVISORY PROCESS
Len Bergantino, Ed.D., Ph.D.

A therapist asked for a consultation for hypnosis for her therapy patient, and re-
quested that she be present. While she did not state it clearly, this was a request at the unconscious level to help the therapist with sexual countertransference issues that were blocking the patient's growth. The patient stated that she wanted hypnosis to help her "peel an onion", getting to deeper levels. It was agreed from the onset that it was going to be one session.

The patient complained of being stuck in the past, feeling like a four year old. She recalled an incident of wetting her pants following her teacher around screaming. She complained of washing her hands at the time - "everything was dirty and the intensity gets worse during my period". She complained of washing her hands forty times per day, living in fear of being an adult, and feelings of chronic empti-
ness and of being "stuck". The patient's therapist sat quietly throughout the ses-
sion.

The hypnotic method entailed my looking at the patient and the therapist, getting an impression of them, and then turning into my unconscious and doing what might be referred to as a "reverse analysis", that is, an insight oriented hypnotic storytelling where the insights occur indi-
rectly relating to both what was going on with the patient and the countertransfer-
ence problem that existed between the patient and her therapist. However, this entire process was metaphorical, and dealt with at the unconscious level. The method is an indirect metaphorical method of hypnosis that is experienced solely as hypnosis by the patient, while at the unconscious level it serves the dual function of being both hypnosis to the patient and supervision regarding countertransference issues for the therapist. The supervision aspects are not as obvi-
ous, because stories were told only to the patient, the therapist was spoken to directly only upon entering and leaving.

The metaphors I set revolve around my work with Milton H. Erickson, M.D. I tell stories about him much as Carlos Casta-
neda wrote about the Tales of Don Juan, only using unconscious specificity de-
pending on the patient or the group to determine which story, which inflection, which pace, the particular wording and refraining, etc. So the same story is never told the same way twice, and always has a purpose that is intended for the unique personality or personalities being treated.

Sensing this woman was quite fearful, I set up the metaphor of amnesia, telling two stories about two patients who had an amnesia, but were cured. One was about a next door neighbor of mine who was a doctor, using hypnosis in medical capacities. The woman was in the midst of making difficult choices in terms of her husband's employment being out of California, not knowing if she should give up a job she liked very much in California, having two children, and going to see Dr. Erickson to learn more about hypnosis for professional reasons. I said that I was curi-
ous about her work with Dr. Erickson, but when I asked her she said the strangest thing happened - "I can't remember any-
thing that happened during the entire week I was there. The only thing that is different is that every time I go into a restaurant and see a bottle of red catch-
up, I have a visual image of Dr. Erickson and I taking a hot pouch together". Then I said, can you believe that! She had an amnesia for everything else, and all her problems were resolved. She moved out of state, has a nice ranch, enjoys her work, is a good mother to her children, and enjoys her husband, and the only thing she remembered was a bottle of red catchup! I told one other Erickson story, the punchline being, "and he looked at this 25 year old woman, and said - eat it from an authoritarian old man like me that you have very unstable bowels". To deal

with the resistance I said Dr. Erickson was always concerned about the conscious and the unconscious mind. The woman's conscious mind tended to discount her unconscious wisdom, and as she got up to leave she said, "But Dr. Erickson, how is that I going to help me stop coughing and sleep tonight?" Dr. Erickson turned over his right shoulder and began to sing, with his paralyzed lips and dislocated tongue, "The lip bone is connected to the chest bone, and the chest bone is connected to the neck bone, and the neck bone is connected to the chest bone", and then he turned around to the group with an all-
knowing chuckle and said that he knew that Barbara would sleep very well that night. (The patient's original complaint was an asthma attack and up at night coughing, but I generalized the company that the red catchup and I suasable to metaphors would get the sexual job done.

When the patient came to see me she looked sexless and masculine. When I asked her at the end of the session if there was anything she wanted to say, she said she had the realization that she could just change, and she didn't have to wait a long time or suffer a lot to do it. When I asked the therapist if there were any thoughts or feelings she had, she said, "Only that you have given me a great deal with which to think about and continue my work", indicating that there had been a shift in the therapist's countertransference relation-
ship to the patient. Later, the woman's therapist reported to me that the patient showed up for her next session with a new hairstyle, "a permanent", and was wearing a stylish new red outfit.

When the patient was leaving my office, her conscious doubts took over and she asked, "Can one hypnosis session make a difference?" I firmly and with gusto and challenge replied, "You only had to be born once, didn't you?" The patient replied, "Yes".

Professional Exchange

A Little Bit of Outrageousness Goes a Long Way

By Len Bergantino, Ed. D. ABPP American Board of Professional Psychology • Diplomate in Family Psychology

Upon physician referal, father telephoned. He said the entire family was upset because his youngest son would not report to his new job because he insisted his hair was too thin and too kinky. I told father that mother and older brother would have to come. He agreed.

Mother, father, and older brother sat down and younger brother plopped his chair right in the middle of the floor while emanating an emotional response of taking up all the space in the office.

"Move your chair out of the center" I said to him in an offhanded authoritarian manner. The tone of command, ordering him around, and not treating him with kid gloves, established my authority, and reframed him as someone who wasn't fragile. He moved and there was a feeling of relief in the family.

The older brother said he had been to a psychotherapist and he thought people of my profession were for the birds. I said,"I've often had the same thought myself. Obviously you are an intelligent man." He was off balance in that I had joined him and identified him as being an intelligent man because we had the same thought.

When patients are thrown off balance, there exists opportunities for life shifts to relieve the chaos of not knowing.

After speaking with all family members I told them that baby brother was trying to keep his older brother from withdrawing from the family and bring some heat to the family because there wasn't much there between the parents and they needed him to keep their marriage together. I told the younger brother that he was doing an ingenius thing to save the family and that every family needed a sacrificial lamb. It was obvious, I said, that he remain the problem to focus upon but that it was a shame he was practicing family therapy without a license and not being paid for it.

He looked all knowing. Even though he didn't say a word, his look was that of a paranoid sort who would never speak his thoughts or feelings, I told him he had a great deal of wisdom. He was taken off balance when I treated him as if he were all-knowing in that he did not know how I knew that, given he said nothing. When patients are thrown off balance, there exists opportunities for life shifts to relieve the chaos of not knowing.

When the family tried to persuade him that his hair was normal, and it was, he became more entrenched in his position.

Having established myself as an authority with an unusual but credible perspective, I then used this position. I told him, in an insulting way that had to be believed because of its impoliteness, that he had a lot more to worry about than his hair --namely,

all that "baby fat" and the fact he shakes hands like a "wimp". I forcefully suggested he should join a gym, get rid of his baby fat, and he should develop a firm handshake and that these changes would solve his problem.

I shifted the ground or reframed the situation whereby the boy could utilize his own power in such a way that would get him out of the family enmeshment as much as all parties could tolerate, but with a solution he could work upon as opposed to one he could not--his kinky hair.

Two days later the family came back for a second session. They reported that the boy had joined a gym, begun to work out, and that he did report for work. The boy said he felt much more confident. When the family left, he looked me square in the eye and gave me a very firm handshake. All members of the family were pleased with the life shift. ♥♥♥♥

LEN BERGANTINO, Ed.D., ABPP (310) 207-8818 12301 Wilshire Blvd. Los Angeles, CA 9002!
Doctorate-University of Southern California -1971
Diplomate in Family Psychology-American Board of Professional Psychology
Private Practice of Clinical Psychology
Specialty: Family Therapy

116

Guest Editorial

Get Informed
By: Kenny Matinel

As of press time, Prime Minister of Hon. Honorable Dean Barrow was addressing the country in his State of the nation address. During his speech, Honorable Barrow is touching on issues that affect our day to day life, our bread and butter and our future. It was being aired live through the frequency of Love FM Radio and parlous stations gathered at the Radisson Fort George Hotel to listen to the Prime Minister's presentation.

As we listened, Honorable Barrow spoke of issues on tourism and future projects which may be implemented on the island. He spoke of police issues which have been affecting the towns across the nation and the fact that soon, we may have more human resources joining the force. Such an important speech and live coverage, did you listen to it?

Speeches such as the one presented by Honorable Dean Barrow shape up our country and shed light into our economy. At times there, these issues make headline news, whether it be print, television or radio. However, as Belizeans these issues were discussed prior to media before submitting to the public.

On the island, Her Worship Mayor Elsa Paz offers similar presentations, which we have had the privilege of attending. At these meetings, the attendees can be counted, what does this say about our involvement as citizens? The notion

leaders can know how much money was generated through taxes, through donations, told how much was spent for infrastructure, streets and education, etc. During the meeting, the opportunity is given for expansion and answer sessions where residents can either voice their concerns or clarify issues which might not have been too clear.

Consultations for developments are also carried out in the same manner. Before a development is set to begin construction, the Government requires the investor to submit an Environmental Impact Assessment (EIA) and then carry out public consultations. These meetings are advertised and the general public is invited to attend. During the meeting, the proposed plan is laid out and again, residents are given the opportunity to ask questions or voice their concerns.

Throughout these meetings, attendance is low, why? These are issues that affect our community, our island, our Belize. These meetings do not happen every day or every week, they happen once in a while. Taking the time to sit through these meetings provides us with important information that lets us know what direction we are heading into. In the end of the day, it is our future, and if we keep ignoring our country it is imperative that we all, as Belizeans, take more interest in these sort of meetings and speeches.

By taking a role and being informed,

The San Pedro Sun welcomes letters from its readers. Letters cannot be libelous or slanderous and must be signed, with a return address, a telephone number and mailed to The San Pedro Sun, P.O. Box 35, San Pedro Town, Ambergris Caye, Belize. Letters are not the views of The San Pedro Sun. The San Pedro Sun reserves the right to edit and shorten letters. Please do not exceed 300 words when submitting letters.

Dear Editor,

I Love San Pedro

I was here for two days in April 2008 and knew I had to come back. What I love about San Pedro:

1. You fly in from Belize City on a 12 seat – Tropic or Maya Air – and land two streets away from the Main Road.
2. If you travel light you just carry your bags across two streets and are at a hotel.
3. You do not have to rent a car and walk Front Street, Middle Street and Back Street it is probably just as healthy to walk or get a golf cart.
4. I stayed at Ruby's Hotel and both times which is at the beginning of the cobblestoned Barrier Reef Drive. You walk out the back door and you are on the beach. You walk out the front door and you are at the beginning of a pleasant walk.
5. The airport here has a sign that says something to the effect that nobody is a stranger in San Pedro. The people are naturally friendly to visitors.
6. Most of all I feel good here. I walk out the door of Ruby's Hotel around 7:15 a.m. and usually I see three or four people I know on the empty cobblestone streets ahead of me.
7. It gives one the feeling of "It's good to be alive every day!"
8. It is pleasant to walk the cobble lined streets uncrowded by masses of bodies as you would find in many big cities.
9. The weather is warm and balmy with some wind and not too hot but you don't get chilled either.

IN OTHER WORDS SAN PEDRO IS LIKE A LITTLE SLICE OF HEAVEN ON EARTH

/s/ Dr. Lou Bergantino
Los Angeles, CA. U.S.A.

Dear Editor,

I have been asked the question why ... world and continue to be ...

... are precariously bordering near chaos with all these senseless murders and assaults with no end seemingly in

THE SAN PEDRO SUN

P.O. Box 35
San Pedro Town
Ambergris Caye
Belize
Central America
(501) 226-2070
(501) 226-2905
tamara@sanpedrosun.net
www.sanpedrosun.com

March 19, 2019

Whom It May Concern,

As the owner and editor of The San Pedro Sun I give re-print permission for a Letter to the Editor that was submitted and printed by The San Pedro Sun on February 11, 2010

The letter, titled "I Love San Pedro" was submitted by Dr. Len Bergantino.

Feel free to contact me should you require further information.

Regards,
Tamara Sniffin

Owner/Editor
The San Pedro Sun

118

UNSOLICITED REVIEW OF "WIZARD OF THE STRINGS: A PORTRAIT OF ROY SMECK"
(VIDEO-VHS)

by Dr. Len Bergantino

When I was twelve years old I bought a guitar method book by Roy Smeck in 1955. In my father's old tenor banjo music of the twenties and early thirties there were tenor banjo solos written by him. The photographs of course were twenty to twenty five years different. When I asked my dad about Roy Smeck he said, "Oh, he was the Wizard of the Strings. He played everything well". However, I never got a chance to hear or see him. Thus, when I read the article in April/May 2001 issue of FIGA magazine regarding Roy Smeck, I wrote to FIGA requesting the address of The Ukulele Hall of Fame to purchase the video.

The video is a delightfully unusual experience in a way I had not expected. Roy Smeck was a character and one half from the vaudeville era. If one had not lived through the era it would be difficult to understand the kind of personality and character he is. In certain scenes, he hams it up a bit, realizing that, he is, an entertainer first and foremost, and that his craft is to entertain with a variety of his string instruments.

He was a bit different than I expected. My dad's heros, the musicians he modeled himself

after...were Harry Res.. on the tenor banjo, Django Reinhardt and Charlie Christian on the guitar, an Dave Appollon on the mandolin. After carefu attention to these players, I had come to see them a both musically and technically in terms of playing their respective instruments. They were, perhaps the best in the world in their time and certainly up for consideration as such for all time. I did not see Smeck in this regard on either the banjo or the guitar and on the Hawaiian guitar I have no frame o reference from which to make any comments.

One thing I wondered was why a tenor banjo player, my first exposure to Roy Smeck's work, was in the *Ukulele* Hall of Fame. Until seeing this video, my exposure to the ukulele had been confined to Arthur Godfrey. However, when I saw this video, I had the answer. The ukulele was Roy Smeck's best instrument and he played it in a manner that one could easily say, "No one does it better!" Smeck is awesome on the ukulele and does things with incredible speed and fluidity. Whether you like ukulele or not, it is worth getting the video to see this, perhaps the best ukulele player of all time.

In person, Smeck resembles a Bela Lugosi or Eddie Cantor, again out of the vaudeville era. In a way it is kind of funny to refer to a great musical artist in this way. His comments at the beginning of the video were made without any false sense of modesty saying, "Look, I'm not going to talk too much because I have something to offer, so let's show people what I have to offer." and he did!

The video included film clips of the eras in which Smeck lived and played. From his earliest film appearance in *Pastimes* (1926) to a live, in concert appearance in 1995. Roy Smeck's entire career is recalled and documented with amazing footage. This video is a must for collectors in that you get a first hand experience with one of the truly delightful characters of our rich musical past and his relationship to an American musical entertainment long gone by the wayside - Vaudeville

("WIZARD OF THE STRINGS, A PORTRAIT OF ROY SMECK" can be purchased by sending $29.00 -which includes postage- to. Ukelele Hall of Fame Museum, c/o 15 Concord Avenue, Cranston, RI 02910)

Herbert Ohta   7/25/05

Dear Len!

Just a short note. I just returned from the orient & am quite tied up with 'uke fest this weekend. I don't give lessons anymore but in Sept. I'll be in California 9/23/05 at the Rio in Santa Cruz. 9/24/05 at Whittier College in Whittier, Calif. 2 concerts in Whittier.

I listened to the CD and I don't thing (think) you need lessons.

Aloka
Herb.

Becoming A Jazz Player

In 1998 at 55 years old I decided it was time to attempt to learn to play the music I listened to for the last thirty years - progressive jazz. So I signed up for a Jamey Abersoll camp in Louisville, Kentucky in the summer.

Jamey Abersoll became a multi millionaire with this idea of teaching jazz to wanna be's. He had academic classes at 8 a.m. laying out the rudiments of what every self respecting jazz player ought to know. At 8:08 I left class and was back in bed by 8:15 a.m. I had no intention of attempting to learn jazz by filling in the gaps of the thirty years experience I had missed. Like Maynard Ferguson, if it ain't fun, I ain't doin it!

I cut all the classes. However, I did go to the afternoon ensemble, where one of the few African American jazz player instructors was teaching. His name was Hank Marr, an organ player from Columbus, Ohio! Boy, did I luck out! He was the best jazz player in the whole place!

I was the trumpet player, then there were a trombone, a tenor sax, a guitar, a bass fiddle, a piano and drums.. Hank Marr went around the circle asking everyone to play a jazz solo. He got to me and I said "I don't know how to play a jazz solo! He said, "Well, then go home! You either have to play a jazz solo or go home! Hank Marr became more of a Zen Master putting me head on in touch with my terror of getting away from the written note- a problem most lead trumpet players have!

I started to play and what came out of my horn shocked me and every one else there. All the stuff I had been listening to on the All Jazz All The Time Radio station for 30 years, began to come out!

Hank Marr was so excited he nearly jumped out of his skin! He excitedly said "Do you want to know what you just did? It was incredible!" I said, true to my "existential moment" and being fully absorbed in the moment said "No, this is jazz! I'm never going to play it again quite the same way!" Hank didn't play cliches, but in retrospect I made a mistake not finding out in that it could have been a trademark for me. Like Miles, or Chet play three notes and you know who they are!

A bunch of younger students began following me around as if I were a find, the golden boy, so to speak. It was cool!

There was a Thursday night evening concert and Hank Marr was near the end of the list of performers. He said to me "Watch this!" And he tore the house down! He was so far superior as a jazz player to anyone there and I hate organ!

I called him in Columbus a few years later to thank him and let him know his efforts were not wasted in that I was getting experience playing and studying jazz after he made it possible for me to begin with his "play or go home!"

I CAME BACK TO LOS ANGELES

DANNY LITTLE -TRUMPET PLAYER FOR JACK TEAGARDEN IN 1941.

Danny's only problem was that all his referral sources died! I was eager to learn and get experience. He was eager to make a few bucks. He correctly saw me as someone who could make something happen. I got a tenor and plectrum banjo playing rhythm and he played dixieland trumpet and I played dixieland solos on cornet and mandolin banjo. I was still a bit timid and a trumpet could not play forever, so when Danny couldn't get another note out he yelled at me "PLAY YOU SON OF A BITCH! PLAY!" AND THAt'S HOW I LEARNED HOW TO PLAY DIXIELAND ON THIRd STREET PROMENADE IN SANTA MONICA WHERE PEOPLE THREW MONEY IN THE BASKET. Danny sold me one of Conrad Gozzo's mouthpiece's for $40. I think it was a Rudy Muck (custom made). Like Maynard's and Al Hirt's, I couldn't play it!

We got hired to play a book signing high society party in Santa Monica and followed a classical guitarist. We got a standing ovation every number. After we finished one of the younger set by 30 years said, "I never heard anybody play more than three chords before! You guys were great!"

BILL WATROUS -THE WORLD'S GREATEST TROMBONE PLAYER

I heard him play at a jazz festival. He sounded a little like Chet Baker -in any case more like Chet Baker than anyone else at the jazz festival. I was in the first row about five feet in front of Charlie Mingus at the Lighthouse. Watrous mentioned that Charlie Mingus hated him.

One thing I learned from Milton H. Erickson, M.D. was that if you didn't get someone's attention right off the bat you probably weren't going to get it. I wanted Bill Watrous to give me jazz lessons.

I WALKED UP TO HIM, LOOKED HIM RIGHT IN THE EYE, AND SAID, "I KNOW WHY CHARLIE MINGUS HATED YOU!" HE STOPPED EVERYTHING AND SAID, "WHY!" I SAID, "BECAUSE YOU PLAY PRETTY AND HE WAS A MEAN ANGRY BASTARD!" (AND HE WAS THE NIGHT I SAW HIM!) WATROUS SEEMED SATISFIED WITH MY VERSION OF HELLO. THEN I SAID, "YOU SOUND LIKE CHET BAKER! I AM A TRUMPET PLAYER AND I WANT TO TAKE JAZZ LESSONS FROM YOU!" HE SAID "I DON'T TEACH! I SAID "HOW MUCH!" HE SAID "$100 AN HOUR!" (TWICE THE GOING RATE AT THE TIME!)

I SAID "WHEN DO WE START!" (IT WAS GOOD TO BE A MILLIONAIRE HAVING MADE THE MONEY AS A CLINICAL PSYCHOLOGIST)

WATROUS CHARGED TWICE THE GOING RATE AT THE TIME BUT HE NEVER GAVE ME A LESSON THAT WAS NOT TWO HOURS IN LENGTH DURING THE SIX MONTHS I STUDIED WITH HIM.

WATROUS COULD PLAY A SLIDE TROMBONE WITH THE SAME TECHNICAL SPEED AS RAPHAEL MENDEZ PLAYED MOTO PERPETUO (PAGANINI VIOLIN SOLO) ON THE TRUMPET. HE HAD A SOUND LIKE CHET BAKER WHEN HE PLAYED JAZZ. HE HAD SOME KIND OF TECHNIQUE WHERE HE COULD PLAY SIMULTANEOUS MELODY LINES OUT OF ONE MOUTHPIECE AT THE SAME TIME. I HAD NEVER SEEN OR HEARD ANYTHING LIKE IT! (see exhibit - p 143b)

BEING AS GOOD AS HE WAS WHY DID MILES DAVIS WANT TO KILL HIM!

My father used to say "musician is only an eight letter word but it encompasses a lot." After studying with Bill Watrous for awhile I realized he played at least some canned phrases that he had memorized in his head that fit in beautifully with a particular song he was playing a jazz solo on. When I first heard Watrous I did not recognize this and if I did I would not

LEN BERGANTINO, ED.D., ABPP
1215 Brockton Avenue, Suite 104
Los Angeles, California 90025

Dr. Len Bergantino's
Banjo Band (Old Standards)

s2.webstarts.com/lenbergantino
(37,700 internet hits)

Call (310) 207-9397

May 17, 2011

Dear Bill,

An unusual occurrence about ten years ago. There was one cornet
player at one of these trad jazz Festivals in San Diego that
could actually play jazz. He had a silver cornet made in Boston
around 1886.; He was tall and thin and not famous. He said he
played in Rhode Island and New London, Connecticut areas. I said
"Oh, I studied jazz for about six months with Bill Watrous.
He began looking at the floor and began to say words in French
that I did not understand. "Le terrible enfante" "Le terrible
enfante!" Then he said in English, "The terrible infant!
Bill Watrous! He played that way since he was sixteen years old'"

    I can't remember his name and that is my bad. He sounded like
a Chet Baker who played trad jazz!

Warm Regards.

Len

124

have thought much about it at the time. This was similar to what everyone at the Abersoll Jazz Camp did in teaching and playing jazz learning it externally - except for Hank Marr, who did it internally.

BY COMBINING THE AUTHENTICITY OF HIS ENTIRE BEING -THE QUALITY OF HIS BEING, HIS SOUL, WITH HIS INSTRUMENT AND THEN SOMETHING CAME OUT CALLED JAZZ THAT WAS SO DISTINGUISHABLE FROM WHAT EVERYONE ELSE PLAYED WITHOUT KNOWING THE REASONS WHY AT THE TIME, THAT THE ENTIRE AUDIENCE TORE THE HOUSE DOWN WITH APPLAUSE!

ONLY SOMEONE AS FAR ALONG AS MILES OR CHARLIE MINGUS WOULD NOTICE THE DIFFERENCE, AND HAVING "ABNORMAL INTEGRITY", WOULD INDEED FIND IT AS A JUSTIFICATION FOR MURDER!

"MAESTRO", TOSCANINI, WOULD HAVE PICKED IT UP. AS MY FATHER'S STORY GOES WHEN THE BATON FLEW OUT OF HIS HAND AND PUT OUT A MAN'S EYE IN THE FIRST VIOLIN SECTION, WHEN ASKED IF HE WAS GOING TO SUE TOSCANINI, HE SAID "NO, IF IT WAS ANYBODY BUT TOSCANINI I WOULD SUE THE SHIT OUT OF HIM! BUT WITH TOSCANINI! HE HAD NO CHOICE!" IN OTHER WORDS A DISCONNECTION BETWEEN THE INSTRUMENT AND THE FULL QUALITY OF A MUSICIAN'S BEING IS SO OFFENSIVE TO ONE IS CONNECTED UP AT THE DEGREES OF "THE HIGHER SENSITIVE" SO AS AT "THE MOST PRIMITIVE LEVEL" TO EVOKE "THE FEELINGS OF MURDEROUS RAGE IN THE OFFENDED PARTY", SOMETHING THE MASSES WOULD INTERPRET AS PSYCHOTIC BUT MAY JUST BE A CORRECT RESPONSE TO THOSE WHO DESPITE EXTRAORDINARY TALENT HAVE NOT LIVED HIS OR HER LIFE IN A WAY TO PURSUE FINER AND FINER DISCRIMINATIONS OF PURE BEING IN THE IMAGE OF GOD AS LIFE'S WORK! Personally, I always hated ordinary people for this reason!

Toscanini after hearing a performance conducted by world renown conducter Bruno Walter was yelling at him at the top of his lungs "YOU EAT THE NOTES! YOU EAT THE NOTES!" OF ALL THE PSYCHOANALYSTS WILFRED R. BION, M.R.C.S. (MEDICAL ROYAL COLLEGE OF SURGEONS) HAD THIS DOWN BEST WHEN HE DESCRIBED THE PURPOSE OF AN ANALYSIS WAS IN "BECOMING "O" (WITH "O" BEING FINER AND FINER DISCRIMINATIONS OF ONE'S BEING, AND WHILE "O" IS NEVER ATTAINABLE IT IS ONE'S LIFE'S WORK TO MOVE TOWARD FINER AND FINER DISCRIMINATIONS OF "O". I GUESS ACCORDING TO TOSCANINI BRUNO WALTER DIDN'T COME CLOSE ENOUGH!

BACK TO WATROUS

After spending six hours learning "I'm In The Mood For Love" by memory and then its form of AB AA or whatever it was, I then played a rather stiff solo and Watrous asked me if I knew the words. In my family of musicians, which included everybody, no one ever paid attention to the

126

words. He said, while you played a nice lick harmonically it did not make any sense in that it did not fit the words of the song - and then he insisted I learn the words of the song.

I was clearly too old for this and it didn't fit my unique talents which were more on the kinesthetic side as in feeling as opposed to the auditory side as in singing or visual side as in AABA and form.

As I was attracted to Watrous because he was the closest thing I could find to Chet Baker in Los Angeles in the late nineties I told him what I was willing to do which was for him to put on a record of Chet Baker and he would take a solo and then I would take one and then we would play one off of each other like Gerry Mulligan and Chet Baker used to do. One day his wife Marianne walked out and said "Hey, your solo sounded really good today!"

Prior to just playing solos with the cd's of Chet Baker there was one early cd with Russ Freeman playing piano which had "Russ Job", "Maid in Mexico", "No Ties" "Happy Little Sunbeam", and others (BAND AID) written down note for note and Watrous started by having me play what I read while playing along with the CD to get the feel of exactly how Chet played it as well as the technical capacity to get it down cold.

AFTER HANK MARR WHEN I CAME BACK TO LOS ANGELES

For six months I practiced six hours a day playing along with the records of Miles Davis and Chet Baker, matching the sound and in Baker's case the beautiful lyrical quality of his moment to moment compositions on already beautiful songs such as written by Loerner and Loewe such as "On The Street Where You Live" and "I Could Have Danced All Night". With Miles it was the purity of his sound as I EXTENDED BY EAR (AND IT TOOK THREE TIMES THE CONCENTRATION IT WOULD TAKE TO PLAY NON MODAL MUSIC) MY ABILITY TO PLAY THE DISCORDANT NOTE IN THE MOMENT, THEREBY LEARNING TO PLAY MODAL MUSIC WITHOUT FORMALLY HAVING STUDIED IT!

ALL THE WHILE WERE JOE DIORIO'S WORDS RUMBLING IN MY HEAD. "THE GREATEST JAZZ PLAYER I EVER MET WAS JOHN COLTRANE!" WHY JOE? "BECAUSE COLTRANE COULD PLAY FOR SIX HOURS WITHOUT REPEATING HIMSELF!"

GIVEN I ALSO PLAY STRING INSTRUMENTS (MANDOLIN, TENOR BANJO, TENOR GUITAR, BANJO MANDOLIN,

CONCERT AND SOPRANO SIZE UKELELES) I ALSO PUT ON MY FAVORITE STRING PLAYERS TO PLAY ALONG WITH THEM. THEY WERE JOHNNY SMITH (GUITAR), CHARLIE BYRD (GUITAR, THE CD WHERE CLARK TERRY PLAYED HORN AND I LEFT MY HEART IN SAN FRANCISCO WAS ON THE CD) (with Charlie Byrd at the Village Vanguard); Django Reinhardt and Stephan Grappellie (The Hot Club of France - a cd made in France as it was better than English copies - and the one where Django was yelling "Common!", on "Them There Eyes" was also on it. I put on the best of the best and they became my teachers. Miles two best discordant sounds were on "Porgy and Bess" and SKETCHES IN SPAIN (NOT SURE OF EXAct TITLE). (ITS CLOSE ENOUGH FOR YOU TO FIND IT).

I CAN PLAY SIX HOURS WITHOUT REPEATING MYSELF using my God Given Gift "the existential moment" to pay such full attention in the moment I am either able to create beautiful lyrical solos on the spot or play a series of discordant modal notes that are magnificent.

WATROUS AND I WENT SEPARATE WAYS WHEN I SAID I WANTED HIM TO TEACH ME THE MODAL MUSIC. HE FLIPPED OUT, SAYING THAT HE WOULD NOT TEACH ME THE MILES STYLE BECAUSE MILES TRIED TO GET HIM KILLED IN A CLUB IN HARLEM AND FREDDIE HUBBARD SAVED HIM. MILES SAID ABOUT FREDDIE HUBBARD, "HE DOESN'T PLAY THROUGH HIS CHORDS!"

**********I COULD PLAY SIX HOURS WITHOUT REPEATING MYSELF HOWEVER I DEVELOPED ANOTHER PROBLEM BY FOCUSING IN THAT MANNER. I HAD NO IDEA WHEN THIRTY TWO BARS WERE UP WHICH IS THE USUAL AND CUSTOMARY TIME ALLOTTED TO A SOLOIST BEFORE THE NEXT MUSICIAN PLAYS HIS OR HER SOLO! THIS LEFT WHITE AND BLACK MUSICIANS ALIKE IN A HOMICIDAL FRAME OF MIND TOWARD ME NO MATTER HOW GREAT EVERYTHING ELSE WAS.

RECOMMENDATION: GET THE THIRTY TWO BAR ENDINGS DOWN BEFORE YOU BECOME A MUSICAL ZEN MASTER IN TERMS OF TOTAL AND FULL ABSORBPTION IN THE MOMENT, ELSE YOU MIGHT GET KILLED BY SOME MEDIOCRE ASSHOLE WHO THINKS HE OR SHE KNOWS HOW TO PLAY JAZZ!

THE WHITE BOYS PLAY "TRAD JAZZ"

which means they are more familiar with major, minor and 7th chords than stretching their eyes in discordant manners with the soul and suffering that comes along with being BLACK! Joe Diorio was a White guitar player who became the best in the world for about 20 years, but he married a BLACK CHICK AND LIVED THE BLACK LIFE!

BLACKS PLAY BETTER JAZZ THAN WHITES!

I played a good deal with both and the difference is in addition to stretching out modal tones, and discordant tones, BLACKS play with a lot more feeling. In other words when I play with them through what Melanie Klein referred to as "projective identification" I am able to feel myself deeper and more soulfully and more creatively without as many imposed limitations. I AM FREER!

By feeling more I mean I can actually feel my body well up with feeling with about 73% of the Black progressive jazz players I have played with. In terms of the White progressive jazz players I have PLAYED WITH AS WELL AS THE TRAD JAZZ (DIXIELAND STYLE) I WOULD SAY I HAVE ZERO TO ONE PER CENT FEELING PROJECTED FROM THEY WHEN THEY PLAY. THEY ARE MORE INTERESTED IN "GOOD IDEAS" AS IF THE IDEAS ARE DISCONNECTED FROM THE SOUL AND THE BODY. I FIND IT HARD TO BELIEVE THIS IS WHAT THE ORIGINATORS OF TRAD JAZZ WHEN IT WAS ALL THERE WAS HAD IN MIND, CATS SUCH AS LOUIS ARMSTRONG. LOUIS WAS SO GOOD EVEN THE GREAT LEAD PLAYER CONRAD GOZZO USED TO HAVE HIS COLLEAGUES CALL HIM "SATCH" AFTER SATCHMO LOUIS ARMSTRONG.

AFTER HANK MARR AND BILL WATROUS
GETTING THE EXPERIENCE

I hear tell that Chet Baker used to sit in everywhere he could to get experience before he made it. This is what I did and there were a few problems with missing thirty years playing experience plus playing too much baseball instead of taking the opportunities I had when I was a young boy. So:

a)\ The Black jazz players wanted me to learn about 50 tunes from "The REAL BOOK" THEY SAID ALL PROGRESSIVE JAZZ PLAYERS HAD MEMORIZED SO WHEN THEY SHOWED UP ON A GIG THEY HAD A COMMON LANGUAGE. THEY SAID I SHOULD KNOW THE CHORD PROGRESSIONS TO EASH TUNE. THIS WAS AFTER MY LEGEND COUSIN FREDDIE BREDICE WHO TAUGHT JOE DIORIO HOW TO PLAY GUITAR TOLD ME "I DON'T PLAY CHORDS, IT FUCKS UP YOUR HANDS!"

b)\ The WHITE trad jazz dixieland crowd wanted me to memorize fifty of those tunes with all the original chord progressions, even though many of those tunes were obscure even to me who knew everything that came out from 1940 to 1970, my area of expertise.

c)\ I was 55 years old and my memory was such that I could barely remember my own name, let alone memorize 100 new tunes! So anyone who insisted on teaching me the ordinary way that people learn such kinds of music before they fail to play it I thought to be both ridiculous and disrespectful to my own unique talents and ways to achieve my own personal goals, which was to have fun in a second career after I had retired from clinical psychology.

d)\ And then there was the issue of the 32 bar solo and my not knowing when it ended, albeit my solos were georgeous and I could play them not only for 32 bars but sometimes for six hours, and from their point of view, often did. This was easy enough to remedy. My timing was good enough that if someone in the band was willing to cue me when I was approaching 32 bars. I would wind up in the right place. However, my problem so incensed them there were very few that wanted to be team players in that respect, and in many cases preferred to start primitively homicidal rage situations. Of course, this was fine with me because I am trained by the best psychiatrists and clinical psychologists who ever lived and utilizing those methods when combined with those of Erwin Rommel and Heinz Guderian, German tank commanders whose work I have studied intensively, I am somewhat like a martial artist legal combatant who cannot be defeated. Erickson said "Much has been said about the solid rock of truth but little has been said about the shifting sands!" When you can do both at a moment's notice, you can do anything because you are confident that if things go sideways you are so skillful you will be able to take the next step. So I enjoyed kicking the shit out of those who would thwart my musical aspirations! (Milton H. Erickson, M.D. - the Father of Modern Medical Hypnosis trained me from September 11, 1977 to March, 1980 when he died! He was unbelievable!)

I highly recommend reading "UNCOMMON THERAPY: THE PSYCHIATRIC TECHNIQUES OF MILTON H. ERICKSON, M.D. written by Jay Haley Norton Press, 1973.

Dr. Erickson also trained me "how to utilize the resistance" so I applied this to playing jazz.

WHITE BOYS WHO PLAYED SO PRETTY IT DIDN'T MAKE ANY DIFFERENCE IF THEY DIDN'T SOUND MODALLY BLACK!

1.\ Chet Baker. When Charlie Parker was interviewing for a trumpet player in Los Angeles Chet played one or two numbers and BIRD cancelled all the other auditions. Then he called Miles Davis and said "Hey, Miles, there is a White Boy out here in Los Angeles whose going to give you some trouble!" By trouble, he meant who might take your title away as the best progressive jazz trumpet player who ever lived! Charlie Parker had the insight and wisdom to know that after hearing two numbers Chet played and the statement was just as true in the early fifties as it is today!

2.\ Gerry Mulligan, who I saw play three times and talked with the last time I saw him at the JAZZ Festival put on by the radio station. He played the most georgeous sounding jazz on the baritone sax I have ever heard in my life. IN REFERENCE TO CHET BAKER'S DEATH IN 1988 I ASKED HIM IF BAKER JUMPED OR HE WAS PUSHED OUT THE WINDOW ON A DRUG DEAL GONE BAD! MULLIGAN LOOKED ME RIGHT IN THE EYE AND SAID "I THINK HE HAD A LITTLE HELP!"

3.\ Paul Desmond -Alto saxophone player with Dave Brubeck. First time I heard him play was in the food halls at the University of Connecticut in the Fall of 1961 where they played "TAKE FIVE" over and over. It is the only record I remember ever being played. I heard Paul Desmond on many records over the years and I never heard him play a note where the sound was not spectaculor! And saxophone is not one of my favorite sounds. In fact, it is one of my least favorite. So perhaps his jazz solos were inconsequential in that anything he played would have sounded magnificent and it just happened to be jazz. After he died I saw Brubeck a few times and he never did it for me!

4.\ Paul Desmond and Harry James were stupid bastards! They both had the best sounds of their respective eras on their respective instruments and they were both chain smokers and they both died of lung cancer! Albeit there were not as many warnings in those days but anyone could have figured out biologically speaking that you have more wind and better breathing when you don't have smoke coming out of your ears! I am pissed at both of them for dying on me! I take it personally when they were that good and meant so much to my life!

I HAD HARRY RESER'S TENOR BANJO SOLOS "THE CLOCK AND THE BANJO" AND "LOLLIPOPS" AS WELL AS HARRY JAMES' "YOU MADE ME LOVE YOU" AND "THE SLEEPY LAGOON" BURNT INTO MY MIND. THIS WAS TOLD TO ME BY BUDDY WACHTER, A CURRENTLY WORLD RENOWN TENOR BANJO PLAYER WHO HAS TAKEN THE INSTRUMENT TO THE LEVEL OF CARNEGIE HALL AND THE BOSTON POPS. THIS COMMENT CAME OUT OF HIS MOUTH IN RELATION TO HOW I HAPPEN TO KNOW MORE ABOUT TENOR BANJO AND ITS PLAYERS AND ITS SOUND THAN ANYONE ELSE IN THE WORLD. I MENTIONED TO BUDDY THAT I LISTENED TO HARRY RESER AND HARRY JAMES ON 78 rpm's 10,000 times each.. That is when Buddy, one of the best music teacher's who ever lived said "Oh, so it is burnt into your head." While, at the time he was referring to the tenor banjo, it also explains how I had a sound like Harry James after two weeks of playing the trumpet. That sound was "burnt into my entire being" and by the time I got around to the trumpet that was the only thing that could come out. There are many strange things that people do not believe are possible and those mental constrictions or limitations make the world full of sad ass mother fuckers! Pimples On The Ass Of Progress! so to speak!

My cousin Lou Bredice used to play 7 nights a week at the San Souci Hotel in Miami Beach. He had an eighth grade education but he was a genius. I was studying for my doctoral exams at The University of Southern California in Los Angeles in 1970 and Lou was staying with me for a few weeks. I had hundreds of books to review and not enough time to read all my notes. Lou said "Go to sleep. I will read to you while you are sleeping and all your notes will seep into your mind and during the test you will know all of it." I thought he was loonier than a bedbug, but I was desperate, exhausted and I had nothing to lose. WHEN I TOOK THE EXAM I HAD RECOGNITION OF EACH AND EVERY ITEM COVERED IN HIS READING TO ME WHILE I WAS ASLEEP AND I AM NOW DR. LEN BERGANTINO. I LATER FOUND OUT IN AN EDUCATIONAL PSYCHOLOGY COURSE THAT WHAT HE DID IS REFERRED TO AS "MNEUMONIC MEMORY". BUT HOW THE HELL DID HE LEARN IT IN THE EIGHTH GRADE WHEN I NEVER HEARD OF UNTIL LATE AS A DOCTORAL STUDENT?!?!?!?!?!? Lou played 7 nights a week from 9 p.m. until 2 a.m. and he had a date with a nurse. She said "Lou, Let's go to a night club!" He said, "No, Let's go to a hospital!"

THE BEST JAZZ TEACHER I EVER HAD WAS STACY ROWLES
1955-2009

Stacy Rowles was the daughter of Jimmy Rowles, the piano player who Chet Baker studied harmony with from eight a.m. until 3 p.m. for four years while Stacy was in high school. While she was not well known she was soulful with every note she played. I loved playing the flugelhorn with her -me taking one and her taking one - often with a cd either she or I would select. I loved the way she played. She sounded like Chet. Her father taught Chet and he taught her to the degree such soulfully connected playing is possible to teach. It was the more I hung around her and played the more I was able to play like me, like Chet. Image 30 is an article I wrote for her obituary in the Musicians Local 47 Newsletter. I cried when I heard of her death. I had only cried when my parents and my maternal grandmother died. She moved me that much!

******I PLAYED THE MOST LIKE PEOPLE I LOVED OR THOSE WHO WERE GOOD TO ME AS A YOUNGSTER.

**********I STUDIED WITH RON STOUT TAKING JAZZ LESSONS FOR SIX MONTHS. While he played the jazz chair for Bill Holman's big band what thrilled me about his jazz solos is that when I asked him to he is the only one I ever heard who had the technical ability to play dixieland solos like Al Hirt Al Hirt was nice to me as a kid (see Image 31- A Good Deed -Local 47 Newsletter -Overture) so when I play dixieland solos even in my own band they always had an Al Hirt flavor to them. In fact I have two Holton Al Hirt Model Cornets with a Large Bore and the valves move faster than most cornets, kind of like the valves on the Olds Mendez Models in that they had to move fast for Mendez! He played at the speed of light!

OVERTURE

12

Final Notes

The officers and members of Local 47 extend our sincere sympathies to the families and friends of our departed members.

Stacy Rowles (1955 - 2009)

BY DR. LEN BERGANTINO, LOCAL 47 MEMBER

In Memoriam

Les Paul

Life Member, Guitar

Keep Your Beneficiary Card Current

Harold Wolf (1921 - 2009)

F. 153 e

overture

THE OFFICIAL PUBLICATION OF PROFESSIONAL MUSICIANS LOCAL 47, LOS ANGELES, AFM, AFL-CIO, CLC

MAY, 2003

Important Change in Dues Payment Policy

As of March 31, 2003, you no longer are able to designate how dues payments shall be applied.

As of March 31, 2003, all late membership dues and all work dues ments to Local 47 will be applied in the following order:

1. Reinstatement fees
2. Membership
3. Outstanding fines/Hearing Board
4. Late fees

A Good Deed

By Dr. Len Erlgantino

Rex Merriweather, another Local 47 member, and I were playing trumpet duets out of St. Jacome's — something we hadn't done since our time with our original trumpet teachers, mine being Carl Berg who played for Harry James. We met at Rex's house to do this because playing a trumpet is something we both love to do – like two little kids in a sandbox.

I began telling him of the well known trumpet players who were kind to me along the way. They included Miles Davis, Maynard Ferguson, Harry James, Lee Morgan, and Al Hirt. I told Rex that when Al Hirt was playing a show at Oakdale Summer Theatre in Connecticut in 1963, he talked to me for a long time about playing trumpet with the same enthusiasm that Rex and I had, as if he were a little kid in a sandbox. Then Rex told me a story that has deeply moved everyone I have told.

Rex lived in Wisconsin. He got his first regular job in a band as a young teenager (13 or 14), but they wanted him to have a fluegelhorn as well as a trumpet. He took a train to a well known trumpet shop in Chicago,

which was quite a distance. The only way he could do it was if they gave him credit for his cornet and took perhaps $100 extra. All the time he was trying the horn, there was a big heavy-set man in the corner playing trumpet and trying horns. The shopkeeper said that Rex would have to come back the following day, despite having to take the train a long way back to Wisconsin, and then back again.

When Rex came back the following day, he had his mother come with him. She brought some extra money just in case, but they were not wealthy and it was a stretch. When they got to the store, the man said, "Here is your fluegelhorn and here is your cornet back." Rex said, "How much do I owe you?" The man said, "Nothing. You remember that heavy-set fellow over there in the corner? He heard you play and he thought you were pretty good, so he bought you the fluegelhorn. His name is Al Hirt."

It's kind of funny when someone touches your heart in that way. It keeps the love of the trumpet, the love of the music, and the transmission of culture to future generations alive."

ike a Stan

one of their friends and

, even though the new ...kind in and protected ...feeling of profound ...asn't gone away for a ...many others, the disa ...pered by a profound ...s horn from the bitte

Guidelines For Use of the Relief Fund

136

TOSCANINI, MILES, OR MYSELF FOR THAT MATTER HAD AND HAVE NO SOCIAL SELF.

1.\ Toscanini was introduced to Tommy Dorsey. His only statement was "YOU PLAY FLAT!"

2.\ Miles asked Maynard to play Christmas Carols at Birdland when they both were playing there on Christmas Eve one year. The DJ, Symphony Sid, said to Miles, "What's with Maynard! This is Birdland and he's playing Christmas Carols! This is a jazz joint!" Miles said "What the fuck are you deaf!" (as he hit him with one punch knocking him out (Miles was a good boxer).

3.\ MORT SAHL TOLD ME "NEVER BETRAY THE MUSE". While I attained the prowess as a musician at 66 years old I did as an internationally renown clinical psychologist who had extrasensory perception and THERE WAS ALWAYS THE FEELING THAT UNLESS YOU PUT YOUR FULL BEING ON AUTOMATIC PILOT, WHERE YOU DO NOT DECIDE IF YOU ARE GOING TO SELL OUT EACH AND EVERY TIME A CHOICE COMES UP, THEN THE FEAR IS YOU NEVER KNOW WHICH YOU WILL SHOW UP WHEN YOU NEED THAT YOU THE MOST! YOU Don't get to be a Toscanini or a Miles Davis unless your wire is so **fine tuned as to be above and beyond normal human perception.** WE ARE TALKING ABOUT A DIFFERENT BREED OF CAT HERE WHO PLAY TO THE BEAT OF THEIR OWN DRUMMER ALL THE TIME AND PISS OFF THE MASSES AND ARE HIGHLY MISUNDERSTOOD AND OFTEN PERSECUTED BY "ORDINARY PEOPLE!"

4.\ It was to Mussolini's credit that he understood this about Toscanini, that he had no choice when he refused to perform at La Scala Opera House in Milan for Mussolini, and Mussolini did let him leave the country instead of putting him to death, which was foremost on his mind at the time!

BILL WATROUS HAD EARS LIKE A DOG!

One day I drove to his house for a 9 a.m. lesson and Watrous had a little plastic toy bell on the outside of his gate - sort of like you would put on a Christmas tree. I rang it twice and it made such a feint sound I almost could not hear it. Watrous did not come out so five minutes later I rang it again, and it was just as feint a sound as the first time. Only this time he came running out asking me if I was trying to wake up the entire nieghborhood!

One lesson he just had me sit in the living room and listen to intense classical music so loud that the floor was vibrating with sound. I assume his objective was to get me to feel deeply into the music instead of just listening to it, as in waves of sound.

For gifted people they often have sensitivities there is no way to describe and you learn things that are otherwise unteachable!

When I was President of the Hypnosis Society composed of MD's, Dentists and Clinical Psychologists one woman psychiatrist said after seeing me do a demo (at the time I was the best alive) -"Dr. Bergantino, your work was magnificent. I admire you greatly. However, I would have to live my entire life like a Buddhist Monk to do what you did. I have a husband and kids. I want to give a few hypnotic suggestions, have people lose a few pounds or stop smoking, and go home after work and enjoy the rest of my life." (A perfectly valid out front position in which she did not blame me for being too good, and actually appreciated what I did). During the same evening at the very end a woman psychologist yelled out, "Hey Bergantino, when the fuck are you going to teach something somebody can learn!" Same work sample. Same evening. Quite a different response. Most people do not consider what they bring to the table in making their evaluation.

While I primarily consider myself a mandolin and a trumpet player JAZZ IS JAZZ AND YOU EITHER HAVE A SOUL THAT COMES THROUGH YOUR AXE OR YOU DON'T!; so I did not care if I was being taught by a trumpet player, a guitar player, or a trombone player.

I had a few lessons with "Clay Jenkins" -a jazz trumpet and fluegelhorn player at the beginning of my return to music after a 30 year layoff!

I had lunch with Marcus Printup who was more interested in what I knew as a shrink than my interest in him as a jazz trumpet player.

Nicholas Payton and Wallace Roney agreed to give me jazz lessons when they came through Los Angeles again, but I never got the timing right. They were both good guys as they saw me as a serious intent person of interest.

The most beautiful sounds out of a flugelhorn come from Roy Hargrove -born in Texas. I tracked him down over several years every time he came to Catalina's and I finally got to ask him for jazz lessons and he gave me his phone number. When I called he said he was leaving that morning to play for President Bush at the White House. When I asked him what the fuck he would want to do that for he thought I was busting his chops! I meant it as a compliment, that President or no president, Bush was not in his league!

Roy turned me on to the Swiss manufacturer Thomas Inderbinen (Zurich, Switzerland) a "WOOD" model flugelhorn. It had a better sound than anything made in the United States and cost $1000 more at that time ($3300) It was worth it. I can't remember the name of it. The maker's Inderbinen name is Tom.

I took six months of jazz lessons with Ron Stout who played the jazz chair for Bill Holman as well as Phil Norman's Tentet. A couple of things stuck. He played Herbert Clarke's etudes in double tongue, triple tongue, slurs and single tongue (I think it is page 8 of the Characteristics Book). I made it part of my daily routine! He is the only one who could play upbeat Al Hirt solos and technically actually sound like Al Hirt!!! Herbert Clarke. The best trumpet player technically I ever heard person to person in my lifetime was Raphael Mendez. I had always assumed he did things that never were done before until THE INTERNATIONAL TRUMPET GUILD MADE A CD OF HERBERT L. CLARKE'S CORNET SOLOS, SOME OF WHICH WERE WITH JOHN PHILLIP SOUZA'S CONCERT BAND. CLARKE, AS WAS MENDEZ, WERE BEYOND HUMAN BELIEF! THE ONLY OTHER TRUMPET PLAYER I HEARD IN A CLASS WITH THEM, OR PERHAPS EVEN IN A CLASS BY HIMSELF, WAS THE RUSSIAN TIMOFEI DOKSHIZER!. The Soviets, for whatever else they were or were not, once they had a sense that you were gifted in music, grabbed you at six years old, put you in music school until you graduated from The Russian Conservatory some twenty years later and then you could play like no one had ever heard before! In terms of classical technique the Soviets were the best in the world! I got to see several of their string players and Dokshizer's cd was sent out one year by the International Trumpet Guild. He had Mendez's technique, only a sound that was as big and round and warm as a house that was a home! I only listened to the cd once! As an aspiring trumpet player I could not stand how bad I was in comparison! (I had a great sound.) Once was enough! As I write this I would have to say that Dokshizer was the best that ever lived! Mendez's tone was a little too much on the bullfighter style. Then again, he was Pancho Villa (The Great Mexican Freedom Fighter or Bandit - depending on who you ask) trumpet player at four years old!

JOHNNY SMITH -THE GUITAR LEGEND! (NEW YORK IN THE FIFTIES!) who retired at the top of his game when he was the first call in recording studios and the top jazz player in the country on guitar when his wife died and a psychiatrist told him that if he did not give it up to raise his infant daughter she would grow up in a looney bin, moved to Colorado and opened a music store. IF YOU EVER HEAR JOHNNY SMITH PLAYING PAVANNE ALL BY HIMSELF OR HIS RENDITION OF "MOONLIGHT IN VERMONT" WITH HIS OWN GROUP ON HIS OWN CD, HE IS ONE OF THOSE IN THE CLASS WITH MILES, TOSCANINI, ET. AL, WHO HAS UNIFED THE FULL QUALITY OF HIS BEING WITH HIS INSTRUMENT AND THE PURITY THEREOF IS WHAT YOU HEAR COME OUT! I ALMOST HAD JOHNNY SMITH AGREE FOR ME TO GO TO COLORADO FOR A COUPLE OF WEEKS WHERE I WOULD PLAY JAZZ ON THE GIBSON F-2 MANDOLIN HOWEVER ALTHOUGH HE WAS POSITIVELY INCLINED HE KEPT SAYING THAT HE "COULDN'T SPOOL UP!" HE SAID IT WAS NOT JUST A MATTER OF HIM TAKING THE GUITAR OUT OF THE CASE. JOHNNY SMITH PLAYED TENOR BANJO BEFORE HE PLAYED GUITAR. HE SENT ME COPIES OF NEWSPAPER CLIPPINGS THAT ONCE HE DECIDED TO PUT THE GUITAR AWAY IT WAS FOR GOOD AND NO ONE WOULD EVER GET HIM TO PLAY IT AGAIN! HE SENT ME A VERY KIND NOTE AND I HAD A STRANGE REACTION, IT WAS RELIEF! I SENT HIM A NOTE I REGRET SENDING STATING THAT IT WAS PROBABLY FOR THE BEST IN THAT I WOULD HAVE BEEN IN OVER MY HEAD FOR TWO WEEKS! I WAS TRUTHFUL BUT IT WAS NOT THE LETTER OF A DEDICATED WARRIOR!

SHADES OF SOUND

Bob Reeves in Valencia California was a mouthpiece maker and machinist extraordinaire. He said to me regarding trumpet "The only thing you have to sell is sound!" He made me over $3000 of combinations of screw rims and bottoms. For what I was doing most of the time the best combination I remember (although they were all good at different times depending upon what shade of sound I wanted to play (he copied the old Jet Tone underpart cup from the 1960's Jet tone #7 and matched it with a copy of the #6 rim of a Parduba by the fellow now making them in Oakland, California. For the fluegelhorn I used the under cup of the Bobby Shew Yahama model with the Parduba #6 rim made by Reeves. It had a deep rich sound.

OTHERS ALONG THE WAY

WAYNE BERGERON WAS BIG ON WARBURTON AND I HAD QUITE A FEW DIFFERENT RIMS AND UNDERCUPS. I NEVER GOT QUITE THE SOUND I WANTED SO THEY WERE NOT FOR ME!

Marcinkewiczs' were popular for awhile. I had a Bobby Shew 1.5 which was good on the high notes but a little thin on the sound. I could not play the Bobby Shew #1 and the #2 just wasn't my bag.

Parduba #5 and 6 I was told were used by Harry James in different situations and a #4 1/2 when he did high note stuff. I played the #5 with a lot of satisfaction before moving to the #6 in which I gave up a little range for a better sound. But when I had Bob Reeves customize for me I got both the sound and the range!

I got a chance to play at a United States Navy Alumni Reunion band where I played revolving lead during the day and jazz at night. some great musicians thought I shined on both. Many of these guys were Las Vegas show guys and were terrific players with nothing to prove! I remember one guy who liked me said, "Kid, I'll play this one!" It was so difficult, so fast and so high had I attempted to play it I would have made a fool out of myself. His only purpose in taking that chart was to save me the embarrassment. I let him know how grateful I was as soon as the tune was over! (Red Bank)

I HATED THE MUSIC BUSINESS!!!!!!!!!!!!!!!!!!!!!!!!!!!!!!!!!!!! As a clinical psychologist I made $240,000 a year in the mid 1980's and I commanded $300 per hour in the 1990's. As a musician those that hired musicians for the most part gave one the feeling that you ought to pay them for letting you play at their establishment!

********BENNY GOODMAN HAD A REPUTATION. "HEY BENNY, WE WANT YOU AND TO PLAY FOR US." BENNY, WITH COLD STEELY EYES LOOKED THE PERPETRATOR RIGHT IN THE EYE AND SAID "HOW MUCH AND WHEN DO I GET PAID!" A LOT OF PEOPLE DISLIKED HIM FOR THIS QUALITY BUT

THE WORD IS HE ALWAYS PAID THE BAND ON TIME! GOD BLESS BENNY GOODMAN! THE PROBLEM FOR ME IN THE MUSIC BUSINESS WAS THAT I WAS NOT AS GOOD AS BENNY GOODMAN!

THE BANJO BAND -GETTING EXPERIENCE PLAYING WHITE MAN'S MUSIC!

Mostly in the keys of C, B flat, E flat, F, A Flat, G or D, the banjo band played tunes from about 1915 through the roaring twenties at up tempo. IT WASN'T DIXIELAND BUT THEN AGAIN IT WASN'T NOT DIXIELAND!!!

I played about 500 gigs where I sat next to a baritone player who played bass notes, so I played walking bass lines and jazz improvisation all night long. It was great experience.

My father was the best tenor banjo player in New England and only Harry Reser was better. I heard Harry's solos ten thousand times until I got them burnt into my being, as told to me by Buddy Wachter, current day virtuoso.

I became good friends with Don Vappie who played tenor banjo for Preservation Hall and I wrote articles about him, Howard Alden who played guitar in the Woody Allen movie "Sweet and Lowdown," and Buddy Wachter as well as my father. The articles I can find will be pages (160 a) through whatever.

While I was not in the calibre of a Toscanini as a musician I was as a psychologist with extra sensory perception and my areas of exquisite expertise upon which I could evaluate who was doing what were jazz trumpet, big band trumpet, tenor banjo, mandolin and jazz guitar. The current day masters of the tenor banjo all respected my feedback. Vappie once introduced me to his bass player after a gig saying, "This is Dr. Len Bergantino! If you want to KNOW THE AWFUL TRUTH ABOUT YOUR PERFORMANCE, JUST ASK HIM! HE WILL TELL YOU!" Those I became good friends with appreciated this quality of mine even though they were much better players than me!

I DID IT MY WAY!

Paul Anka wrote it! Frank Sinatra sang it! I lived it! Being Green isn't easy! Neither is having extra sensory perception. My daughter once shouted at me when she was five years old in total frustration. "Daddy, everybody in the world is one way! And you are the other! I just don't know what to do with you!" IF YOU ARE IDIOSYNCRATIC, START YOUR OWN BAND EVEN THOUGH IT IS A PAIN IN THE ASS!

MY BANDS

One way to reduce the number of shit sandwiches you get served as a professional musician is to start your own bands. I started three along the lines of my musical interest. I got the best musicians I could find who were willing to come to weekly rehearsal sessions at PROFESSIONAL MUSICIANS LOCAL 47 in their practice rooms. Most of these musicians were Local 47 Members. Some were not. The groups I had were

1.\ <u>Brass Quintet</u>. A moment to remember is when another top LA professional trumpet player heard me playing a classical piece and came running into the room to listen, telling other Local 47 Members how well I played that number. With music as a second profession this really made my day!

2.\ Dixieland Band - I named it "Alexander's Ragtime Band" after my son, Alexander, a developmentally delayed young man strangled at birth with a lack of oxygen. He got a big kick out of fronting the band. I got him a baritone horn so he wouldn't feel lonely and as we all took solos one day he boldly announced it was his turn to play a solo, which shocked the hell out of me because with his muscle tone deficiency he couldn't blow a note. Nevertheless other good natured band members shared a solo with him where he stood up and in his own mind played solos like everybody else in the group. THE MOST FAMOUS OF MY BAND MEMBERS WAS GEORGE PROBERT ON SOPRANO SAXAPHONE WHO PLAYED FOR THE "FIREHOUSE FIVE PLUS TWO!"

3.\ PROGRESSIVE JAZZ OCTET This was my favorite band. I had a guy writing original pieces for it who was a graduate of the Berkelee College of Music in Boston, Massachusetts and I had some great jazz musicians in the band. My drummer was a student of Shelley Manne. The band was so good that JED CURTIS, CHET BAKER'S PIANO PLAYER, A LAS VEGAS WORKING MUSICIAN AT THE TIME, USED TO DRIVE IN ABOUT ONCE A MONTH FROM

Dr. Len Bergantino, Ed.D., Ph.D.

LAS VEGAS TO SIT IN. IN FACT, HE LIKED THE GROUP SO MUCH HE WROTE AN ORIGINAL COMPOSITION FOR THE GROUP.

ONE OF MY FAVORITE CHET BAKER SOLOS WAS A TUNE CALLED "BORN TO BE BLUE" WRITTEN BY MEL TORME. I played this on my Callichio Copper Trumpet with a 3 Bell and a 9 pipe and it sounded just like Chet Baker on the record of the same title. In regard to my playing of jazz Jed Curtis noticed something there wasn't much I could do about in that I came from an era where it was burnt into my soul and that of my family's soul! Jed Curtis said "When Chet Baker plays jazz he plays the eight notes evenly as in da, da, da, da. You play them more out of the swing era as Da, Dah, Da Dah, Da Dah,. Mind you, as much as I focused on this I could not really hear or feel it, feel it or play it much different after he told me that than before he told me.

As I was the band leader I always took two solos to one for everybody else. As I saw it there was a necessity in that one of them was on trumpet or flugelhorn in the progressive jazz band and one was on trumpet or cornet in the dixieland band and the other was on a string instrument, mandolin, tenor guitar, tenor banjo, ukelele, et. al, depending on which group and which sound I thought fit better.

GIARDINELLI MOUTHPIECES

MADE BY BOB GIARDINELLI HIMSELF
THE SIX MONTHS I STUDIED WITH WATROUS I USED A GIARDINELLI 10V V stands for V cup and is much deeper than the regular trumpet mouthpieces and gives you a mellow progressive jazz feeling, or if you are playing dixieland a sound similar to Bobby Hackett on a good day

Furthur, Watrous was a Bach fanatic so I bought a couple of Stradivarius Bach T rumpets - the well tested one to which the number 37 is significant. I used that Bach with a Giardinelli 10V to get enough of a Chet Baker sound that Watrous was as satisfied as he was going to be with what he had to work with. His wife Marianne came out one day and said "Hey, your solo sounded good! That's when I knew I had arrived!"

Then Giardinelli was going out of business and they were selling mouthpieces for some ridiculous price such as $3 so I bought out the entire

144

stock of 10V for trumpet, a 12 m and 12 s for lead trumpet and a 12 V and 3V for fluegelhorn, a few 1VM's for trumpet which I now use playing first trumpet for the German Blaskapelle Brass Band or for classical music. Since I had a stroke this is all I do with a trumpet as jazz and high notes put pressure on my head that I do not want. I use a 1VM with an Olds Mendez Model trumpet.

Robb Stewart is one of the two best repair men in Los Angeles (Manny at The Horn's Connection in Hollywood, CA is the other.) and he also sells cornets and trumpets. Its like a toy store. I bought this particular Olds Mendez Model from him after Malcolm McNabb returned it after using it to play his version of Raphael Mendez's life put to trumpet music at the Music Center. I figured the horn couldn't be all bad. Its valves are extremely fast as they would have to be on a Mendez model and the V CUP takes care of the Bullfighter sound to the Olds horns and turns it into a mellow, rich full beautiful sound, something like Timofei Dokshizer of the Soviet Russian Conservatories! I only had to hear it once to have influenced the rest of my life! He was that good!

MOMENTS TO REMEMBER

One night in my dixieland band I was taking a trumpet solo and whaling up there on high F's and G's above high C with a technique influenced by my 3 live attendances of Al Hirt and the way he put energy through a horn. The lead trumpet players from the practice rooms on both side of the room my band was in came in to watch and applaud!

BRINGING THE PLACE TO LIFE!

My father was like the pied piper when he played guitar, tenor banjo or mandolin in that he brought an entire band to life which by comparison when he was missing was lifeless. They played the right notes but it didn't make any difference. I USED TO BE IN AWE OF HIS ABILITY TO BRING A BAND AND SOON AN ENTIRE AUDIENCE TO LIFE!

By the time I started doing professional training workshops in psychotherapy I could do this and my work was described as "a kind of mental precision that electrified the Australian Therapeutic Community and had lasting therapeutic impact." I could do that as a clinical psychologist when I was 40 years old! I was one of the best in the world having been trained by 17 world renown psychiatrists and psychologists and being able to stay connected to my inner source of power at all times, ala "the existential moment". SO I knew how to do it! The problem was it took me until I was 67 years old to be able to do it in a big band setting with a trumpet!. I knew I had succeeded when a couple of Black twenty year olds were jumping up and down giving me high fives after my solos and doing that only in relationship to my solos. Furthur, I did it on gigs in a banjo band with a tenor banjo and in my own trio with a banjo mandolin. SO IT TOOK ME SIXTY ONE YEARS TO BE ABLE TO DO IT WITH A MUSICAL INSTRUMENT AND THEN IT DID NOT MAKE ANY DIFFERENCE IF IT WAS STRINGS OR HORNS! While this was much too late to make a career of it, IT WAS EXTREMELY SATISFYING TO HAVE BEEN ABLE TO DO IT AT ALL IN MY LIFETIME, AS IT SEEMED SO FAR OUT OF MY REACH AS TO BE HOPELESS! COME HELL OR HIGH WATER I WAS DETERMINED TO DO ALL THAT I COULD TO SUCCEED AT THIS LEVEL IN BOTH PSYCHOLOGY AND MUSIC! I LOVED HAVING MY OWN REHEARSAL BANDS AT THE MUSICIANS' UNION MUCH MORE THAN I WOULD HAVING TO GO OUT AND GET SHIT ON FOR CRUMBS ATTEMPTING TO EARN A LIVING BY WHATEVER MUSICAL FETISH IS BEHOLDIN TO THE EARS OF THE LISTENER ON THAT GIVEN DAY! *****I ALWAYS HAD AN APPRECIATION FOR HOW DIFFICULT IT WAS FOR MY FATHER TO DEAL WITH THE BUSINESS OF MUSIC EVEN WHEN TIMES WERE GOOD, AS OPPOSED TO NOW WHEN "MUSIC IS SAID TO BE THE BEST HOBBY IN LOS ANGELES!"

JOE VENTO OF THE THREE SONS IN THE LATE FIFTIES

JOE was a piece of work! No one never knew what the hell he was going to do. Nevertheless when I met him he had a big band that played at Las Hadas in Northridge, CA on Wednesday nights and I got about five years experience with him in two phases several years apart.

Joe had a way to respond to band members out of the blue that felt like you got kicked in the solar plexus for no good reason; or at least whatever Joe's victim of the week was had no idea why Joe did what he did. Joe went on undaunted oblivious to any feedback that was contrary to his nature and homicidal instincts.

146

I kept saying he was a genius and I am convinced he was. He was on a total wave length of his own. He played too much Glen Miller stuff to suit my tastes, but it wasn't my band and I needed the experience.

One night, the only night this ever happened, I had another engagement but showed up on the last number of the gig. This was after I could hit the high notes. Joe said, "TAKE THE HORN OUT OF THE CASE AND HIT A HIGH, HARD, LOUD ONE AS THE LAST NOTE OF THE NIGHT! SO WITHOUT ANY WARMUPS I HIT A LOUD SCREAMING "Double High C"! ADMITTEDLY ONE OF MY BETTER SHOTS AND COMING IN COLD TOO! WELL, THE LEAD PLAYER, MEL BADER, A BANKER BY DAY BUT A HIGH NOTE PLAYER AT BIRTH ALSO HIT A "Double High C" AS WRITTEN ON THE CHART! HE WAS LIVID WITH ME (CUSTOMARILY A GOOD NATURED GUY!) HE SAID, "I DON'T CARE IF YOU PLAY A HIGHER NOTE THAN ME! BUT DON'T HIT THE SAME NOTE!" Anyway that was the kind of problem I had always wished that I had and I think my first thought was "OK POPS MC LAUGHLIN!" (my high note teacher from DeSoto Texas (I think his first name might be Clint). As I said earlier there are only two in DeSoto Texas and you won't play em from reading this book! You have to spend a week there!

UNUSUAL EVENTS

Joe Vento often said to me "PEOPLE LOVE TO BE LIED TO!" One night Bobby Shew showed up with a group of trumpet students who came to study with him from Holland. I said "Hey Joe, there's Bobby Shew! Why don't you ask him to sit in!" Joe went up to Bobby Shew and said "Hey, Bobby, do you want to sit in!" Bobby Shew was rather nasty in his tone and said "Joe, I don't sit in!"

Earlier in the evening Joe took credit for writing some famous songs, at least two of them, for example such as Stardust or Misty, that he did not write. This drove Bobby Shew bananas! Joe asked Bobby a second time, "Hey, Bobby, come on sit in!" Bobby said, "Joe, I don't sit in, but if I did it would not be with someone who takes credit for songs he did not write!!!!!" Of course the word spread throughout the nightclub that Bobby Shew had just refused to sit in at Joe Vento's request.

Joe always had someone who set up the band, his personal lacky. The third trumpet player at that time was named Al. He came up to me the following week and said "Hey, I heard Joe wouldn't let Bobby Shew sit in!" No matter how many times I tried to convince Al that it went down exactly the opposite he would not believe me. I guess Joe Vento was right. "People love to be lied to!" I would add "And most of the time they believe the lies!" (Joe was into "Fake News" long before it became an issue in the 2016 Presidential Election.)

WHEN I WAS PIMPING FOR THE BANJO BAND

The banjo band did not play jazz however what they played was for example upbeat roaring twenties music that sounded like trad jazz so we got invited to play at a number of jazz festivals in Orange County, Costa Mesa and San Diego. It was great fun! The leader had a riff with the people who ran the "Hot and Sweet" Jazz Festival in Los Angeles around Labor Day. The swing vote was carried by Margaret Teagarden who was married to Jack Teagarden's brother. Someone had just given me a video of Jack Teagarden playing at the top of his game. I had a copy and brought it to her on the morning of 9/11 when the twin Towers were hit by a terrorist attack and my younger cousins husband was killed and she had to raise three children by herself. MARGARET TEAGARDEN WAS AS CRUSTY AN OLD BATTLEAXE AS I HAD EVER MET. SHE SAID "I used to be married to Jack Teagarden's brother. I am divorced from him and I am glad to be rid of the whole bunch of those Teagarden's. They drank too much and were irresponsible!" Then she commented about my request to get the banjo band on the schedule. she said "Twelve banjos! Maybe one, but TWELVE!!!!!'"

BACK TO GIARDINELLI MOUTHPIECES

Bob Reeves made me all copies of a Parduba six rim and matched them with undercups from Giardinelli and rescrewed them to fit his mold instead of Giardinelli screw fits. I am now using a 1M on the trumpet. A BOBBY HACKET SOUND CAN BEST BE HAD ON THE IVS. IT IS NOT ALL THAT SMALL, AND IT GETS A DEEPER RICH SOUND. I USED A 3-F Cup on the flugelhorns. Bobby Hacket used to use a V cup. He made a 33 1p with an organ player where he plays "Stardust, Misty, Kiss Me Again" in the most lyrical romantic way one could imagine. He used to be a guitar player and knew all the chord progressions such as Chet Baker did with the progressive jazz lyrical sounds when Chet studied chord progressions and harmonies with Jimmy Rowles from 8 a.m. to 3 p.m. for four years that his daughter was in high school.

I FELT DIXIELAND ON THE TENOR BANJO AND BIG BAND AND PROGRESSIVE JAZZ ON THE TRUMPET. SOMETIMES I FELT DIXIELAND ON THE CORNET, BUT NEVER LIKED TO PLAY IT ON THE TRUMPET. Brass Quintet Music I like on both the cornet and the trumpet. I came in with Harry James on the trumpet. Before that the music I heard was my father on the tenor banjo. Thus, from swing, big band, and progressive jazz I felt it on the trumpet and the flugelhorn, but I did not feel dixieland on them. It was more NATURAL FOR ME TO PLAY TENOR BANJO IN DIXIELAND SITUATIONS!

LEARNING TO TRUST YOUR UNCONSCIOUS MIND

Before being trained by Milton Erickson I was so rationally consciously controlled that I did not have access to the storehouse of "thoughts, memories, feelings and actions stored in my unconscious mind nor did I trust in them if one did peek through into conscious awareness." After being trained by Erickson I had moment to moment awareness with what went through my unconscious mind and used it as a guide for daily living, trusting in the messages of my unconscious mind as being the correct path for me even when the direction seemed bizarre or very risky according to the mores of the times and culture bind.

THE MANDOLIN

The mandolin always seemed to be a natural extension of my body, but a part of my body. I almost cannot remember a time when the mandolin was not part of me; and this is the Gibson F-2 mandolin and not the Italian roundback mandolin.

In the documentary called "Let's Get Lost" about Chet Baker's life after he died his good friend Jack Sheldon said "All us trumpet players used to go home and practice Arban's for hours (Arban's is about 3 inches thick trumpet method). Chettie's dad bought him a horn when he was eleven and he just picked it up and played it. Everybody else used to practice Arban's! Chettie just picked it up and played it!" In many respects it was like that for me on the mandolin and like Jack Sheldon said on the trumpet with Arbans.

For example I made a cd with world renown jazz guitarist Joe Diorio and I had not practiced for six months and just picked up the mandolin for an hour each day for four days prior to the recording date of December 22, 1997 at Musicians Local 47.

149

In so many words my mother sensed my frustration at being my father's son with musical aspirations in that he was a monster player and faster than the speed of light technically. Her advise to me was something like. "Keep your day job! Don't mess with him technically or he will bury you alive! YOU PLAY PRETTIER THAN HIM!" What I did not realize is that to play prettier than him I COULD PLAY THE MANDOLIN AND GET A PRETTIER MORE BEAUTIFUL AND WARMER RICHER SOUND THAN ANYONE WHO EVER RECORDED ON THE INSTRUMENT. WHEN YOU LISTEN TO THE CD "FALLING IN LOVE" I MADE WITH JOE DIORIO YOU CAN HEAR THAT MY TONE IS MORE PURE THAN JOE'S TONE.

THROUGH MY PSYCHOTHERAPY TRAINING I BECAME AWARE OF HOW CONNECTED I AM TO THE SOURCE OF MY PURE BEING AND THIS IS WHAT COMES THROUGH THE MANDOLIN WHEN I PLAY IT.

I HAVE DEVELOPED A SPECIALTY TO PLAY FOR A COUPLE FOR ONE HOUR FOR $500 AN HOUR WITH THE NOTION IT WILL BOTH ENHANCE THE DEPTH TO WHICH THEY FALL IN LOVE AND CONSEQUENTLY THE HEAT AND PASSION OF THEIR SEX LIFE!

CHARLIE MINGUS DID NOT HATE ALL WHITE PEOPLE IF THEY WERE CONNECTED UP TO THEIR TOTAL BEING WHEN THEY PLAYED MUSIC!

Kara DioGuardi in her book "A HELLUVA HIGH NOTE", Harper Collins Publishers, 2011, wrote of her musical family "My mother's family consisted of many aspiring opera singers. My great-grandfather had made quite a lot of money in the stonemasonry business, helping to build many of the older buildings in New York City. He rewarded his children with trips to Italy, where they would study music and voice. The star of the family was my great-aunt Theresa, who as a six year old was even praised by the Italian composer Respighi, St. Cecilia's Conservatory of Music in Rome. Years later she would find herself playing alongside Charles Mingus. As the story goes, she liked a recording she had heard of Lenny Tristano, a famous blind pianist, so she wandered into his midtown studio and introduced herself. All these jazz heavyweights like Charlie Mingus, Stan Getz, Max Roach and Bud Powell were there, stoned and laughing as my prim and proper, red-lipstick-wearing, Jackie Kennedy-pillbox-hat-toting, walking dichotomy of an aunt asked to play a four-hand with Tristano! She let loose and tore it up that day, and became friends with all of them, including Mingus, with whom she eventually got the chance to play.....Unfortunately, success in music, or any field for that matter, is about taking the chances, absorbing the blows, and staying in the fight. Come to think of it, maybe I've been channeling a bit of my aunt Theresa all these years."

TRUMPETS, FLUGELHORNS AND CORNETS

Flugelhorns. I have two - a French Quesnon which was not an expensive flugelhorn in its day but many of the pros in LA feel that as a second horn behind the trumpet it is adequate to the task.

The second flugelhorn I own is an Inderbinen made by Tom Inderbinen outside of Zurich, Switzerland. It is a WOOD Model, not that it is made of Wood, that is just the name of the model. It is the flugelhorn played by Roy Hargrove who in my estimation has the best sound of all persons who ever played romantic ballads on a flugelhorn. He has an Inderbinen trumpet two, but has an edge that I do not find becoming to his sound on that instrument.

Trumpets - depends on what sound you want for the particular kind of job you are doing. This took a lot more practice because I was practicing on different mouthpieces and different horns for different situations.

Lead Trumpets:

1.\ Olds Mendez with the very large Calicchio leadpipe that Dominic Callichio sold to Olds for barrels of pitch after WWII. I have three Mendez horns and only one has this leadpipe. It is good for a note and one half higher than you are able to play with any other pro lead trumpet, which is why Los Angeles' top lead men used Callicho's before Dominic sold the mandle to make the leadpipe to Olds as he could never reproduce it.

2.\ Schilke S-32's. Renaud Schilke made them especially tailored to the tasks of the lead players. It was the last trumpet that he personally designed prior to his death. Also, of the modern day trumpets it is the only one I was able to come pretty close to the Harry James Sound as a solo trumpet burnt into my unconscious mind.

3.\ King Silver Bell Symphonic Dual Bore as advertised by Harry James. Has a great sound on solos such as "The Sleepy Lagoon, You Made Me Love You, and Bunny Berrigan's I Can't Get Started".

4.\ Selmer Paris 1939 Medium Bore Horn (that is when Harry James played a Selmer Balanced Action Trumpet, the same as did Louis Armstrong is also great on Harry James solos.

5.\ I have two Selmer K Modified Trumpets made in the 1950's and 1960's One is a good lead and high note horn with a brass player's roar. The other is a great big band jazz horn and is mellower than the first. Both are good high note horns.

6.\ & 7 I have two pre WWII French Bessons One is a Miha and the other is a Brevette. The Miha is Silver and the sound is a little thin but it is a good high note horn.

The Brevette is the most beautiful sounding jazz solo horn that I own ala Miles and Chet Baker sound. The Silver one is played out in that I bought it from a man who was 100 years old. Sometimes a trumpet has played all the notes the metal will tolerate and it loses its warmth and charm.

8.\ I have a Calicchio lead trumpet as used by Frank Szabo with a #1S Bell and a #2 leadpipe. This was made by Chris Callichio Weik, who later sold the business. At the time it was right up there with the Schilke S 32 as the best lead horn of modern day late 1990's!

9.\ I have another Calicchio made by Chris which he had in mind as a competitor for the Bach 37 Stradivarious. It has a 7 lead pipe and a 2 Bell. It has a nice lively sound for brass quintet work and regular trumpet gigs as an all around horn. In comparing it to the Bach Strad it does not fit the bill in that it has more of an edge and people who use the Bach Strad want uniformity in fitting into a symphony or an orchestra or a trumpet section. I was never the kind of guy who wanted to fit in so Bach's were a little stuffy for me and I always liked Callichio's bright edge!

THEN AGAIN ONE NIGHT I PLAYED FOR A NEW YORK GROUP CALLED "SPANISH HARLEM" SALSA MUSIC NEXT TO A MONSTER PLAYER FROM NEW YORK NAMED HECTOR COLON. I ASKED HIM WHAT HE WAS PLAYING AND HE RESPONDED AS IF THE QUESTION WAS RIDICULOUS "A NEW YORK BACH! WHAT ELSE WOULD I BE PLAYING!" Johnny Pacheco was the leader and he commented that he loved my sound playing third trumpet. I don't remember what mouthpiece or trumpet I played that night.

The East Coast Bias is Bach. My college buddy Carmen

Joseph D'Agostino owned the Burritt Music Store in New Britain, Connecticut and later expanded by buying out Tirkott's in Hartford Connecticut which serviced upper State New York. When I mentioned Schilke's, Callichio's, et. al. he said, "I ONLY NEED TO STOCK BACH. IT IS THE ONLY TRUMPET THAT SELLS ON THE EAST COAST." THIS WAS ABOUT 1999. Then again the East Coast is much more of a jacket and tie kind of place than the hang loose experimental West Coast where wearing a suit and tie is liable to get you accused of "looking like you just fell off of a wedding cake!"

10.\ My second best jazz trumpet is a Callichio made by Chris that is all copper with a 9 lead pipe and a #3 bell. The copper gives it the Miles, Chet sound. Freddie Hubbard used a Callichio with a 9 leadpipe and a 3 bell but it was not copper. Chuck Mangione used a copper flugelhorn made by Callichio which had a great mass market sound as in the song "CHASE THE CLOUDS AWAY!" The copper horn cost me $2700 cash on discount when other top horns were going for $1500. Chris felt the price was prohibitive. I felt the copper made such a difference in the sound as a jazz horn that it was worth the extra money. Then again I was a millionaire psychologist and not a starving musician who he mostly had to sell his trumpets to.

As a jazz player I can put more of my own personality and my own soul into the French Besson Brevette (Pre WWII) than I can any other trumpet. One professional musician once heard me play lead with it and said I had a sound that sounded like it was coming from Heaven! (Maybe it was!)

The Inderbinen cost me $3300 when the Calicchio Copper trumpet cost me $2700 when most other top pro horns in the United States sold for $1500. I am pointing this out in terms of a relative value scale because I see the price of those trumpets I paid $1500 for is now $3000 in 2011. I am glad I bought what I did when I could!

KANSTUL TRUMPETS AND FLUGELHORNS AND "C" CORNETS.

I am certain that as of 2011 a Kanstul Copper Flugelhorn is the best sounding flugelhorn made in America. I know Zig Kanstul who currently makes Kanstuls and he bought the trademark for French Bessons at his factory in Anaheim, California. I said to him once, around 1995, "Your name is Kanstul! Why do you make French Bessons?" His answer was "Two and one half million a year!"

I had a model number 1500 Kanstul trumpet when I was studying with Wayne Bergeron. Kanstul made a special model for Wayne Bergeron before he went with Yamaha. The horn played well, but I could never play it with feeling, so I sold it.

Zig Kanstul used to work for Chicago Benge, for Olds when they were in Fullerton, California, for Benge when they were in Burbank, prior to making his own trumpets. These days big conglomerates make Selmer, Conn, Bach, et. al. Kanstul is one of the few American independent brass makers still in existence.

I had a good time playing the Kanstul "C" cornet, which was the best "C" cornet for the buck. Other names were about $1000 more and that is when you were put on a waiting list for six months.

I have two "C" trumpets. One is an old Conn that is easy to get around on and the other is an Amati which I got inexpensively and plays well.

The two Bach Stradivarius #37's I have are exquisitely in tune! I have a "Stomvi 1925" that Carlos Mireles assembled in Valencia, CA. - 1925 is the model number. Carlos is a great guy! That is the closest all purpose trumpet other than the Bach if you are only going to buy one. It is also exquisitely in tune.

I have a Martin Large Bore Committee Model which is my third best jazz horn trumpet. This is not the Martin Committee Horn made by Martin in the mid fifties. This is made by Holton who bought out Martin and is a copy. If I had bought the Martin Committee Model Large Bore down at Manny's Music Store in New York when Kenny Dorham wanted to sell it to me (1962), it would be worth $3000 when other top horns were $1500. Miles, Chet, Dizzy Gillespie, and Kenny Dorham all used the Martin Committee Model in the 1950's. They were designed by a Commttee of five. I think Zig Kanstul was on that committee of 1950's Martin Committee Models.

I do have an original Martin Committee Model cornet which is very solid, as in a lot of heavy metal went into making it. (LARGE BORE)

I have a Maynard Ferguson Holton trumpet, a good solid horn. I never really gave this horn a fair test in that I had so many others I was already using. It had a big sound and I could go up pretty well with it. Another horn I never used much was a 1950's Conn Constellation which was the horn Maynard Ferguson played his most powerful solos on. It is silver and has a duller sound than the Harry James sound I was after with the King and the Selmer. It has some kind of a tapered bore that helps the high register. My teacher Carl Berg played one and swore by them. When I studied with him in 1957 they were $300.

Robb Stewart Brass Instruments Repair in Arcadia California sold me most of my cornets. Every time I went there for a trumpet repair he had a stockpile of cornets selling from $450 to $1000. I was an addict. The reason I bought so many cornets was I was looking for an authentic dixieland sound that pleased me with my two models being Louis Armstrong and Bobby Hackett. What I did not realize was that the problem wasn't the cornet; it was that I felt the music on the tenor banjo and not on trumpet or cornet. My father was the second best tenor banjo player whoever lived. Harry Reser was the best! Listen to Harry play "Lollipops" on a CD named Crackerjacks!

Given that personal problem I will spell out what I like about the ones I have.

1.\ King Silversonic - is both sweet, loud and in tune. Used by Chicago cornetists Wild Bill Davison and Tommy Saunders, his protege.
2.\ A 1937 New York Bach has a classical sound and is one of the best New York Bach's I have ever played (made around 1960). I also have a New York Bach silver plated trumpet with all kinds of designs engraved on it. Beautiful sounding horn. I paid $2200 for that when everything else was going for $1500.
3.\ I have 3 Conn Victor Cornets. They are very much in tune with a great sound. They do not have tuning slides. They have some kind of slide that screws upward or downward and you can get the horn in perfect tune and it stays there. When I played classical and had to be on the dime as far as being in tune I used one of these Conn Victors. They are not made any more. I paid about $450 apiece for them. This was the cornet used by Bix Biederbecke.
4.\ I have two Holton Large Bore Al Hirt Models that I sound a little like Al Hirt when I play. The valves like the Olds Mendez horns really move. Al Hirt could play the ass off of a trumpet and a cornet technically.
5.\ Holton is jointly owned by LeBlanc who used to make Al Hirt and Conrad Gozzo Model trumpets in the sixties, and I bought a LeBlanc cornet that is precisely the same horn as the Al Hirt Model Holtons,

only this particular one has a richer sound and slower valves. You always give up something somewhere. There is no perfect trumpet or cornet. It boils down to what you can live with on a daily basis!

6.\ I have an early 1940's Martin, made by Martin before they made the Martin Committee Model. It is a good sounding horn of high quality.

7.\ My favorite cornet was made by Holton in the late twenties or early thirties and is the exact same model horn used by Herbert Clarke. With a little Bob Reeves magic that is my prettiest progressive jazz sound on a cornet and would be great for recording studios if I were to make such a cd.

8.\ I have a couple of mongrels that have a great sound.

9.\ I have a French made cornet that is long like a trumpet that has some kind of a tuning slide you turn that turns the cornet into an A cornet from a B flat cornet. It has a beautiful mellow sound, as do many of the French trumpets and cornets.

I have about 23 trumpets, cornets and flugelhorns in all and I mix and match the arsenal Bob Reeves has custom made for me TO GET PRECISELY THE SHADE OF SOUND I AM LOOKING FOR ON THE PARTICULAR GIG IN QUESTION.

I HOPE YOU ENJOYED THE BOOK!

THE END!

Articles I published related to:

1) Clinical Psychology
2) Trumpet
3) Mandolin
4) Tenor Banjo

overture

THE OFFICIAL PUBLICATION OF PROFESSIONAL MUSICIANS LOCAL 47, LOS ANGELES, AFM, AFL-CIO, CLC

MAY, 2003

Important Change in Dues Payment Policy

As of March 31, 2003, you no longer are able to designate how dues payments shall be applied.

As of March 31, 2003, all late membership dues and all work dues ments to Local 47 will be applied in the following order:

1. Reinstatement fees
2. Membership
3. Outstanding fines/Hearing Board
4. Late fees

A Good Deed

By Dr. Les Benedetto

Rex Merriweather, another Local 47 member, and I were playing trumpet duets out of St. Jacome's — something we hadn't done since our teens — with our original trumpet teachers, mine being Carl Berg who played for Harry James. We met at Rex's house to do this because playing a trumpet is something we both love to do - like two little kids in a sandbox.

I began telling him of the well known trumpet players who were kind to me along the way. They included Miles Davis, Maynard Ferguson, Harry James, Lee Morgan, and Al Hirt. I told Rex that when Al Hirt was playing a show at Oakdale Summer Theatre in Connecticut in 1963, he talked to me for a long time about playing trumpet with the same enthusiasm that Rex and I had, as if he were a little kid in a sandbox. Then Rex told me a story that has deeply moved everyone I have told.

Rex lived in Wisconsin. He got his first regular job in a band as a young teenager (13 or 14), but they wanted him to have a fluegelhorn as well as a trumpet. He took a train to a well known trumpet shop in Chicago,

which was quite a distance. The only way he could do it was if they gave him credit for his cornet and took perhaps $100 extra. All the time he was trying the horn, there was a big heavy-set man in the corner playing trumpet and trying horns. The shopkeeper said that Rex would have to come back the following day, despite having to take the train a long way back to Wisconsin, and then back again.

When Rex came back the following day, he had his mother come with him. She brought some extra money just in case, but they were not wealthy and it was a stretch. When they got to the store, the man said, "Here is your fluegelhorn and here is your cornet back." Rex said, "How much do I owe you?" The man said, "Nothing. You remember that heavy-set fellow over there in the corner? He heard you play and he thought you were pretty good, so he bought you the fluegelhorn. His name is Al Hirt."

It's kind of funny when someone touches your heart in that way. It keeps the love of the trumpet, the love of the music, and the transmission of culture to future generations alive?

...t funeral procession in ...
(Photo by Don ...

...ike a Stan...

...ne of their friends and

..., even though the news ...cked in and protected ... feeling of profound ...asn't gone away for s... many others, the diss... pered by a profound ... is born from the bitte...

Guidelines For Use of the Relief Fund

(Continued ...)

A Review

By DONALD B. RINSLEY, M.D., F.R.S.H., Fellow, American College
of Psychoanalysis; Fellow, American Psychiatric Association
Psychotherapy, Insight and Style. By Len Bergantino, Ed.D., Ph.D.
Boston: Allyn and Bacon, 1981, 288 pp. Published in Bulletin of the
Menninger Clinic, Vol. 47, No. 5, September 1983.

There is no doubt that some people possess a healing capacity and
that others do not; nor is there any doubt that a Zulu witch doctor, a Puerto
Rican curandero, a Navaho medicine man or a voodoo spiritist may
remit symptoms more effectively than the best trained psychotherapist
or psychoanalyst. The differences between healing and therapy are not
inconspicuous even as both may readily dissolve into quackery in the hands
of the exploitive and the unscrupulous. A wise Freud once commented that
the function of psychoanalysis is to convert neurotic misery into ordinary
human suffering, a point of view to be dismissed only at one's peril even
though it doubtless reflected the essence of Freud's depressive personality.
From such few considerations as these emerge questions concerning the
differences separating healing and therapy, the features that unite them
and the goals and objectives they may be noted to share. And whatever
answers to these questions may satisfy those who propound them will
reflect whether one's Weltanschauung considers the world to be a vale
of tears or, after the fashion of the Gallic optimist, Coué, a place where
everything keeps getting better and better.

Dr. Bergantino's book in scholarly and even entertaining fashion
sets out to address issues such as these. The blurb on its bookjacket
states that it "integrates 17 prominent therapists' styles and problem
solving techniques . . ."

Its more accurate subtitle, The Existential Moment reflects the author's searching awareness that effective psychological healing, or psychotherapy, or whatever one chooses to call such interpersonal transactional processes ultimately expands one's awareness, hence one's knowledge of one's self, one's surround and the relationship between them; and further, that such awareness and knowledge develops in saltatory fashion, deriving from unheralded and even momentary experiences of insight, illumination ("aha!") or unconscious internal change. So far so good, but there is after all nothing new in that, so why read yet another book devoted to arresting human experiences that many believe to be inexplicable and unteachable?

There are at least two answers to that question. To begin with, the book reflects the personal odyssey of a trained, disciplined yet openminded professional psychologist who has drunk deeply at the wells of an number of acknowledged healer-therapists whose work he has carefully studied and evaluated, among them, Viktor Frankl, Wilfred Bion, the Gouldings, Frederick Perls, Milton Erickson and Carl Whitaker. A unique feature of Dr. Bergantino's presentation is his detailed accounts of these therapists' hourto- hour work, drawn from his own personal experience and from verbatim descriptions provided by their students and analysands, offering fascinating and instructive insights into the therapeutic labors of admittedly gifted treaters. The book is thus replete with clinical material, excerpts from therapeutic encounters and direct reports of those precious "aha"-type moments, conveyed within a disciplined epistemic context that presents each example in terms of ethical professionalism rather than exemplary amateurishness.

Again, the book reflects its author's ongoing growth and development as both thinker and therapist. Dr. Bergantino has gone to great length to converse and consult with both primary and secondary sources, delving into the what and the how, ferreting out illustrative clinical situations and indicating how he has proceeded to synthesize and integrate what he has learned from them and from his own therapeutic work. His book is indeed a literate statement of how one clinician has made of himself a therapist and his statement is both informative and poignant.

As I read this book my thoughts returned to a little-known 1962 Psychiatric Quarterly paper by Ernst Federn, the son of the psychoanalyst Paul Federn, entitled "The Therapeutic Personality, As Illustrated by Paul Federn and August Aichorn." It described in some detail the uniquely intuitive therapeutic work of these two outstanding clinicians, drawn from the author's own experience of knowing them both; Federn and Aichorn brought disciplined artistry to their respective therapeutic tasks in working psychoanalytically with "difficult" cases, Federn with psychoties. Aichorn with disturbed adolescents; both readily sensed suffering and never flinched from addressing it; both could occupy honored places in Dr. Bergantino's book. I learned much from that paper and I have learned much from Dr. Bergantino's book as well.

Psychotherapy, Insight and Style is an absorbing work, to be returned to time and again after one has read it through, to be thought about, mulled over and placed on one's bedside table if not under one's pillow. It is a book that the experienced clinician will read with knowledgeable satisfaction and that the nascent therapist will read with excitement. And both will profit from what it has to tell.

Donald Rinsley, M.D., F.R.S.H.
Senior Faculty Member in Adult and
Child Psychiatry, Karl Menninger
School of Psychiatry

Associate Chief for Education, Psychiatry
Service, Colmery-O'Neil
Veterans Administration Medical Center

Dr. Rinsley was on the speaking circuit with Dr. Harold Seinles, M. D. (the best American Psychoanalyst) and Dr. Otto Hernsberg, M.D, If you read between the books Dr. Rinsley wrote that I was the best alive then (1981-1983).

THE QUALITY OF BEING: PSYCHOANALYSIS - STATE OF THE ART

A REVOLUTIONARY Approach by Len Bergantino, Ed.D., Ph.D

"The Discipline of Being IN THE PRACTICE OF PSYCHOANALYSIS

Beta Elements: An Expansion of the conceptual work of Wilfred R. Bion, M.R.C.S. into Psychoanalytic Technique.

- **VHS VIDEO TAPE - ONE HOUR - $45**
Seminar by Len Bergantino, Ed.D., Ph.D.
Working with a professional audience.

MAKING AN IMPACT IN THERAPY: HOW MASTER CLINICIANS INTERVENE, Jason Aronson Publ., Northvale, N.J.,1993. 288 pages. Author: Bergantino, L.

- For Physicians who want their patients to get better psychologically and for Training Analysts and Psychiatrists who want to learn to succeed at doing these jobs in paragraph 1.

This kind of work permits psychoanalysts to develop techniques to do jobs that have either never or rarely been done:

1. Form a solid nuclear self in a patient who never had one - a job Kohut wrote couldn't be done.

2. Work successfully with the kind of archaic liquid symbiotic transferences that Searles wrote about treating with limited success over 13 and 18 year cases;

3. Detect and work with underlying psychotic thinking disorders - such as Bion wrote about even in narcissistic, borderline and neurotic patients;

4. Detoxify psychotoxic states of being (Kernberg's work stops here) and return patients to natural states of being where affect is connected and life force and the fight for that life force is sustained;

5. Help psychoanalysts' quality of being (Becoming 'O'-Bion) become enhanced so they may be curative of primitive mental states at deep emotional levels, even in patients thought not to be in treatment for that problem. Otherwise, patients will respond to the primitive mental states of the analyst even though the analyst does not act out. The end result would be an analysis whereby the analyst's blocked quality of being would leave patients in prematurely stuck places with self and a significant other whereby that patient's life would remain tragic even after a long analysis.

- Beta elements that Bion wrote about from a conceptual frame of reference actually exist. The question then becomes how can one do an analysis if they do not perceive with their senses these beta elements because they would not know what needed to be contained, therefore the underlying psychotic thinking disorder aspects of patients personalities, even those thought to be neurotic, narcissistic or borderline, could not be dealt with authentically beyond the point with which a psychoanalysis could 'detect', 'detoxify' and 'interpret' these beta elements.

- Donald Rinsley, M.D., Fellow, American College of Psychoanalysts, in a review of Dr. Bergantino's book, Psychotherapy, Insight and Style: The Existential Moment, Jason Aronson Publishers, 1986, made reference to Dr. Bergantino and his work in the following way: "There is no doubt that some people possess a healing capacity and that others do not. Nor is there any doubt that a Zulu witch doctor, a Puerto Rican curandero, a Navaho Medicine man, or a voodoo spiritist may remit symptoms more effectively than the best trained psychotherapist or psychoanalyst." Bulletin of the Menninger Clinic, Vol. 47, No. 5.

- Len Bergantino, Ed.D., Ph.D is in the private practice of psychoanalysis in Beverly Hills, CA.

For book send $ was $100 to Len Bergantino, Ed.D. Ph.D

1215 Brockton Avenue, Suite 104
Los Angeles, California 90025 USA

For Training Analysis or psychoanalysis Call (310) 207-9397

Foreword

Making an Impact in Therapy:

How Master Clinicians Intervene

The plethora of how-to books is increasing. This is not one of those. Barbara Betz stated that the dynamics of psychotherapy is in the person of the therapist. Abraham Maslow stated that the peak experience lasts two weeks. Winicott insisted that if you haven't been hated by your psychotherapist you have been cheated. Erenwald has stated that psychotherapy is the effort to evolve an existential shift.

Len Bergantino is trying to expand this operational territory by stretching the psychotherapeutic geology. He succeeds. Describing the therapist as a person of liberated wisdom, he dares to the chaos and anxiety of not knowing; he opens a gate to see and make the impact of psychotherapy more clearly. His description of beingness as a process is reminiscent of Paul Tillich. His grasp of responsible involvement with the patient as a discipline of self shows his own search for creative options. He makes no pretense of camouflaging the psychotherapist as a wounded healer. Furthermore, Len makes crucial the pattern of the therapist's search for his own healing and successfully validates the authentic trickery of the psychotherapist as a liberated spirit. The approach to his own craziness, the freedom from the culture bind, and the discipline of self each emerged as obtainable goals of that professional parent we call the psychotherapist.

Further evidence of his own search is illustrated by his impersonalized impressionistic response to the other searchers he uses as models.

164

Simply reading his book leaves me feeling it would be meaningful to join in his search for his beingness. Though he would be enjoying himself and enjoying me as a patient, he would not be doing things to keep from being himself and thus I could be more fully myself.

Carl A. Whitaker, M.D.
Professor of Psychiatry
School of Medicine
University of Wisconsin

8th September, 1986.

TO WHOM IT MAY CONCERN

Dr. Len Bergantino has conducted workshops on Family Therapy and Existential Psychotherapy for us in Brisbane, Australia in 1984 and 1986.

We have had various individuals giving workshops for us each year since 1979. Some of the Leaders were Dr. Jim Simkin, Dr. Stella Resnick, Dr. Tom Munson and others.

We find Dr. Bergantino's calibre of work equal and even superior to some of the presenters. Dr. Bergantino's teaching and demonstrations of his therapeutic style are exceptional in the area of Family Therapy, Gestalt, Existential Psychotherapy and Ericksonian hypnosis via story telling.

Dr. Bergantino has a unique ability to transfer his teaching methods in a live and expressive manner that has proven to have lasting impact on his audience. He has our highest recommendation as a workshop leader.

FOR THE GESTALT INSTITUTE OF QLD. FACULTY

YARO STARAK
CO-ORDINATOR

166

The Centre for Experiential Learning

Director
rry Blicharski
M.A. Dip. B.P.M. M.A.P.s.s.

141 Be : Street,
Balmain.
N.S.W. 2041
Phone 818 6188

5th September 1986.

TO WHOM IT MAY CONCERN

Len Bergantino Ed.D, Ph.D., has recently conducted workshops at this Centre on Existential Family Therapy and Ericksonian Hypnotic Storytelling. He also conducted some workshops for the Gestalt Institute of Queensland during this visit to Australia. He also conducted a workshop with the students in the Gestalt Therapy Training Programme in Sydney.

I am happy to recommend Len Bergantino as an excellent workshop leader, trainer and psychotherapist. His work with our Gestalt trainees was of the highest order and his Gestalt work is enhanced by his breadth of training in Family Therapy, Ericksonian Hypnotherapy etc. His work was extremely well received both here and in Queensland.

I am a Psychotherapist, accredited Psychodrama Director and Gestalt Therapist and have trained with Erv and Miriam Polster, Jim Simkin, Jorge Rosner and have had workshop experience with a number of other Gestalt Therapists visiting Australia during the last ten years.

We will be inviting Len Bergantino to return to Australia and I recommend his work, both clinical and teaching, in any situation.

Barry Blicharski,
Director.

167

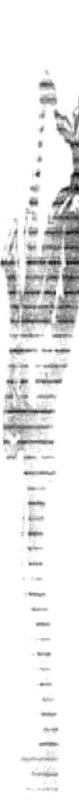

ALEXANDER'S
RAGTIME BAND
WITH
DR. LEN BERGANTINO

L.A.'S BEST MUSICIANS

FOR BOOKINGS CALL:
DR. LEN BERGANTINO (310-869-4110)

Letters to the Editor

On December 1, 2000, Screen Actors Guild and AFTRA members voted overwhelmingly to approve our Television & Radio Commercial Contract, thus officially ending our strike. Our members are now back to work in full force and our union are stronger than ever.

We know we could not have reached a fair agreement without the resounding support of our sister unions, the AFL-CIO, state and local labor federations, legislators, and the dedication of so many others. This combined effort made the advertising industry realize that our solidarity would not falter, and that we had your commitment, and that of your members and supporters.

On behalf of the 124,000 members of SAG and AFTRA, thank you for standing proudly with us through this difficult time. We applaud your commitment and look forward to working with you in the future.

Best regards,
William Daniels, National President, Screen Actors Guild
Shelby Scott, National President, AFTRA

"I've Always Been Dependent Upon the Kindness of Strangers"

The quote from Kenny "Snake" Stabler former quarterback – Oakland Raiders. Kenny Stabler was a roving vagabond with a gift for playing quarterback that brought him acclaim under Bear Bryant at Alabama and later The Oakland Raiders. He was a hitchhiking vagabond that always seems to wind up in the right place at the right time in the right situation. In many ways this time and lifestyle was similar to the plight of the musician of past eras. I remember my dad who was a sixty-year member of Waterbury, Connecticut and his fellow musicians. I went to many meetings as a youngster and I went on many gigs and heard the musicians talk of the gigs. I never recall anything but hearing of the kindness of those who hired the musicians in that each set they bought a round of drinks for the musicians and on many occasions they gave them dinner along with the gig. However, the round of drinks each set was just about an automatic.

After being in the Union for my fourth year here I notice this is no longer the custom of those who hire musicians. While this is no longer a letter about alcohol consumption, it is a letter about how the musician is treated. Is he or she treated as a first class citizen? Is the musician treated in a way that is evocative of the musician having the most fun and most enjoyment of the gig as possible? This is extremely important because when the musician is the happiest, having the most fun, enjoying himself or herself the most, the music is congruently the absolute best that musician has to offer to the employer.

Unfortunately many employers today do not realize this and they offer musicians the bare minimum of Union wages and do not think to offer drinks, dinner on occasion and/or perhaps paying for parking where that is required. This has happened on enough occasions for me to realize that one cannot demand generosity where it does not exist, and that the musician may want to consider an alternative to playing a job where the musician is less than emotionally satisfied.

Musicians may want to add a fee of $20 per man as an entertainment fee for the musicians, whereby a couple of drinks are purchased for the musician, or a bite to eat when hungry, or parking, or just a bonus the musician can do what he or she wishes with.

I do believe the day and age upon which "one is able to depend upon the kindness of strangers" is over, and the musician would do well to make explicit what they want, what they don't want, what they will do and what they won't do in Union contracts prior to the gig.

Dr. Len Bergantino, Local 47 Member

Danny Little, by David Schubach

Danny Little, a trumpeter often rehearsing at our Union Hall in the last few years, recently succumbed to liver cancer.

Danny began his professional career when he moved from West Virginia to New York City in 1934. Dan played in all the major venues including Roseland, El Morocco, Laura Lei, and the Copa Cabana. He was the featured trumpeter with several of the era's most renowned big bands including Gardner Benedict, Enoch Light, and Jack Teagarden.

In Los Angeles Danny freelanced with society and dixieland bands, and gave private lessons. In later years Danny was an avid tennis player. Even after his health started to fail, he was often heard practicing at the Union just to keep in shape.

I have often listened, fascinated, to Danny tell tales of the good old days. To the people who knew him he made these good old days even better. Danny will be missed.

Danny Little, by Dr. Len Bergantino

Knowing Danny Little was a transmission of the culture in that he gave me the feeling of how it was to play for and with Jack Teagarden, and through knowing him, I learned and developed my ability to play Dixieland Trumpet as well as banjo-mandolin. Danny was unselfish in his encouragement for me to take more and more solos on the trumpet as well as the mandolin banjo. He made a lifelong imprint and for that I am forever grateful, and I told him so before he died.

On June 12, 1999 we got hired for a book signing party by a 26 year old very attractive young lady. We played from 10:30 p.m. to midnight at what used to be a very large home in Santa Monica that was now rented out for such occasions. They hired a classical guitarist from 9 to 10:30. There were wooden floors, and the acoustics were such that the classical guitarist's notes were bouncing off the walls. We were going to play Dixieland. The crowd was primarily a younger crowd of between 25 and 35 years old, many of them looking like Timothy Leary did in the old days when he was tuning in, turning on and dropping out. I thought, we are going to bomb. Everything is working against us in this kind of environment.

We had Al Vescovo on tenor banjo, me on banjo-mandolin and Danny Little on trumpet. By the way, Danny's only problem was that he got old and he was not hired as much as he used to be, but make no mistake about it, he could blow his ever lovin' ass off on a gig and he did. He was 85 years old the night of the gig.

Danny called all the tunes. He played the first course and a Dixie improv course, then I would take one and Al Vescovo would take one. What happened shocked the hell out of all three of us, there was a standing ovation after every solo, and while Al and I certainly held our own and did our part, it was clear the audience wanted to love Danny Little! There was something about the way he played, the fire in it—not only was there a standing ovation after every number but the kids were dancing to Dixieland! This was Danny Little's last gig!

Labor CALENDAR

November

5 Labor leader and socialist Eugene V. Debs was born in Terre Haute, Ind. in 1855. "The strike is a weapon of the oppressed, of men capable of appreciating justice and having the courage to resist wrong and contend for principle," he said.

9 The Congress of Industrial Organizations (CIO) was formed in 1935 to expand industrial unionism. It merged with the American Federation of Labor (AFL) in 1955 to form the AFL-CIO.

11 Veterans Day. World War I ended on this day in 1918.

19 In 1903, the Women's Trade Union League was formed to educate women about the advantages of union membership, to support women's demands for better working conditions, and to raise awareness about the exploitation of women workers.

19 Industrial Workers of the World (IWW) labor organizer and balladeer Joe Hill was executed by a Salt Lake City, Utah firing squad in 1915. Hill was arrested and condemned to death for a murder, though supporters claim no clear evidence existed to convict him. The IWW and others rushed to defend Hill, believing he was unfairly prosecuted because of his labor background. Hill died a martyr and has been celebrated in song and legend... death, time in words day.

29 ...

30 ...

In ... war to ... the largest gathering in AFL-CIO history of union members and their families with community allies, the clergy, and elected officials, roughly 10,000 people packed the L.A. Convention Center on October 9 to participate in the Working Families Convocation. Speakers Miguel Contreras, John Sweeney, the Rev. Jesse Jackson, Tipper Gore, Governor Gray Davis, and Senator Diane Feinstein reflected on the celebration's themes— good jobs, strong communities and a voice for working families. A group of union musicians were hired through the Local 47 Musicians Network (see photos on pages 1 and 24).

500 Newly Organized Workers March into the Convention Hall

Miguel Contreras, the Executive Secretary-Treasurer of the Los Angeles County Federation of Labor and the honor of opening the 23rd Biennial AFL-CIO Convention on Monday, October 11. Welcoming the National Executive Board and Delegates, he told the L.A. Union story—highlighting our...

170

The Three Days I Met Buddy Collette

BY DR. LEN BERGANTINO, LOCAL 47 MEMBER

THE OFFICIAL PUBLICATION OF PROFESSIONAL MUSICIANS LOCAL 47, LOS ANGELES, AFM, AFL-CIO, CLC

APRIL 2002   NO. 1

Dear Serena,

I can't thank you and Overture enough for the article and photo of our dear Peggy Gilbert receiving The Lil Harden Armstrong Award. I also thank the person responsible for bringing it to you and Overture — "Kimberly M. Cord" who also included June Sapen.

Peg has been overlooked and I am thrilled that she has achieved the recognition she deserves as leader of the Dixie Belles and as a reed player I thank you again for making our friend and member of Local 47 aware of the prestigious award given our friend and member.

Most sincerely,

Nellie Lutcher, Local 47 Life Member

Dear Editor,

A contract is a contract, and when a recording artist signs one they must fulfill their obligations, or hire a lawyer to try to get out of it. Just because a musician doesn't have the "expressive power" or "desire to question" the contract is no reason to whine for the government to bail them out after the fact. Somebody often comes with a price.

I admit I was very amused by Don Henley using the "open marketplace" line. He should know that contracts are part of that marketplace. Signing them is optional.

**Gregory Smith, Local 47 Member
Former Recording Artist/Polygram Records**

continued on page 25

Len Bergantino
CD Falling in Love

Local 47 member Len Bergantino was born in Waterbury, Connecticut. At the age of five years his father Dan had him taking college lessons and at six mandolin lessons.

Len played for seniors and leisure ties in college at The University of Connecticut and finding the mandolin to be a very romantic instrument, he often played for the girl he was courting at the time.

Len received his doctorate from the University of Southern California and then entered private practice of clinical

psychology for 30 years, retiring in 1999.

In 1979 he saw Mischa Shenkyman play mandolin at the Bonaventure and he remembers being in awe of what Shenkyman could do with a mandolin. He asked Mischa if he could teach him a technique good for recording studios and Shenkyman taught him the method taught in the Russian conservatories.

About 1995 Len began playing mandolin professionally. He customarily uses guitar accompaniment for Italian mandolin music and romantic mandolin music. His usual accompanist is Dei Cacher, a guitar player formerly with The Three Sons, and whose ethnic background gives him a good feel for what Len wants to do with the Italian and American old standards.

On *Falling in Love* CD Len is accompanied by Joe Diorio, world renowned jazz guitarist, who on this CD is not playing jazz. The CD is a romantic compilation of Italian and American Old Standards. Some of the songs are Aluta, Anniversary Roma, New Domenticas, I'm in The Mood for Love, Come Back to Sorrento, Tre Veglia E Sorora and Love Theme From La Strada.

Falling in Love CD is available through Local 47.

The Mandolin Journal August 1, 1999 Vol XIII #3 p.173

"FALLING IN LOVE" WITH RIGHT-HAND TECHNIQUE

Who was recently asked to listen to, and offer his critique of, a 1998 mandolin CD, "Falling in Love," featuring Dr. Len Bergantino on mandolin, and Joe Diorio on guitar. After listening to the disc six times, Who did indeed fall in love with the right-hand technique of Bergantino. His playing on the CD is clean and clear. His tremolo is faultless, fast, accurate and expressive. As most of the selections were slow 4/4 numbers, Who at first wondered why Bergantino didn't use the tremolo more often, but the more Who listened, the better Bergantino sounded. Who gradually discerned a slight left-hand vibrato on the mandolin (Does Len perchance play the violin or trumpet? Or zither?) and an exaggerated vibrato on the electric guitar of Diorio. However, the combination of the instruments' sounds makes for an enjoyable product.

The music on the CD is slow and dreamy, and very listenable. Three of the 22 numbers are mandolin solos: "St Mary's Waltz," the mazurka "Tra Veglia e Sonno," and "Spanish Eyes." The latter number, beautifully played as a beguine, certainly reminded Who of Rose Nemoto's* showing off her pyrotechnics at La Bella Roma in Dale City VA ten years ago.

Perhaps the best feature of the CD is the selection of the music - all "Schlagers"** - half of them Italian standards, and the other half American. It begins with Mona, Arrivederci Roma, and Non Dimenticar, and winds up with Kiss Me Again. Who noticed that in choosing numbers Bergantino selected several songs which made effective use of a solo mandolin pickup (introductions) of six or seven eighth notes followed on the down beat by a tremoloed whole and quarter note tied, giving the guitarist an opportunity to do his thing, which jazzman Diorio has reduced to a science. (Who would like very much to hear Ellington's *Don't Get Around Much Anymore* and Green's *What a Difference a Day Made* performed by these two artists using this same technique.)

A CD entitled "Falling in Love" does not, per se, call for "cut time" or "pop tunes" but the talents of this pair of performers make Who wonder if a tarantella or polka might not have been included along with the mazurka and the beguine (both of which are "toe-tappers)." We hope their next opus will include more dance numbers, plus a few doublestops, and as our bluegrass brethren say, more "playin' down the neck!"

* *The reference to Rose Nemoto is not a misspelling; the Italian gentleman who owned La Bella Roma asked Rose to spell it that way. I kidded her about it but she and her staff I substituted for them occasionally made that restaurant thousands of dollars. I have a shirt full showing that spelling.*

** *"Schlager" is a German slang word meaning No. 1 on the hit parade; top of the charts; etc. - a "monster hit."*

by Russell Who

INVITATION TO AN INTERNATIONAL COMPETITION OF PLUCKED STRING ORCHESTRAS

Ladies and Gentlemen, dear fellow musicians

On occasion of the 75th anniversary of our orchestra we will organize another **International Mandolin Competition on June 3rd & 4th, 2000.** We wish to invite your orchestra to participate in this contest.

The enthusiastic participation and the positive feedback we received from many contestants after our two previous International Mandolin Competitions makes us hope for positive replies from orchestras from a number of different countries again. We will do our best to let you have a pleasant stay in the Taunus area, not far from Frankfurt am Main.

The competition will be presented at a local hall. An international jury consisting of three renowned specialists for plucked string orchestra music will assure adequate judgement of the pieces played.

Since organizing such a competition requires careful preparation, may we ask you to complete and return to us the enclosed questionnaire. Should your orchestra not be able to participate, we would appreciate a short reply nonetheless. In case of a positive response we will send you the conditions of the competition.

We look forward to your positive reply and would be pleased to have your orchestra with us in Falkenstein next year in June.

Yours sincerely, Hans Klee
Mandolinenclub Falkenstein e.V.

Please answer these questions in your reply:

1. We will / will not participate in the international competition of plucked string orchestras in Falkenstein/Taunus on June 3rd & 4th, 2000.
2. Our orchestra consists of _____ players
3. We need to spend the night ❑ Yes ❑ No
4. If yes, the approximate number of persons is _____
5. Expected dates of   Arrival _____   Departure _____
6. Name of Orchestra _____

Return to:
Mandolinea Club e.V., Falkenstein im Taunus, Wiesbadener Str. 11, D 61462 Königstein • Phone: (06174) 78 90 • email: mandolinen-club e.v., wiesbadener str. 11 61462 königstein

Mandolins Galore and More

The Bloomfield Federation of Music and the Bloomfield **Mandolin Orchestra,** Gabriel L. Novola, Director presented its 5th Spring Concert on May 2, 1999 "Mandolins Galore and More". Barry Mitterhoff, mandolinist and Peter Stan, accordionist were special guest artists.

their 57th

Spring Concert

RadioGold

FM 88.800 MHz

via Melgora 10 - 15048 Valenza (al)
Tel   +39 0131 941117
Fax   +39 0131 953025
Web   http://www.radiogold.it
e-mail radiogold@radiogold.it

p. 149

ARTISTA	CD	TRACCIA	DATA
EMANUIL SHENKMAN	LIN EB	NN 3-4	1A-II-01
LEN BERGANTINO	FALLING	N 3	28-II-01
EMANUIL SHENKMAN	LIN EB	N 1	5-IV-01
EMANUIL SHENKMAN	LIN EB	N 6	6-IV-01
LEN BERGANTINO	FALLING	N 6	11-VI-01
EMANUIL SHENKMAN	LIN EB	N 1	1V-VI-01
LEN BERGANTINO	FALLING	N 10	13-IV-01
LEN BERGANTINO	FALLING	N 6	1A-VI-01
EMANUIL SHENKMAN	LIN EB	NN 3-4	2A-VI-01
LEN BERGANTINO	FALLING	N 1	9-I-02
EMANUIL SHENKMAN	LIN EB	NN 1-2	9-I-02
EMANUIL SHENKMAN	LIN EB	N 4	13-I-02
EMANUIL SHENKMAN	LIN EB	NN 6-7	16-I-02
LEN BERGANTINO	FALLING	N 1	30-I-02
EMANUIL SHENKMAN	LIN EB	N 5	31-I-02
EMANUIL SHENKMAN	LIN EB	N 8	5-II-02
LEN BERGANTINO	FALLING	N 11	6-II-02
LAN BERGANTINO	TENOR BANJO	N 3	13-V-02
LAN BERGANTINO	TENOR BANJO	N 4	19-V-02
LAN BERGANTINO	TENOR BANJO	N 1	20-V-02
EMANUIL SHENKMAN	LIN EB	N 5	1L-I-02

174

Howard Alden

November 10, 2003

Dear Dr. Bergantino,

This is a very late thank you for sending me your CD, with Joe Diorio and yourself. Beautiful tone and articulation, and great accompaniment from Joe–very enjoyable. Have a good holiday season, and I hope to see you next time I'm in LA.

All the best,

Howard

Howard Alden

EDITOR'S NOTE:
MANDOLIN STORIES FOR CHILDREN

At last! We have responses to appeals for mandolin stories for children. One called "Larry the Luthier and The Bucking Fingerboard" was sent in by **Tyrus Reiman**. **Bernard Zinar** has agreed to illustrate it. On the same day I heard from **Dee Darlington**, a published author, who said she had already outlined a story. Another member expressed interest, as well.

This rush of responses made me think that a book containing several stories might have broader appeal. I even resurrected "Belinda", the bowlback mandolin that wound up on Broadway and, or course, as Bernard Zinar suggested, Larry the Luthier could become a series of stories

When I spoke to Norman Levine about the project he was delighted. The presses are ready any time we are. We still need stories and people who are willing to illustrate them. Stick figures can be very effective, you know.

Thank you contributors for a great beginning to a worthwhile project! If you are interested in brainstorming a story at the convention, let me know. Call - 516-271-9518.

ELMER:

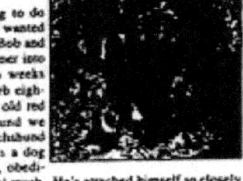

This has nothing to do with mandolins, but I wanted to share it with you. Bob and I welcomed a newcomer into our home about two weeks ago. - Elmer, a superb eighteen pound 2-3 year old red long haired dachshund we adopted through Dachshund Rescue. Now, this is a dog who is housebroken, obedience trained and a real mush. He's attached himself so closely to us, we could easily have named him "Velcro". It's less than two weeks and he already has adapted to the rest of our menagerie (a minidachs, a toy poodle, two very old cats and a bird). They hang out with each other as if they've been buddies for years. Chloe, our minidachs, is particularly smitten.

As close as anyone can figure Elmer (original name unknown) had been stolen to sell for drug money and later confiscated by police when they raided a crack house. The police then brought him to a veterinarian who contacted Rescue. They contact prospective adoptive owners and carefully screen them to be sure that a good match is made. The sole purpose of the organization is to see that foundling dachshunds wind up in a happy household rather than a pound.

I only recently learned that there are breed rescue organizations all over the United States, and was astounded to hear that

in our area alone more than one hundred dachshunds are rescued a year, and that's just one breed. So if you are of a mind to open your homes to a dog, or even if you aren't, I urge you to do so. You won't be sorry.

Continued on page 11

THE CURE OF THE PARAPLEGIC RIGHT HAND FOR MANDOLIN PLAYERS
written by Dr. Len Bergantino

I was a clinical psychologist with a very busy practice and hadn't devoted much time to music or playing the mandolin in years. It was 1979 and I happened to be passing through the Bonaventure Hotel when I heard Emanuil Shenkman playing the mandolin. I heard Dave Appollon on records, but Shenkman was the only one of that calibre I ever heard in person. He did stuff on that mandolin I couldn't even begin to describe. I found myself asking him if he gave lessons, and if he could teach me to play with a technique for recording studios. He said yes, and we began. In retrospect, the amazing part to me was that I had asked him to teach me something I had no idea I would ever use, but in December, 1997 Joe Diorio, world renowned jazz guitarist and I completed a CD of romantic Italian and old American Standards entitled "Falling In Love".*

Mischa (as he was called) began by taking away my mandolin and my pick. With my left hand he made me hold a book to my lower chest and the top of my abdomen. Then he made a paper pick folded in a variety of ways that somewhat resembled the pick he had brought from Russia where he had been a soloist for the Leningrad Symphony. He later played in the United States at Carnegie Hall.

For three months my lessons consisted solely of loosening of the right wrist while simulating picking movements as if the book I was holding was the mandolin. My right hand became looser and looser and more and more flexible in the right wrist. Then, at the end of three months I got my mandolin and pick back.

There were no books to study in the following two years that I took weekly lessons from Mischa. He wrote about 8 half pages totaling four full pages of music in two years. His method was so different from the new lesson each week procedure that had been my experience, typical of music lessons in America. But Mischa did not appear to be interested in moving on, only in the detail and the precision in which I was to develop the right hand and consequently the kinds of pickings and eventual speed with which I developed the left hand. So I played four pages of music over two years and it was taking me two hours a day of practice which was going to increase. With the practice of clinical psychology as full as it was I became exasperated and told Mischa I was going to quit. He said to me, "Take it easy, but take it!" I felt total relief and broke out laughing when he said this.

In retrospect I was very fortunate to be exposed to the way the Russian Conservatories trained musicians. There was a dedication to detail and repetition that I had never seen before. I find that while I need to do some practice on the positions for the left hand, the right hand always comes back to the same level of proficiency with what Mischa taught me even if I never practice. I pick it up and there it is! Without what he taught me a mandolin has difficulty being expressed as full and as rich an instrument as it is, without feeling pinched, cramped, or sometimes a little tinny. At least that is how it seems to me with the mandolins I have heard over the past twenty years. Thus, although the reader will not have Mischa's personal guidance, it may be worth experimenting with the paper pick if you think your right hand needs work.

The CD, "Falling In Love", with the Italian Mandolin of Dr. Len Bergantino accompanied by world renowned guitarist, Joe Diorio, is available, write to: Dr. Len Bergantino, 1215 Brockton Avenue # 104, Los Angeles, CA 90025 Send $15 or call (310)-207-9397

Len Bergantino - Falling In Love

Len Bergantino & Joe Diorio – Falling In Love and Dan
Bergantino and the Mandolin

by Terry Pender

These two recordings come from the collection
of Len Bergantino, a clinical psychologist and mandolin
player from Los Angeles, California. Len's father, Dan
Bergantino, was a well-known mandolin player, born in
Waterbury, CT in 1906. He made his living as a
professional mandolin player and also worked as a
violinist with the Waterbury Symphony. He was one of
those unsung players – a huge talent in the Waterbury/
New Haven, CT area, but one that never went out on
the road or recorded and, subsequently, is not very well
known today.

Len remembers his father's great musicianship
and his ability to blend fast single note playing with
agile chordal work. As Len says, "He had fire in his
hands!" Dan Bergantino was the son of immigrants
who came through Ellis Island from San Marco La
Catola, Italy. As a young man, Dan helped support his
large family through his music when times were tough.
Along with his uncle and brothers, there was quite a bit
of music in the Bergantino household. It was Dan's
uncle, Soledad Bredice, who taught him the mandolin.
Soledad also taught his own sons, Fred and Louie
Bredice, who were well known guitarists in the
Connecticut area. The Bredice brothers turned out to
be Joe Diorio's teachers and that's where the
connection between Len and Joe was established. Joe
Diorio is considered to be one of the world's greatest
guitar players. He's an expert in mainstream jazz
performance and in free-form jazz improvisation.

Dan Bergantino taught his young son Len
solfeggio when he was five and began to teach him the
mandolin at age six using the Christoforo books. Dan
made his living primarily with the guitar, violin and
tenor banjo, but mandolin was his first love. He played
all the old Italian music whenever he picked up his
mandolin – songs that were played at Italian weddings
that no one had ever written down. In the summer of
1979, Len had his father write out some of those old
tunes. Len also has a cassette tape available of his
father playing exclusively Italian music. It is a solo
medley of Italian songs that includes all the classics and
more. This 15-minute demonstration of solo Italian
music on a cheap borrowed mandolin played near the
end of his life shows that Dan could really play. His
musicality and precision are evident, as well as his
marvelous skill at arranging Italian classics. Len is
offering to duplicate this cassette for anyone interested
for $10, including tax and postage. Although quite
short, it is a wonderful document, and I recommend it
to fans of Italian mandolin.

Dan Bergantino

After receiving training from his father, Len
Bergantino pursued a career as a clinical psychologist.
But one evening at the Bonaventure Hotel, Len heard
the Russian mandolin virtuoso Emanuil Sheynkman
and began a period of study with him. Len's goal was to
learn as much as he could so that he could record his
own mandolin CD. During this process, Len became
good friends with "Mischa" Sheynkman and, after his
death, had one of Sheynkman's out-of-print Russian
recordings re-mastered for CD. This recording, Emanuil
Sheynkman: The Paganini of the Mandolin, is available on
CD from Len for $15.00. This is a great CD that I
highly recommend. Norman Levine reviewed it when
it was first released in a past issue of MQ.

Finally, after his studies with Sheynkman, Len
did record his own mandolin CD called Falling In Love.
This recording brings us full circle, with Len playing the
beautiful Italian melodies he had heard during his
childhood – and with his family friend, Joe Diorio, on
guitar. Their friendship is a wonderful coincidence
because Joe Diorio is a consummate musician, and he
provides everything that Bergantino could ask for,
playing a beautiful accompaniment on jazz guitar as Len
plays the melodies on his 1913 Gibson F-2. Falling In
Love is just what you might expect – a very mellow,
relaxed reading of Italian and jazz standards played with

a lot of love and feeling. Together, Diorio and Bergantino play through tunes like "Arrivederci Rome," "Come Prima," "Come Back To Sorrento," "Misty," "Tre Veglia e Sonno" and "Speak Softly Love."

These self-produced recordings and tapes present a unique glimpse of the mandolin world from the point of view of someone who grew up during the heyday of the Italian/American mandolin popularity, and they provide us with some interesting recordings of music that is not generally available elsewhere.

Len Bergantino's *Falling In Love* is also $15.00, and all of the recordings can be obtained by writing to Len at:

Len Bergantino
1215 Brockton Avenue
Suite 104
Los Angeles, CA 90025.

Radim Zenkl – Restless Joy

Restless Joy - Radim Zenkl
Ventana 3401.

by Terry Pender

Restless Joy is the fifth and latest recording by mandolinist Radim Zenkl. His first outing on CD since 1996's *Strings and Wings*, this recording finds Radim in a contemplative mood playing quite a bit of Celtic-influenced music on his nylon stringed mandolin and bouzouki. Radim, a new member of the Modern Mandolin Quartet, is well known for his experimental bent. His earlier recording, *Galactic Mandolin*, featured a series of compositions, each using a different tuning system. Radim is also known for his great speed and dexterity. Although this CD is more focused and traditional in some aspects, it still has the edge supplied by Radim's rhythmic energy and command of the mandolin. Overall, I'd have to say that this recording struck me as Radim's most introspective CD to date. There are a lot of quiet, beautiful moments on this recording. The energy level and experimental demeanor are still there, but there are several moments that are simply quiet and thoughtful, and a melodic lushness radiates from many of the tunes on this collection.

The 13 pieces range from poignant Irish-influenced melodies to the rhythmically charged "Revival," where Radim reaches into the Sam Bush playbook for some powerful, drum-like mandolin rhythms. "Ventana Breeze" is just that – a cool breeze floating by on the mandolin with a smooth tremolo and an irresistible melody. "Once Upon A Time" features Radim playing his Irish bouzouki fingerstyle. This

smooth, mellow fingerstyle technique is quite attractive, and it works well both on the melody and for accompanying the pennywhistle in this duet. "Twin Peaks" is a fast-paced mandolin fiddle tune with the same twisting and turning phrases that Chris Thile likes to play. "At The End Of Summer" is Radim's gorgeous slide mandolin showpiece. When Sam Bush plays the slide mandolin, it's almost always in a blues or rock vein, influenced by blues slide guitar. Radim takes the idea and smoothes it out by writing a lush melody in a major key and using a very supple and warm tone that ends up sounding nothing like Sam Bush.

Originally from Czechoslovakia, Radim's music encompasses eastern European folk music. It's classical mandolin with American bluegrass, jazz and folk all mixed in. And the new emphasis on Celtic music fits right in with Radim's interest in world music. This is an interesting, original perspective on mandolin music. I can't wait to hear how Radim and the Modern Mandolin Quartet sound together. The journey continues for one of our more adventurous and ambitious mandolin players.

Captain Corelli's Mandolin The Original Motion Picture Soundtrack

Captain Corelli's Mandolin - The Original Motion Picture Soundtrack with music composed by Steven Warbick, Decca Records.

by Terry Pender

This is not really a mandolin CD. Rather, it's a CD of music from the movie that often uses the

MY FATHER, DAN BERGANTINO, AND THE MANDOLIN:
MELODY, CHORDS, SPEED, CLEAN, AND HE HAD FIRE IN HIS HANDS

My father was born in 1906 in Waterbury, Connecticut where he was a professional musician from the time he was fourteen until he was 75 when he moved to California to be with me the last two years of his life. He played two to four nights a week, and he had "fire in his hands". Whenever I saw him play, on whatever instrument I saw him play (mandolin, guitar, tenor banjo or violin) he had incredible speed and cleanliness of technique and played with such an inner fire that he lit up an entire audience and/or band that he was playing with. He customarily played in night clubs or restaurants with small combos, but played violin in the Waterbury Symphony.

My father was one of those unsung heroes. He was one of the most talented musicians in the Waterbury and New Haven Connecticut areas, where he customarily played, but never went on the road and never became famous. Yet some of the things he could do well and his sense of musicality, one would only hear in those who were world renown. He knew how to blend blazing speed, single string technique with chords at the same time with a sense of musicality and with fire in his hands and the music.

My father's parents came through Ellis Island from Italy. San Marco La Catola, Province of Foggia around the turn of the century. His father, Leonardo, was a stone mason. There were several layoffs and my father supported the family (seven brothers and sisters) lived out of sisters through music.

In a sense music was the family business. My father's uncle taught him solfeggio (reading music - do, re, mi, fa, sol, la, si, do) for a year and then gave him a few years of mandolin lessons. He then had violin lessons for six months and was self taught in terms of tenor banjo and guitar. He was one of those was a natural. That is what he was born to do.

His uncle, Soledad Bredice, who taught him mandolin, and had two sons - Fred Bredice was one of the first single string soloists with blazing speed - and a legend around the Connecticut area. He did it in the early thirties, radio show and all. His brother Inique Bredice was tenth in the country in Downbeat Magazine Poll for piano one year. He told me when he first started playing jazz, he played a lot of notes, then he realized all he needed were the right ones. Soledad had a brother Charlie Bredice whose son was Vinnie Bredice, a well schooled classical and jazz guitar player (Hartt School of Music in Hartford Connecticut). Vinnie wrote a few jazz guitar books for Mel Bay Publications. Fred and Vinnie Bredice were Joe Dorns's teachers (Joe is a world renowned jazz guitarist who accompanied me on the CD "Falling In Love"). It's all in the family. All of this began with the mandolin and with Soledad Bredice teaching his sons and nephews the mandolin as the first instrument from which they had a "foundation" in music and could move in any direction they wished from there.

When I was five years old my father stuck me in a room with a solfeggio book and gave me the one half hour lesson per week on reading music. He said by the time you get an instrument you will only have to concern yourself with learning to play it. You will already know how to read music.

At six years old he took me to the violin repair man, Louis Volpe, who had a Gibson F-2 mandolin that was gorgeous. He sold it to my father for $55. I remember Louis Volpe had a big Saint Bernard who leaped up that day and licked me in the face knocking me on my rear. To this day for some strange reason I always liked Saint Bernards and I have never had any fear of them.

My father always emphasized the looseness of the wrist in the right hand saying that if the right hand worked all else would fall into place.

He took me through DeCristoforo Method Books One and Two. I remember there were a lot of nice duets for first and second mandolin in those books.

While my Dad made his living primarily with the guitar, violin and tenor banjo, mandolin was a first love for him and he always felt it was the basic instrument that string players should begin with at the very least. When he played it he remembered all the old Italian music that you hear at weddings, but was never written down anywhere. One of the one's he did not write down was "The Poet and Peasant Overture". If anyone reading this article has a written arrangement of it I would be most grateful to purchase it from them.

In the summer of 1979 when my father was staying at my home in Los Angeles for a few weeks of summer vacation he wrote out several numbers he thought would keep the heritage alive. One selection "Elvira" follows this article.

Also, there was one audio tape on which he played mandolin exclusively for about fifteen minutes that demonstrates his talent: MUSICALITY, SPEED, CLEANLINESS WITH SPEED, SINGLE STRING SOLOS MIXED WITH CHORDS IMPROVISATION, AND FIRE IN HIS HANDS.

If you wish to purchase a copy of this tape send $10.

Dr. Len Bergantino
1235 Brockton Avenue #104
Los Angeles, CA 90025

JIRO NAKANO

Jiro Nakano, a well known researcher and composer for mandolin music passed away at the age of 96 on June 10, 2000 from heart failure. He was born on April 30th so birth certificate says, but actual birth date is April 4, 1902. After graduated from the High School of Technology majoring designing, he started to study solo mandolin and guitar playing by himself. In his younger years, he was active as a soloist of mandolin and guitar. Besides playing, he composed more than 100 pieces of music for the mandolin orchestra, mandolin solo and guitar solo. He also wrote many nursery rhymes and when talking about these compositions, he said "Although this is very different to plectrum music, when talking about myself, I have to make mention of these children's songs (otherwise half of my work is lost)." In 1946 and 1999, at the age of 94 and 97 respectively, he conducted a mandolin orchestra to record several romantic mandolin music and publish two CDs titled 'Profumo Romantico di Mandolino'. The music scores of those music in the CD were handwritten by Nakano himself and published together with the CD.

Below listed are popular numbers out of many and varied Nakano's compositions.

Mandolin solo	Tre Studi - Sol maggiore, Re maggiore, Re minore
	Haru-ga-Kita con variazioni
	Tema 'Ryosho' e variazioni
	2a Fantasia
Mandolin Orchestra	La Iglesia sobre la Colina (Chapel on the Hill)
	Una Notte di Villaggio Pescatori (One Night in a Fishing village)
	Hamabe no Uta (Song on a seashore)
	Foggia di Maggio (Melancholy on a rainy day in May)
	Juego de Peloota (Playing with a Ball)

179

181

A Musical Journey to Russia and Italy
- Mildred Sokol

On Sunday, October 25 I attended a concert at St. Peter's Church in Manhattan. The performers included a lively professional group named the "Russian Carnival Ensemble". Their performance included varied folk instruments (domras, balalaikas and bayon - a button type accordion)

What is important about this performance is that the group included members of one of the newest and most promising plucked string ensembles: The Mandolin Quartet "Rondo", organized by the ever dynamic and talented prima donna and mandolinist, **Tamara Volskaya**, and her partner in life as well as in music, the creative arranger and bayonist, **Anatoly Trofimov**.

The quartet consists of **Tamara Volskaya** and **Mayya Kalikhman**, mandolin; **Victoria Chernokhlebova**, mandola; and **Natalya Vsevolodskaya**, guitar.

The first half of the program included a wide range of compositions from baroque to contemporary, starting with the full Carnival Ensemble's rendition of Alfred Schnitke's, *"Minuet and Fugue"*, followed by duets, trios and quartet. Each selection highlighted the musicianship and skill of the individual performer. Included also were pieces by Cangiello, **Roeser**, **Calace and Pender** (a member of CMSA who wrote *"A Letter to Gorbachev"*). The program included two duos for domra and bayon, *"Neapolitan Dance"* by Tchaikovsky and a brilliant *"Carnival of Venice"* by Paganini. This last was accompanied by the full Russian Carnival Ensemble

The threads of Tamara's silver stringed presence woven throughout every segment of the program enhanced the carefully and colorfully blended tapestry that made the program a joy to the ear.

Singers, **Irina Zagurnova** and the basso, **Anatoly Panchasenky** provided toetapping folk songs for the second half of the program.

All in all I had no idea of what a musical surprise was in store for me that day. I suspect there will be more such programs in the future.

Note: Thank you's to Toni Negrelli for "volunteering me to write this article" and to Terry Pender for his "Letter" and for letting me hear the beautiful hauntingly reflective and delicate sounds from the CD "Mandolin 84 (PSDoo06).

From Italy In Their Only Area Appearance
Submitted by Mildred Sokol

Beppe Gambetta, guitar, with Carlo Aonzo, mandolin, performed music from the turn-of-the-century Italy on March 13 at the First Reformed Church, New Brunswick, New Jersey.

This internationally renowned duo brought to life turn of the century virtuosos in this historical glimpse in the fascinating folk and classical genres of the time, boleros, mazurkas, serenades, tangos, czardas and more.

The performance was presented by the Mine Street Coffeehouse, a not-for profit, volunteer concert series. This concert was the annual fund raiser to help defray operational costs for the Saturday night series. Information: 732-249-7873

More About Mischa Sheynkman -
Len Bergantino's "Man of the Century"
- Edited for space considerations

. . . Mischa was an "all star" of the Soviet music world, known to many as the "Paganini of the Mandolin", but to the rest of the world before emigrating to the United States he remained unknown. When asked in 1979 "Why did you come to the United States when you had everything you wanted musically in the Soviet Union?", he replied that the Soviet Union had a policy that would deprive his children of anything more than a high school education because they were Jewish. He wanted to give his children the best life they could have so he emigrated to the United States even though he knew his chances of great success as a musician here were slim.

Some twenty years later, Mischa is dead and I know that one of his sons graduated from MIT. He gave his life and his celebrated musical career for his sons. Yet, he did achieve a measure of success and has left a deep impression on those whom he managed to reach. He did, after all, play at Carnegie Hall and tour the United States. He also became a teacher. But he was never able to connect with the caliber of players of the kind of music he played, on a scale wide enough for him to take his rightful place with greats like Dave Appollon and David Grisman.

To that end I have had three of his LP recordings professionally taped. These recordings are no longer available anywhere in the world. For details about purchasing copies of these tapes, please contact me at (308) 207-9397 or write to me at 1215 Brockton Avenue, Suite 104, Los Angeles, CA 90025

13

Mischa Sheynkman:
The Soviet Paganini of the Mandolin
by Len Bergantino

p. 204

After sending a cd of Emanuil "Mischa" Sheynkman to the *Mandolin Journal* editor, I asked if she would be interested in an article about Mischa to which she happily agreed. The cd features Sheynkman playing mandolin with his peers – those who graduated from Russian conservatories with a major in Russian folk music. He was never able to find those kinds of peers when he defected to the United States in 1972. The Soviet government destroyed all of the masters of his work but I made a copy from a recording that he gave me when he was my teacher from 1979 – 1981.

While this is an article about Sheynkman, in that I am claiming from all that I know he was the best that ever lived (and fellow mandolinist Bill Bloom backs me up on it) I must say a little about both of us in that you will know that such praise does not come lightly.

Bill Bloom is about 83 years old and I am 67. I am not even sure where I met him and how we have been friends for twenty years. Bill is an eccentric who loves mandolin, he is a Russian Jew born in the United States with a deep appreciation of Russian mandolin and domra music. Sheynkman defected to New York in 1977 and Bill Bloom worked for two years to transplant Sheynkman and his family to Los Angeles. Sheynkman, along with his wife and two children, lived with Bill and Letha Bloom for about six months before they got an apartment in the San Fernando Valley, which is where I took lessons from him.

In 1966, a professional mandolin player in Waterbury, Connecticut — Ray Amicone, who had a handmade D'Angelico mandolin let me borrow a record of the legendary mandolinist Dave Apollon, whose arrangement of "Smoke Gets in Your Eyes" was written out for me by my father, Daniel Bergantino, who had fire in his hands and brought every stage to life I ever saw him play on, and which version I played on my own CD "Falling In Love" which I made with jazz guitarist Joe Diorio. Until I met Sheynkman, Dave Apollon was the best I had ever heard play the mandolin in my lifetime.

I met Sheynkman in 1979 when I heard him play at the Bonaventure Hotel in Los Angeles. He and his group wore red tunics and he had a lot of black hair bobbing and weaving all over the place as he played with a technique where his speed was blinding. His fingers never left the fingerboard, and his sense of musicality touched my soul many times during the engagement. I had sold my mandolin and my trumpet and was not playing music at the time, and yet, all I could think was "I want to take lessons from this guy! This is the chance of a lifetime!" My parents were visiting me so I brought my father to hear him the following week. He too thought Sheynkman was beyond human belief. In other words, keep in mind that no matter how good I attempt to show you a picture of his ability, I can never give you the full extent of it any more than I can bring Paganini himself back to life (I have read two volumes of his life and work).

So that night I went up to Sheynkman during a break and said, "Sir, do you teach? I want to take mandolin lessons from you." He said, "Yes." I said "How much do you charge?" He said "$20 a lesson." I said, blurting it out for no conscious reason, "Can you teach me a technique I can use in a recording studio?" He said "yes." And we were off and running. I was studying with the Paganini of the mandolin from the Soviet Union for $20 a lesson. I went out and bought a 1913 Gibson F-2 round hole mellow sounding mandolin. I told Sheynkman that my mandolin was better than his. He said that was true but in the Soviet Union he only paid five dollars for his

I brought a mandolin book for him to use when he taught me. He made a paper pick and had me work on the right hand wrist flexibility until it was so automatic I could do it in my sleep. When I had the right hand at a level acceptable to him, he said to bring the mandolin, but he gave me a Soviet made pick different than any pick I had ever seen and insisted I use that pick. He began to write out each lesson, and each week he would add a few lines that built on the week before. He used to play for me during the lessons and he was inspirational in this way.

The way he was in the world took the torture out of studying to be the best you could. One time I said, "Mischa, you are killing me! You are killing me!" I was on the verge of quitting in total exasperation and frustration. He put

(continued on page 25)

Mischa Sheynkman:
The Soviet Pagan... ...d of the Mandolin

(continued from page 24)

his arm on my shoulder with a gentle grin and said "Len, take it easy, but take it!"

Los Angeles wasn't exactly a Mecca for mandolin players. In fact I had not run into one between 1968 and the time I Sheynkman in 1979. I asked him what made him so sure he would make it playing mandolin in a town where no one knew what a mandolin looked like. A situation was later described to me where a certain top session guitarist who actually played mandolin on one of the Tijuana Brass early records, used to hire Mischa to play first in the studios while he took the credit for the fancy mandolin playing and Sheynkman told him he was primarily interested in supporting his family and any way this guitarist wanted to do it he was more than grateful.

I am certain that if I looked around I still have the original copies of what he wrote out for lessons each week. In the United States we are used to buying method books. In the Soviet Union they had no money for such books, so the teacher would write out the lesson with the specific objectives more pinpointed.

I forget his exact words but the idea and the feeling was something like this. When he was six years old his teachers in elementary school knew he was gifted and the Soviet government said to his parents, "Your kid is going to be a musician and he is going to graduate from a Russian Conservatory!" And that is all Mischa ever did his entire life! There is certainly something to be said for the pursuit of excellence in classical music as one might say "the proof is in the pudding." There is almost no way I can describe the refinement of technique to which I refer. It is perfection beyond my capacity to discriminate. My father always mentioned that Paganini never wrote down

any of his methods for future violin players to study. Maybe there was no way to write them down?

About the recordings of Mischa Sheynkman:

During the time that I was his student, he gave me two 33 long play rpm records that he made in the Soviet Union. I was able to make one cd from the two records –this is the only recording where you can hear Sheynkman play with those who were trained in the Soviet conservatory system.

Sheynkman died in the mid to late 1990's when he was in his late fifties. He was a soloist for the Leningrad Symphony and he had his own radio show featuring his mandolin playing in the Soviet Union. When he defected to the United States in 1977 the Soviet Government destroyed all the masters of his musical performances that earned him the reputation of "the Paganini of the Mandolin" in the Soviet Union. To my knowledge what I put together on this cd is the only opportunity those in the United States will ever get to hear Sheynkman play the music he was trained in, Russian folk music, with those who were trained in it with him at the Russian conservatories.

A limited edition was made and copies can be purchased for $20 a cd which includes postage and the cd. Orders can be sent to Dr. Len Bergantino and the check made out to Dr. Len Bergantino at 1215 Brockton Avenue, #104, Los Angeles, CA 90025-1366.

Dr. Len Bergantino is a clinical psychologist and musician who plays mandolin, trumpet, and tenor banjo.

-News about Keith Harris-

Every four years, the Federal Association of German Orchestral Organizations holds a competition for the best of the numerous amateur orchestras in the country.

On Saturday, November 6th, 2010, 38 selective orchestras with 1,700 players met for the competition in the beautiful city of Bamberg.

In the section plucked strings, two equal first places were awarded this time, each with 95 out of 100 points. A sensation was that for the first time, an orchestra of

zithers astounded with the quality of their music and skill.

The two winners were (for the first time) the State Zither Orchestra of Baden-Wuerttemberg – conducted by the Australian Keith Harris – and the State Plucked String Orchestra of Baden-Wuerttemberg, which Harris had also conducted for two years over a decade ago.

The winner in the section four years ago was the Hessian State Plucked String Orchestra, which Harris had directed for 12 years (1986-1998), with numerous recordings and many concert tours, including those to Australia, America

DEADLINE FOR SUBMISSIONS TO THE FEBRUARY JOURNAL IS JANUARY 15th
PLEASE SEND SUBMISSIONS TO: CMSAjournal@gmail.com

25

Danny Bergantino - My Dad

by Dr. Len Bergantino

Dan Bergantino, my dad, was born in Waterbury, Connecticut in 1906. He came of age with the tenor banjo in the mid to late 1920s. You know, there are some people who are just born to play an instrument and they can do no wrong on it - Benny Goodman with a clarinet...Harry James with a trumpet. Well, my old man was like that with a tenor banjo.

If a tenor banjo player is judged on speed, cleanliness and musicianship, my dad may not have been as good as Harry Reser. But, he was the best that most people who came across him had ever heard. In his day, he used to cut the Harry Reser solos clean as a whistle as the tenor banjo player in Harry Brinkman's band in the Connecticut area.

My introduction to my dad's tenor banjo playing came in 1954 when I was 11 years old. Even though it was winter, I decided to crawl through the trap-door that led to our unheated attic. There I saw this instrument with broken strings and what looked to me like a broken drum head. I dragged it down

stairs and said, "Daddy, what's this?" He said, "It's a tenor banjo - but nobody uses it anymore." When I persisted and asked "Why?", dad said, "I used to play it all the time - then radio came in. First I was on the bandstand with the band and they said I was too loud. Then they had me play near the door while the band was on the stage and they still said it was too loud. Finally they moved me outside the door and said, 'Danny, if you want to play with this band, you'd better learn to play the guitar." So, he did!

As a result, my dad's tenor banjo was relegated to the attic where it remained until I dragged it back into his life. I don't know what it was, but I loved the banjo at first sight and pleaded with my dad to get it fixed. While he hadn't played the banjo in years, his hand were in pretty good shape as he had worked regularly on guitar and violin. When he picked up the banjo and rattled off *Lollipops, Nola and The Cat and the Dog*, I just sat there in awe. He had gotten me started on mandolin at the age of six, but now I wanted him to teach me the tenor banjo. Too bad for me, my hands were very small and I didn't seem to have the strength and speed necessary to play the tenor banjo and quickly gave up. But I fondly recall listening to dad, who continued to play the banjo for his own enjoyment.

185

When the nostalgia craze of the late 1950s and early 60s came around, dad and his tenor banjo were ready. He ended up working a couple of nights a week in New Haven and the surrounding area. In addition to his superb musicianship, dad knew how to light up a stage. He was like a magician who was able to bring an audience to life though his fire and speed. Dad had made the choice many years earlier to raise his family and stay close to home. But, I'm confident that he could have played anywhere with anybody had he chosen that path. The fact that he didn't makes him one of those unsung heroes in the musical world.

Knowing that his incredible talent wouldn't be around forever, I made a point of coaxing dad to sit in front of a tape recorder and document his abilities. While he was past his years of blazing speed, his musicality and technical powers did not desert him. He played a wide range of music - from *Lollypops* to the (then) current hits, *Honey* and *The Way We Were*. Yes, even though this recording captured him at the ages of 75, he was still keeping up to date with the tunes. Later, I also found one of

dad's rehearsal tapes made about ten years earlier. Since editing both of the tapes (made in 1971 and 1981) I have often listened to them and experienced the same sense of awe that I had as a youngster. When dad passed away in 1983, these recordings took their place among my prized possessions.

Over the years, I had continued to play the mandolin and, through my friend Bill Bloom, became associated with the San Fernando Valley Banjo Band. While I'd gotten a false start trying to work in the banjo-mandolin, I found that playing jazz riffs and bass lines on a real tenor banjo suited my style and my small hands just fine. Having been a member of the band for about a year, I decided to make the other band members a present of the audio tapes I had of my dad's playing. The band members raved about the recordings (and still do). This reaction gave me the notion that other banjo players might like to hear these recordings and may find value in the things dad was able to do. So, I decided to make these tapes available to everyone.

Danny Bergantino was a soulful musician with masterful technique. When I pressed him, he'd comment, "You should have heard me 50 years ago." Based on what I *did* hear, I can only imagine. He may not have been Harry Reser. But, he was the best banjo player I ever heard. If it sounds like I'm idealizing him a little bit, remember, he was my old man!

To purchase a copy of "Danny Bergantino on his tenor banjo" send $15.00 to Dr. Len Bergantino, 1215 Brockton Avenue, #104, Los Angeles, CA 90025.

THE VINACCIA

written by Dr. Lou Bergantino

I boarded a plane for Italy, on my way to Torino for a psychoanalytic conference, and then to visit my relatives in Naples, the owners of Bergantino's Restorante since 1848. I began reading **The Mandolin Journal**, the official newsletter of the Classical Mandolin Society of America. An article was written describing the best of the how I back mandolins as the Vinaccia, made in Naples, Italy. Wow! That is where I was going and I planned to see if I could find some, play them and see what I thought. I have played a Gibson F-2 with a sound as mellow as a cello since 1976, so I certainly was well acquainted with what a good sound on a mandolin happened to be.

My cousins had to make several calls for me since rock guitars are much more popular in Italy than mandolins these days. In all of Naples only one store had three Vinaccias and three Calaces. I think only one of the Calace's was in playable condition. That is, in terms of fingerboard, a new set of strings, ease of fingering, etc. However, for sound quality it was easy to determine how each of them sounded as they were playable enough for those purposes. Again, the standard of sound I used for compared was my Gibson F-2. None of the Calaces moved me to consider buying one instead of my 1913.

This old music store had been in existence since about 1860 and repair men in the store would do the work necessary to put a mandolin in top condition if you were definitely going to purchase it. Instruments of the Vinaccias did not particularly impress me. However, one Vinaccia had a sound that was so beautiful, so delicate, so rich, so mellow, that it goes beyond anything I can describe. In other words if Gabriel plays trumpet at the right hand of God and there is a mandolin counterpart, he or she must be playing a Vinaccia.

The storeowner, like my relatives at Bergantino's Ristorante, his father, grandfather and great grandfather owned the store since about 1860. He showed me old phone books where his great grandfather as a violin maker. The two Vinaccia Brothers were advertised (about 1890) as well. He informed me that the Vinaccia was known as the Stradivarious of Italian mandolins and the brothers were known for making mandolins for the King of Savoy's family. (handwritten)

The old man who ran the store wanted between $2200 and $3000 each for the Calaces and the Vinaccias. You guessed it. The one I wanted was $3000. For whatever reason I could not bring myself to pay more than $2700 and the next day the owner's granddaughter, to whom it belonged, decided not to sell it.

I had been told by many vintage instrument dealers that Vinaccias and Calaces in the United States were not highly valued and perhaps I would be able to get one for between $500 and $700. This was in the back of my mind when negotiating for the Vinaccia. I was also told that Vinaccias were not the most playable.

So I came back to the United States empty handed but with an indelible impression of that sound. I called all of the vintage instrument places that are well known throughout the United States. No Vinaccias were to be had. Then I called a local store in Santa Monica just by chance and they said they had two, one had just been sold and they had one left. They wanted $1200. It was in excellent condition and the sound was great, but not the same as the one I had liked in Naples. The mandolin in Santa Monica had been made for a fair competition in 1926. Nevertheless it has a clarity and fullness of sound that for classical mandolin playing was better than my Gibson F-2 (that is, unamplified). It cost me $1200 for the mandolin. Then I brought it to the best repair man in Los Angeles and had him lower the fingerboard action. It was very difficult to play at first. This cost $40. The case was $200. There was no pickguard, so the repairman who also made Greek instruments similar to the mandolin, researched the exact kind of pickguard made by Vinaccia, and made one for $150. It is very unique and gorgeous. So I now have a mandolin that is quite playable with a Vinaccia sound that is better than all but one of the Vinaccias or Calaces I found in Naples for $1800.

I thought it was important to take the reader on this shopping trip because I wound up paying about half of what the Italians say it is worth and a bit more than double of what the Americans say it is worth! If you find one with the sound", one thing is for sure, "it is worth it!"

"GEORGE, DON'T-A BE A TROUBADOR"

Continued from page 12

Although Rantucci was an appreciative citizen of the U.S.A. he missed his native country. On one occasion he said, "In America everything is-a wonderful. We have-a many great orchestras and musicians. But in Italy music is-a everywhere. Here, music is-a played mainly by the professional music player. The average American no play-a the music. In Italy everyone they sing or play an instrument". Rantucci 's eyes lit up as he continued, "In Italy you go into a barber shop for a haircut or a shave and when it's-a busy you have-a to wait. But you don't sit on a bench and stare-a into space or read-a the magazine. Up against the wall, in the corner of the shop, is-a all kinds of instruments to play - mandolin, guitar or piccolo. You reach-a for a guitar or mandolin and you play it while-a you wait for a haircut. Then the barber or even a customer getting a shave, he sings along with-a the player. Music is-a in the air, all over Italy".

Then, to emphasize his point he would pick up his mandolin and play a rollicking Italian polka or tarantella. When his fingers flew up and down the frets and his pick skillfully struck the strings one could almost picture couples dancing and shaking their tambourines.

The enjoyable two weeks at the workshop had a wonderful high awaiting me during the last few days. One morning a radio reporter from the Interlochen music station came around and interviewed Rantucci and several members of our class. The reporter also made a tape recording of my teacher and me playing the last movement of "Vivaldi's Concerto for Two Mandolins". Rantucci took the first mandolin part and I played second mandolin. When we listened to the broadcast a few days later we all were pleased with the outcome. After the final chords of the movement died down Rantucci leaned over, patted me on the back and exclaimed, "George, you played like a concert musician, not like-a the troubador."

My spirits soared. I really appreciated his compliment. But, if the truth were to be told, I would have given my bottom dollar to have been able to play the mandolin as well as a good troubador.

Friederichshafen

In June, Don Lewis, Silver Spring, MD attended the Mandolin Festival in Friederichshafen, Germany. We are looking forward to his report.

187

Danny Bergantino - My Dad

by Dr. Len Bergantino

stairs and said, "Daddy, what's this?" He said, "It's a tenor banjo - but nobody uses it anymore." When I persisted and asked "Why?", dad said, "I used to play it all the time - then radio came in. First I was on the bandstand with the band and they said I was too loud. Then they had me play near the door while the band was on the stage and they still said it was too loud. Finally they moved me outside the door and said, 'Danny, if you want to play with this band, you'd better learn to play the guitar." So, he did!

Dan Bergantino, my dad, was born in Waterbury, Connecticut in 1906. He came of age with the tenor banjo in the mid to late 1920s. You know, there are some people who are just born to play an instrument and they can do no wrong on it - Benny Goodman with a clarinet...Harry James with a trumpet. Well, my old man was like that with a tenor banjo.

If a tenor banjo player is judged on speed, cleanliness and musicianship, my dad may not have been as good as Harry Reser. But, he was the best that most people who came across him had ever heard. In his day, he used to cut the Harry Reser solos clean as a whistle as the tenor banjo player in Harry Brinkman's band in the Connecticut area.

My introduction to my dad's tenor banjo playing came in 1954 when I was 11 years old. Even though it was winter, I decided to crawl through the trap-door that led to our unheated attic. There I saw this instrument with broken strings and what looked to me like a broken drum head. I dragged it down

As a result, my dad's tenor banjo was relegated to the attic where it remained until I dragged it back into his life. I don't know what it was, but I loved the banjo at first sight and pleaded with my dad to get it fixed. While he hadn't played the banjo in years, his hand were in pretty good shape as he had worked regularly on guitar and violin. When he picked up the banjo and rattled off *Lollipops, Nola and The Cat and the Dog*, I just sat there in awe. He had gotten me started on mandolin at the age of six, but now I wanted him to teach me the tenor banjo. Too bad for me, my hands were very small and I didn't seem to have the strength and speed necessary to play the tenor banjo and quickly gave up. But I fondly recall listening to dad, who continued to play the banjo for his own enjoyment.

When the nostalgia craze of the late 1950s and early 60s came around, dad and his tenor banjo were ready. He ended up working a couple of nights a week in New Haven and the surrounding area. In addition to his superb musicianship, dad knew how to light up a stage. He was like a magician who was able to bring an audience to life though his fire and speed. Dad had made the choice many years earlier to raise his family and stay close to home. But, I'm confident that he could have played anywhere with anybody had he chosen that path. The fact that he didn't makes him one of those unsung heroes in the musical world.

Knowing that his incredible talent wouldn't be around forever, I made a point of coaxing dad to sit in front of a tape recorder and document his abilities. While he was past his years of blazing speed, his musicality and technical powers did not desert him. He played a wide range of music - from *Lollypops* to the (then) current hits, *Honey* and *The Way We Were*. Yes, even though this recording captured him at the ages of 75, he was still keeping up to date with the tunes. Later, I also found one of

dad's rehearsal tapes made about ten years earlier. Since editing both of the tapes (made in 1971 and 1981) I have often listened to them and experienced the same sense of awe that I had as a youngster. When dad passed away in 1983, these recordings took their place among my prized possessions.

Over the years, I had continued to play the mandolin and, through my friend Bill Bloom, became associated with the San Fernando Valley Banjo Band. While I'd gotten a false start trying to work in the banjo-mandolin, I found that playing jazz riffs and bass lines on a real tenor banjo suited my style and my small hands just fine. Having been a member of the band for about a year, I decided to make the other band members a present of the audio tapes I had of my dad's playing. The band members raved about the recordings (and still do). This reaction gave me the notion that other banjo players might like to hear these recordings and may find value in the things dad was able to do. So, I decided to make these tapes available to everyone.

Danny Bergantino was a soulful musician with masterful technique. When I pressed him, he'd comment, "You should have heard me 50 years ago." Based on what I *did* hear, I can only imagine. He may not have been Harry Reser. But, he was the best banjo player I ever heard. If it sounds like I'm idealizing him a little bit, remember, he was my old man!

To purchase a copy of "Danny Bergantino on his tenor banjo" send $15.00 to Dr. Len Bergantino, 1215 Brockton Avenue, #104, Los Angeles, CA 90025.

Mischa Sheynkman:

The Soviet Paganini of the Mandolin

by Len Bergantino

After sending a cd of Emanuil "Mischa" Sheynkman to the *Mandolin Journal* editor, I asked if she would be interested in an article about Mischa to which she happily agreed. The cd features Sheynkman playing mandolin with his peers – those who graduated from Russian conservatories with a major in Russian folk music. He was never able to find those kinds of peers when he defected to the United States in 1977. The Soviet government destroyed all of the masters of his work but I made a copy from a recording that he gave me when he was my teacher from 1979 – 1981.

While this is an article about Sheynkman, in that I am claiming from all that I know he was the best that ever lived (and fellow mandolinist Bill Bloom backs me up on it) I must say a little about both of us in that you will know that such praise does not come lightly.

Bill Bloom is about 83 years old and I am 67. I am not even sure where I met him and how we have been friends for twenty years. Bill is an eccentric who loves mandolin, he is a Russian Jew born in the United States with a deep appreciation of Russian mandolin and domra music. Sheynkman defected to New York in 1977 and Bill Bloom worked for two years to transplant Sheynkman and his family to Los Angeles. Sheynkman, along with his wife and two children, lived with Bill and Letha Bloom for about six months before they got an apartment in the San Fernando Valley, which is where I took lessons from him.

In 1956, a professional mandolin player in Waterbury, Connecticut – Ray Amicone, who had a handmade D'Angelico mandolin let me borrow a record of the legendary mandolinist Dave Apollon, whose arrangements

of "Smoke Gets in Your Eyes" was written out for me by my father, Daniel Bergantino, who had fire in his hands and brought every stage to life I ever saw him play on. and which version I played on my own CD "Falling In Love" which I made with jazz guitarist Joe Diorio. Until I met Sheynkman, Dave Apollon was the best I had ever heard play the mandolin in my lifetime.

I met Sheynkman in 1979 when I heard him play at the Bonaventure Hotel in Los Angeles. He and his group wore red tunics and he had a lot of black hair bobbing and weaving all over the place as he played with a technique where his speed was blinding. His fingers never left the fingerboard, and his sense of musicality touched my soul many times during the engagement. I had sold my mandolin and my trumpet and was not playing music at the time, and yet, all I could think was "I want to take lessons from this guy". This is the chance of a lifetime! My parents were visiting me so I brought my father to hear him the following week. He too thought Sheynkman was beyond human belief. In other words, keep in mind that no matter how good I attempt to show you a picture of his ability, I can never give you the full extent of it any more than I can bring Paganini himself back to life (I have read two volumes of his life and work).

So that night I went up to Sheynkman during a break and said, "Sir, do you teach?" I want to take mandolin lessons from you" He said, "Yes." I said "How much do you charge?" He said "$20 a lesson." I said, blurting it out for no conscious reason, "Can you teach me a technique I can use in a recording studio?" He said "yes." And we were off and running. I was studying with the Paganini of the mandolin from the Soviet Union for $20 a lesson. I went out and bought a 1913 Gibson F-2 round hole mellow sounding mandolin. I told Sheynkman that my mandolin was better than his. He said that was true but in the Soviet Union he only paid five dollars for his

I brought a mandolin book for him to use when he taught me. He took away my mandolin and pick for the first three months. He made a paper pick and had me work on the right hand wrist flexibility until it was so automatic I could do it in my sleep. When I had the right hand at a level acceptable to him, he said to bring the mandolin, but he gave me a Soviet made pick different than any pick I had ever seen and insisted I use that pick. He began to write out each lesson, and each week he would add a few lines that built on the week before. He used to play for me during the lessons and he was inspirational in this way.

The way he was in the world took the torture out of studying to be the best you could. One time I said, "Mischa, you are killing me! You are killing me!" I was on the verge of quitting in total exasperation and frustration. He put

(continued on page 25)

THE MANDOLIN JOURNAL August, 2001 - Vol. XV #3

MY FATHER, DAN BERGANTINO, AND THE MANDOLIN:
MELODY, CHORDS, SPEED, CLEAN, AND HE HAD FIRE IN HIS HANDS

My father was born in 1906 in Waterbury, Connecticut where he was a professional musician from the time he was fourteen until he was 75 when he moved to California to be with me the last two years of his life. He played two to four nights a week, and he had "fire in his hands". Whenever I saw him play, on whatever instrument I saw him play (mandolin, guitar, tenor banjo or violin) he had incredible speed and cleanliness of technique and played with such an inner fire that he lit up an entire audience and or band that he was playing with. He customarily played in night clubs or restaurants with small combos, but played violin in the Waterbury Symphony.

My father was one of those unsung heroes. He was one of the most talented musicians in the Waterbury and New Haven Connecticut areas, where he customarily played, but never went on the road and never became famous. Yet some of the things he could do well and his sense of musicality, one would only hear in those who were world renown. He knew how to blend blazing speed, single string technique with chords at the same time with a sense of musicality and with fire in his hands and the music.

My father's parents came through Ellis Island from Italy, San Marco La Catola, Province of Foggia around the turn of the century. His father Leonardo was a stone mason. There were severe layoffs and my father supported the family (seven brothers and sisters lived out of sixteen) through music.

In a sense music was the family business. My father's uncle taught him solfeggio (reading music: do, re, mi, fa, sol, la, si, do) for a year and then gave him a few years of mandolin lessons. He then had violin lessons for six months and was self taught in terms of tenor banjo and guitar. He was one of those who was a natural. That is what he was born to do.

His uncle, Soledad Bredice, who taught him mandolin also had (a son) Fred Bredice was one of the first single string soloists with blazing speed - and a legend around the Connecticut area. He did it in the early thirties, radio show and all. His brother Louis Bredice was tenth in the country in December Magazine Poll for piano one year. He told me when he first started playing jazz "he played a lot of notes, then he realized all he needed were the right ones. Soledad had a brother Charlie Bredice whose son was Vinnie Bredice, a well schooled classical and jazz guitar player (Hartt School of Music in Hartford, Connecticut). Vinnie wrote a few jazz guitar books for Mel Bay Publications. Fred and Vinnie Bredice were Joe Bono's teachers (Joe is a world renowned jazz guitarist who accompanied me on the CD "Falling In Love"). It's all in the family. All of this (began) with the mandolin and with Soledad Bredice teaching his sons and nephews as the first instrument from which they had a "foundation" in music and could move in any direction they wished from there.

When I was five years old my father stuck me in a room with a solfeggio book and gave me the one half hour lesson per week on reading music. He said by the time you get an instrument you will only have to concern yourself with learning to play it. You will already know how to read music.

At six years old he took me to the violin repair man, Louis Volpe, who had a Gibson F-2 mandolin that was gorgeous. He sold it to my father for $75. I remember Louis Volpe had a big Saint Bernard who leaped up that day and licked me in the face knocking me on my rear. To this day for some strange reason I always liked Saint Bernards and I have never had any fear of them.

My father always emphasized the lightness of the wrist in the right hand saying that if the right hand worked all else would fall into place.

He took me through DeCristofaro Method Books One and Two. I remember there were a lot of nice duets for first and second mandolin in those books.

While my Dad made his living primarily with the guitar, violin and tenor banjo, mandolin was a first love for him and he always felt it was the basic instrument that string players should begin with at the very least. When he played it he remembered all the old Italian music that you hear at weddings, but was never written down anywhere. One of the one's he did not write down was "The Poet and Peasant Overture". If anyone trading this article has a written arrangement of it I would be most grateful to purchase it from them.

In the summer of 1979 when my father was staying at my home in Los Angeles for a few weeks of summer vacation he wrote out several numbers he thought would keep the heritage alive. One selection "Elvira" follows this article.

Also, there was one audio tape on which he played mandolin exclusively for about fifteen minutes that demonstrates his talent "MUSICALITY, SPEED, CLEANLINESS WITH SPEED, SINGLE STRING SOLOS MIXED WITH CHORDS (IMPROVISATION, AND FIRE IN HIS HANDS)".

If you wish to purchase a copy of this tape **send $10**

Dr. Len Bergantino
1233 Brockton Avenue #104
Los Angeles, CA 90025

JIRO NAKANO

Jiro Nakano, a well known researcher and composer for mandolin music passed away at the age of 98 on June 10 2000 from heart failure. He was born on April 30th so birth certificate says, but actual birth date is April 4, 1902. After graduated from the High School of Technology majoring dyeing, he started to study solo mandolin and guitar playing by himself. In his younger years, he was active as a soloist of mandolin and guitar. Besides playing, he composed more than 100 pieces of music for the mandolin orchestra, mandolin solo and guitar solo. He also wrote many nursery rhymes and when talking about these compositions, he said "Although this is very different to plectrum music, when talking about myself, I have to make mention of these children's songs (otherwise half of my work is lost). In 1996 and 1999, at the age of 94 and 97 respectively, he conducted a mandolin orchestra to record several romantic mandolin music and publish two CDs titled "Preludio Romantico di Mandolino". The music scores of those music in the CD were handwritten by Nakano himself and published together with the CD.

Below listed are popular numbers out of many and varied Nakano's compositions.

Mandolin solo	Tre Studi - Sol maggiore, Re maggiore, Re minore
	Haru ga-Kita con variazioni
	Tema "Ryusha" e variazioni
	Za Fantasia
Mandolin Orchestra	La Iglesia sobre la Colina (Chapel on the Hill)
	Una Notte di Villaggio Pescatori (One Night in a Fishing village)
	Hamabe no Uta (Song on a Seashore)
	Pioggia di Maggio (Melancholy on a rainy day in May)
	Juego de Pelotita (Playing with a Ball)

EDITOR'S NOTE:

MANDOLIN STORIES FOR CHILDREN

At last! We have responses to appeals for mandolin stories for children. One called "Larry the Luthier and The Bucking Fingerboard" was sent in by Tyrus Relman. Bernard Zinar has agreed to illustrate it. On the same day I heard from Dee Darlington, a published author, who said she had already outlined a story. Another member expressed interest, as well.

This rush of responses made me think that a book containing several stories might have broader appeal. I even resurrected "Belinda", the bowlback mandolin that wound up on Broadway and, of course, as Bernard Zinar suggested, Larry the Luthier could become a series of stories.

When I spoke to Norman Levine about the project he was delighted. The presses are ready any time we are. We still need stories and people who are willing to illustrate them. Stick figures can be very effective, you know.

Thank you contributors for a great beginning to a worthwhile project! If you are interested in brainstorming a story at the convention, let me know. Call - 516-271-9518.

ELMER:

This has nothing to do with mandolins, but I wanted to share it with you. Bob and I welcomed a newcomer into our home about two weeks ago. - Elmer, a superb eighteen pound 2-3 year old red long haired dachshund we adopted through Dachshund Rescue. Now, this is a dog who is housebroken, obedi-

ence trained and a real mesh. He's attached himself so closely to us, we could easily have named him "Velcro". It's less than two weeks and he already has adapted to the rest of our menagerie (a minidachs, a toy poodle, two very old cats and a bird). They hang out with each other as if they've been buddies for years. Chloe, our minidachs, is particularly smitten.

As close as anyone can figure Elmer (original name unknown) had been stolen to sell for drug money and later confiscated by police when they raided a crack house. The police then brought him to a veterinarian who contacted Rescue. They contact prospective adoptive owners and carefully screen them to be sure that a good match is made. The sole purpose of the organization is to see that foundling dachshunds wind up in a happy household rather than a pound.

I only recently learned that there are breed rescue organizations all over the United States, and was astounded to hear that in our area alone more than one hundred dachshunds are rescued a year, and that's just one breed. So if you are of a mind to open your homes to a dog, or even if you aren't, I urge you to do so. You won't be sorry.

Continued on page 11

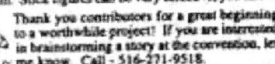

written by Dr. Len Bergantino

I was a clinical psychologist with a very busy practice and hadn't devoted much time to music or playing the mandolin in years. It was 1979 and I happened to be passing through the Bonaventure Hotel when I heard Emanuil Shenkman playing the mandolin. I heard Dave Appollon on records, but Shenkman was the only one of that caliber I ever heard in person. He did stuff on that mandolin I couldn't even begin to describe. I found myself asking him if he gave lessons, and if he could teach me to play with a technique for recording studios. He said yes, and we began. In retrospect, the amazing part to me was that I had asked him to teach me something I had no idea I would ever use, but in December, 1997 Joe Diorio, world renowned jazz guitarist and I completed a CD of romantic Italian and old American Standards entitled "Falling In Love".*

Mischa (as he was called) began by taking away my mandolin and my pick. With my left hand he made me hold a book to my lower chest and the top of my abdomen. Then he made a paper pick folded in a variety of ways that somewhat resembled the pick he had brought from Russia where he had been a soloist for the Leningrad Symphony. He later played in the United States at Carnegie Hall.

For three months my lessons consisted solely of loosening of the right wrist while simulating picking movements as if the book I was holding was the mandolin. My right hand became looser and looser and more and more flexible in the right wrist. Then, at the end of three months I got my mandolin and pick back.

There were no books to study in the following two years that I took weekly lessons from Mischa. He wrote about 8 half pages totaling four full pages of music in two years. His method was so different from the new lesson each week procedure that had been my experience, typical of music lessons in America. But Mischa did not appear to be interested in moving on, only in the detail and the precision in which I was to develop the right hand and consequently the kinds of pickings and eventual speed with which I developed the left hand. So I played four pages of music over two years and it was taking me two hours a day of practice which was going to increase. With the practice of clinical psychology as full as it was I became exasperated and told Mischa I was going to quit. He said to me, "Take it easy, but take it!" I felt total relief and broke out laughing when he said this.

In retrospect I was very fortunate to be exposed to the way the Russian Conservatories trained musicians. There was a dedication to detail and repetition that I had never seen before. I find that while I need to do some practice on the positions for the left hand, the right hand always comes back to the same level of proficiency with what Mischa taught me even if I never practice. I pick it up and there it is! Without what he taught me a mandolin has difficulty being expressed as full and as rich an instrument as it is, without feeling pinched, cramped, or sometimes a little tinny. At least that is how it seems to me with the mandolins I have heard over the past twenty years. Thus, although the reader will not have Mischa's personal guidance, it may be worth experimenting with the paper pick if you think your right hand needs work.

*The CD, "Falling In Love", with the Italian Mandolin of Dr. Len Bergantino accompanied by world renowned guitarist, Joe Diorio, is available, write to: Dr. Len Bergantino, 1215 Brockton Avenue # 104, Los Angeles, CA 90025 Send $15 or call (310)-207-9397

3

The Day I Met Raphael Mendez

In 1955 I began studying trumpet with Carl Berg in Waterbury, Connecticut. He played for Harry James and often spoke with great reverance about Raphael Mendez. In 1960 I bought a few 33 rpms long play of Raphael Mendez. One of his features was "MOTO PERPETUO" where it sounds as if he did not take a breath for 4 1/2 minutes.

In 1971 I had a full time job as a junior high school counselor while I was a full time doctoral student at the University of Southern California. The music teacher said one afternoon in May, "Do you want to go hear Raphael Mendez today after school at La Puente Junior High School?" I couldn't believe my ears and said with great enthusiasm that I would love to attend. Raphael Mendez gave free concerts for the children in an impoverished area of Los Angeles County.

I got there early, at approximately 4 p.m. for a 5 p.m. concert. All attendees, both children and faculty, were dressed casually. Mendez was dressed in his customary Mexican style tuxedo. I walked up to talk trumpet with him. He seemed to appreciate my interest. We discussed the following subjects:

1.\ He practiced twelve hours a day.
2.\ The first two hours were at a whisper.
3.\ He only taught double and triple tonguing to those who spoke Spanish because the language was spoken so much faster than English, the students had a chance to get the appropriate speed. He strongly felt (not racially biased) that people who spoke English had no chance to develop the kind of speed he was trying to teach with double and triple tonguing.

4.\ He recorded Moto Perpetuo (a Paganini violin solo) in 4 segments, not one segment, as it sounds on the recording. He demonstrated a method of circular breathing where he breathed in, choked air in his throat, and continued to blow into the trumpet at the same time.

5.\ He apologized telling me it was going to be the worst performance of his life, because he was receiving cortisone shots in the face that made his lips feel like tire tubes over which he had no control.

BE THAT AS IT MAY, IT WAS THE BEST TECHNICAL PERFORMANCE I EVER HEARD ON A TRUMPET IN MY ENTIRE LIFE!!!!!!!!!!!

LIFELONG EFFECTS OF MY HALF HOUR
WITH RAPHAEL MENDEZ

1.\ I practice three hours a day as a seventy year old, very softly, and totally absorbed in quality of sound on the production of each note.

2.\ I put my best foot forward in dressing my best for trumpet performances in that musicians be given the respect that is in accord with the long hours of unpaid practice it takes to achieve musical competency.

3.\ I maintain a human generosity toward the less fortunate.

4.\ I gauged the speed of how fast people speak in Spanish and practice double and triple tonguing at that speed as opposed to the speed at which I can only speak English. I am particularly good at guaging the speed at which people speak but for those who are not the same results can be achieved by having a person speak Spanish in front of a metronone and then setting the pace.

ALL IN ALL THAT HALF HOUR AND TWO HOUR CONCERT BY RAPHAEL MENDEZ WAS ONE OF THE MAJOR HIGHLIGHTS OF MY LIFE AND HAD LASTING PERSONAL AND MUSICAL IMPACT!

submitted by DR. LEN BERGANTINO, ED.D., PH.D.
CLINICAL PSYCHOLOGIST & PROFESSIONAL TRUMPET PLAYER (Musician)
1215 Brockton Avenue #104 Los Angeles, CA 90025
424-293-9511 Tel. (Let it ring 7 times)

A PSYCHOLOGIST AND HIS MANDOLIN: REFLECTIONS OVER THIS LIFETIME!

My father was a professional musician. Wherever he played the entire orchestra and venue came alive!

When I was five years old he stuck me in a room with a solfeggi book and by the time I was six he said "This is a mandolin. Everybody in our family plays it. Now that you can read music all you have to worry about is the instrument. At the same time he kept telling me a story about a time long before I was born. My Godfather, his brother, my uncle Tony was about twelve years old and my father was already playing professionally at about 14 years old. He said he was giving Tony mandolin lessons and one Sunday morning before Church my father came to an epiphane. He was standing behind Tony and ripped his white shirt in half down the middle and with the Italian round back mandolin he smashed it over Tony's head as he said "Tony, YOU ARE NOT GOING TO MAKE IT!" The message was clear. I gave up my dream of pitching for the New York Yankees and practiced mandolin one half hour a day, realizing that my American made Gibson 1913 F-2 mandolin was made of hardwood and would do much more damage than the Italian roundback did to my Uncle Tony's head!

At the time, before being trained by Carl Whitaker, M.D. to invade the unconscious and play in everybody when you do it, and being trained by Milton Erickson, M.D. to put them in a double bind straight jacket when you do it, and being trained by Jim Simkin and Walter Kempler to make my interventions with smoke coming in on the fastball, a story from when I was six years old - which if I had any sense at all would have made me realize that it was I who was "The Natural" and not Robert Redford and a shoo in to take Che Gueverra's place after his assassination.

It was Thanksgiving and I was at Baby Anne's house along with my then cousin-brother Dennis, and all of our parents went into the kitchen to discuss Italian politics. I suggested the two six year olds and five year old Baby Anne take the fruit bowl upstairs to the toilet. I found great delight with the avid support of my two cousins in stuffing oranges down the toilet! Baby Anne's father came into the room looking somewhat homicidal as I continued stuffing oranges down the toilet and said, as his face was shaking, "What are you doing?" I said, "Uncle Joe! I am stuffing oranges down the toilet!" As his face kept shaking, only now his neck was bulging too, he said, "WHY ARE YOU DOING THAT!" I matter of factly and calmly said, realizing that my parents were in the kitchen so that it was unlikely Uncle Joe was going to kill me then, "Because It is fun Uncle Joe!"

From Walt Kempler who used to play banjo when I played mandolin, I learned that one should UTILIZE HIS OWN PERSONALITY CHARACTERISTICS TO GIVE THE CLIENT OR PATIENT SOMETHING TO RUB UP AGAINST RATHER THAN ATTEMPTING TO CURE ONESELF IT IT. Kempler often referred to himself as a "rotten personality disorder, warts and all".

Of course my father was a monster player and in comparison whatever I did the local community of Waterbury Connecticut said "Well, the kid is alright, but he is no Danny!" On the other hand my mother had the good sense to tell me, "Don't mess with him technically because he will bury you alive (he used to keep grumbling that Paganini didn't write down his violin method). BUT YOU PLAY PRETTIER THAN HIM!"

So I took her words to heart. I dated six Miss Connecticut's in a row and played love songs on the mandolin for all of them. I didn't think they were particularly fond of me so it must have been the mandolin.

From 1979-1981 I took mandolin lessons from Mischa Shenkyman, the Paganini of the Mandolin in the Soviet Union. In 1997 I made a cd entitled "FALLING IN LOVE" where I was accompanied by the foremost jazz guitarist in the world at that time, Joe Diorio. Old Man Lovari of Lovari's Music Store in Naples Italy since 1848 said "When Italians leave Italy to come to America they become Italian Americans and then American Italians, but they never get the musical feeling back of being Italian Italians. You did. I don't know how you did it. In Italy everybody plays like Pavarotti sings!"

What I figured out with Crime running rampant and the United States on the verge of bankruptcy, that character disordered sorts would continue on attempting to create THE RISE AND FALL OF THE UNITED STATES GOVERNMENT, THAT I MUST TAKE THE PRINCIPLES AND PERSONALITY CHARCTERISTICS THAT ARE MY GOD GIVEN GIFTS AND TREAT THE UNITED STATES GOVERNMENT AND ITS AFFILIATE GOVERNMENTAL SUBSIDIARIES AS ONE BIG FAMILY DOING FAMILY THERAPY WITH THEM WHETHER THEY WANT IT OR NOT!

RESPECTFULLY SUBMITTED BY
THE REVEREND DR. LEN BERGANTINO, Ed.D.,
Ph.D.
RETIRED LICENSED PSYCHOLOGIST IN CA, AZ
AND HI
AND
DIPLOMATE IN FAMILY PSYCHOLOGY
AMERICAN BOARD OF PROFESSIONAL
PSYCHOLOGY
DR. LEN BERGANTINO CURRENTLY DOES
FAMILY THERAPY WITH THE WORLD AT LARGE
WHETHER THEY WANT IT OR NOT! CALL 424
293-9511. (Let it ring 7 times)

DR. LEN BERGANTINO

Doctorate - University of Southern California - 1971

Tel/Fax (310) 207-9397

Trumpet - Progressive Jazz & Lead
Solo Tenor Banjo - Mandolin Banjo for
Dixieland & Roaring Twenties

Mandolin - Romantic Italian
& American Old Standards
& Classical Mandolin

LETTER OF REFERENCE FOR LISA FRANCESCA BERGANTINO IN THE FIELD OF MUSIC

LISA FRANCESCA BERGANTINO'S USE OF SELF AS AN INSTRUMENT IN
THE FIELD OF MUSIC APPRECIATION THAT CUTS ACROSS ALL
KINDS OF MUSIC AS WELL AS HER QUALITATIVE JUDGEMENT THEROF
ARE WITHOUT PEER. HER PERFORMANCE SURPASSES DOCTORS OF MUSIC
IN ACADEMIC SETTINGS IN TERMS OF THOSE WHO MIGHT TEACH MUSIC
APPRECIATION AND OR SIT ON PERFORMANCE JURIES IN SCHOOLS OF MUSIC!

AS LISA BERGANTINO DOES NOT HAVE FORMAL TRAINING AS A MUSICIAN
ONE CAN ONLY SPECULATIVE AS TO HOW SHE CAME UPON SUCH ABILITY!

THE BERGANTINO-BREDICE FAMILY HAVE PRODUCED OUTSTANDING MUSICIANS
TO MY KNOWLEDGE SINCE THE 1900's AND PERHAPS PRIOR TO THAT DATE!
THUS, THERE IS BOTH A HEREDITY AND A GENETIC FACTOR INVOLVED.

HER FATHER, DR. LEN BERGANTINO, WAS TRAINED AS A CLINICAL
PSYCHOLOGIST AND MUSICIAN BY MANY WORLD RENOWN PSYCHIATRISTS,
CLINICAL PSYCHOLOGISTS AND MUSICIANS AT THE HIGHEST LEVELS OF
ACHIEVEMENT AND HAS DONE HIS BEST TO IMPART HIS KNOWLEDGE
BOTH DIRECTLY AND INDIRECTLY IN ALL TRANSACTIONS OVER THE COURSE
OF TWENTY NINE YEARS!. FOR EXAMPLE, DR. BERGANTINO, A LIFETIME
FAMILIAL STUDENT OF MUSIC HAS STUDIED WITH THE PAGANINI OF
THE MANDOLIN IN THE SOVIET UNION AS WELL AS MANY OF THE TOP
LEAD AND JAZZ TRUMPET PLAYERS INTERNATIONALLY. IN ADDITION
DR. BERGANTINO'S FATHER AND COUSINS WERE KNOWN TO BE PROFESSIONAL
MUSICIANS WHO HAD A UNIQUE ABILITY TO BRING ANY AUDIENCE ALIVE
EACH AND EVERY TIME THEY PERFORMED. IN ADDITION DR. BERGANTINO
HAS WRITTEN A BOOK THAT BECAME A MASTER CLASSIC IN THE FIELD
OF PSYCHOTHERAPY AND HAS NINETY PUBLICATIONS, SEVENTY OF WHICH
ARE IN CLINICAL PSYCHOLOGY AND TWENTY OF WHICH ARE IN THE FIELD
OF MUSIC. HE MADE A CD PLAYING MANDOLIN ACCOMPANIED BY WORLD
RENOWN GUITARIST JOE DIORIO.

SO ONE MIGHT SPECULATE THAT WITH ALL OF THIS BACKGROUND AND THE
UNIQUE GENIUS OF LISA BERGANTINO, WE HAVE A PERSON LIKE
EINSTEIN, WHEREBY A POSITION NEEDS TO BE CREATED AT THE
UNIVERSITY LEVEL NOT TO WASTE THE GENIUS QUALITY OF LISA
BERGANTINO, IN THAT NO SUCH POSITION CURRENTLY EXISTS FOR
THOSE WHO DO NOT POSSESS A DOCTORATE IN MUSIC NO MATTER OF
ONE'S CAPACITY TO ASSESS MUSIC QUALITATIVELY AS A SOULFUL
PERFORMANCE WITH IMPECCABLE TASTE AS EXEMPLIFIED BY THE QUALITY
OF BEING AND SENSITIVITY OF THE LISTENER IN THE PERSONHOOD
OF LISA FRANCESCA BERGANTINO!

I RECOMMEND HER WITHOUT RESERVATION FOR THE CREATION OF SUCH
A POSITION AT THE DOCTORAL LEVEL IN SCHOOLS OF MUSIC AS A FULL
PROFESSOR MUCH AS ERIK ERICKSON TAUGHT PSYCHOLOGY AT HARVARD
IN DOCTORAL PROGRAMS WITHOUT A DOCTORATE HIMSELF

1215 Brockton Avenue, Suite 104, Los Angeles, California 90025 USA

Respectfully Submitted, Dr. Len Bergantino, Ed.D., Ph.D.

198

CD Review: Tamara Volskaya's "My Journey" p. 245
Reviewed by Len Bergantino, clinical psychologist and musician

I am listening with the ears of a mandolin player and in all other situations the domra cuts more than I care to hear, but this is not true with Tamara Volskaya who makes the domra sound mellower.

I have heard three world class Russian domra players and technically I am not in a place to discriminate except to say that Soviet trained classical and Russian folk musicians are technically the best I ever heard, and the Soviet's for all their faults did right by musicians they trained in the Russian Conservatories, Tamara Volskaya of course reflects this kind of mastery over the instrument. However, unlike the others I have heard she has no need to prove her point in that she chooses some slow pieces in her repertoire that focus on MUSICALITY!

Musicality is where she is most different than anyone I have ever heard on any instrument in that she is consistently dark and soulful. This puts a demand on the listener in that the listener has to be able to stay with his or her own feelings of depth, darkness and soulfulness to appreciate what Tamara is doing. When I used to do

psychoanalysis it was customarily not until the third year of the analysis seeing people five days a week that they were able to stay with the depth and darkness of their most soulful feelings.

Tamara Volskaya plays "Flight of the Bumblebee". Her technique is faster, cleaner, and clearer than anyone I have ever heard play "Flight of the Bumblebee" on any instrument. While this includes all string instruments – even Harry Reser on the tenor banjo and Dave Apollon on the mandolin, it also includes Harry James and Raphael Mendes on the trumpet. Prior to hearing Tamara's virtuosity I was of the belief that it was humanly impossible to play faster, cleaner and clearer on a string instrument than on a trumpet (I play both), even if you are Paganini!

Recommendation: Buy the CD and sit down in a quiet room where you can enter a meditative state and feel and listen as deeply as you are able and it will be an experience you will not regret! A must buy!

22

200

*** "FALLING IN LOVE" AND THE MANDOLIN GIBSON F-2
MADE IN 1913 IN KALAMAZOO, MICHIGAN PLAYED BY
DR. LEN BERGANTINO COMES THE CLOSEST TO PURE
SOUND AS ANY MANDOLIN EVER RECORDED!!!

IT IS THE EQUIVALENT OF JOHNNY SMITH'S GUITAR
SOUND ON HIS CD "MOONLIGHT IN VERMONT"

ONCE IN AWHILE YOU HEAR A SOUND AND YOU HAVE
THE THOUGHT "THAT SOUND COMES DIRECTLY FROM
GOD!!! KAREN CARPENTER SINGING "CLOSE TO YOU"
AND WE'VE ONLY JUST BEGUN IS ONE OF THOSE!

WHAT MAKES "THE PAGANINI OF THE MANDOLIN EXTRAORDINARY
IS THE FACT IT WAS MADE IN THE SOVIET UNION WITH ALL
GRADUATES FROM RUSSIAN CONSERVATORIES OF MUSIC IN
"RUSSIAN FOLK MUSIC!" NO MATTER HOW GOOD MISCHA
SHENKMAN WAS PLAYING IN THE UNITED STATES HE WAS
EVEN BETTER ACCOMPANIED BY THE BEST RUSSIAN FOLK
MUSICIANS IN THE WORLD.

HOW THAT WORKED WAS THE RUSSIAN GOVERNMENT SAW MISCHA'S
TALENT AT AGE SIX AND SAID, "YOU ARE GOING TO BE A
MANDOLIN, BALILIKA AND DOMRA PLAYER AND YOU ARE GOING
TO THE RUSSIAN CONSERVATORY!" AND THAT IS ALL MISCHA
DID HIS ENTIRE LIFE! I HAVE HEARD SEVERAL RUSSIAN
CONSERVATORY GRADUATES! THEY ARE UNBELIEVABLE!:
TIMOFEI DOKSHIZER WAS THAT GOOD ON THE TRUMPET!!!

201

Aloha-Mahalo: Slyde Hyde, Ollie Mitchell and The Pres – Hal Espinosa

By Local 47 member Dr. Len Bergantino

Editor's Note: The following article is an unsolicited contribution submitted to the Overture.

This is an article that was motivated by graciousness and hospitality extended by two former L.A. musicians of institutional repute and the president of Local 47 Hal Espinosa on my recent journey to Hawaii for two ukulele conventions.

As I play jazz ukulele and I was interested in establishing a livelihood playing with a jazz group at the ukulele conventions, I had sent a demo to both Slyde Hyde and Ollie Mitchell in the hopes they would join me in a proposal for the conventions in 2006.

When I called Slyde he invited me to hear him play backing up a former L.A. singer, Paulina Wilson. He had a gorgeous, full, deep sound. My daughter Lisa and I were invited to sit at Slyde's table by his wife, Nola – an absolutely delightful woman. They invited us to their home the following day. They have the personal characteristics of playing with a couple of folks both as a sandbox. In other words, they are agreeable people who have never out their...

...to them." Then he demonstrated the way he blew air on the high notes and it was like a hurricane coming out of a fire hose. The strength and focus of the tone was incredible, and he is 78 years old now. He picked one solo for me to hear and as I suspected, I will never forget what he did and how he played it.

Ollie gave me a couple of CDs which are not for sale, but I suppose if you wrote and asked him for them he would be glad to send them to you. They demonstrate very high-level brass intricacies in a big band. Ollie has a big band that meets every Monday night on the Big Island of Hawaii. Ollie is a retired lifetime member of Local 47.

Slyde Hyde's CD is on the marketplace and is titled *Late Night Jazz*. He stated he has sold 100,000 copies in Europe via the Internet. Local 47 member Pete Christlieb plays sax, Jim Hughart plays bass, and Charlie Harris plays drums. Slyde plays beautiful ballads on the trombone.

The Pres - Hal Espinosa

When I got to Honolulu, Waikiki, I was in touch with Local 47 and was informed that Hal Espinosa was there for a Union meeting. I was able to locate...

While I had spoken to him on the phone once before, Hawaii was the first time I actually met him - and as I said, he was the sort of person who made himself available to a Local 47 member at a very busy time for no other reason in particular that I was a member of Local 47. In other words, I very much appreciated his making himself accessible and available.

When I told Hal that Ollie had played 400 gigs a year for 20 years in Los Angeles, he said, "I am surprised it was only 400. He played two and three gigs a day many times." He stated that he had played many times with Slyde Hyde when Slyde was a member of Local 47 between 1989 and 1992.

Now work talk aside, I had the most fun with him when he told me stories about his trumpet playing, all the big bands he played for, and some great anecdotes. Hal has pretty much lived every trumpet player's fantasies while growing up during these times. He said he played for Harry James, Maynard Ferguson, Henry Mancini and Les Brown, among others. I said, "Harry James was the reason I started playing trumpet - his recordings of 'The Sleepy Lagoon' and 'You Made Me Love You'."

202

A Letter from the Super Nova Quartet To Friends and Colleagues of Local 47 Member Ludvig Girdland

By now, many of you know about the tragic accident Ludvig was involved in two months ago. Performing and making an album with an artist of Ludvig's stature was one of the great honors of our lives. All of us who knew and were fortunate enough to perform with LG will forever be inspired by the uncompromisingly high standards he set as an artist and it is in that spirit that we will donate 75 percent of the proceeds of album sales to help with Ludvig's medical expenses. We want to thank everyone for their support not just to Ludvig and his family but also of the other members of the quartet in this difficult time. — Jacob Seitsch/Robert Anderson

If you would like to purchase Super Nova Quartet CDs, visit the band's website at www.supernovaquartet.com.

LEN BERGANTINO, ED.D., ABPP
1215 Brockton Avenue, Suite 104
Los Angeles, California 90025

TO HIRE ME AS A CONSULTANT
CALL (424) 293-0911
(7 RINGS)

CD PURCHASES

Several cd's are advertised in this book. A few are professionally done in studios with sound engineers and several of the DEMOS ARE NOT PROFESSIONALLY DONE, YET THEY DEMONSTRATE SOME OF THE QUALITIES WRITTEN ABOUT IN THIS BOOK

THE ESSENCE OF MUSIC

As of MAY, 2019 I am willing to sell you cd's separately from the book.

professionally done cd's are $25 each.

DEMOS are $15 each.

It is wise to call and leave a message with your return phone number. While I expect this book to be around for 200 years, I do not expect I will be around that long, as I am 75 now, an 76 on May 29, 2019.

If you are serious about pursuing the fullness of your being, and playing music from the inside out, YOU SHOULD PROBABLY BUY ALL OF THE CD's as they will only be sold during my lifetime. The address to send the check and the telephone number are at the top of this page of the stationary.

Call twice a few days apart in case the cell phone drops a call.

Sincerely,

Dr. Len Bergantino

Dr. Len Bergantino

Dr. Len Bergantino
Plays
Two Soulful Cornet Ballads

1. Black & Blue
2. Georgia On My Mind

Contact Dr. Len Bergantino
at (424) 293-9511
(7 rings)

205

Musicality
Pure Sound
The Art of Melody
Peace

1. Alex's Song

3. CD Overview
4. Around The World
5. Some Enchanted Evening
6. Medley
   (It's Been A Long, Long Time,
   Teresa, Maria, Stardust,
   Tammy, Maria Elena)
7. Guitarbara / My Regards
8. Misty

9. I'm In The Mood For Love
10. Autumn In New York
11. Old Cape Cod
12. Arrivederci Roma
13. Memento
14. Younger Than Springtime
15. Wake The Town And Tell The People
16. If I Give My Heart To You
17. Do I Dare Disturb The Musical Universe

" Alex's Songs Written For My Son "

Played by Dr. Len Bergantino
© 2018 L.D. Bergantino Music LLC

Recorded Feb.16 2018

Call (424) 293-9511
(7 Rings)

Falling In Love

Dr. Len Bergantino - Mandolin
Featuring: Joe Diorio - Guitar

1. Misty
2. Ambrodora's Roma
3. New Dimension
4. I'm In The Mood For Love
5. Come Prima
6. Phalsport
7. Come Back To Sorrentino
8. Smoke Gets In Your Eyes
9. St. Mary's Waltz
10. In The Chapel In The Moonlight
11. Imtermovista

12. Love Theme From La Strada
13. The Virgin e Stamp
14. Wake The Town And Tell The People
15. Per Condessor
16. Speak Softly Love
17. Spanish Eyes
18. Adesria e Cora
19. Sottovortices In Venice
20. It's Been A Long, Long Time
21. I'll Give My Heart To You
22. Kiss Me Again

(424) 293-9511
(7 rings)

© 1998

207

EMANUIL (Mischa) SHENKMAN

The Paganini of The Mandolin

1. CAPRICCIOSO - F.Riss 2. MADRIGAL - A. Simonetti
3. SLAVONIC LULLABY - F. Nerukh 4. Tango - M. Colen
5. CONCERT WALTZ - E. Manuzelli 6. MARCH - E. Mezzacapo

7. CANZONETTA - B. Godar 8. GONDOLIERA - F. Riss
9. SERANADE WALTZ - R. Drigo 10. BOLERO - E. Mezzacapo

LIMITED EDITION PRODUCED BY
DR. LEN BERGANTINO - HIS STUDENT

(424) 293-9511
(7 Rings)

208

209

Falling In Love

Dr. Len Bergantino - Mandolin
Featuring: Joe Diorio - Guitar

1. Misty
2. Arrivederci Roma
3. Non Dimenticar
4. I'm In The Mood For Love
5. Come Prima
6. Pietà!
7. Come Back To Sorrento
8. Smoke Gets In Your Eyes
9. St. Mary's Waltz
10. In The Chapel In The Moonlight
11. Innamorata

12. Love Theme From La Strada
13. Tre Voglia e Scirop
14. Wake The Town And Tell The People
15. I'm Confessin'
16. Speak Softly Love
17. Spanish Eyes
18. Anema e Core
19. Somewhere In Verona
20. It's Been A Long, Long Time
21. If I Give My Heart To You
22. Kiss Me Again

COMPACT

Digital Audio

(424) 293-9511
(7 rings)

© 1998

210

HEALING CD

This cd has a healing effect and has the potential to positively
effect and affect and to somewhat ameliorate medical symptomatology
in many vital areas as an assistance to medical treatment where
no such amelioration of medical symptomatology currently exists!

For this to occur the cd has to be played 'repetitively and well'
each time suffering outweighs wellbeing!

122 VETS A DAY COMMIT
SUICIDE!!!

VETS WHO LISTEN TO
THIS CD FOR TWO
ONE AND ONE HALF
HOUR BLOCKS OF
TIME WILL REDUCE
SUICIDE RATE
BY 60%

(PER DAY FOR
SIX MONTHS!

MY MOTHER WAS A
WITCH DOCTOR!

HALF THE TOWN CAME
TO SEE HER WHEN
THEY WERE ILL. IF
SHE COULDN'T GET
RID OF THEIR
SYMPTOMS, THEN THE
WENT TO THE DOCTOR

On a pure musical level this cd is good enough that I am able to
make a statement that I have played THE DEFINITIVE INTERPRETATION
OF THE SONG "ALFIE" Written by Mr. Burt Bacharach!

To purchase this cd send a check for $25 to

Dr. Len Bergantino
Editor-in-Chief
Publish or Perish Press
1215 Brockton Avenue # 104
Los Angeles, CA 90025-1366

P.S. This cd is one of a kind in that I am the healing
ingredient and I never plan to make another one!
I have been likened to a 'voodoo spiritist and a
Zulu Witch Doctor' by Dr. Donald Rinsley, M.D.-
Fellow-American College of Psychoanalysts in his
Review of my book -Psychotherapy Insight & Style: The
Existential Moment, Published by Allyn & Bacon, Inc.,
Boston, 288 pp., 1981, in Bulletin of The Menninger Clinic
Vol. 47, No.5, September 1983.

The Jazz Trumpet of
Dr. Len Bergantino

Piano and Vocals
Nohwas Tennert
Contact Dr. Len Bergantino
(424) 293-9511
(7 rings)

HEALING CD

This cd has a healing effect and has the potential to positively
effect and affect and to somewhat ameliorate medical symptomatology
in many vital areas as an assistance to medical treatment where
no such amelioration of medical symptomatology currently exists!

For this to occur the cd has to be played 'repetitively and well'
each time suffering outweighs wellbeing!

122 VETS A DAY COMMIT
SUICIDE!''

VETS WHO LISTEN TO
THIS CD FOR TWO
ONE AND ONE HALF
HOUR BLOCKS OF
TIME WILL REDUCE
SUICIDE RATE
BY 60%

(PER DAY FOR
SIX MONTHS)

MY MOTHER WAS A
WITCH DOCTOR!

HALF THE TOWN CAME
TO SEE HER WHEN
THEY WERE ILL. IF
SHE COULDN'T GET
RID OF THEIR
SYMPTOMS, THEN THEY
WENT TO THE DOCTOR

On a pure musical level this cd is good enough that I am able to
make a statement that I have played THE DEFINITIVE INTERPRETATION
OF THE SONG 'ALFIE' written by Mr. Burt Bacharach!

To purchase this cd send a check for $25 to

Dr. Len Bergantino
Editor-in-Chief
Publish or Perish Press
1215 Brockton Avenue # 104
Los Angeles, CA 90025-1366

P.S. This cd is one of a kind in that I am the healing
ingredient and I never plan to make another one!
I have been likened to a 'voodoo spiritist and a
Zulu Witch Doctor' by Dr. Donald Rinsley, M.D.-
Fellow-American College of Psychoanalysts in his
Review of my book -Psychotherapy Insight & Style: The
Existential Moment, Published by Allyn & Bacon, Inc.,
Boston. 788 pp., 1981, in Bulletin of The Menninger Clinic
Vol. 47, No.5, September 1983.

Dr. Len Bergantino's
Progressive Jazz Octet

Contact
Dr. Len Bergantino
at (424) 293-9511
(7 rings)

1. Song - Meditation

Dr. Bergantino plays a concert size
ukelele on second solo and
a fluegelhorn solo

214

HEALING CD

This cd has a healing effect and has the potential to positively
effect and affect and to somewhat ameliorate medical symptomatology
in many vital areas as an assistance to medical treatment where
no such amelioration of medical symptomatology currently exists!

For this to occur the cd has to be played 'repetitively and well'
each time suffering outweighs wellbeing!

122 VETS A DAY COMMIT
SUICIDE!!!

VETS WHO LISTEN TO
THIS CD FOR TWO
ONE AND ONE HALF
HOUR BLOCKS OF
TIME WILL REDUCE
SUICIDE RATE
BY 60%

(PER DAY FOR
SIX MONTHS)

MY MOTHER WAS A
WITCH DOCTOR!

HALF THE TOWN CAME
TO SEE HER WHEN
THEY WERE ILL. IF
SHE COULDN'T GET
RID OF THEIR
SYMPTOMS, THEN THEY
WENT TO THE DOCTOR

On a pure musical level this cd is good enough that I am able to
make a statement that I have played THE DEFINITIVE INTERPRETATION
OF THE SONG "ALFIE" written by Mr. Burt Bacharach!

To purchase this cd send a check for $25 to

Dr. Len Bergantino
Editor-in-Chief
Publish or Perish Press
1215 Brockton Avenue # 104
Los Angeles, CA 90025-1366

P.S. This cd is one of a kind in that I am the healing
     ingredient and I never plan to make another one!
     I have been likened to a "voodoo spiritist and a
     Zulu Witch Doctor" by Dr. Donald Rinsley, M.D.-
     'Fellow-American College of Psychoanalysts in his
     Review of my book -Psychotherapy Insight & Style: The
     Existential Moment, Published by Allyn & Bacon, Inc.,
     Boston, 288 pp., 1981, in Bulletin of The Menninger Clinic,
     Vol. 47, No.5, September 1983.

Dr. Len Bergantino
Plays
Jazz Ukelele

Contact Dr. Len Bergantino
at (424) 293-9511
(7 rings)

216

Lenny's Song
Musicality
Pure Sound
The Art of Melody
Peace

1. Lenny's Song
2. Italian-American Love Song
3. Me Too
4. Opie's Otus
5. I Love Baseball
6. I Miss You, Ma

12/2/17

Songs written and played
on Kamaka Concert Size Ohta - San Ukelele
by Dr. Len Bergantino
© 2017 LD Bergantino Music LLC
Call (424) 293-9511
(7 Rings)

Dan Bergantino
on his Tenor Banjo

Produced by
Dr Len Bergantino
© 2017 LD Bergantino Music LLC
Call (424) 293-9511
(7 Rings)

DR. LEN BERGANTINO
Doctorate - University of Southern California - 1971
Tel/Fax (310) 207-9397

Trumpet - Progressive Jazz & Lead
Solo Tenor Banjo - Mandolin Banjo for
Dixieland & Roaring Twenties

Mandolin - Romantic Italian
& American Old Standard
& Classical Mandolin

1215 Brockton Avenue, Suite 104, Los Angeles, California 90025 USA

Musicality
Pure Sound
The Art of Melody
Peace

1. Alex's Song

3. CD Overview
4. Around The World
5. Some Enchanted Evening
6. Medley
    (It's Been A Long, Long Time,
    Teresa, Maria, Stardust,
    Tammy, Maria Elena)
7. Guitariana / My Regards
8. Misty

9. I'm In The Mood For Love
10. Autumn In New York
11. Old Cape Cod
12. Arriverdici Roma
13. Sorrento
14. Younger Than Springtime
15. Wake The Town And Tell The People
16. If I Give My Heart To You
17. Do I Dare Disturb The Musical Universe

" Alex's Songs Written For My Son "

Played by Dr. Len Bergantino
© 2018 L.D. Bergantino Music LLC

Recorded Feb.16 2018

Call (424) 293-9511
(7 Rings)

Steven Prasinos, Ph.D.
Psychologist

phone/fax: 203-266-4003
website: doctorsteven.net

39 Sherman Hill Rd., Suite C202B
Woodbury, Connecticut 06798

2/27/19

Hi Len -

Really enjoying your CD. The melodies are gorgeous + your playing is very clean + openly spaced. Your brief comments between songs are charming + interesting. Thanks a lot.

Here is my CD #1 with my band playing my songs. Enjoy —

Steven

DR. LEN BERGANTINO
Doctorate - University of Southern California - 1971
Tel/Fax (310) 207-9397

Trumpet - Progressive Jazz & Lead
Solo Tenor Banjo - Mandolin Banjo for
Dixieland & Roaring Twenties

Mandolin - Romantic Italian
& American Old Standards
& Classical Mandolin

03/03/19

UNSOLICITED REVIEW OF DR. STEVEN PRASINOS CD "WHATEVER"

I enjoyed this cd from the very first note to it's entirety.
The first thought I had was what kind of electric guitar
would produce that kind of sound? Furthur. Dr. Steven Prasinos
wrote the songs for the cd and demonstrates a kind of micro-
scopic thought patterns that are both tight and brilliant!
As he is both a musician and a professional psychologist
the second selection on the cd, "Problems" has to make you
laugh because most mortals suffering from the human condition
have had the same mental ramblims as stated by Prasinos.

As for the music it is rare that someone can play from the
inside out and transcend musical technique in reaching the
essence of music on a consistent basis throughout the cd.
Prasinos succeeds! No matter what tempo he plays or what genre
of music he selects. That is, the entire cd is georgeous!

This review is written for Dr. Prasinos to use in whatever way
he sees fit.

Respectfully submitted by,

Dr. Len Bergantino

Dr. Len Bergantino

1215 Brockton Avenue, Suite 104, Los Angeles, California 90025 USA

223

Howard Alden STILL plays the Tenor Banjo!

by Dr. Len Bergantino

In September 2003, I had my first experience with Howard Alden while he was playing guitar at the annual Hot and Sweet Jazz Festival. I had never seen him in person, but did hear him performing on the soundtrack of Woody Allen's movie *Sweet and Lowdown*. What stood out about his guitar playing was the smoothness of his technique - almost like silk. There was a flawless quality that gave you the feeling you wouldn't run into someone who could do this very often - who also played beautifully.

I introduced myself after his set, and told him about a mandolin CD I had made with Joe Diorio backing me on guitar, and asked if he would like a copy. He said to send him one. I asked him to let me know what he thought of it, but didn't really expect such a famous person in the music business to do so. However, a couple of months later I got the following letter from him:

Dear Dr. Bergantino: This is a very late thank you for sending me your CD, with Joe Diorio and yourself. Beautiful tone and articulation, and great accompaniment from Joe - very enjoyable. Have a good holiday season, and I hope to see you next time I'm in LA. All the best,

Howard Alden

After the letter from him I sent him a CD of my father playing tenor banjo, having heard that he "used to play banjo." Then prior to an upcoming appearance at guitar night with John Pisano at *Spazio's* along with Mundell Lowe, I telephoned him to confirm that we would meet. That's when he surprised me. He said he had just played a tenor banjo gig the prior weekend in New York City. Del Casher, another fine guitar player who has accompanied me on gigs in the past told me that Howard Alden was the best tenor banjo player in Los Angeles at one time and he earned his living doing so from about the age of thirteen years old onward. However, I AND MANY OTHER PEOPLE MADE THE ERRONEOUS ASSUMPTION THAT WHEN HOWARD ALDEN SWITCHED TO GUITAR HE STOPPED PLAYING THE TENOR BANJO. THE IMPORTANCE OF THIS ARTICLE TO FIGA IS THAT THIS IS NOT TRUE. HOWARD ALDEN STILL PLAYS TENOR BANJO AND HIS PRIOR RECORDINGS ARE WELL WORTH LISTENING TO.

During our conversation, he told me he liked my father's CD and that he would bring me an audio tape recording of him playing the tenor banjo. When we met he presented me with a copy of the cassette, *Howard Alden Plays The Music of Harry Reser*. On the cover photo, he looks 20 years younger than he is now. He looked to be just a teenager! My first reaction was, "How could such a young kid play the music of Harry Reser?" However, upon listening to Alden breeze through some of Reser's most difficult arrangements in his own style, I became convinced of both the young man's talent as well as the timeless nature of the recording. His style is different than Harry Reser's in that it softer, intended to sound prettier as opposed to the fire coming out of Reser's hands with that crisp full ringing sound. It is

ALL FRETS JULY/AUGUST 2004

224

a different version of how Reser's solos can be played adding a sense of musicality that is Howard Alden and is well worth hearing.

Hopefully, this article will spark an interest in the music of Howard Alden within FIGA and possibly persuade him to attend our FIGA Conventions. If he does, whether playing tenor banjo or guitar, we are all in for a musical treat of the highest order.

"Howard Alden Plays The Music of Harry Reser" is available from Stomp Off Records, PO Box 342, York PA 17405 or directly from Howard Alden, 310 W. 97th St, Apt. 41, New York, NY 10025.

ALL FRETS JULY/AUGUST 2004

Glossary for R.'s new letter

DR. LEN BERGANTINO

Doctorate - University of Southern California - 1971

Tel/Fax (310) 207-9397

Trumpet - Progressive Jazz & Lead
Solo Tenor Banjo - Mandolin Banjo for
Dixieland & Roaring Twenties

16 year Retired Local 47
Member for Good Standing

Mandolin - Romantic Italian
& American Old Standards
& Classical Mandolin

July 17, 2018

UNSOLICITED REVIEW OF TOM BRUNER'S CD "HOMAGE TO A HERO"
Played a gig with him when he was in Local 47
(To be used in any way that Tom Bruner sees fit!)

I am not a guitar player. I am a retired musician writing
this review as a Musicologist.

When you hear the first three notes of a cd you know if
you like it and you know if it is music. Tom Bruner's
FIRST 3 NOTES GRAB YOU IMMEDIATELY AND TELL YOU THAT
TOM BRUNER IS A MUSICIAN IN THE FULL SENSE OF THE WORD,
THAT HE IS A CLASS ACT HUMAN BEING WHO PLAYS MUSIC FROM
HIS SOUL, AND THAT THE PRODUCTION OF HIS SOUND ON THE
GUITARS CONNECTED TO HIS INNER BEING!

Further, Tom Bruner plays jazz to song melodies. While this
sounds simple unfortunately Tom is of the generation
where people actually played and wrote songs, and then
played jazz to those songs. CURRENT GENERATIONS PLAY NOISE!!!

Taken from Tom's cd jacket, quoting his hero directly, is
the most important thing I ever read about playing jazz:

"Wes has been quoted many times as saying that he did not
practice, that what he played came basically from the spur of
the moment. After years of listening to him, I feel that when
he started an improvised solo, he would play a note - whether
it would necessarily be within the basic harmony or not - and
then build improvisational melodic ideas and variations by free
association from that note...to another note...sequentially as
to how he heard that ad-libbed melody unfolding inside his
consciousness... and not generally from a specific organization
of pitches learned through a prescribed scale, finger position
on the neck, or mode. Possibly this is the result of his
playing so fluently with octaves, as in doing so, "notes"
relating to harmonic structures become more important where they
lay on the neck than do "positions". This is not to say he
didn't have favorite "places" to go when starting a single-note
solo, only that those places were uniquely Wes Montgomery."

Last but not least, anyone that could write the above
paragraph must of graduated from North Texas State
University, the finest jazz school and one of the finest
music schools in The United States. Tom Bruner went to North
Texas State. I spent a week there basically through the
good graces of jazz instructor Mike Steinel. I attended
a North Texas State college football game and it is the only
school where the fans went to hear the band!!!

1215 Brockton Avenue, Suite 104, Los Angeles, California 90025 USA

written by   DR. Len Bergantino

226

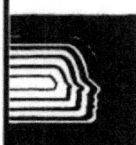

THE MILTON H. ERICKSON FOUNDATION, INC.

3606 North 24th Street • Phoenix, Arizona 85016-6500 • USA
Telephone: (602) 956-6196 • Fax: (602) 956-0519
e-mail: office@erickson-foundation.org
http://www.erickson-foundation.org

SM

February 16, 2008

To Whom This May Concern:

I am the daughter of Milton H. Erickson M.D., and a member of the Board of Directors of the Milton Erickson Foundation.

Prior to and during the 1970's, Dr. Erickson held weeklong professional teaching seminars in the home office. The content of the seminars included basic and advanced techniques of clinical hypnosis and uncommon therapy. The teaching involved didactic, metaphorical and experiential methodology.

Dr. Len Bergantino first participated in this educational opportunity on September 11, 1977, returning several times for more in depth study with Dr. Erickson. Dr. Bergantino breadth of knowledge is remarkable in that he has studied under numerous world-renowned psychotherapists. Dr Erickson remarked to him that he "respected your dedication to the work". The mutual respect that Dr. Erickson and Dr. Bergantino held for each other was reflected in the friendship that continued until Dr. Erickson's death in 1980, and has continued with Dr. Erickson's widow, Elizabeth Erickson, now 92 years old.

Sincerely

Roxanna Erickson Klein RN PhD

Roxanna Erickson Klein

GEORGE G. KATZ, J.D., Ph.D.
Board Certified in Clinical Psychology
Board Certified in Forensic Psychology
American Board of Professional Psychology

(310) 454-8643
Email:bb283@latn.org

April 12, 2000

To whom it may concern:

I am writing this letter on behalf of Dr. Leonard Bergantino who is applying for the position of counselor at your facility.

I have known Dr. Bergantino for over twenty-five years, having first met him when he was a staff psychologist at the West Los Angeles VA Medical Center. He was most impressive as a highly empathic therapist who showed exceptional creativity in assisting patients' reintegration into the community. His sensitivity and manner makes it easy for folks to talk to him and share problems. I believe that he is eminently qualified to assume any position requiring finely honed people skills.

As for his experience in dealing with multi-cultural situations, he can best describe the details of his extensive travels and professional background in conducting workshops throughout Europe and elsewhere.

I would conclude with one final characterization. Dr. Bergantino is a multi-faceted individual; he is a first rate trumpet player and a mandolin virtuoso. While these abilities may not appear germane to the role of counselor, it does round out the description of this gifted person applying for this position.

Yours truly,

17337 Tramonto Drive . Pacific Palisades . California . 90272. Psychology License PL-3193

228

LEN BERGANTINO, ED.D., ABPP
1215 Brockton Avenue, Suite 104
Los Angeles, California 90025

RE: PICTURES ON BACK COVER OF BOOK

Top Picture:

My children and myself with my Callichio Trumpet made by the
great Italian trumpet maker Dominic Callichio and sold to me
in 1967. The picture was taken in the early 1990's and my
daughter Lisa Francesca Bergantino and my son Alexander
Leonardo Bergantino are on either side of me.

Bottom Picture:

Harry James whose 1941 record "The Sleepy Lagoon" forever
influenced my musical life. The picture is of Harry James
in 1942.

Around 2003 I met with then President Hal Espinosa of Musicians
Local 47 in Honolulu, Hawaii. Hal played lead trumpet for Les
Brown and His Band of Renown before he became Union President.
I said to him, "Harry James is the reason I started playing
trumpet!" He said to me "Harry James is the reason we all
started playing trumpet!"

PICTURE ON FRONT COVER OF BOOK

The front cover of the book is a picture of Dr. Len Bergantino
around 1979. This is the time I simultaneously began the
private practice of psychoanalysis in Beverly Hills, California
and I began working on my recording studio technique on the
mandolin with The Paganini of the Mandolin in the Soviet Union,
Mischa Shenkyman.

This picture exudes PSYCHOSEXUAL CONNECTEDNESS AS IN HAVING BOTH
WORKED THROUGH THE OEDIPAL COMPLEX WHILE SIMULTANEOUSLY
RECONNECTING THE LIFE FORCE WITH ALL COMPONENTS OF YOUR MENTAL
AND PHYSICAL BODY!!!

LEN BERGANTINO, ED.D., ABPP
1215 Brockton Avenue, Suite 104
Los Angeles, California 90025

Beautiful Melodies

Music Duo For Hire

CD Demo on Request
310.207.9397

Chet Baker (Renown Jazz Trumpeter) meets Romano
Mussolini (Renown jazz pianist and son of fascist dictator
Benito Mussolini) in Milan, Italy in 1960.

Background

Benito Mussolini (tl Duce- the creator of Fascism) was
captured along with his mistress Ciara Petacci (extremely
attractive) in Lake Como, Italy in 1945 and they were both
shot by the partisans, hung upside down in the center of
town and urinated on! Ciara Petacci ran in front of
Mussolini to get shot first!!! a trait none of the women I
dated manifested!!!

230

Chet Baker, smashed out of his mind on drugs was playing jazz trumpet at a nightclub in Milan, Italy in 1960. It was a dark nightclub.

Roman Mussolini was sitting at the back end of the dark club and sent one of his friends to tell Chet Baker he wanted to meet him. Now, Chet, true to form was blasted out of his mind on drugs and as he stumbled to the back of the room he walked up to Romano Mussolini and said, "Hey man, I am sorry about your old man! What a drag!" Baker said it as if there was not time lag between 1945 and 1960, as if it happened yesterday. Romano Mussolini was in disbelief but said nothing in response the comment in that he understood it was Chet Baker blasted out of his mind!

LEN BERGANTINO, ED.D., ABPP
1215 Brockton Avenue, Suite 104
Los Angeles, California 90025

Beautiful Melodies

Music Duo For Hire

CD Demo on Request
310.207.9397

BOBBY HACKETT-TRUMPET-CORNET-PURE
SOUND

Bobby Hackett had the closest to pure sound on a trumpet
and cornet that I ever heard. When Jackie Gleason (The
Great One) had a big band Bobby Hackett was the trumpet
player.

Bobby Hackett was known among the musicians as never
saying a bad word about anybody, nor could the musicians
get him to do so. Right after Hitler's demise at his lowest
ebb the musicians placed a bet they could get him to say
something negative so they said to Bobby Hackett, "Hey
Bobby? What do you think of Adolph Hitler?" Hackett
paused for an over a minute and then said, " HE WAS THE

232

BEST IN HIS CATEGORY!". Of course the category was
Benito Mussolini, Joseph Stalin and Generalissimo Franco!

My excellent Gestalt therapy trainer Dr. James Simkin,
Ph.D., Diplomate in Clinical Psychology, referred to such
phenomena as "Unconditional Positive Disregard!", a fate
from which he considered there was no cure!

LEN BERGANTINO, ED.D., ABPP
1215 Brockton Avenue, Suite 104
Los Angeles, California 90025

To Hire Me As A Consultant

Call (424)293-9511

(7 Rings)

The above logo was made and given to me as a gift by Phil
Urso- who played Saxophone for Chet Baker in the ealry
1950's. I met Phil at a Jazz conert around 2003. Phil played
with Chet Baker at original Lighthouse in Hermosa Beach-
run by Howard Ramsey.

234

LEN BERGANTINO, ED.D., ABPP

1215 Brockton Avenue, Suite 104
Los Angeles, California 90025

**TO HIRE ME AS A CONSULTANT
CALL (424) 293-9511
(7 RINGS)**

MP 3's

p. 3

Trumpet- Progressive Jazz
& Lead
Solo Tenor Bano-Mandolin
Banjo
for Dixieland & Roaring
Twenties

Mandolin-
Romantic
Italian
&
American
Old
Standards
& Classical
Mandolin

www.drlenbergantino.com

These MP3's have a medically healing quality and at the very least will provide a healing pace that strengthens the immune system.

This healing pace cuts across not only music but also the fields of psychoanalysis, psychotherapy, clinical hypnosis and is at the core of the pursuit of Shakespeare's question "TO BE OR NOT TO BE' WHICH IS AT THE CORE OF

235

THE CREATION OF AN UPWARD SPIRALING SOCIETY AS OPPOSED TO THE DOWNWARD SPIRALING SOCIETY WE HAVE TODAY!

FURTHER, THE TRANSPOSITION OF THIS MUSICAL PACING THROUGHOUT SOCIETY IS SPIRITUAL IN NATURE AND WILL LEAD TO THE SIGNIFICANT INCREASE IN THE CURRENT STATISTICAL COUNT OF PERSONS OUT OF EVERY ONE HUNDRED MILLION THAT CROSS OVER INTO THE PEARLY GATES KNOWN AS HEAVEN!

AS ME AND MY CHILDREN HAVE BEEN SENT BACK ON A KARMIC MISSION TO EVOKE THESE RESULTS AND AS A THE ALMIGHTY HAS HAD IT WITH "DOUBTING THOMASES" IT IS AS CERTAIN AS DEATH AND TAXES THAT ALL "DOUBTING THOMASES" WILL BE SENT DIRECTLY TO HELL AND WILL NOT PASS GOAL!

These MP3's need to be linked to all of my published books as specified in www.drlenbergantinobooks.com.

While I come from a musical family, it was three persons breaking out into uncontrollable tears when I played music that led my contribution to mankind to incorporate THE ESSENCE OF MUSIC!

a. While seeing a patient for psychoanalysis I played Come Back to Sorrento on my mandolin and he cried for 45 minutes. As he left he said, "Boy, you sure earned your money today!".

b. While recording my CD, "Falling In Love-Dr. Len Bergantino' sold through Amazon Digital as an MP3-World renown guitar accompanist Joe Diorio broke out into tears when I played The St. Mary's Waltz, written by my father's uncle Soledad Bredice in 1920.

c. My daughter, Lisa Francesca Bergantino, broke out in tears while listening to a five song Demo where I played mandolin with jazz choruses including HERE COMES SANTA CLAUS FOR THE CHRISTMAS HOLIDAYS!

LEN BERGANTINO, ED.D., ABPP
1215 Brockton Avenue, Suite 104
Los Angeles, California 90025

TO HIRE ME AS A CONSULTANT
CALL (424) 293-9511
(7 RINGS)

MP 3's

ρ. 3

www.drlenbergantino.com

1. Falling In Love- Dr. Len Bergantino sold by Amazon Digital 22 Songs accompanied by World Renown jazz guitarist Joe Diorio. Joe cried during my mandolin recording!

2. Alex's Song - A Healing CD- focus on healing pace and SHOULD BE LISTENED TO IN IT'S Entirety (45 minutes). I listen to it every night before bed. Additional focus on the melody!!! I WROTE ALEX'S SONG!!!

3. 2 Soulful Cornet Solos 2 days after I mailed out this Demo I was hired by the President of The Italian American Lawyers. In the prior two monthly meetings he hired IL Vuolo from Italy and The Beach Boys. After hearing me play the first set on the cornet, HE PAID ME DOUBLE FOR THE ENGAGEMENT! THIS IS UNHEARD OF

BOTH IN THE MUSIC BUSINESS AND AMONG
MUSICIAN UNION MEMBERS-LOCAL 47 in Los
Angeles.

4. Dr. Len Bergantino - 5 Song Demo- My daughter cried
when hearing this Demo. I go back and forth between this
demo and Falling In Love in terms of THE HIGHEST
QUALITY MANDOLIN SOUND EVER RECORDED.
THEY BOTH MOVED PEOPLE TO TEARS!!!!

5. Choro-The Music of the People in Brazil has me playing
Choro and Jazz solos on both the BANDOLIM AND THE
CORNET AND WAS RECORDED BY A MEMBER OF
THE BAND ON A LIVE GIG!!!

I went to Rio De Janeiro for a couple of weeks to study
with some of the best bandolim players in Brazil. I
remember Joel Nasciemento in particular. Although he
spoke only Portuguese he changed my sound forever!
Bandolim was like a mandolin only with a bigger top more
like a large size pizza. When they heard me play they said "
NOT BAD FOR A GRINGO!".

6. PROGRESSIVE JAZZ OCTET recorded one eight-
minute song entitled MEDITATION written by Tom
Jobim. They named the International Airport after him in
Rio de Janeiro. I play solos on concert size Kamaka
Ukelele and Flugelhorn recommended to me by Roy
Hargrove and made in Zurich Switzerland made by Tom
Inderbinen, Roy Hargrove had the best sound on a
flugelhorn I ever heard!!!

I had lunch with Tom Jobim's son in Rio de Janeiro. He informed me that Tom Jobim International Airport was the only time an international airport was named after a musician. He further said that he never left his residence when writing his songs. He looked out of one window and saw a girl walking on the beach and wrote THE GIRL FROM IPANEMA. He looked out another window and saw a statue of Christ and wrote Corcovado.

7. Lenny's Song- I wrote 5 melodies for this CD. The one for my daughter is ME TOO. Another is about baseball. For each song I wrote I felt as deeply as I could in my heart and then wrote the melody.

8. Dr. Len Bergantino plays jazz trumpet is a demo that demonstrates playing from the heart while also playing rapid technical passages using triple and double tonguing.

9. MISCHA SHENKYMAN WAS THE PAGANINI OF THE MANDOLIN IN THE SOVIET UNION AND DID GIVE A CONCERT AT CARNEGIE HALL IN THE UNITED STATES. HE WAS MY teacher from 1979-2981. He graduated from a Russian Conservatory. Russian Conservatory Graduates (the four that I have met) have superior technical abilities.

10. Dr. Len Bergantino plays Jazz Ukelele. I am experimenting with a Kamaka Soprano size and a Kamaka Concert size Ukelele. I made this Demo in my bedroom

using different cd's to play the background as if I were playing for their band.

Jazz musicians refer to the term WOODSHEDDING as in hours per day of practice to develop their art form. On trumpet, I played with cd's of Miles Davis and Chet Baker and on mandolin I played along with guitarists Johnny Smith and Charlie Byrd. When you listen to FALLING IN LOVE YOU WILL HEAR A SOUND SIMILAR TO JOHNNY SMITH PLAYING MOONLIGHT IN VERMONT ON MY GIBSON F-2 1913 MANDOLIN. My father said if you don't put in the highest quality, the quality does not come out.

I LOVED THE SOUND OF THE UKELELE WHEN PLAYING PROGRESSIVE JAZZ! Herb Ohta Sr. liked the way I played. He was the best in Hawaii.

11. DAN BERGANTINO AND HIS TENOR BANJO. Dan Bergantino was my father and the second best tenor banjo player I ever heard. Harry Reser was the best. I loved when my father played Nola. Lollipops and The Clock and The Banjo for me! My Mother told me "Don't compete with your father technically. He will bury you alive! BUT YOU PLAY PRETTIER THAN HIM!"

12. The Romantic Music of Dr. Len Bergantino- where I play romantic song I love that I haven't recorded on any other demo.

242

Dr. Len Bergantino, ED.D. (USC), PH.D.

*Musicality,
Pure Sound,
The Art of Melody
and Inner Peace*

The
Essence
of
Music

THE MILTON H. ERICKSON FOUNDATION, INC

3606 North 24th Street • Phoenix, Arizona 85016-6500 • USA
Telephone: (602) 956-6196 • Fax: (602) 956-0519
e-mail: office@erickson-foundation.org
http://www.erickson-foundation.org

SM

February 16, 2008

To Whom This May Concern:

I am the daughter of Milton H. Erickson M.D., and a member of the Board of Directors
of the Milton Erickson Foundation.

Prior to and during the 1970's, Dr. Erickson held weeklong professional teaching
seminars in the home office. The content of the seminars included basic and advanced
techniques of clinical hypnosis and uncommon therapy. The teaching involved didactic,
metaphorical and experiential methodology.

Dr. Len Bergantino first participated in this educational opportunity on September 11,
1977, returning several times for more in depth study with Dr. Erickson. Dr. Bergantino
breadth of knowledge is remarkable in that he has studied under numerous world-
renowned psychotherapists. Dr Erickson remarked to him that he "respected your
dedication to the work". The mutual respect that Dr. Erickson and Dr. Bergantino held
for each other was reflected in the friendship that continued until Dr. Erickson's death in
1980, and has continued with Dr. Erickson's widow, Elizabeth Erickson, now 92 years
old.

Sincerely

Roxana Erickson Klein RN PhD
Roxanna Erickson Klein

244

Ex-City Teacher's Article Published

A Waterbury native and former Wilby High School teacher recently had an article published in the magazine "Voices," journal of the American Association of Psychotherapy.

Dr. Len Bergantino also is writing two books in the field of psychotherapy and expects them to be published in a few months.

Dr. Len Bergantino

The article describes Bergantino's experiences with patients in private practice after a 50-minute session supposedly ended therapy for that day.

His experience has taught him that intensive therapy frequently takes place after the 50-minute session is over, Bergantino said.

Bergantino described how he dealt with the problem, citing examples.

Bergantino is the son of Mr. and Mrs. Daniel Bergantino of 25 Houston St. The senior Bergantino is a well-known area music instructor.

Mrs. Bergantino is president of the auxiliary at St. Mary's Hospital.

Dr. Bergantino is a graduate of Sacred Heart High School. He

received a B.A. in political science and history from the University of Connecticut at Storrs. He has two master's degrees, one from Fairfield University in education and social studies and the other from the University of Southern California at Los Angeles in education.

He received his doctorate in education and psychology from USC.

Dr. Bergantino taught at Wilby High School in 1967 and 1968. He worked as a psychologist for the U.S. Civil Service in California. He taught at USC on both the San Diego and Los Angeles campuses and at Chapman College. He currently teaches for the California Graduate Institute of Los Angeles, in addition to teaching weekend marathon counseling courses for USC at San Diego.

He is married to the former Barbara Tiexson of Beverly Hills, Calif., where he also maintains a private practice.

1975
Published I
Waterbury (Conn)
Republican -
American.

At the time I had
a private practice in
clinical Psychology
on 3760 Third Avenue
San Diego, California

246

Chuck Cecil's Swingin' Years

7 May 2013

Dear Len ...

    With a little luck your track of "Misty" will
be part of a TURNING-TIME-AROUND feature scheduled
to be heard Saturday, June 29, about 7:45am on KKJZ.
Your performance will be heard along with the original
by Errol Garner, plus samples of the song by Sarah
Vaughn and Johnny Mathis. It's all on the enclosed CD.

    Thanks for listening and for contributing to
the SWINGIN' YEARS.

Sincerely ...

chuck cecil's

Swingin' Years

Show #104
Disc #2

---

theme

TRACK - 1

7:47

"Don't Get Around Much Anymore" - Duke Ellington

"But Not For Me" - Judy Garland

segment 1

(cue: "The Swingin' Years")

COMMERCIAL BREAK #1

TRACK - 2

5:34

"Misty" - Len Bergantino
"Misty" - Errol Garner
"Misty" - Sarah Vaughn (sample)
"Misty" - Johnny Mathis (sample)
"Misty" - Len Bergantino (reprise)

segment 2
TURNING TIME AROUND

(cue: "The Swingin' Years")

COMMERCIAL BREAK #2

5:57

"It's Torture" - Count Basie
"I Want a Little Girl" - Count Basie

segment 3
DOUBLE PLAY

(cue: "The Swingin' Years")

COMMERCIAL BREAK #3

"Soft Shoe Shuffle" - Jan Garber

7:01

(theme with program identification & :10 bed for
station or sponsor ID, cue: "The Swingin' Years")

segment 4

"Skyliner" - Charlie Barnet

(cue: "The Swingin' Years")

COMMERCIAL BREAK #4

2:56

"Cielito Lindo" - King Sisters

segment 5

(cue: "The Swingin' Years")

COMMERCIAL BREAK #5

15:05

theme
"Solid As a Stone Wall Jackson" - Glenn Miller
"Walking By the River" - Glenn Miller
"Frenesi" - Glenn Miller
"A Stone's Throw From Heaven" - Glenn Miller
theme

segment 6
ON LOCATION

(cue: "The Swingin' Years")

COMMERCIAL BREAK #6

3:40

"Memories Of You" - Benny Goodman

segment 7

theme

(cue: "The Swingin' Years" & theme tag)

total pgm time: 48:00

248

Danny Bergantino - My Dad

by Dr. Len Bergantino

stairs and said. "Daddy, what's this?" He said. "It's a tenor banjo - but nobody uses it anymore." When I persisted and asked "Why?". dad said. "I used to play it all the time - then radio came in. First I was on the bandstand with the band and they said I was too loud. Then they had me play near the door while the band was on the stage and they still said it was too loud. Finally they moved me outside the door and said. 'Danny, if you want to play with this band, you'd better learn to play the guitar." So, he did!

As a result, my dad's tenor banjo was relegated to the attic where it remained until I dragged it back into his life. I don't know what it was, but I loved the banjo at first sight and pleaded with my dad to get it fixed. While he hadn't played the banjo in years, his hand were in pretty good shape as he had worked regularly on guitar and violin. When he picked up the banjo and rattled off *Lollipops, Nola and The Cat and the Dog*, I just sat there in awe. He had gotten me started on mandolin at the age of six, but now I wanted him to teach me the tenor banjo. Too bad for me, my hands were very small and I didn't seem to have the strength and speed necessary to play the tenor banjo and quickly gave up. But I fondly recall listening to dad, who continued to play the banjo for his own enjoyment.

Dan Bergantino, my dad, was born in Waterbury, Connecticut in 1906. He came of age with the tenor banjo in the mid to late 1920s. You know, there are some people who are just born to play an instrument and they can do no wrong on it - Benny Goodman with a clarinet... Harry James with a trumpet. Well, my old man was like that with a tenor banjo.

If a tenor banjo player is judged on speed, cleanliness and musicianship, my dad may not have been as good as Harry Reser. But, he was the best that most people who came across him had ever heard. In his day, he used to cut the Harry Reser solos clean as a whistle as the tenor banjo player in Harry Brinkman's band in the Connecticut area.

My introduction to my dad's tenor banjo playing came in 1954 when I was 11 years old. Even though it was winter, I decided to crawl through the trap-door that led to our unheated attic. There I saw this instrument with broken strings and what looked to me like a broken drum head. I dragged it down

When the nostalgia craze of the late 1950s and early 60s came around, dad and his tenor banjo were ready. He ended up working a couple of nights a week in New Haven and the surrounding area. In addition to his superb musicianship, dad knew how to light up a stage. He was like a magician who was able to bring an audience to life though his fire and speed. Dad had made the choice many years earlier to raise his family and stay close to home. But, I'm confident that he could have played anywhere with anybody had he chosen that path. The fact that he didn't makes him one of those unsung heroes in the musical world.

Knowing that his incredible talent wouldn't be around forever, I made a point of coaxing dad to sit in front of a tape recorder and document his abilities. While he was past his years of blazing speed, his musicality and technical powers did not desert him. He played a wide range of music - from *Lollypops* to the (then) current hits, *Honey* and *The Way We Were*. Yes, even though this recording captured him at the ages of 75, he was still keeping up to date with the tunes. Later, I also found one of

dad's memorial tapes made about ten years earlier. Since editing both of the tapes (made in 1971 and 1981) I have often listened to them and experienced the same sense of awe that I had as a youngster. When dad passed away in 1983, these recordings took their place among my prized possessions.

Over the years, I had continued to play the mandolin and, through my friend Bill Bloom, became associated with the San Fernando Valley Banjo Band. While I'd gotten a false start trying to work in the banjo-mandolin, I found that playing jazz riffs and bass lines on a real tenor banjo suited my style and my small hands just fine. Having been a member of the band for about a year, I decided to make the other band members a present of the audio tapes I had of my dad's playing. The band members raved about the recordings (and still do). This reaction gave me the notion that other banjo players might like to hear these recordings and may find value in the things dad was able to do. So, I decided to make these tapes available to everyone.

Danny Bergantino was a soulful musician with masterful technique. When I pressed him, he'd comment, "You should have heard me 50 years ago." Based on what I *did* hear, I can only imagine. He may not have been Harry Reser. But, he was the best banjo player I ever heard. If it sounds like I'm idealizing him a little bit, remember, he was my old man!

To purchase a copy of "Danny Bergantino on his tenor banjo" send $15.00 to Dr. Len Bergantino, 1215 Brockton Avenue, #104, Los Angeles, CA 90025.

Dan Bergan true AND
HIS TENOR BANSO

Arbson
Top
1. For World is WAITING
2. ? The Sunrise
3. Lollipops - a Harry Reser
Solo - A Novelty few can play!
4 ?

5 Theme from The Broadway Show The Boyfriend
6. ? (The Boy friend - mid 1950's)
7. Dueling Banjos from Movie Deliverance
8. ? with Burt Reynolds -1970's
9. ? from "The Boy friend"
10. ?
11 Oh Susuan's
12 The World is WAITING for The Sunrise
13 Alabamy Bound - clean speed
14 Bye Bye Blues
15 Ralph Colacchio Banjo Novelty - Cute riff
16 my old Kentucky Home
17. World is WAITING for The Sunrise
18.
19 AN WAITING for The Sunrise   Harry Reser
    The Octode and The Banjo   solo
20 (-NOLA - Great Solo
21 MAME (Ethel Merman -Broadway)
22
23 Bye Bye Blues - Arbson Banjo

252

*24. Alabamy Bound speed, cram; char

*25? 11 Paramount Banjo

26. Those Were The Days

27 Theme from Love story

28 Movie - Ryan O'Neal & Ali McGraw
    Honey

29 Five Foot Two, Eyes of Blue

JC 30 When Day is Done

* 31 Go Go (Ralph Calichto)
       Novelty Number - Cuts off

* 32. Nola - Novelty written by Felix Arndt

JC 33 Dueling Banjos from Deliverance

253

Len Bergantino - Falling In Love

Len Bergantino & Joe Diorio – Falling In Love and Dan Bergantino and the Mandolin

by Terry Pender

These two recordings come from the collection of Len Bergantino, a clinical psychologist and mandolin player from Los Angeles, California. Len's father, Dan Bergantino, was a well-known mandolin player, born in Waterbury, CT in 1906. He made his living as a professional mandolin player and also worked as a violinist with the Waterbury Symphony. He was one of those unsung players – a huge talent in the Waterbury/New Haven, CT area, but one that never went out on the road or recorded and, subsequently, is not very well known today.

Len remembers his father's great musicianship and his ability to blend fast single note playing with agile chordal work. As Len says, "He had fire in his hands!" Dan Bergantino was the son of immigrants who came through Ellis Island from San Marco La Catola, Italy. As a young man, Dan helped support his large family through his music when times were tough. Along with his uncle and brothers, there was quite a bit of music in the Bergantino household. It was Dan's uncle, Soledad Bredice, who taught him the mandolin. Soledad also taught his own sons, Fred and Louie Bredice, who were well known guitarists in the Connecticut area. The Bredice brothers named out to be Joe Diorio's teachers and that's where the connection between Len and Joe was established. Joe Diorio is considered to be one of the world's greatest guitar players. He's an expert in mainstream jazz performance and in free-form jazz improvisation.

Dan Bergantino taught his young son Len solfeggio when he was five and began to teach him the mandolin at age six using the Christofaro books. Dan made his living primarily with the guitar, violin and tenor banjo, but mandolin was his first love. He played all the old Italian music whenever he picked up his mandolin – songs that were played at Italian weddings that no one had ever written down. In the summer of 1979, Len had his father write out some of those old tunes. Len also has a cassette tape available of his father playing exclusively Italian music. It is a solo medley of Italian songs that includes all the classics and more. This 15-minute demonstration of solo Italian music on a cheap borrowed mandolin played near the end of his life shows that Dan could really play. His musicality and precision are evident, as well as his marvelous skill at arranging Italian classics. Len is offering to duplicate this cassette for anyone interested for $10, including tax and postage. Although quite short, it is a wonderful document, and I recommend it to fans of Italian mandolin.

Dan Bergantino

After receiving training from his father, Len Bergantino pursued a career as a clinical psychologist. But one evening at the Bonaventure Hotel, Len heard the Russian mandolin virtuoso Emanuil Sheynkman and began a period of study with him. Len's goal was to learn as much as he could so that he could record his own mandolin CD. During this process, Len became good friends with "Mischa" Sheynkman and, after his death, had one of Sheynkman's out-of-print Russian recordings re-mastered for CD. This recording, Emanuil Sheynkman: The Paganini of the Mandolin, is available on CD from Len for $15.00. This is a great CD that I highly recommend. Norman Levine reviewed it when it was first released in a past issue of MQ.

Finally, after his studies with Sheynkman, Len did record his own mandolin CD called Falling In Love. This recording brings us full circle, with Len playing the beautiful Italian melodies he had heard during his childhood – and with his family friend, Joe Diorio, on guitar. Their friendship is a wonderful coincidence because Joe Diorio is a consummate musician, and he provides everything that Bergantino could ask for, playing a beautiful accompaniment on jazz guitar as Len plays the melodies on his 1913 Gibson F-2. Falling In Love is just what you might expect – a very mellow, relaxed reading of Italian and jazz standards played with a lot of love and feeling. Together, Diorio and Bergantino play through tunes like "Arrivederci Roma," "Come Prima," "Come Back To Sorrento," "Misty," "Tre Viglia e Sonno" and "Speak Softly Love."

These self-produced recordings and tapes present a unique glimpse of the mandolin world from the point of view of someone who grew up during the heyday of the Italian/American mandolin popularity, and they provide us with some interesting recordings of music that is not generally available elsewhere.

Len Bergantino's *Falling In Love* is also $15.00, and all of the recordings can be obtained by writing to Len at:

Len Bergantino
1215 Brockton Avenue
Suite 104
Los Angeles, CA 90025

Radim Zenkl – Restless Joy

Restless Joy - Radim Zenkl
Ventana 3401.

by Terry Pender

Restless Joy is the fifth and latest recording by mandolinist Radim Zenkl. His first outing on CD since 1996's *Strings and Wings*, this recording finds Radim in a contemplative mood playing quite a bit of Celtic-influenced music on his nylon stringed mandolin and bouzouki. Radim, a new member of the Modern Mandolin Quartet, is well known for his experimental bent. His earlier recording, *Galactic Mandolin*, featured a series of compositions, each using a different tuning system. Radim is also known for his great speed and dexterity. Although this CD is more focused and traditional in some aspects, it still has the edge supplied by Radim's rhythmic energy and command of the mandolin. Overall, I'd have to say that this recording struck me as Radim's most introspective CD to date. There are a lot of quiet, beautiful moments on this recording. The energy level and experimental demeanor are still there, but there are several moments that are simply quiet and thoughtful, and a melodic lushness radiates from many of the tunes on this collection.

The 13 pieces range from poignant Irish-influenced melodies to the rhythmically charged "Revival," where Radim reaches into the Sam Bush playbook for some powerful, drum-like mandolin rhythms. "Ventana Breeze" is just that – a cool breeze floating by on the mandolin with a smooth tremolo and an irresistible melody. "Once Upon A Time" features Radim playing his Irish bouzouki fingerstyle. This

smooth, mellow fingerstyle technique is quite attractive, and it works well both on the melody and for accompanying the pennywhistle in this duet. "Twin Peaks" is a fast-paced mandolin fiddle tune with the same twisting and turning phrases that Chris Thile likes to play. "At The End Of Summer" is Radim's gorgeous slide mandolin showpiece. When Sam Bush plays the slide mandolin, it's almost always in a blues or rock vein, influenced by blues slide guitar. Radim takes the idea and smoothes it out by writing a lush melody in a major key and using a very supple and warm tone that ends up sounding nothing like Sam Bush.

Originally from Czechoslovakia, Radim's music encompasses eastern European folk music. It's classical mandolin with American bluegrass, jazz and folk all mixed in. And the new emphasis on Celtic music fits right in with Radim's interest in world music. This is an interesting, original perspective on mandolin music. I can't wait to hear how Radim and the Modern Mandolin Quartet sound together. The journey continues for one of our more adventurous and ambitious mandolin players.

Captain Corelli's Mandolin The Original Motion Picture Soundtrack

Captain Corelli's Mandolin - The Original Motion Picture Soundtrack with music composed by Steven Warbeck. Decca Records.

by Terry Pender

This is not really a mandolin CD. Rather, it's a CD of music from the movie that often uses the

Mischa Sheynkman:

The Soviet Paganini of the Mandolin

by Len Bergantino

After sending a cd of Emanuil "Mischa" Sheynkman to the *Mandolin Journal* editor, I asked if she would be interested in an article about Mischa to which she happily agreed. The cd features Sheynkman playing mandolin with his peers – those who graduated from Russian conservatories with a major in Russian folk music. He was never able to find those kinds of peers when he defected to the United States in 1977. The Soviet government destroyed all of the masters of his work but I made a copy from a recording that he gave me when he was my teacher from 1979 - 1981.

While this is an article about Sheynkman, in that I am claiming from all that I know he was the best that ever lived (and fellow mandolinist Bill Bloom backs me up on it) I must say a little about both of us in that you will know that such praise does not come lightly.

Bill Bloom is about 83 years old and I am 67. I am not even sure where I met him and how we have been friends for twenty years. Bill is an eccentric who loves mandolin, he is a Russian Jew born in the United States with a deep appreciation of Russian mandolin and domra music. Sheynkman defected to New York in 1977 and Bill Bloom worked for two years to transplant Sheynkman and his family to Los Angeles. Sheynkman, along with his wife and two children, lived with Bill and Letha Bloom for about six months before they got an apartment in the San Fernando Valley, which is where I took lessons from him.

In 1956, a professional mandolin player in Waterbury, Connecticut – Ray Amicone, who had a handmade D'Angelico mandolin let me borrow a record of the legendary mandolinist Dave Apollon, whose arrangement

of "Smoke Gets in Your Eyes" was written out for me by my father, Daniel Bergantino, who had fire in his hands and brought every stage to life I ever saw him play on, and which version I played on my own CD "Falling In Love" which I made with jazz guitarist Joe Diorio. Until I met Sheynkman, Dave Apollon was the best I had ever heard play the mandolin in my lifetime.

I met Sheynkman in 1979 when I heard him play at the Bonaventure Hotel in Los Angeles. He and his group wore red tunics and he had a lot of black hair bobbing and weaving all over the place as he played with a technique where his speed was blinding. His fingers never left the fingerboard, and his sense of musicality touched my soul many times during the engagement. I had sold my mandolin and my trumpet and was not playing music at the time, and yet, all I could think was "I want to take lessons from this guy! This is the chance of a lifetime!" My parents were visiting me so I brought my father to hear him the following week. He too thought Sheynkman was beyond human belief. In other words, keep in mind that no matter how good I attempt to show you a picture of his ability, I can never give you the full extent of it any more than I can bring Paganini himself back to life (I have read two volumes of his life and work).

So that night I went up to Sheynkman during a break and said, "Sir, do you teach?" I want to take mandolin lessons from you" He said, "Yes" I said "How much do you charge?" He said "$20 a lesson." I said, blurting it out for no conscious reason, "Can you teach me a technique I can use in a recording studio?" He said "yes" And we were off and running. I was studying with the Paganini of the mandolin from the Soviet Union for $20 a lesson. I went out and bought a 1913 Gibson F-2 round hole mellow sounding mandolin. I told Sheynkman that my mandolin was better than his. He said that was true but in the Soviet Union he only paid five dollars for his.

I brought a mandolin book for him to use when he taught me. He took away my mandolin and pick for the first three months. He made a paper pick and had me work on the right hand wrist flexibility until it was so automatic I could do it in my sleep. When I had the right hand at a level acceptable to him, he said to bring the mandolin, but he gave me a Soviet made pick different than any pick I had ever seen and insisted I use that pick. He began to write out each lesson, and each week he would add a few lines that built on the week before. He used to play for me during the lessons and he was inspirational in this way.

The way he was in the world took the torture out of studying to be the best you could. One time I said, "Mischa, you are killing me! You are killing me!" I was on the verge of quitting in total exasperation and frustration. He put

(continued on page 25)

Mischa Sheynkman:

The Soviet Paganini of the Mandolin

(continued from page 24)

his arm on my shoulder with a gentle grin and said "Len, take it easy, but take it!"

Los Angeles wasn't exactly a Mecca for mandolin players. In fact I had not run into one between 1968 and the time I Sheynkman in 1979. I asked him what made him so sure he would make it playing mandolin in a town where no one knew what a mandolin looked like. A situation was ater described to me where a certain top session guitarist who actually played mandolin on one of the Tijuana Brass early records, used to hire Mischa to play first in the studios while he took the credit for the fancy mandolin playing and Sheynkman told him he was primarily interested in supporting his family and any way this guitarist wanted to do it he was more than grateful.

am certain that if I looked around I still have the original opies of what he wrote out for lessons each week. In the United States we are used to buying method books. In the Soviet Union they had no money for such books, so he teacher would write out the lesson with the specific bjectives more pinpointed.

forget his exact words but the idea and the feeling vas something like this. When he was six years old his eachers in elementary school knew he was gifted and he Soviet government said to his parents, "Your kid is oing to be a musician and he is going to graduate from a ussian Conservatory!" And that is all Mischa ever did s entire life! There is certainly something to be said for e pursuit of excellence in classical music as one might y "the proof is in the pudding." There is almost no way I n describe the refinement of technique to which I refer. is perfection beyond my capacity to discriminate. My her always mentioned that Paganini never wrote down

any of his methods for future violin players to study. Maybe there was no way to write them down?

About the recordings of Mischa Sheynkman:

During the time that I was his student, he gave me two 33 long play rpm records that he made in the Soviet Union. I was able to make one cd from the two records—this is the only recording where you can hear Sheynkman play with those who were trained in the Soviet conservatory system.

Sheynkman died in the mid to late 1990's when he was in his late fifties. He was a soloist for the Leningrad Symphony and he had his own radio show featuring his mandolin playing in the Soviet Union. When he defected to the United States in 1977 the Soviet Government destroyed all the masters of his musical performances that earned him the reputation of "the Paganini of the Mandolin" in the Soviet Union. To my knowledge what I put together on this cd is the only opportunity those in the United States will ever get to hear Sheynkman play the music he was trained in, Russian folk music, with those were trained in it with him at the Russian conservatories.

A limited edition was made and copies can be purchased for $20 a cd which includes postage and the cd. Orders can be sent to Dr. Len Bergantino and the check made out to Dr. Len Bergantino at 1215 Brockton Avenue, #104, Los Angeles, CA 90025-1886.

Dr. Len Bergantino is a clinical psychologist and musician who plays mandolin, trumpet, and tenor banjo.

-News about Keith Harris-

ery four years, the Federal Association of German chestral Organisations holds a competition for the best he numerous amateur orchestras in the country.

Saturday, November 6th, 2010, 38 selective orchestras h 1,700 players met for the competition in the beautiful of Bamberg.

the section plucked strings, two equal first places e awarded this time, each with 95 out of 100 points. insation was that for the first time, an orchestra of

zithers astounded with the quality of their music and skill.

The two winners were (for the first time) the State Zither Orchestra of Baden-Wuerttemberg – conducted by the Australian Keith Harris – and the State Plucked String Orchestra of Baden-Wuerttemberg, which Harris had also conducted for two years over a decade ago.

The winner in the section four years ago was the Hessian State Plucked String Orchestra, which Harris had directed for 12 years (1986-1998), with numerous recordings and many concert tours, including those to Australia, America

---

DEADLINE FOR SUBMISSIONS TO THE FEBRUARY JOURNAL IS JANUARY 15th
PLEASE SEND SUBMISSIONS TO: CMSAJournal@gmail.com

Joe Diorio, an exquisto jazz guitarist.

Diorio was essentially an uncompromising bop guitarist, as Feather correctly defined him, an aspect that could have influenced his reluctance to record material that had commercial potential, hence he took refuge, so to speak, in teaching where he provided to be an extraordinary teacher creating a guitar school.

He codified his own modern language on the guitar, a transcendent contribution to musical education. He was a mentor to Argentine guitarist Pino Marrone.

LEN BERGANTINO, ED.D., ABPP
1215 Brockton Avenue, Suite 104
Los Angeles, California 90025

TO HIRE ME AS A CONSULTANT
CALL (424) 293-9511
(7 RINGS)

Joe Diorio — one of Waterbury's
Greatest Stars 08/1936 - 02/22.

Joe Diorio was not only a world renown
jazz guitarist - he was the best that
all other jazz guitarists considered
#1 in the world among jazz guitarists.

I met Joe in 1977 when he moved to
Los Angeles, where I was in the private
practice of clinical psychology. I will
share a few anecdotes, comments from Joe
to me, and my reflections about him.

Joe took me to hear Joe Pass one
night. Joe Pass was known as the best
jazz guitar player before Joe Diorio got
to Los Angeles. Joe Pass just came out with
a cd with Ella Fitz Gerald. As we were
leaving Joe Pass yelled out - "Hey Joe! When are
you going to play songs again!" In other

LEN BERGANTINO, ED.D., ABPP
1215 Brockton Avenue, Suite 104
Los Angeles, California 90025

TO HIRE ME AS A CONSULTANT
CALL (424) 293-9511
(7 RINGS)

words Joe Pass was telling Joe Diorio
"Look! I know you are better than me!
But the public will never know it!
I just made a cd with Ella Fitzgerald
and you play strange sounds
sitting in a corner 6 hours a day
and you don't care what the public
thinks about you!!!" Other guitarists
who tried to compete with him
were blown off the stage! One
time Joe invited me, Ada Bredtes, my
mother and father to hear him featured
in Venice Beach, CA (1985?) It looked
from the audience like he had 3 left hands.
I had been watching great guitar players
since I was a boy and I have never seen
or heard anything like that night.

Joe was forever greatful to my
two cousins Fred and Vinnie
Bredice who taught him how to
play guitar, and to Wes Montgomery
a great jazz and a blues and

LEN BERGANTINO, ED.D., ABPP
1215 Brockton Avenue, Suite 104
Los Angeles, California 90025

TO HIRE ME AS A CONSULTANT
CALL (424) 293-9511
(7 RINGS)

invited Joe to come on stage with
him in 1940's and told Joe he was
going to be a world great.

He played with Stan Getz a
few exceptional who with guitarist
Charlie Byrd brought the Bossa
Nova from Brazil to the United
States. On December 22, 1997 I
got Joe to play songs again! We
made a cd entitled <u>Falling In Love</u>
where I played mandolin and Joe
accompanied me on guitar. I chose
many of the American — Italian songs
between 1940 and 1970 and a few
Italian — Italian songs that came
from Italy. As an accompanist
Joe gave me the gift of totally
being there for me in the most non
intrusive way possible; This cd or MP3
can be purchased of Amazon, digital

261

LEN BERGANTINO, ED.D., ABPP
1215 Brockton Avenue, Suite 104
Los Angeles, California 90025

TO HIRE ME AS A CONSULTANT
CALL (424) 293-9511
(7 RINGS)

and two different songs a
week are played by Joe Costa
on WATR - 1320 AM on "Carasello
Italiano".

When I met Joe he was married
to Myrna who dabbled in guitar and
being a competent artist got Joe to
dabble in art. Sometime in the early
eighties he gave me a picture he
painted that said "All the animals
in the jungle except man know
that the principle business of life
is to enjoy it." Myrna died of a brain
tumor. Joe taught at USC in
the Masters Program as did Jascha
Heifetz and other world class musicians.
He got a massive stroke in 2005.
When I asked him if he would miss

262

LEN BERGANTINO, ED.D., ABPP
1215 Brockton Avenue, Suite 104
Los Angeles, California 90025

TO HIRE ME AS A CONSULTANT
CALL (424) 293-9511
(7 RINGS)

being the jazz player on guitar
that all other jazz guitar players
emulated he said, " I'm just
glad to be alive!" When I had
a brush with death Joe
called me every day in the
hospital. When I left the
hospital and called him 3 days
a week he was in dialysis
in Waterbury, Connecticut
where he lived with his wife
Christina - While he had more
than his share of painful days
that were doomed of energy
he always had an upbeat forward
looking attitude about both his
teaching guitar and his writing
music. He gave me one book he
wrote called " Intervallic Designs "

published by Mel Bay for
guitar students.

I kept telling Joe stories! He
kept laughing and saying "You
ought to write and publish
those stories". After the
hundredth time he told me I
did it and those stories are
an integral part of my book
on Reverse Analysis, X.Vibiny
publishing company. The cd
we made Joe and I played
at a pace Margaret Mead told
one of the greatest of my
teachers, Milton H. Erickson, MD,
that she (Margaret Mead) "only heard
in a rare African tribe relatively
free of disease." This pace is
a necessity for healing to occur in
psychoanalysis, psychotherapy and
clinical hypnosis. Joe was like a cousin a brother

264

Regarding Joe Diorio's solo "With a Song In My Heart" I haven't heard this song since Jane Froman made it a hit in early 50's. Froman made a comeback. I remember her walking with a limb. These was the prettiest solo that I ever heard Joe played. And he entered the spirit of place of sweetness and light (Mathew Arnold) after he became disabled. As was the case with Jane Froman, Joe Diorio was a fighter. (Megan Clarkson)

American Federation of Musicians LOCAL 47
of the United States and Canada, AFL-CIO/CLC

STEPHANIE O'KEEFE
President

MARC SAZER
Vice President

DANITA NG POSS
Secretary/Treasurer

March 18, 2022

Dr. Len Bergantino
1215 Brockton Ave. #104
Los Angeles CA 90025

Dear Dr. Bergantino:

Thank you for your Overture Final Notes submission for Joseph Diorio. Please find a copy of the article as it appeared in our March 2022 digital issue. We also have it posted on our 47 blog, of which I have also enclosed a printout.

Please note: Until further notice, AFM Local 47's Overture publication is now an e-magazine and is published digitally only. Our archives may be found online at afm47.org/overture/online.

Sincerely,

Linda   Rapka
Communications director
AFM Local 47

3220 Winona Avenue Burbank CA 91504-2544 323.462.2161 www.afm47.org

266

Joseph Diorio
Life Member. Guitar
8/6/1936 – 2/2/2022

by Dr. Len Bergantino, retired Local 47 member and retired clinical psychiatrist

Joe Diorio died on February 2, 2022 at the age of 85. Joe was known as the jazz guitar players' jazz guitar player! He was the one jazz guitar players thought was the best. He suffered from a stroke in 2005. When I asked him if he would miss being top man and not playing jazz, he said, "I'm just glad to be alive!" He once gave me a painting he did which said, "All the animals in the jungle except man known that the principle business of life is to enjoy it!"

Final Note: Joseph Diorio

Life Member, Guitar
8/6/1936 – 2/2/2022

by Dr. Len Bergantino, retired Local 47 member and retired clinical psychiatrist

Joe Diorio died on February 2, 2022 at the age of 85. Joe was known as the jazz guitar players' jazz guitar player! He was the one jazz guitar players thought was the best. He suffered from a stroke in 2005. When I asked him if he would miss being top man and not playing jazz, he said, "I'm just glad to be alive!" He once gave me a painting he did which said, "All the animals in the jungle except man known that the principle business of life is to enjoy it!"

This entry was posted in All News, Final Notes / In Memoriam and tagged final note, Joseph Diorio on March 1, 2022 [https://www.afm47.org/press/final-note-joseph-diorio/] .

Foreword
Making an
Impact in
Therapy:

Len Bergantino, Ed.D., Ph.D.

JASON ARONSON INC.
Northvale. New Jersey
London

How Master
Clinicians Intervene

The plethora of how-to books is increasing. This is not one of those. Barbara Betz stated that the dynamics of psychotherapy is in the person of the therapist. Abraham Maslow stated that the peak experience lasts two weeks. Winicott insisted that if you haven't been hated by your psychotherapist you have been cheated. Erenwald has stated that psychotherapy is the effort to evolve an existential shift.

Len Bergantino is trying to expand this operational territory by stretching the psychotherapeutic geology. He succeeds. Describing the therapist as a person of liberated wisdom, he dares to the chaos and anxiety of not knowing; he opens a gate to see and make the impact of psychotherapy more clearly. His description of beingness as a process is reminiscent of Paul Tillich. His grasp of responsible involvement with the patient as a discipline of self shows his own search for creative options. He makes no pretense of camouflaging the psychotherapist as a wounded healer. Furthermore, Len makes crucial the pattern of the therapist's search for his own healing and successfully validates the authentic trickery of the psychotherapist as a liberated spirit. The approach to his own craziness, the freedom from the culture bind, and the discipline of self each emerged as obtainable goals of that professional parent we call the psychotherapist.

Further evidence of his own search is illustrated by his impersonalized impressionistic response to the other searchers he uses as models.

Simply reading his book leaves me feeling it would be meaningful to join in his search for his beingness. Though he would be enjoying himself and enjoying me as a patient, he would not be doing things to keep from being himself and thus I could be more fully myself.

Carl A. Whitaker, M.D.
Professor of Psychiatry
School of Medicine
University of Wisconsin

This is a book for all time. As I had extrasensory perception to help me find out things on a primitive level and depth with an ability to pick up split-off, severe pathological projective identifications moment to moment in an era when psychologists were only permitted to be research psychoanalysts by the American Psychoanalytic Association (but tightly controlled where that research was going that in many ways nullified it as true psychoanalytic research). And I will show you how extrasensory perception can be developed and utilized by the therapeutic use of self within the psychoanalytic frame in ways that can enhance the treatment of borderline, narcissistic, obsessive-compulsive, and schizophrenic disorders and other diagnoses, as well as help pinpoint psychophysiological awareness, which through the repetition compulsion, can prevent disease and will circumvent disease in later life. This kind of psychoanalysis will go a long way in preventing the next holocaust!

Dr. Bergantino and his two children were sent back on a karmic mission to complete the work. Dr. Bergantino is the reincarnated soul of Sigmund Freud and Julius Caesar. These skill sets were required to complete the project. His children are Wilfred Bion and Milton Erickson. They taught Dr. Bergantino how to use paranormal abilities. We are all off the karmic wheel and WE WILL NOT BE BACK!!! GOODBYE!!!

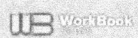

ISBN 978-0-0000-0000-0

WB WorkBook

DR. LEN BERGANTINO, ED.D., PH.D.

I AM FREUD!

I am Freud! I am Caesar!
I am the Worlds Greatest Psychoanalyst!
Psychoanalysis-Reincarnation-Extra
Sensory Perception

Karmic Law- Natural Law- Civil Law

DR. LEN BERGANTINO, ED.D., PH.D.

What the Reviewers Say:

Psychotherapy, Insight and Style
The Existential Moment

by Len Bergantino, Ed. D., ABPP

The book sells for $26.95 / Send check to *1215 Brockton Ave. #104, Los Angeles, C 90025*
Interested? Contact Dr.Bergantino / (310) 207-8818

Dr. Carl A. Whitaker, M.D. Professor of Psychiatry / School of Medicine, University of Wisconsin

"The plethora of how-to books is increasing. Barbara Betz stated that the dynamics of psychotherapy is in the person of the therapist. Abraham Maslow stated that the peak experience lasts two weeks. Winicott insisted that if you haven't been hated by your psychotherapist you have been cheated. Erenwald has stated that psychotherapy is the effort to evolve an existential shift.

Len Bergantino is trying to expand this operational territory by streching the psychotherapeutic geology He succeeds. Describing the therapist as a person of liberated wisdom, he dares to the chaos and anxiety of not knowing; he opens a gate to see and make the impact of psychotherapy more clearly. His description of beingness as a process is reminiscent of Paul Tillich. His grasp of responsible involvement with the patient as a discipline of self shows his own search for creative options. He makes no pretense of camouflaging the psychotherapist as a wounded healer. Furthermore, Len makes crucial the pattern of the therapist's search for his own healing and successfully validates the authentic trickery of the psychotherapist as a liberated spirit. The approach to his own craziness, the freedom from the culture bind, and the discipline of self each emerged as obtainable goals of that professional parent we call the psychotherapist.

Further evidence of his own search is illustrated by his impersonalized impressionistic response to the other searchers he uses as models. Simply reading his book leaves me feeling it would be meaningful to join in his search for his own beingness. Though he would be enjoying himself and enjoying me as a patient, he would not be doing things to keep from being himself and thus I could be more fully myself."

Dr. Donald Rinsley, M.D., F. R.S.H. Fellow American College of Psychoanalysts in his

review of Dr. Bergantino's book published in Bulletin of the Menninger Clinic, Vol. 47, No. 5, September, 1983 wrote:

"The book reflects the personal odyssey of a trained, disciplined yet openminded professional psychologist who has drunk at the wells of an number of acknowledged healer-therapists whose work he has carefully studied and evaluated, among them, Viktor Frankl, Wilfred Bion. the Gouldings, Frederick Perls, Milton Erickson and Carl Whitaker. A unique feature of Dr. Bergantino's presentation is his detailed accounts of these therapists' hour-to-hour work, drawn from his own personal experience and from verbatim descriptions provided by their students and analysands, offering fascinating and instructive insights into the therapeutic labors of admittedly gifted treaters "

Dr. Martin Grotjahn, M.D., Training and Supervising Analyst Emeritus Southern California

Psychoanalytic Institute in a pre-publication review wrote:

"Dr. Bergantino is obviously a gifted therapist ...Most cases as reported in the literature describe the patient's associations and productions while the therapist remains hidden in the mystery of darkness unrevealed. Dr. B is an exception: the great advantage of his work is the openness and frankness with which the author reveals his experiences when treating patients or when accepting himself as a patient of another therapist.

Dr. Walter Kempler, M.D. The Kempler Institute - Costa Mesa CA

"Len's writing is intelligent and lucid...engrossing......
I think his book is valuable...an interesting and pro pellingwork...His ideas ride the crest of current thought in the field, provides clean reviews of popular modes, formulates in the popular jargon of the day using traditional interpretions and terminology. His personal touch is enchancing."

Dr. James S. Simkin, Ph.D. American Board of Examiners in Professional Psychology - Big Sur CA

"Professionals could benefit directly from this book in that Bergantino describes how it is possible to integrate a variety of psychotherapeutic approaches."

Dr. Ernest Lawrence Rossi, Ph.D. Diplomate in Clinical Psychology - Los Angeles CA

"A deeply moving floodof insights and approaches to becoming oneself as a psychotherapist.....It is a highly readable record of (Bergantino's) development as a therapist via his personal contacts and training with a variety of current-day psychotherapists...a new understanding of what it means to be a creative therapist continually living in the present's potential for change and transformation...
......focuses on the precise and often provocative and shocking techniques that are useful in helping patients break out of their learned limitations to realize their potentials for creative change."

This book is being republished by Jason Aronson Publishers Inc. as part of The Master Classic Series under a new title, Moments of Impact in Psychotherapy: How The Masters Intervene

LEN BERGANTINO Ed. D., ABPP
In-Depth Family Therapy • Ericksonian Hypnosis
American Board of Professional Psychology • Diplomate in Family Psychology

Dr. Len Bergantino, Ed.D., Ph.D.,
Book Collections

www.drlenbergantinobooks.com

1. I AM FREUD! Psychoanalysis Is the Only Method of Cure:

It's Too Bad No One Knows How to Do One!!!

2. I DARED TO DISTURB THE UNIVERSE!!!

3. Reverse Analysis, the Existential Shift, Gestalt Family Therapy and the Prevention of the Next Holocaust

4. The Art of Psychotherapy and the Liberation of the Therapist

5. The Essence of Music

6. When Baseball was King The New York Yankees were King of Baseball

This book, The Essence of Music, along with the music itself provides the Spirit of place linking the phasing (metronome) of psychoanalysis and music to the practice of psychoanalysis and music with the phrasing that makes effective psychoanalytic treatment probable and music healing.

www.ingramcontent.com/pod-product-compliance
Lightning Source LLC
Chambersburg PA
CBHW070905120626
46546CB00001B/144